MEDIA, POPULAR

CULTURE, AND

THE AMERICAN

CENTURY

MEDIA, POPULAR CULTURE, AND THE AMERICAN CENTURY

Edited by
KINGSLEY BOLTON
and JAN OLSSON

NATIONAL LIBRARY OF SWEDEN

P. O. BOX 5039, 102 41 STOCKHOLM, SWEDEN

©THE AUTHORS & NATIONAL LIBRARY OF SWEDEN 2010

DESIGNED BY JENS ANDERSSON/WWW.BOKOCHFORM.SE

PRINTED IN SWEDEN BY FÄLTH & HÄSSLER, 2010

ISSN 1654-6601

ISBN 978-0-86196-698-1

MEDIEHISTORISKT ARKIV 20

CONTENTS

INTRODUCTION

MEDIATED AMERICA: AMERICANA AS HOLLYWOODIANA

JAN OLSSON AND KINGSLEY BOLTON

"All civilization is the product of fenced-in lack of freedom."
— Haruki Murakami

THERE ARE NO fencings-in here, no ground rules, nor any territorial claims. Instead this volume started out as a road map for exploring avenues of shared scholarly interest. In broad terms, we envisioned synergetic overlaps across fences and unaccounted-for connections between the global spread of American popular culture and the mechanisms for language change in the age of modernity. As an example, a particular case in point that provides an emblematic discursive backdrop is the inventive study of national cinemas—in terms of the vernacular in relation to Hollywood's classic idiom—by Miriam Hansen and Zhen Zhang.[1] Hansen's influential essay takes stock of the market value of classic Hollywood and how its domineering storytelling regime has been appropriated, inflected, and negotiated in national film contexts. In her magisterial work on the emergence of Chinese cinema in Shanghai, Zhen Zhang elegantly mobilizes vernacular perspectives as the key critical pivot for the celluloid encounter between West and East. In this spirit, Hollywood's styles, genres, and codes—linguistic and otherwise—loom large for our project. With different, more consciousness-related emphasis, one could have invoked Roland Robertson's usage of the original Japanese term, glocalization, when referring to the practices of local embodiments, reverberations, and *mise-en-scenès* of global templates.[2]

7

FIGURE 1: Burlesque poster from 1897.
Courtesy of the Theatrical Poster Collection, Library of Congress.

UNFENCING AMERICAN STUDIES

The editors' academic habitats are Cinema Studies and English, with our respective research interests the consolidation of American film culture in the silent era and the many Englishes in Asia. Stockholm served as the point of departure for our road trip: a crossroads where our travel plans happened to intersect. To be sure, the Swedish academic geography bears some significance in that the study of English in Sweden traditionally pays minimal heed to popular culture, American or not, while Cinema Studies in Stockholm has been somewhat reluctant to fully engage with Hollywood cinema as well as American television. We therefore envisioned opportunities for novel excitements for a new generation of students and young scholars attuned to and symbolically milk-fed on the many guises and inflections of American popular culture. Our ambition was however not to start up a full-scale American Studies program from scratch in Stockholm, but to organize encounters, events, speaker series, workshop, conferences, and possibly a mobile research center—and to edit this collection as a first draft or travelogue.

In order for us to get a grip on the role of Americana and its media and language practices—inside the U.S. as Americanization (a somewhat dated term) as well as in the form of hard and/or soft export—we have elected to invite a select group of both American and non-American scholars as contributors to this volume. Our team comes from a diverse humanities background and offers insightful responses to our call for critical reflections on mediated—as in media-filtered, media-messaged, and media-projected—Americana, American English, as well as current changes in the development of domestic U.S. media. By choice we have included neither historians proper nor political scientists. These two groups are otherwise the most prominent when it comes to an "external" research interest concerning American society in- or outside the banner of American Studies. As a teaser and preamble for a research field *in spe*, we've vouched for a differently pivoted area of expertise and an international team.

On U.S. campuses, and half century or so after Henry Nash Smith's classic study *Virgin Land*—in many ways a foundational work—American Studies is still not a clear-cut and fenced-in area of research. It is, instead, a highly productive and malleable field of inquiry traversing vast facets of American endeavors, experiences, and identities across centuries and in the process skirting multiple disciplines.[3] In the 1940s and during the 1950s, according to Stanley Bailis' historiographic sketch, the prime pioneers of American Studies came from literature and history and many preferred to stay put after occasional forays into new programs and seminars. Partly rooted in ideas of American exceptionalism and a realm of putative unique American experiences as a new nation built on immigration, scholars tried to capture salient traces of this special American condition, often in studies featuring grand historical sweeps. In the process, a focus on English literature shifted to American letters. Again the most influential studies were animated by the elongated lifespan of myths, images, and symbols for coming to terms with the American mind, imagination or some other broad category.[4]

FIGURE 2: Frame enlargement from Alfred Hitchcock's
Saboteur (Universal, 1942).

AMERICA'S TIME

Emblematic for our approach to Americana in this volume is not only scholarly efforts, but foremost a non-academic text, namely Henry R. Luce's landmark essay "The American Century" from 1941. H.G Wells, however, probably first used the phrase "American Century."[5] The intertwined nature of mediated Americana and the role of America's position on the global political scene resonates with the backdrop for the analysis outlined by Luce, perhaps the most renowned American publisher of the 20th century. Discounting the daily newspapers tycoons, Pulitzer, Hearst, and Ochs, *the* American Editor-in-Chief was undoubtedly Henry R. Luce. Born in China to missionary parents, educated at Yale and Oxford, Luce became the most prominent publisher of his generation. *Time*, the first venture, emerged in collaboration with Briton Hadden in 1923, and after Hadden's death Luce launched *Fortune, Life,* and *Sports Illustrated*, and on radio and screen two innovative news digests, both named *March of Time*.

In 1941 Orson Welles effectively parodied the *March of Time* in *Citizen Kane* and the style Hadden and Luce had crafted for *Time*, which seemingly effortlessly spilled over to other publications and media. Prior to the opening of *Citizen Kane* in May and the attack on Pearl Harbor in December, Luce was ready to affix the label "American" onto the 20th century in a classic essay in *Life* straightforwardly titled "The American Century." Here Luce waxed poetic on key facets of Americana as the sole common currency across the globe, namely: "American jazz, Hollywood movies, American slang, American machines and patented products." Thus, he claimed, they are "the only things that every community in the world, from Zanzibar to Hamburg, recognizes in common."[6] To single out Hamburg was of course a calculated move in the middle of the Second World War, just prior to the American entry that was to come after Pearl Harbor. For Luce, the ubiquitous cultural presence of Americana was a bridgehead and signpost for America's inevitable political role in the 20th century. Non-visionary American politicians, he maintained, had dodged this role since 1919. Luce prime's mission at this time was to convince the Roosevelt administration to abandon isolationism and to act according to America's manifest purpose and bring leadership to a brave new world. The world, Luce argued, was in need of American civilization and values as a bulwark against totalitarianism at a time when Europe and Great Britain had been backed into a corner by tyranny.

The attack on Pearl Harbor ten months later was to vindicate his argument, and, during the Cold War that followed, America's role in the global arena expanded along lines first sketched by Luce. A son of a missionary with both an internal and external perspective on America, Luce's publications were welcomed by a jazz-age America driven by business and consumerism and led by a generation of well-educated, young businessmen—*tycoon* was a term popularized by *Time*. Luce and Hadden reasoned that busy, modern people needed a new type of entertaining, condensed, and well-written information to keep abreast with the national and world affairs of the time. In the eyes of the public, traditional newspapers like the *New York Times* were long-winded and dull. *Time* was not the first news magazine to be published in the U.S., but its streamlined digest of topical events was to be successful beyond expectations—in spite of competition from the *Literary Digest* and *Reader's Digest*. The time-savvy philosophy that underpinned *Time* resonated with the burgeoning culture of speed that was gaining hold in the U.S. during these decades, for which the automobile, cinema, Fordism, and Taylorism provide shared discursive links in the current academic literature.

FIGURE 3: "Come To America." Immigration poster from 1919.
Courtesy of Getty Images.

FROM MANIFEST DESTINY TO RONALD MCDONALD

Luce's overall vision of America's larger mission in world affairs—his internationalist Manifest Destiny—is however not our concern. Instead, we have singled out Luce's critical lines on American popular culture as an enduring strand of his analytical argument. His almost casual observations on the global spread of American popular culture still strike us a timely and timeless observation (at least for the time being) and are still pertinent decades later, even when the blessings of the American way are less obvious than they were before the assassination of the Kennedys, Martin Luther King, Vietnam, and Watergate. More recently, prison-camp reports from Guantanamo Bay, renditions across Europe, and Abu Ghraib have further dampened the enthusiasm of even America's allies worldwide.

Following Luce, the overall rationale for this volume is that, crucially, "mediated Americana" (i.e. key aspects of U.S. culture filtered, interpreted and presented through the popular media) and its language together gain a singular presence across the globe after circa 1914. This did not occur in uniform fashion, however, because this very process itself was mediated by diverse geographical vernaculars in its reception across the world. At the point in time when the American feature film became conspicuous after years in the shadow of Europe, Hollywood simultaneously emerged as the epicenter of American cinema. This chain of events leading up to the prominence of the American feature film, or at least aspects of this process, is highlighted in Joel Frykholm's essay on the writer Rex Beach's cinematic endeavors. Apart from selling literary material to the film industry, most prominently his novel *The Spoilers* (Selig, 1914), Beach started ed his own film company. So did several other authors, but less successfully. With the gradual ascendance of the feature film as a dominant commodity, film culture was not only produced and programmed differently, but also marketed and experienced in novel ways in palace-like movie theaters. Not least the atmospheric architecture, often replete with exotic elements, encouraged and further sustained the flight of fancy of the story world. In its desire for middle-class patrons, the industry sought to establish a mass market by its diverse tier of exhibition venues and levels of run. After World War I, Hollywood's reach was no longer domestic only, but global. Corrado Neri, in his essay on filmmaker Sun Yu, details how a young Chinese student, who witnessed the consolidation of film culture and its representational practices up-close in America, took his filmmaking insights to the fledgling film production in China.

Negotiated by arbiters, embraced by fans, and despised by foes, the momentum of mediated Americana from this time has seemed unstoppable until the present. As early as the 1920s, England, for example, deemed it necessary to deploy a quota system for the import of American titles in order to safeguard the national production of films. Savvy Hollywood, however, elegantly bypassed the regulations by mounting the

13

FIGURE 4: Hebrew poster in support for the allies cause. In translation:
Food will win the war—You came here seeking freedom, now you must
help to preserve it—Wheat is needed for the allies—waste nothing.
Poster designed by Charles Edward Chambers in 1917. Courtesy of Getty Images.

14

production in England of so-called "quota quickies" to secure the unhindered passage of its regular fare. French media later came up with schemes for rationing American tunes on radio to stem the tide of American lyrics, and France and many other countries still mute American voices on big and small screens by choosing to dub motion pictures, with original, sub-titled versions as the connoisseur alternative in select theaters. Such endeavors have only underscored the fact that mediated modernity and "modern life" generally have been projected beneath the banner of American mediated sights and sounds, ideas and ideals, to the accompaniment U.S. commodities and consumerism.

Globalization is open to debate and interpretation, but for many it is unequivocally steeped in the shimmering light of U.S. brands. CocaCola, Nike, and McDonald's are among the most symbolic global brands, along with Disney, Dreamworks, Paramount, and the other Hollywood studios. As Andy Warhol put it in 1975: "The most beautiful thing in Tokyo is McDonald's. The most beautiful thing in Stockholm is McDonald's. The most beautiful thing in Florence is McDonald's. Peking and Moscow don't have anything beautiful yet."[7] Following the 1980s economic boom and political changes in the former Eastern Europe and elsewhere, the aesthetics of premier American brands are globally celebrated and buttressed to varying degrees by shared domains of popular culture, from cinema to fashion to hip-hop. This in turn has favored the spread of American English—alongside burgers, blue jeans and their accompanying aesthetics.

FROM SOFT POWER TO HARD REALITIES

The American export of complex patterns of popular culture has run its course parallel to the rise and expression of American imperial ambitions through military means, which, following Luce, has often been presented in terms of promoting the unrivaled benefits of American civilization. At the same time, another strand in the long American century has been the traffic in people to the U.S., which has occurred through a variety of means—through brute force on slave ships, through the enrollment of gullible colonizers and immigrants from Europe and Asia, and, currently, through the steady stream of people risking their lives in the hope of becoming an illegal alien in the U.S. Southwest.

During his long tenure at CNN, Lou Dobbs hammered away on a daily basis concerning the allegedly eroding effects of the NAFTA tariff treaties, outsourcing, and illegal immigration, with all these issues subsumed under the catchphrase "broken borders." For Dobbs the United States had reached a critical crossroads with grave repercussions for the American middle class, which was further imperiled by the so-called corporate greed of Wall Street. Eventually, Dobbs' daily rants forced him out from CNN, but by then he had published a trilogy of discontents with titles unequivocally advertising his dismay concerning American politics.[8] As we write, Arizona is now the battleground for issues of immigration that engage and contest very different interpretations of the American dream.

The traffic across American borders has always been divisive and controversial. From inside and afar, America has stood as a symbol of freedom and opportunity. Internationally, U.S. ambitions, ideological missions, and power have sometimes been welcomed, but as often they have been feared and fought. The historical trail of blood, imperialism, and jingoism cannot be balanced or erased by the global embrace of American media and related commodities.[9] Indeed, our enthusiasm for the discussion of media and popular culture in this volume should not be read as some kind of celebratory self-indulgence, but despite this it is a hard fact that, ironically, empire and media do make good dancing partners. And the attraction of that dance may explain the often love-hate tempo of the international intellectual reception of America as Fordian standardization, mass-consumerism, and popular culture from critics as diverse as the Dutch historian Johan Huizinga to America's own Sinclair Lewis with his invention of the narrow-minded and eponymous "Babittism," from the 1920s.[10]

At the same time, the freedom sought after in America was deeply entangled in a structural racism, which inspired self-contained urban colonies in the metropolises. Today, the dilemma of racism still persists, despite the establishment of the Obama administration. In many senses, America is unthinkable without the culture of violence that inspires the section in this book devoted to gangster movies, while Michael Renov discusses issues of racism and civil rights in the light of Barack Obama's election to the Presidency, and Jan Olsson immigration politics from the perspective of Italian immigrants around 1900. The mass immigration of Italians and others powered U.S. industrialization and simultaneously

16

FIGURE 5: Pitch for liberty bonds to support the allies in World War I.
Poster designed by Z.P. Nikolaki in 1918. Courtesy of Getty Images.

expanded its consumer base, which in turn led to the development of a mass-consumer society, prior to the eclipse of the cultural dominance of old Europe.

The "huddled masses" yearning for a better life in America, and the export of media underpinning a wide range of American imaginaries, intertwine with hegemonic ambitions to secure markets and influence. This American specter has provided the contours for a wide range of hopes and dreams, experiences and imaginaries, in which the crossing of borders has been a central strand. Sadly, some hopeful immigrants never managed to arrived at their dream destination, as Gregory Lee vividly shows in his reading of Chinese emigration to the Americas. Conversely, sometimes the traffic flowed in other directions, and some Americans, if only imaginatively, did arrive on rural Sweden's arcadian streets, as in the film discussed by Ann-Kristin Wallengren. In the mid-1970s Swedish film she discusses, an American gangster arrives in a Swedish backwater and inspires admiration and fear, before meeting a suitably sticky end. Assembled as a media constellation, our essays feature slaves and immigrants, gangsters and entrepreneurs, rappers and civil-right activists and range from the marionette theater to satellites and digital television, the spread of which is mapped against the domestic culture of the U.S. by Lisa Parks.

The argument sketched out here and imbricated in all the essays of this volume, to a greater or lesser degree, is that soft Americanization took place, and still takes place—both inside and outside the U.S.—through the propagation of U.S. media and consumer products, while the hard sell of American interests and hegemony has been conducted overtly through diplomacy backed by the armed forces, as well as by clandestine operations of various intelligence agencies. Such intersections have been widely studied, and also fictionalized through the intriguing lens of conspiracy by James Ellroy in his massive and recently completed "Underworld USA" trilogy. This covers the Kennedy-era and its aftermath, and presents a bleak take on the meanings and practices of modern America.[11] Ellroy's depiction of state-sponsored gangsterism thus provides a cynical counterpoint to Luce's idealistic optimism about the benefits of American civilization.

COWBOYS AND GANGSTERS

The gangster genre takes center stage in several essays in this collection—in the texts by Sonnet, Stanfield, and Wallengren. Arguably, the figure of the gangster is the most prominent American fiction character alongside the cowboy. The fictional versions of these mythical figures survive and sometimes thrive in the grey area between lily-white idealism and dark cynicism. The violence in stories featuring cowboy/gangster protagonists are indicative of a defense-oriented society still practicing capital punishment, with a sizable amount of its population behind bars, and with many citizens still having firearms within easy reach in their daily lives. A more contemporary gauge of the strength of the key components of American civilization was played out in Rome, Wisconsin, in David E. Kelley's aptly-named television series, *Picket Fences*. For two seasons, the episodes gravitated between three domains, the mayor's office, the police station, and the courthouse, presided over by the stern but unconventional judge facing the perennial defense lawyer, a human, humane, and most colorful shyster. Add to this the civil society and its institutions, the school, the hospital, for example, as the fourth line of fencing-in.

In 1925, when Hollywood had already flexed its media muscles for a number of years, the Swedish author and poet Erik Lindorm claimed: "The globe is on the verge of being completely Americanized, and the Swedish patch is being pushed up on the edge of the Arctic Circle." The background for his newspaper essay, "Adieu Swedish Film," was that film director Victor Sjöström had turned into "Victor Seastrom" by defecting from the studio at Råsunda to Samuel Goldwyn's studio in the heart of Hollywood. Now Mauritz Stiller followed suit with his entourage, Garbo included. Not content with drowning out other movie stars and film cultures, Lindorm opined, Hollywood had also hired away all the local talent and recruited them for a film industry devoid of vernacular tints. Prophetically, he mused, Seastrom and actor Lars Hanson would not survive in a Hollywood that produced talking motion pictures. Both Swedes returned in the wake of the talkies, while Garbo stayed and continued to excel, partly due to the allure of her exotic accent and charismatic appeal. In the era of the talkies, Garbo became *The Divine Woman* of Seastrom's 1927-film featuring Garbo and Hanson. Irrespective of the screen's silence, early cinema came with a soundscape and noise culture of its own, which in her essay in this volume is teased out in gender terms by

Meredith C. Ward. For Ward, the figure of the prostitute is seamlessly aligned with and speaks for early film culture as an intricately-patterned blend of carnal and carnival. Frivolous female display had been part of theater life in general for a long time, as Stephen Gundle vividly portrays in his dazzling history of glamour.[12] For Ward, the regulation of the soundscape was critical for a shift from auditorium to screen eroticism aligned with the overall trajectory of American film culture in the 1910s.

Taking the melting-pot metaphor for Americanization to the screen, "the facial expression," Lindorm continued, "of our compatriots will not even come across with a whiff of Swedish accent, but will melt together with the other actors, whose nationality only will be known to the cognoscenti." Once the wishful metaphor "melting pot" papered over the realities of national and ethnic colonies and enclaves inside American metropolises. The melting sought to capture a form of cultural automatism for a multitude of projects later known as Americanization, mapping out quick fixes for absorption and blending in. The term soon lost its currency as guiding principle of how to cope in the new country, and has, in more recent times, been supplanted with a celebration of cultural diversity, hyphenated or not. As we know, the talkies did not hamper the global attraction of Hollywood movies, rather it fueled the projection of American English, as discussed by Bolton. The American variety of language has also been harnessed with a whole range of sound-based American popular culture, from jazz to pop and rap, an idiom explored in relation to technology by Evelyn Ch'ien in her contribution to this volume.

British newspaperman W.G. Faulkner had voiced cultural anxieties concerning the language consequences of the American screen dominance well in advance of Lindorm's spiel. The intertitles in American films, he warned, threatened to "corrupt the English language."[13] This alarmist observation sets the stage for a much-needed and yet-to-be-undertaken research project concerning the emergence of mediated American English as the lingua franca and hard currency for global culture and as the lingo for the American century. Faulkner's worried contention—cum disdain—offers a productive point of departure for the type of studies this collection offers: on the one hand mapping development inside American popular culture and on the other hand following the trajectory of the export of American entertainment products.[14]

To backtrack even further, but still from a British perspective (albeit from the print media), W.T. Stead had predicted an escalating American dominance as early as 1901 in a cross-continental analysis of journalism, as Pulitzer and Hearst scooped up new readers—including immigrants, mechanics, and women—by the million. In passing, Stead mentioned the "mission of the cinematograph" and its educative potential, which he claimed would engineer a visual turn under the rubric "Eye-gate." Fifteen years later, roughly, Hollywood followed the general path delineated by Stead, with "the United States of America as the greatest of world-powers [and] the greatest political, social, and commercial phenomenon of our times," thereby resonating with the anxieties of Faulkner over the impact of American intertitles a decade later.[15] Comments on the overwhelming success of mediated Americana during the last century by Stead, Faulkner, Lindorm, and their ilk soon evolved into a genre of their own, striving for a larger historical and cultural trajectory in the manner of Huizinga.

Via cinema screens, CDs, DVDs, the Internet and bit torrents, popular culture across much of the globe is inflected in American English, typically parallel to locally-produced material, increasingly repackaged by Hollywood, as with film versions of Swedish writer Stieg Larsson's hit novels, which are now being remade for international audiences with a face associated with James Bond. In this context, media conversion across digital platforms is the most recent aspect of the intricate processes of mediated popular culture. This process and its wide-ranging consequences for copyright, archival practices, and access to research material is at the center of Pelle Snickars' essay.

In a series of lectures from the early 1930s delivered in Berlin, the American historian George Norlin elaborated on the key elements of the European reception of Americana a decade before Luce's celebratory list of popular American cultural creations. Norlin mused: "the skyscraper, the multimillionaire, Fordism, Hollywood, prohibition, Al Capone, and the like, impinge themselves upon the eye and obscure the less picturesque and the more normal aspects of the American landscape."[16] His list—featuring among other things gangsters and movies—brings to mind a short text by James Truslow Adams, which, in concentrated form, offers an historical explanation for the popularity of gangster films in the 1930s. In this iconic film genre, the American Dream is seen in a glass darkly. James Truslow Adams is best known for his study *The Epic of America*, published in September 1931 at a time when a speculation-driven crisis had pushed the country into the great depression. The background for Adams' short text was a talk delivered by President Herbert Hoover at a conference for International Police Chiefs, which inspired an impromptu historiography concerning the roots for American popular culture. In contrast to England and the countries still part of its empire, Adams argues, the independent U.S. lacked an historical tradition of heroes to celebrate. Instead we have an assortment of tough-cookie odd-fellows from the frontier that included Daniel Boone, Jim Bowie, Bill Hickok, and Billy the Kid. Adams notes that, whatever the reality, such figures became mythologized in terms of qualities such as fearlessness, recklessness, self-reliance, and a disregard for the law, whether as gunsels or lawmen.

The American resentment of the authorities and affection for the underdog—combined with a missing historical tradition—conspired to celebrate such characters in mass-market literature and Wild West shows. According to Adams: "These bad men of the frontier became the folk heroes of the people, the one great people of the world which had lost their past and were unconsciously forming myths and heroes for themselves afresh out of the scanty contemporary material at hand." Adams further comments that "the attitude of the general reading and movie public reflects to some extent that of people who, in political vendettas, family feuds and crimes of love, see what the Englishman calls a criminal in a different light." In his conclusion, Adams does not foresee a brisk shift in popular sentiment, instead, he predicts, "the tabloids will fatten for long yet on gangster-folk-hero lore," thus "the public with its under-dog complex, will be more interested in the gangster who shoots up a town than in the policeman who, unjustly perhaps in individual cases, it believes will graft for a ten-dollar bill." And, "if as a nation we do not take crime seriously no matter who commits it, we can scarcely take the tabloid readers and movie-fans to task for liking their criminal heroes served up to them picturesque and hot."[17] The success of the American popular heroes and their 1930s incarnations in the form of movie gangsters did not stop at the borders, but spread to England and everywhere, thus adding new dimensions to Adams' analysis. And in the 1950s, a new gangster cycle came to the fore as analyzed by Peter Stanfield by way of the colorful designation punks. Parallel to Stanfield's work, Ester Sonnet productively separates the gangster cycles from scores of other film types foremost of the *noir* variety.

FIGURE 6: Civil-rights rally around the Statue of Liberty in 1960.
Photo by Al Fenn. Courtesy of Getty Images.

JACK BAUER AT CENTURY'S END

Did the American century in Luce's terms come to a close in 2001, lasting roughly from Stead's prediction of 1901 up until, say 9/11? From such a perspective, the Fox series *24*, which was scheduled to open in the fall of 2001, can be viewed in terms of a post-9/11 America negotiating novel security protocols after an attack as psychologically devastating as Pearl Harbor. The series' protagonist, Jack Bauer, emerged as the sole savior of a U.S. besieged by terrorist attacks, in a television drama series loved by the brass in the Bush administration and the GOP's new poster boy, broadcaster Rush Limbaugh.

Setting the limits of the American Century differently and less jestingly, one may argue that the financial meltdown of 2008 signaled the beginning of an end of sorts, if not an eclipse. Philip J. Deloria underwrites such a contention in his expose over the many forks of American Studies, which leads to the claim that "the American century is truly over" from the dual vantage point after the 2008-election and the collapse of Lehman Brothers. If we believe that this is the case, a plausible candidate for inception of the American Century might be the formation of the so-called Edison trust late 1908. This trust reined in domestic and key foreign film companies under an industrial structure dismantled a decade later by the government as in violation of the Sherman Act and the antitrust laws. But by then Hollywood already reigned supreme, and still does, at least in name, due to its dazzling products, unrivaled distribution, and marketing machine.

Although one can propose all kinds of bookends for Luce's century, eventually America may still surprise us with its resilience in the face of shifting economic and cultural exigencies. Whether "hope," "change," and "yes, we can" will reignite a new set of American dreams, richer in scope and color, with the power to alter the current economic trajectory is for future historians record. In former industrial hotspots with a collapsed housing market to deal with, the future looks bleak indeed. The dreams of a better future may well have been outsourced along with the jobs. Related to this, Thomas L. Friedman has recently claimed that globalization has now "flattened" the earth by creating unprecedented opportunities for developing economies through the Internet and global communications, with particular reference to China and India. Finer-grained analyses of financial expertise and intellectual prowess, for ex-

FIGURE 7: Henry R. Luce. Courtesy of Getty Images.

ample in terms of academic citations and medical patents, suggest that the world predominantly still revolves around familiar hubs in the U.S. and to a lesser extent Europe. But for how long, one wonders?

An important insight from the cultural geography of Jane Jacobs and Edward W. Soja is that nation states now play second fiddle to cities and or sub-national regions and that the "flatness" or "spikiness" of economic and intellectual impact must be gauged in such terms. We thus need to study the Pearl River Delta rather than China, Mumbai rather than India, Lagos rather than Nigeria, and perhaps Hollywood rather than the U.S. Such research programs may then have an interesting potential for the U.S., if, say, one pivots studies of Americana predominantly as Hollywoodiana.

FROM LUCE TO LUCE

Henry R. Luce was the son of an American missionary, who spent his early years in China, and a number of commentators have pointed out that much of his essay on "The American Century" resonates with an almost missionary zeal for the cause he espoused. Towards the end of his essay, Luce identified four key elements ("areas of life and thought") crucial to his vision of America, first, its economic system, second, its technical skills, third, its duty to be a global Good Samaritan, and, fourth, its devotion to its ideals. On this latter issue, Luce declaimed:

We have some things in this country which are infinitely precious and especially American—a love of freedom, a feeling for the equality of opportunity, a tradition of self-reliance and independence and also of co-operation. In addition to ideals and notions which are especially American, we are the inheritors of all the great principles of Western civilization —above all Justice, the love of Truth, the ideal of Charity. [...] America as the dynamic center of ever-widening spheres of enterprise, America as the training center of the skillful servants of mankind, America as the Good Samaritan, really believing again that it is more blessed to give than to receive, and America as the powerhouse of the ideals of Freedom and Justice—out of these elements surely can be fashioned a vision of the 20th Century to which we can and will devote ourselves in joy and gladness and vigor and enthusiasm.

For Luce, one imagines that the term "mission" came with a gravitas and idealism that recalled his childhood in Presbyterian missions in China. Today, however, following George W. Bush's "Mission Accomplished" speech of 2003, the very term has been devalued by its brash and premature use in *faux* Top Gun-style by a failed U.S. President. Nevertheless, the military supremacy of the U.S. remains overwhelming (despite a war still ongoing in Afghanistan and with Iraq in transition), with more than seven hundred military bases in 130 countries worldwide, and huge allocations of funding to the Pentagon and Armed Forces continuing to flow.[18]

Domestically, however, morale seems at low ebb. In a recent article in the *Financial Times*, authored by one Edward Luce (of the British clan, no obvious relation to Henry R.), and titled "Goodbye American Dream," the author documents the current trials of middle America. Luce argues persuasively that the crisis for middle-class Americans began long before 2008, noting that, according to reliable economic analysis, the annual incomes of ninety per cent of U.S. families have been flat since 1973, in line with Lou Dobbs' analysis. By contrast, the incomes of the top one per cent have tripled, while most of those with stagnating incomes have been affected by what economists have dubbed "declining income mobility." This, Luce states, means that America is now longer a fabled land of opportunity, explaining that:

Alexis de Tocqueville, the great French chronicler of early America, was once misquoted as having said: 'America is the best country in the world to be poor.' That is no longer the case. Nowadays in America, you have a smaller chance of swapping your lower income bracket for a higher one than in almost any other developed economy—even Britain on some measures. To invert the classic Horatio Alger stories, in today's America if you are born in rags, you are likelier to stay in rags than in almost any corner of old Europe.[19]

All of which, Luce finally notes, contributes to the current "slow-burning crisis of American capitalism." In similar, yet still darker vein, Pulitzer Prize winning journalist Chris Hedges recently reported that "[t]here are 50 million Americans in real poverty and tens of millions of Americans in a category called 'near poverty.' "[20]

FIGURE 8: Mae West posing as a striped Statue of Liberty in a publicity still for Mike Sarne's comedy *Myra Breckinridge* (Twentieth-Century Fox, 1970). Photo by Terry O'Neill. Courtesy of Getty Images.

In a recent essay that lambasts the illusory cult of celebrity and of self purveyed by the U.S. mass media, in a culture that "spends its emotional and intellectual energy on the trivial and the absurd," particularly through the medium of television, Chris Hedges asserts that:

> The virtues that sustain a nation-state and build community, from honesty to self-sacrifice to transparency to sharing, are ridiculed each night on television as rubes stupid enough to cling to this antiquated behavior are voted off reality shows. […] Our culture of flagrant self-exaltation, hardwired in the American character, permits the humiliation of all those who oppose us. We believe, after all, that because we have the capacity to wage war we have a right to wage war. Those who lose deserve to be erased. Those who fail, those who are deemed ugly, ignorant or poor, should be belittled and mocked. Human beings are used and discarded like Styrofoam boxes that held junk food. And the numbers of superfluous human beings are swelling the unemployment offices, the prisons and the soup kitchens.[21]

Following historian Charles Maier, he argues that the decline of America began when the nation was transformed from an "empire of production" to an "empire of consumption":

> By the end of the Vietnam War, when the costs of the war ate away at Lyndon Johnson's Great Society and domestic oil production began its steady, inexorable decline, we saw our country transformed from one that primarily produced to one that primarily consumed. We started borrowing to maintain a level of consumption as well as an empire we could no longer afford. We began to use force, especially in the Middle East, to feed our insatiable thirst for cheap oil. We substituted the illusion of growth and prosperity for real growth and prosperity. The bill is now due. America's most dangerous enemies are not Islamic radicals but those who sold us the perverted ideology of free-market capitalism and globalization. They have dynamited the very foundations of our society. In the 17th century these speculators would have been hung. Today they run the government and consume billions in taxpayer subsidies.[22]

Hedges charges the U.S. media with deep complicity in the decline of the very values Luce extolled some seventy years earlier, not least in the erosion of the personal freedoms occasioned by the suspension of habeas corpus, the implementation of the Patriot Act, as well as rendition and wire-tapping. On these issues, he argues, the media are mostly silent, offering instead the "cultural retreat into illusion," so that:

> This cultural retreat into illusion, whether peddled by positive psychologists, by Hollywood or by Christian preachers, is magical thinking. It turns worthless mortgages and debt into wealth. It turns the destruction of our manufacturing base into an opportunity for growth. It turns alienation and anxiety into a cheerful conformity. It turns a nation that wages illegal wars and administers offshore penal colonies where it openly practices torture into the greatest democracy on earth.[23]

MEDIA AND POPULAR CULTURE

Whatever the dark side of contemporary U.S. politics, the rationale for this collection of essays, we trust, has by now been sketched out. Taking as its starting point the massive and undeniable impact of U.S. media and popular culture on Americanization at home and abroad, this volume presents a number of explorations that—imaginatively, if not comprehensively— traverse at least some of the important territory as well as a number of key issues of intellectual interest. These include early American and Chinese cinema, border crossings, the gangster movie and film noir, race and the cinema, the spread of American English, and aspects of digital culture in archivism, popular music, television, and the Internet.

Luce's trope of the American Century worked well for the last century, at a time when the U.S.'s military power was matched by an astounding economic and industrial capability that had turned the country into only the bread-basket but also the new workshop of the world. What, one again wonders, of the future? In the current economic climate, there has been much discussion of the U.S. financial system in crisis, the U.S. economy with its declining industries now dependent on cheap imports of manufactures from low-cost countries abroad, and much talk of a coming Asian Century or Chinese Century as the international economy of the world reconfigures itself. Yet to speak so may be premature. Even though the Chinese economy now seems to be the economic powerhouse fuelling much of the world's economic growth, the evidence that U.S. hegemonic power has reached its limits is fragmentary. The Harvard historian Niall

Ferguson has written at length on the American Empire, reasoning, in essence, that "Empires in short are always with us," that the U.S. (an "Empire in denial") should fully embrace its role as an imperial power, and that there is no viable alternative to the U.S. as the world's superpower:

[W]hat is the alternative to American empire? If, as so many people seem to wish, the United States were to scale back its military commitments overseas, then what? We tend to assume that power, like nature, abhors a vacuum. In the history of world politics, it seems, someone is always the hegemon, or is bidding to play that role. Today, it is the United States; a century ago, it was the United Kingdom. [. . .] Anyone who looks forward eagerly to an American retreat from hegemony should bear in mind that, rather than a multipolar world of competing great powers, a world with no hegemon may be the real alternative to U.S. primacy. Apolarity could turn out to mean not the pacifist utopia envisaged in John Lennon's dirge 'Imagine,' but an anarchic new Dark Age.[24]

Ferguson goes on to argue that the case for the American empire is that the alternative—of international anarchy—is far worse, and in spite of the imperfections of the U.S., "there seems to be no better alternative."[25]

Although such issues of *Weltpolitik* may seem irrelevant to the discussion of media and popular culture, they were certainly central to Luce's original vision, where "American jazz, Hollywood movies, American slang, American machines and patented products" had become the common currency of the mid-twentieth century. Even today, we would argue, America continues to create and export its mediated products, along with its language. The common cultural denominator for many worldwide remains the gloss and frisson of American popular culture, either in its unadulterated forms—direct from Hollywood, New York or elsewhere in the U.S.—or through self-styled regional or national vernacular versions. Our hope with this volume is that the exploratory essays here presented go some way at least towards charting the complexities of media and popular culture representations and reception, as mediated America has sought to define itself both domestically and internationally.

Jan Olsson and Kingsley Bolton
Capitana and Hong Kong, August 2010

ENDNOTES

1. Miriam Hansen, "The Mass Production of the Senses: Classical Cinema as Vernacular Modernism," *Modernism/Modernity*, Vol. 6, No. 2 (1999): 59–77; Zhen Zhang, *An Amorous History of the Silver Screen: Shanghai Cinema, 1896–1937* (Chicago: University of Chicago Press, 2006).

2. Roland Robertson, *Globalization: Social Theory and Global Culture* (London: Sage, 1992).

3. Henry Nash Smith, *Virgin Land: The American West as Symbol and Myth* (Cambridge, MA: Harvard University Press, 1950).

4. Stanley Bailis, "The Social Sciences in American Studies: An Integrative Conception," *American Quarterly*, Vol. 26, No. 3 (1974): 202–224; see also Gene Wise, " 'Paradigm Dramas' in American Studies: A Cultural and Institutional History of the Movement," *American Quarterly*, Vol. 31, No. 3 (1979): 293–337.

5. Among a multitude of appraisals of Wells'/Luce's concept and America's global role, see Norman F. Cantor, ed., *The American Century: Varieties of Culture in Modern Times* (New York: HarperCollins, 1997); David Slater and Peter J. Taylor, eds., *The American Century: Consensus and Coercion in the Projection of American Power* (Malden, MA: Blackwell, 1999); Henry Louis Gates, Jr. and Cornel West, *The African-American Century: How Black Americans Have Shaped Our Country* (New York: Free Press, 2000); Helena Michie and Ronald Thomas, eds., *Nineteenth-Century Geography: The Transformation of Space from the Victorian Age to the American Century* (New Brunswick, N.J.: Rutgers University Press, 2003); R. Laurence Moore and Maurizio Vaudagna, eds., *The American Century in Europe* (Ithaca, N.Y.: Cornell University Press, 2003); William Henry Chafe, *The Rise and Fall of the American Century: United States from 1890–2009* (New York: Oxford University Press, 2009).

6. Henry R. Luce, "The American Century," *Life*, Vol. 10, No. 7 (17 February 1941): 61–65. For a recent account of Luce's career, see Alan Brinkley, *The Publisher: Henry Luce and His American Century* (New York: Knopf, 2010).

7. Andy Warhol, *The Philosophy of Andy Warhol: From A to B and Back Again* (New York: Harcourt Brace Jovanovich, 1975), 71.

8. Lou Dobbs, *Exporting America: Why Corporate Greed Is Shipping American Jobs Overseas* (New York: Warner Business Books, 2004); *War on the Middle Class: How the Government, Big Business Are Waging War on the American Dream and how to Fight Back* (New York: Viking, 2006); *Independents Day: Awakening the American Spirit* (New York: Viking, 2007).

9. For "the triumph of American consumer society over Europe's bourgeois civilization," see Victoria de Grazia, *Irresistible Empire: America's Advance through 20th-Century Europe* (Cambridge, MA: The Belknap Press of Harvard University Press, 2005).

10. Johan Huizinga, *Man and Masses in America*, published in Dutch in 1918, and *Life and Thought in America*, published in 1926; they are combined in an American translation from 1972 by Herbert H. Rowen as *America: A Dutch Historian's Vision, from Afar and Near* (New York: Harper & Row, 1972). Sinclair Lewis, *Babbitt* (New York: Harcourt, Brace and Company, 1922).

11. James Ellroy, *American Tabloid: A Novel* (New York: Knopf, 1995); *The Cold Six Thousand: A Novel* (New York: Knopf, 2001); *Blood's a Rover: A Novel* (New York: Knopf, 2009). Ellroy's trilogy can be productively read alongside John Updike's tetralogy featuring one Harry "Rabbit" Angstrom during more or less the same time span.

12. Stephen Gundle, *Glamour: A History* (Oxford: Oxford University Press, 2008).

13. Faulkner's article from the London *Daily Mail* was summarized in *The Literary Digest*, Vol. 47, No. 3 (19 July 1913): 97–98.

14. For Hollywood's early success prior to Luce's observation, see Kristin Thompson, *Exporting Entertainment: America in the World Film Market 1907–1934* (London: BFI Publishing, 1985).

15. W.T. Stead, *The Americanisation of the World, or The Trend of the Twentieth Century* (London: Review of Reviews, 1901). For perspectives on Stead's analysis, see Robert Frankel, *Observing America: The Commentary of British Visitors to the United States, 1890–1950* (Madison, Wis.: University of Wisconsin Press, 2007).

16. George Norlin, *Things in the Saddle: Selected Essays and Addresses* (Cambridge, MA: Harvard University Press, 1940), 96.

17. James Truslow Adams, "Why We Glorify Our Gangsters," *New York Times*, 13 December 1931, SM1.

18. Niall Ferguson, *Colossus: The Rise and Fall of the American Empire* (New York: Penguin, 2005), 16.

19. Edward Luce, "Goodbye American Dream," *Financial Times*, 1 August 2010, Life and Arts; 1–2, both quotes from page 1.

20. Chris Hedges, "American Psychosis." In *Adbusters*, Summer 2010, no page numbers, Vancouver, British Columbia.

21. Ibid.

22. Ibid.

23. Ibid.
24. Ferguson (2005), xxii–xxiii.
25. Ibid., xxviii.

PART 1

CINEMA AND AMERICANIZATION

CHAPTER 1

ITALIAN MARIONETTES MEET CINEMATIC MODERNITY

JAN OLSSON

HIGH HOPES FOR a better life in the new world animated those that fled unforgiving conditions in the old world. For the first wave of colonizers, the so-called "old immigrants" from northwestern Europe that pushed the frontier westward, the American dream took on a reality very different from the conditions faced by the new immigrants from Eastern and Southern Europe in the metropolitan enclaves after 1880. At that time, after the revolutionary war, land purchases in the Southeast and Southwest, and a civil war to boot, the push of the frontier had taken settlers and new citizens all the way to the Pacific slopes. Manifest Destiny was an accomplished mission, and historian Frederick Jackson Turner could pronounce the frontier closed in a landmark talk delivered at the 1893 Chicago Exhibition.

With a disregard to the pull of the melting pot or crucible, and to the utopian idea of fusion across ethnic and national boundaries, the new immigrants tended to nest in ghetto-like colonies of their own especially in the congested parts of New York City's Lower Manhattan. Italians, mostly from southern Italy and Sicily, followed the Irish and Jews—from Eastern Europe and Russia—and poured into the city. Manhattan's lower East Side thus emerged as laboratory for negotiating cultural fusion and Americanization around 1900.

35

COLONIZATION, IMMIGRATION, AND AMERICANIZATION

The topic of this essay is the discursive negotiations of a vanishing cultural form, the Italian marionette theater, in relation to the popularity of the movies, which was intertwined with the unstoppable inroads of modernity. In this context, Americanization emerged as a discursive horizon for coming to terms with a posited cultural shift and its entangled meanings at a time when immigration was under intense Congressional scrutiny. The downfall of the metonymic marionette theater singled out here also coincided with the publication of one of the most sensational volumes from the Committee on Immigration set up by Congress in 1907, with Senator Dillingham as its Chairman. I will use this shared news window to connect the two debates and especially the framing of cinema as an agent for modernity. In this context, the Americanization of immigrants emerged as a key facet of malleable cultural proclivities and plastic physical forms.

Around 1900, the debate within the U.S. on immigration oftentimes expressed progressive hopes for integrative processes respecting cultural diversity. The melting-pot scenario steeped in ideas of cosmopolitan democracy, however, enjoyed with only a feather-light foundation in real societal processes. Gradually, the very concept of Americanization became discredited as nativists and race theorists gained the upper hand by pushing the envelope for full-fledged integration in an atmosphere of xenophobic fear of alien elements and their loyalties, especially when World War I broke out. In this polarized context, cinema, by way of its diverse screen advocacy of modernity, was perceived as a visual stimulus package for integrative processes en route to citizenship and civic awareness for immigrants. As the Edison trust began to operate in 1909, the industry, once totally dominated by French Pathé, took on an American veneer, and the Red-Rooster brand became only one cog in the larger wheel of cinema. In the following, I will zoom in on Little Italy to discuss discourses of screen modernity as a vehicle for indirect Americanization from the perspectives of culture, ethnicity, and language.

According to historian Donna Gabaccia, "Little Italy's decline began around 1910, just as the number of Italians entering New York came to its peak."[1] This downward spiral for one of the most congested areas in the U.S., she explains, was abetted by faltering real-estate values, the relocation of the garment industry to other parts of town, and improved public transportation, which enabled Italian immigrants to live and/ or to work elsewhere. For the sake of argument, let us narrow down the timeline in order to hinge this putative decline on one emblematic event: the closing down of Antonio Parisi's marionette theater on 418 E. 11th Street in New York City in December 1909.

THE CLOSING OF ANTONIO PARISI'S MARIONETTE THEATER

As I will show, the mounting adversity faced by this traditional theatrical form was read as a symbol of the presumed melting away of the cultural cohesiveness of Italians in Diaspora. The decline in the infrastructure noted by Gabaccia hence runs in tandem with dramatic changes in the cultural arena, which, by commentators of the day, were interpreted as a result of a voluntary and self-styled brand of Americanization amongst Italians. At this juncture, the preferred reading frame to deploy for this particular event was that the artistic forms immigrants brought with them to the new country could no longer withstand the pull from *the* medium of modernity in its American inflection: cinema. Still, as recent scholarship has demonstrated, Italians predominantly watched

FIGURE 1: After a drawing by Helen Wood, *Harper's Weekly*, Vol. 52, No. 2702 (3 October 1908): 16.

movies in variety contexts billing movies together with popular live performances in Italian and continued to do so for years to come, irrespective of whether the scenarios for Americanization were couched in benign or xenophobic terms.

Inflection is not an innocent noun in this context. Language, ranging from language proper to moving images with legends/intertitles in American English, offered a key avenue for a perceived cultural shift signified by the demise of the Italian-speaking marionettes brought over from Messina to Boston by Antonio Parisi and his family in 1888. Circa 1896, the Parisis moved their business to New York City. Soon enough all commentators agreed that Parisi's theater was the most advanced of its kind in New York City with more and bigger marionettes, higher artistic ambitions than the competitors, and in command of multiple playbooks, each with several hundred stories to bill. According to Victor Rousseau in 1908: "this is *the* theatre: the others are imitations."[2] After Parisi's shutdown as 1909 turned into 1910, only one marionette theater remained, it was less flamboyant and had its home on 112th Street far from Little Italy and was run by Joseffi Caldo as the Tripoli Marionette Theater.[3]

In his 1911-book on medieval culture, William Witherle Lawrence ascribes a crucial role for the marionette theater, which is elucidated by an account of a visit to one such show, in all likelihood Parisi's. In a register I've elsewhere labeled metaspectatorship, the visitor provides an account of the show interspersed with audience observations, here noticing the "greatest enthusiasm among the audience," and that the "spectators can hardly restrain themselves for emotion." "Even in their homes in the New World," writes Lawrence, "they still celebrate" the medieval tales "so that the newsboys in the streets of modern American are keeping alive the heroic traditions of the age of Charlemagne." The hero is thereby assured of "immortality by his popularity in foreign land."[4] The stories depicted, the heroic deeds from the era of Charles the Great around the year 800 and the so-called Paladin heroes like Roland from the French *Chansons de Geste*, or Orlando in Italian, were chronicled in early medieval times.[5] The marionette theater's story cycles were long and complex, and serialized in installments evening after evening for a full season. The format thus corresponded to the latter film serials, albeit longer. It is important to note that the marionette theater, at least in its last innings, was a predominantly homosocial affair after the children's exodus. Thus "pushcart peddlers, ditch diggers and small merchants, as well as the theatergoer from Broadway," made up the audience according to one report from a Parisi show.[6] In Italian women's life, cinema allegedly played a much more important role, if we are to believe, at least one, perhaps biased, observer, which we will return to.

In his optimistic chronicle from 1911, Lawrence was apparently unaware of the recent withering away of the old marionette culture. To use his vocabulary, the newsboys had found new heroes. Victor Rousseau, in his piece from a visit to the Parisi's theater in 1908, offered a fine-grained description of the history of the art form, the atmosphere of the place, and the work backstage. He sprinkled the account with audience observations on "the eager faces of the spectators," while noticing the precarious situation for this traditional form of Italian culture in Diaspora. Rousseau's article hence ends on a troubled note foreshadowing the demise of the marionettes, which took place a year later—and he identifies the slayer:

> But this is the passing of Romance. She is dying in this tawdry theater […] the cinematograph is killing her. For the Sicilian has transferred his allegiance to this new rival; the spectators grow fewer; the little heaps of nickel and dimes become more pitifully small; the benches and chairs are more and more in evidence; even the leisurely piano-player grows dispirited as he hammers his syncopated marches. (p. 16)

Rousseau's prophetic comments were penned in October 1908, a year before Parisi's shutdown. Taking cues from this analysis, we will rivet our attention on the marionette theater's last hurrah and its discursive context, blending race theories, Americanization practices pivoted around literacy and language, and a consideration of how cinematic modernity was cast as a featured explanatory culprit in this cultural web.

December 1909 hence represents a critical timeframe fraught with discourses of immigrant life and culture as the temporal backdrop to Parisi's withdrawal from the scene. During this month novel practices and reading frames for cinema were ushered in as critics read the closing down of the marionette theater as a result of the unstoppable popularity of movies. For some this in turn bore on the bigger picture of Americanization from a sensibility all too eager to paper over differences and turn immigrants into loyal subjects. For editorial commentators in several New York dailies, it was not the movies' draw in general that killed off the attractiveness of the marionette's medieval story world. Rather, it was the cultural appeal of the representational palette of the movies and especially its manner of capturing the essence of modernity, as it were, that effected a definitive cultural severing from the old country and its traditional artistic forms. Freed from the putative tyranny of the old, immigrant audiences were propelled to the non-picturesque beauty of American modernity spelled out on the screen as succinct intertitles in American English supplanted the voices of Italian-speaking marionettes. Wishful thinking along crucible lines perhaps, albeit tinged with a modicum of nostalgia, but still a train of thought positing the downfall of the marionettes as part of a series of binary oppositions with cinema at the receiving end of the spectrum, so to speak: slow medieval cultural forms versus modernity's hectic cultural palette, immigrant nostalgia versus liberating future prospects, unforgiving conditions versus novel opportunities, the picturesque versus the poetry of the modern industrial world, Italian versus English, cosmopolitan identity versus American grounding.

THE MOVIES AS LINGUA FRANCA
IN IMMIGRANT NEW YORK

In terms of language, Little Italy operated in three languages, if not four: Italian in its multiple regional and vernacular versions, Italglish, the minimalistic mixture of English and Italian used for the most basic, mundane exchanges, and English.[7] Add to this, if you will, the lingua franca of the movies for visually communicating modern life. Before returning to the marionettes, we will embark on a series of contextual detours beginning with the movies and the state of the cinematic art in late 1909.

In hindsight, two films from December 1909 stand out as indicative of the so-called transitional cinema's diverse representational practices: *A Corner in Wheat* (Biograph Co., 1909) and *The Fly Pest* (Charles Urban, 1909). These two emblematic films foreshadow a heightened complexity in terms of storytelling as well as a rhetorical engagement with politics, body politics, and the vicissitudes of everyday life. At more or less the same time as Antonio Parisi closed down his theater, D.W. Griffith's film *A Corner in Wheat* opened. This film, to great effect, demonstrated the storytelling capabilities of cinema by crosscutting between three story strands unrelated in time and space in order to build a moral argument about the way in which speculation in wheat squeezed both small-time farmers and impoverished consumers.

In 1909, films received shorter than short shrift in the daily press, but one writer in a trade journal singled out this film for its editorial stance, claiming that the film was not a picture drama, but an editorial, an argument, an essay.[8] The immense amount of scholarship devoted to *A Corner in Wheat* primarily bespeaks Griffith's storytelling feat and intertextual play, but few have noticed the film's rootedness in contemporary events— the corner in wheat orchestrated by James Patten at the Chicago Board of Trade in the spring of 1909 and the ensuing bread crisis it provoked, not least on the Lower East Side.[9] A film in a different register attracted much more press attention in December 1909. *The Fly Pest* showed that cinema could be used as a tool for shaping public awareness, in this case concerning health issues. Emerging out of longstanding campaigns against diseases spread by houseflies, the fly-pest discourse came to the screen after years of campaigning in print form, as Marina Dahlquist has showed in a well-documented analysis. This lost film, she concludes, demonstrated the hitherto untapped clout for making cinematic cases both inside and outside picture theaters concerning social problems and health hazards in a style drawing on several genres.[10] So, at this moment of crisis for the Parisi family and their medieval warriors, cinema simultaneously showed off its capacity to abstract storytelling via novel forms of editing in order to expose à la muckraking the inner workings of capitalist economy, while the production of *The Fly Pest* demonstrated cinema's rhetorical wherewithal for building instructive visible arguments concerning matters impacting daily life, not least for immigrants.

Next detour: language, which is embroiled in politics and body politics and intertwined with anthropological frames of reference. The latter aspect will take some space to introduce, but it is critically important as groundwork for today's analysis of ethnicity as dynamic and constructed, rather than given and fixed.

In 1909, as cinema depleted the audience for the marionette culture, the Immigration Commission, formed by the Congress in 1907 and chaired by Senator William P. Dillingham, began publishing its reports. The 41 volumes of reports generated a vast amount of materials and data concerning all aspects of immigration. Overall, however, the report reinforced opposition to immigration from Eastern Europe and Italy, and some commentators, for example historian Oscar Handlin, maintained that the Commission's central assumption concerning fundamental differences between old and new immigrants mars the work by foregone

41

conclusions.[11] This contention does not stand up under serious scrutiny as Robert F. Zeidel shows in his monograph on the Dillingham Commission.[12] Senator Dillingham himself later regularly introduced Congressional bills seeking to make literacy tests mandatory for entering the U.S. Supported by Congress, these bills were vetoed by several Presidents until Woodrow Wilson signed a literacy requirement into law in 1917 as the U.S. entered WWI.

IMMIGRANTS AND ENGLISH

The underlying impetus behind the Commission's work was to put Americanization on the fast track and halt the flow of illiterate immigrants and the likes of Antonio Parisi. In this respect language command was key. Among the multiple cultural practices subsumed under the rubric Americanization, language instruction was the most important. Command of the new country's language is evidently a *sine qua non* for active citizenship and cultural belonging. At the time, language was an issue charged with political controversy, ranging from the nativists' clamor for a literacy test to put restrictions on immigration to employer-sponsored initiatives for teaching primarily a factory-relevant version of English. Peter Roberts' work for the industrial branch of Y.M.C.A. seems particularly relevant in this context.

FIGURE 2: Dr. Peter Roberts, the prime mover behind Y.M.C.A.'s language program *English for Coming Americans*. Photograph courtesy of Kautz Family YMCA Archives, University of Minnesota Libraries.

FIGURE 3: A language class in session at Y.M.C.A.'s McBurney branch in Brooklyn. Photograph courtesy of Kautz Family YMCA Archives, University of Minnesota Libraries.

FIGURE 4: A group of students with Chinese background studying English in Minneapolis c. 1907. The students are clearly holding the book *A First Book in English for Foreigners* by Isabel Richman Wallach. The book was published in New York by Boston, Silver, and Burdett Co. in 1906. Photograph courtesy of Kautz Family YMCA Archives, University of Minnesota Libraries.

Peter Roberts language-course program *English for Coming Americans* was first published in our key year, 1909, and reprinted multiple times parallel to his other publications on education for immigrants, among them songs for immigrants and a reader for immigrants. Roberts' pedagogical model was based on the conviction that language was more effectively learned via speech rather than by way of books; the ear, as he phrases it, is "the door to language command." Practice and conversation in daily life are therefore superior to mere reading, and logic and relevant contexts function more effectively than memorizing meaningless sentences. It seems as if Roberts took advantage of the movies for language training in 1913, but the evidence is scant, and only visible in a very limited sense in a featured newspaper article with illustrations apparently from a film. A sole surviving photograph (Figure 5) is identical with one of the illustrations. If there was a film it has vanished without a trace.[13]

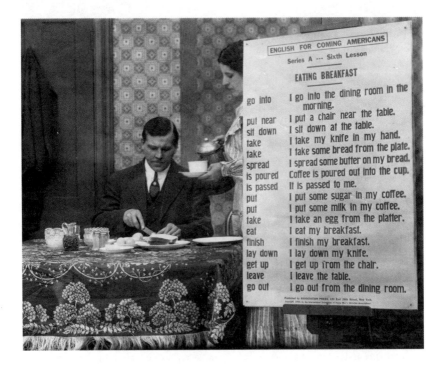

FIGURE 5: Photograph courtesy of Kautz Family YMCA Archives, University of Minnesota Libraries. This photograph and three additional ones from the same series were published in *The Sun* (New York), 1 June 1913, IV:12.

In tune with the assumptions animating the Dillingham Commission, many corporations adopted Roberts' methods and promoted a model of the English language that ensured loyalty to the company as well as allegiance to American values and life styles. Many of the students in Roberts-inspired classes were Italians. More research is called for regarding Roberts' and Y.M.C.A.'s language project and its adoption by American corporations.[14]

FRANZ BOAS AND IMMIGRANT ANTHROPOLOGY

As the marionette theater closed down, the newspapers reported on the summary version of one of the Dillingham Commission's volumes, the one conducted under the auspices of a team headed by renowned anthropologist Franz Boas from Columbia University. From the perspective of immigration, Boas' findings and conclusions concerning changes in bodily form for immigrant children born in the United States were sensational and still stir controversy among anthropologists. Some of the press accounts greeted the report in a celebratory manner with headlines like "Aliens Absorbed" or "Racial Characteristics Disappearing in Melting Pot."[15]

The research methodology came out of a discipline that, not least thanks to Boas' own landmark achievements in pioneering fieldwork, linguistics, and physical anthropology, had moved out of the museums to academia proper. His analysis of changes in bodily form in several respects reframed the discourse of physical anthropology as he abandoned the concept of *race*—and this is key—for *type* thereby supplanting a prejudiced optics pigeonholing immigrant groups in fixed racial terms.

Boas' findings shattered the default theory among physical anthropologists that humankind was made up of a roster of permanent forms, which by way of heredity conveniently translated into a limited set of races labeled in terms of geographical grounding and other loose categories, for example Hebrew. Boas convincingly showed that that there are substantial differences in terms of bodily form within all groups however defined, but his most controversial finding was that he could show that bodily form is not a genetic affair only. The environment, and this was a deathblow to traditional race theory, plays a role as well. Albeit

45

small, the changes he found were significant when he measured head forms for children born by mothers in the old country and head forms for offspring born by immigrant mothers in the U.S.

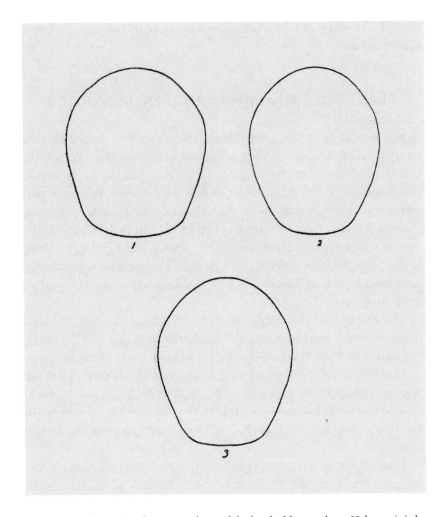

FIGURE 6: "Showing (1) the average form of the head of foreign-born Hebrew; (2) the average form of head of the foreign-born Sicilian; (3) the average form of the American-born Hebrew and Sicilian born more than ten years after the arrival of mother in America. These sketches are intended only to give an impression of the change in proportion. They do not represent the head form in detail." U.S. Immigration Commission, *Reports of the Immigration Commission*, Vol. 38, *Changes in Bodily Form of Descendants of Immigrants* (Washington, D.C.: U.S. Government Printing Office, 1911): 9.

When discussing bodily changes, Boas did not resort to average measurements; bodily and cranial plasticity in the offspring were instead measured in relation to the mother. Thus his material evidenced that a round head form, traditionally associated with East European immigrants, were slightly less round for offspring born in the U.S. by immigrant mothers from this region, while the long head form associated with immigrants from south of Europe, were less long for the U.S. born offspring to mothers from, for example, Sicily. This did not translate to a progressive tendency that eventually would collapse future generations into a common American type with bodily differences melted away, but it demonstrated that the environment, irrespective of mechanisms for selection à la Darwin or Spencer, impacted even what previously was perceived as the most stable genetic determinants. In fact Boas' terminology clashed with another of the commission's reports titled "A Dictionary of Races and Peoples (Vol. 5)," which, as Handlin aptly describes it, "ran a persistent, though not a consistent, tendency to determine race by physical type, to differentiate the old from the new immigrants racially, and to indicate the superiority of the former to the latter." (105)

Boas' conclusions concerning cranial plasticity have generated intense debate among anthropologists the last few years as two research teams using up-to-date methods for measuring have revisited his material and arrived at conflicting conclusions, and I shall not elaborate on the complexities of the debate. From a perspective outside the discipline, it does however seem that Boas' supporters convincingly demonstrate that the detractors misstate his case concerning cranial plasticity and operate with flawed methodological assumptions.[16] Previews of Boas' report were published in the press more or less the same week as the marionette theater's downfall was discussed.[17]

Boas did not convince everybody concerning malleability in Diaspora, physical and otherwise. Edward A. Ross, a leading sociologist, was a staunch and representative proponent of old-fashioned race theory and spread the word in several books and articles. In a 1914 book he does not mince words concerning the alleged racial and cultural inferiority of immigrants from the southern parts of Italy, which he profiles in physiological and psychological terms. The lengthy passage below is indicative of his hardliner analysis and its division between old and new immigrants spelled out in racial/racist terms.

Steerage passengers from a Naples boat show a distressing frequency of low foreheads, open mouths, weak chins, poor features, skew faces, small or knobby crania, and backless heads. Such people lack the power to take rational care of themselves; hence their death-rate in New York is twice the general death-rate and thrice that of the Germans [...] If it be demurred that the ignorant, superstitious Neapolitan or Sicilian, heir to centuries of Bourbon misgovernment, cannot be expected to prove us his race mettle, there are his children, born in America. What showing do they make? Teachers agree that the children of the South Italians rank below the children of the North Italians. They hate study, make slow progress, and quit school at the first opportunity. While they take to drawing and music, they are poor in spelling and language and very weak in abstract mathematics. In the words of one superintendent, 'they lack the conveniences for thinking.' More than any other children, they fall behind their grade [...] As grinding rusty iron reveals the bright metal, so American competition brings to light the race stuff in poverty-crushed immigrants. But not all this stuff is of value in a democracy like ours. Only a people endowed with a steady attention, a slow-fuse temper, and a persistent will can organize itself for success in the international rivalries to come. So far as the American people consents to incorporate with itself great numbers of wavering, excitable, impulsive persons who cannot organize themselves, it must in the end resign itself to lower efficiency, to less democracy, or to both.[18]

THE FORTUNES OF MARIONETTE THEATER

As Ross and others noted, Italians passing through the Golden Door into America predominantly clustered on Manhattan's Lower East Side, not least around the infamous Mulberry Bend. But there was another Italian enclave in East Harlem around Pleasant Avenue. It was in Harlem—and now we are back on track after our detours—that Antonio Parisi opened his marionette theater when he moved from Boston in 1896. The Parisi family relocated to the Lower East Side in 1902, to Elisabeth Street; in the vicinity there were 4,000 to 5,000 inhabitants per block. All in all, 650,000 lived in this immensely over-crowded part of Manhattan. The Parisis found a site for their theater close to their tenement home further down on the street, at 258 Elisabeth Street.

FIGURE 7: 258 Elisabeth Street; the location for Antonio Parisi's theater before moving to 11th Street in 1908.

The family's stock of puppets comprised of more than 300 marionettes, of which many were life-sized and some were worth over $150. In the spring of 1908, as Rousseau noted later that year, the patronage of the theater began to dwindle. The show was considered too highbrow for the local audience. At the same time the People's Institute, one of the leading progressive bodies, intervened, but only in a half-hearted manner. The Institute's Committee on Drama and Music did not want to put the marionette plays on their list of cultural valuable offerings for school children, but still recommended and subsidized three shows, one on April 30th, 1908, and two the following day.

> [We] do not care to recommend these performances, not that there is anything objectionable on moral grounds, and not that they are not of literary merit, but because they are not of sufficient artistic merit to warrant such a recommendation. However, in as much as these performances of the Marionettes are of historical interest, both from their long Italian history and from the historical subject which they present. The

Committee is willing to announce these three performances in the public schools, and to arrange half prices for those who care to see them.

The performances will be given in Italian with English explanation, and will be staged in the same way they were in medieval time. The subject of the performances will be from the tales of the Paladins of France, or the legends of Charlemagne.[19]

Antonio Parisi spoke no English and the shows were of course delivered in Italian. The family communicated with authorities through their son Nunzio, he was 16 years old in 1908 and wanted to be an artist. He had painted and renovated the dolls and painted background scenery as well. With support from the People's Institute, it seems, the theater was moved from the heart of the Italian enclave to a locale on the fringe of the Italian quarters, 418 E. 11th Street in the vicinity of First Avenue, and the Institute seems to have arranged for art courses for Nunzio. There are however no documents in the People's Institute's collection concerning their involvement in the relocation.[20] The new venue was for sure no upgrade, rather, a desperate attempt to keep the business afloat. At the new location, Parisi's stand was not as before on the street. "Now the visitor must traverse the dark, narrow passage to an open court, where it is always wash day [. . .] Across the courtyard a flight of steps is mounted, a huge barnlike door is opened and the theatre is attained."[21]

After a year and a half at the new address, the theater was forced to close its doors and the newspapers, in line with Rousseau's reasoning from 1908, framed the story as a defeat incurred by the success of adjacent moving picture shows. According to the headline in *New York Times*, "Moving Pictures Oust the Puppets." The article in the *Times* claimed that the "Sicilians in New York have become just enough Americanized to desert the little theater where the old Italian romances were acted out by puppets." And rhetorically asked: "What are the classic heroes of long ago beside the latest prizefight!" The latter was, of course, shown on the screen. The article claimed that Antonio Parisi even contemplated turning his theater into a picture show, even if he disliked movies. This never happened, instead he returned to his very first occupation as plumber.[22]

Six months after closing the theater, Antonio Parisi, according to the *Times*, began offering shows on Sunday afternoons after plumbing on weekdays. Now, however, the theater operated in a new language regis-ter—instead of a show in Italian, the Parisis had found helpers for offer-ing the tales in English, thereby hoping to attract a new audience, but the change of language was not enough to turn the tide.[23] In the age of the movies, the marionette culture, irrespective of language, was relegated to what Raymond Williams calls the residual domain (within his three intertwined strands for describing cultural change: the emergent, the dominant, and the residual).[24] While marionettes receded into the re-sidual, movies moved from the emergent to the dominant register of culture in pact with modernity's leaps and bounds.

MOVIES AS MODERNITY

The journalistic framing of Antonio Parisi's downfall ties in with dis-courses reading film culture as an exponent of modernity with an Amer-ican inflection, albeit conveniently forgetting that Italians often enjoyed films in a dual language register: films with English intertitles on screen interspersed with live acts in Italian.

As progressive-era reformers repeatedly contended, going to the mov-ies was a learning process—a form of schooling. Film foes and film en-thusiasts alike agreed that cinema was an unrivaled educator and learn-ing tool. This perception was mobilized to make sense of the downfall of the marionettes in the light of cinema. An editorial in *New York Evening World*, labeled "Marionettes and Moving Pictures", outlined the bigger picture as a segue to the symbolic shift:

> This is the twentieth century—the age of the wireless telegraph, the aero-plane and the moving pictures. The world progresses and the old order of things gives place to the new. [...] [N]ow another conquest of the films puts out of business our medieval friend Signor Parisi, for more than twenty years master of the marionettes.[25]

Arthur H. Gleason's account in *Collier's* was even more adamant on cast-ing modernity's culture of speed as the culprit for the downfall of the marionettes. Writing a couple of months before Parisi called it quits, Gleason opined that "the itch for speed and newsy novelties" had only a "brief life till Modernism haunts them down." Within the paradigm of

"Modernism," Gleason singles out cinema as the marionettes have been "exiled by moving pictures and the Americanization of emotion." According to Gleason:

> [m]oving pictures have driven out the Marionettes of New York. The nickelodeon world is the same mad world as that of the Sunday comic supplement. There is the hot speed, the phantasmagoria, lightning change of incident, blur, and frenzy of color. From those twinkling, overheated scenes of accident, seduction, and sudden death, it is gracious to turn to the cool, orderly ways of the Carlovingian manikins, with their unfailing dignity, even under the drums and trampling of massacre, the repose of manner as of haughty generations enobling the blood. [Gleason (1909), p. 26]

An editorial in New York's *Evening Sun* offered the most circumspect analysis of the shift from marionettes to moving pictures maintaining that films taught lessons in modernity to immigrants allegedly eager to escape from the traditions of their home countries. The editorial cut to the chase regarding Americanization by addressing the migratory amusement preferences of Italian immigrants in New York City with reference to the sad case of Parisi's marionette business. If we are to trust the enthusiastic account steeped in the utopian ideology of the melting pot, which also greeted Boas' findings, uprooting and transplanting apparently could not only change the skies and the bodily form of the offspring but also their cultural habits—thus the demise of the marionette theater as a viable cultural form for Italians in Diaspora.

According to the editorial, the new Americans in Little Italy were willing—even eager—to embrace the culture and emblematic vistas indicative of their new country as represented by an imaginary amalgamation on film screens of industrial Chicago, Coney Island, and the Wild West. From such a concept of cultural variety, readily available through nickelodeon programming, cinema offered illuminating dynamite in Walter Benjamin's sense for those that had fled unforgiving conditions in Europe and wanted to branch out from the cultural confines of the ethnic colonies in American metropolises. In this scenario, cinema becomes a prime clearinghouse for process of Americanization by removing immigrant patrons from the cultural forms they carried with them, here literally and symbolically represented by the marionettes.

This perception of a cultural shift as cinema eclipses Italian-speaking marionettes by films sprinkled with intertexts in American English therefore has a deep-seated significance for a reading of the emergent transitional cinema with its stories and non-fiction genres as a key engine for Americanization at a time of decline for Little Italy. Once, the editorialist told the readers of the *Evening Sun:*

> [Paris's Marionette Theater] was the most 'distinctive' place of amusement in New York (so the overeducated will tell you); far more so than the Chinese theatre, or any of the *cafés chantants* of the various 'quarters,' Russian, Syrian, Greek or what-you-like. And sure enough, for a time, the place was packed with the sons and daughters of the Sicilians, comforting their homesick eyes with the play of the old puppets, nursing their nostalgia.

Here we have two important coordinates—the appreciation of the overeducated—whatever this category subsumes—and a hypothesis for the success in the early days: homesickness and nostalgia with a male slant. This interpretation is underwritten by one of the first accounts of a Parisi show published in 1907. In Elisabeth Irwin's male-centered analysis:

> The tired laborer here forgets that the hour is midnight and all is dark without, that the season is winter and ice and dirty snow cover the streets, that the country is America where sweatshops and tenement houses bound his horizon. To him it is the age of chivalry, he basks in eternal sunshine, he smells the ever-blooming flowers, he is again in the land of his dreams, of his youth, of all his romance, under the sea blue skies of his beloved Italy.[26]

But then things changed, and now we return to the editorialist, and "somehow the spell broke and pouf! Away went the audience." For a while, American children apparently carried the show, but now both Italian immigrants and American children "all like the moving picture shows better." This ties in with Parisi's own analysis ventured in the *New York Times*. About ninety per cent of the patrons, he maintained, went around the corner to the picture theater. But there was an even more important change in mindset seemingly exorcising the old nostalgia according to the *Evening Sun*'s editorial. Namely the alleged fact that the new Americans do not look back "to the land which bore them and starved their souls and bodies." And therefore, "away with the foolish old puppets, and the old tales, and the old order. Moving pictures of steel bridges with express trains crossing them, of new scenes, of the new life [...] and never mind about Firenze or Napoli or Amalfi—talk about Coney Island and Chicago; they are all Americans now."[27] Still, it seems as if the eagerness to adapt to the new skies and turn into real Americans applied primarily to the young ones, those born in the new country or who arrived with their families at a tender age, somebody like Nunzio who had mastered the new language that his parents could not learn. In this respect, Gleason's account of a visit to Parisi's theater offers the most poignant generational emphasis:

> At the Eleventh Street show there sat in the row of the well-to-do a part of five smartly dressed, clever Americanized Italians of the second generation. All the imagination had been flattened out of them. Fluent ridicule was the only reaction of which they were capable. They did not, of course, realize that their attitude toward the 'machine Gestientlantes' showed less intelligence than that of the fruit-venders at the rear. [Gleason (1909), p. 24]

The *Evening Sun*'s editorial instead ventured an upbeat utopian blueprint for the role of film culture in relation to the transformation of immigrant experiences in American metropolises. The editorial positions the new Americans in a liminal spatial zone, in the heterotopical context of cinematic modernity, which propelled them or at least their imagined ideas to an America outside their own ethnic enclaves. Simultaneously, cinematic representations relegate the old country, here Italy, and its cultural imprint to a fading series of picturesque vistas, sights, or places. By contrast, the metropolitan experience, the amusement park, and the movies harnessed together, as it were, teach the immigrants exciting modernity lessons.

The editorial in the *Evening Sun* epitomizes a salient shift in the perception of film culture's role within the larger fabric of modernity. The analysis is of course over-eager in its assessment of film culture's potential for transforming the mindset and cultural habits of Italian immigrants. It was never a question of either/or, instead a negotiation à la Williams between the old and the new culture that continued for years to come, ir-

54

respective of the downfall of Parisi's marionettes and the inroads of film culture. The editorial stance is, however, conflicted in its analysis and ends on a nostalgic note when asking: "[…] is there no room for some of the old forms which their fathers and mothers knew? Are the lights out forever in the theatre of the marionettes?"

The editorial's nostalgic coda mirrors an analysis ventured by John Corbin back in 1898 when writing on the shutdown of the Teatro Italiano, which was also predominantly patronized by men. Corbin's explanation for the theater's downfall points to a similar eagerness to assimilate and leave the old culture behind. Already here the analysis posits a generational difference concerning cultural preferences between first generation immigrants and their offspring.

> The trouble is with their assimilative natures. In a few years even the older immigrants are apt to pick up our language, and one by one to abandon their native customs and ways of thought. Even in the theater they spoke to each other mainly in English. In seeking amusement they fall prey to the flash and glare of our variety bill-posters. The new generation, who lack the traditions of the home country, and sometimes the knowledge of Italy to appreciate its drama, are almost certain to become Americanized in their tastes. An Italian theater could appeal only to new arrivals and to those of the past generation who have not forgotten their old life and the joy of true acting.[28]

A small aside, which in its blunt musing calls for more research concerning early film audiences' gender make-up, was published in the Italian press in New York City. Here the vernacular playwright, poet, performer Giovanni De Rosalia from Sicily penned a different take on the relationships between the marionettes and the movies in November 1909 claiming "the cinematograph is nothing else but a new form of Sicilian puppet show." His contention was solely based on the passionate, but gender-split, disposition displayed by the devotees—men for the puppets and women for cinema. To his mind going to the movies was a waste of money and time for women, since they were too ignorant to understand the nature of the fiction and thus try to interact with the story world. It would therefore have been better if women would "stay at home cleaning up, knitting, washing dishes, and mending."[29]

Not only De Rosalia was unimpressed by the posited polarity be-

tween cinema and marionette culture, but others too. In a critical assessment of cinema as the last refuge for a brand of hackneyed, machine-
made romance, a discourse harking back to the first generation of commentators from O. Winter to Gorky, and most systematically probed by
Luigi Pirandello in his novel *Shoot* from 1914, Herman Scheffauer stresses the affinity between cinema and the marionette culture by highlighting their shared inanimate material base—wooden marionettes operated by iron rods and cords and their putative affinity with cinema's soul-
less machinery. This sobering note undercuts the utopian aspirations for
cinema ventured by the *Evening Sun*'s editorialist. Writes Scheffauer in
January 1913: "The new lying moonshine that beguiles the millions of today is no longer reflected sunlight, but the harsher, deadlier white glare
that streams through the lens of the picture machine [...] In their shad-
ow-shapes the villain is hissed and the hero is applauded." After having
paved the ground, comes the comparison with the marionettes' primitive involvement in representations. Obviously unaware that cinema has
killed off the old Italian marionette culture, Scheffauer claims that film
audiences engage with cinema—"just as rapt Italians shout and cry over
the antics of the wooden marionettes operated by heavy cords and thick
iron rods."[30] The dominant reading of film spectatorship at this time is
otherwise that a former interactive engagement had been displaced by a
more disciplined regime devoid of shouts and cries.[31]

Simultaneously, the dispersed marionette culture took on an idealized form in intellectual circles outside the timeless function analyzed
by the medievalist William Witherle Lawrence. As theater legend Gordon Craig supplanted actors with so-called super-marionettes and Mau-
rice Maeterlinck began writing plays for marionettes, a new era dawned
for a novel, avant-garde form of marionette culture. A Marionette Society was organized in New York City in 1913 taking the discourse we
have been tracing full circle by stating "marionettes will vie with moving
pictures in popularity." John Collier of the People's Institute in an interview even hoped that "some of the old Italian puppet shows, perhaps
those that are already in storage in this city, could be set up in our small
city parks." This would "delight not only the children, but these simple-
minded Italians who cling in their old traditions and legends." Here we
are back to perceptions of primitive audiences unaffected by the brand
of modernity posited for cinema in the *Evening Sun*. Hoping for a revival
of an art form already abandoned by Italian audiences and allegedly un-

done by the movies, Collier's stance echoes De Rosalia and Scheffauer: "In our country," he rhetorically asks, "what is the moving picture show, after all, but a realistic marionette show?"[32]

Italians having walked away from the art form they brought with them for cinema and modernity in the 1909-readings are here idealistically re-inserted in their traditional culture by way of an analysis that equates the two forms of representations, marionettes and cinema, through the emphasis on shared symbolism irrespective of material base. Where Collier sees unifying symbolism, Scheffauer only notices hackneyed romance, wood, and machinery, while the editorial writer in 1909 believed that Italian emigrants watching the screen perceived the culturally liberating realities of modern life.

POSTSCRIPT FOR THE PARISIS

Our discursive analysis of the undoing of one aspect of the culture of Little Italy by popular non-demand in 1909 mirrors the overall decline noted by Gabaccia. Decline here signals a shift, which for certain did not Americanize Italians once and for all, but, instead, spelled an enlarged fabric of Italian culture, even without the marionettes, spread across the overall tapestry of greater New York. The movies might have killed off the marionettes, but not Italian culture in New York City. And, surprise, surprise—a brand new marionette theater emerged in the late 1910s by way of Argentina. It survived well into the 1930s and Agrippino Manteo and his family pulled the cords.

In the context of 1909, as we have shown, the Parisi family was very much a case in point concerning the new immigration. Arriving in 1888, Antonio Parisi would probably not have passed the literacy test Senator Dillingham and others later wanted to adopt to keep undesirable immigrants out. We have no data for the three Parisi sons' head forms, but the two younger ones went to school when Boas conducted his study and could theoretically have been measured by his team. Returning to Victor Rousseau's article from a visit to the theater in 1908, we find a pregnant description of the family in terms of a cultural trajectory along the lines of negotiations discussed here, but with a progressive, cosmopolitan focus in tune with the nostalgic coda in the *Evening Sun*'s editorial. Thus, we may give the last words to Rousseau who reports that "Antonio is from Messina, and a pure medieval; Nunzio [the older son] is an American-Italian, one of those citizens of the next generation who will produce in America some sudden art renaissance by virtue of our commingling with the most gifted race in Europe. There are two boys besides, but they were born after Sicily had become a memory; they are American purely."

FIGURE 8: After a drawing by Helen Wood, *Harper's Weekly*, Vol. 52, No. 2702 (3 October 1908): 15.

ENDNOTES

1. Donna Gabaccia, "Little Italy's Decline: Immigrant Renters and Investors in a Changing City." In David Ward and Oliver Zunz, eds., *The Landscape of Modernity: New York City, 1900–1940* (Baltimore: Johns Hopkins University Press, 1997 [1992]), 244.
2. Victor Rousseau, "A Puppet Play Which Lasts Two Months," *Harper's Weekly*, Vol. 52, No. 2702 (3 October 1908): 15–16.
3. According to puppet historian Paul McPharlin, Caldo's puppets were small and "not so well made." *The Puppet Theater in America: A History* (New York: Harper & Brothers, 1949), 301.
4. William Witherle Lawrence, *Medieval Story and the Beginning of the Social Ideals of English-Speaking People* (New York: Columbia University Press, 1911), 57–59. In his essay, "Puppet Shows, Old and New," Brander Matthews quotes Lawrence account seemingly, too, unaware of the downfall of New York's old

marionette culture. *The Bookman*, Vol. 40, No. 4 (December 1914): 379–388. A survey of the amusements in New York City from 1911 duly noted the demise of this cultural form: "Three years ago one might enjoy three Italian Marionette-shows, two downtown, the third in the uptown Italian quarter. Nothing more replete with local color, more naively mediæval, no more sincere as an expression of folk-life, could be seen in New York. Now only one remains, and it is time to make haste to see it." Michael M. Davis, Jr., *The Exploitation of Pleasure: A Study of Commercial Recreations in New York City* (New York: Department of Child Hygiene of the Russell Sage Foundation, 1911), 35. For my fullest discussion of metaspecatorship, see *Los Angeles Before Hollywood: Journalism and American Film Culture, 1905 to 1915* (Stockholm: The National Library of Sweden, 2008).

5. For an account of a visit to a puppet show in San Francisco with a French-Sicilian tinge, see Lucy B. Jerome, "The Marionettes of Little Sicily," *New England Magazine*, Vol. 41 (February 1910): 745–750. The audience here is described as "a medley of nationalities" from the Quarter, which is inhabited by "French, Portuguese, Spanish, Italian, Russian and Turkish dwellers"; p.745.

6. "Where Puppet Knights Battle Gloriously As Lurid Tale Is Told," *New York Herald*, 20 February 1910, III:8. An earlier report lined up a more or less identical audience composition for Salvatore Lo Cascio's show at 111th Street and First Avenue: "eighty to two hundred push-cart peddlers, candy-store men, ditch-diggers—Italians all." Arthur H. Gleason, "Last Stand Marionette," *Collier's*, Vol. 44, No. 5 (23 October 1909): 16, 24, 26; quotation from p. 16. The audience at Parisi's show was somewhat different according to Gleason.

7. For a discussion of Itaglish, see Michael La Sorte, *La Merica: Images of Italian Greenhorn Experience* (Philadelphia: Temple University Press, 1985), chapter 5.

8. *New York Dramatic Mirror*, Vol. 62, No. 1618 (25 December 1909): 15.

9. See my essay "Trading Places: Griffith, Patten and Agricultural Modernity," *Film History*, Vol. 17, No. 1 (2005): 39–65.

10. Marina Dahlquist, " 'Swat the Fly.' Educational Films and Health Campaigns 1909–1914." In Corinna Müller, ed., *Kinoöffentlichkeit/Cinema's Public Sphere* (Marburg: Schüren Verlag, 2008), 211–225.

11. Oscar Handlin, *Race and Nationality in American Life* (Boston: Little, Brown and Company, 1957 [1948]), 131.

12. Robert F. Zeidel, *Immigrants, Progressives, and Exclusion Politics: The Dillingham Commission, 1900–1927* (DeKalb, Illinois: Northern Illinois University Press, 2004), especially chapter 2.

13. For a discussion of Y.M.C.A. and cinema, see John Collier, "Motion Pictures for Y.M.C.A. Work," *Motography*, Vol. 8, No. 13 (21 December 1912): 493–495. Regarding teaching language by "the aid of the 'movies,' " I have not been able to find any evidence that this happened irrespective of still images and the claim: "The accompanying photographs showing the latest use to which it [the moving picture] has been put was devised by the Young Men's Christian Association to teach English to foreigners and newcomers to this country." *The Sun* (New York), 1 June 1913, IV:12.

14. Gerd Korman has written the best account of Roberts' work, see his *Industrialization, Immigrants, and Americanizers: The View from Milwaukee, 1866–1921* (Madison, Wisconsin: Wisconsin State Historical Society, 1967); see also Korman's essay "Americanization at the Factory Gate," *Industrial and Labor Relations Review*, Vol. 18, No. 3 (April 1965): 396–419.

15. *New York Tribune*, 17 December 1909, 4. One editorialist pushed the envelope even further when speculating on "the physical make-up and aspect of the negro. Is his cranium also altering, and is his skin becoming whiter?" "The American Type," *Globe and Commercial Advertiser*, 17 December 1909, 10.

16. Franz Boas, "Changes in Bodily From of Descendents of Immigrants," *American Anthropologist*, Vol. 14, No. 2 (April–June, 1912): 530–562; for the critical reappraisal of Boas' study, see Corey Sparks and Richard Jantz, "A Reassessment of Human Cranial Plasticity: Boas Revisited," *Proceedings of the National Academy of Sciences*, Vol. 99, No. 23 (2002): 14636–14639; a study confirming Boas' findings was published by Clarence G. Gravlee, H. Russell Bernard, and William R. Leonard, "Heredity, Environment, and Cranial Form: A Re-Analysis of Boas' Immigrant Data," *American Anthropologist*, Vol. 105, No. 1 (2003): 123–136. An "Exchange across Difference" was published with follow-ups from the two research teams: Gravlee et. al., "Boas' *Changes in Bodily Form*: The Immigrant Study, Cranial Plasticity, and Boas' Physical Anthropology," *American Anthropologist*, Vol. 105, No. 2 (2003): 326–332 and Jantz/Sparks, "Changing Times, Changing Faces: Franz Boas' Immigrant Study in Modern Perspective," *American Anthropologist*, Vol. 105, No.2 (2003): 333–337.

17. The congressional commission was not the only investigation concerning immigration, the state of New York launched its own Commission of Immigration and it submitted its report to the legislature in Albany in April 1909.

18. Edward A. Ross, *The Old World and the New* (New York: Century Publishing, 1914), 118.

19. The People's Institute Collection at New York Public Library, Department

of Drama and Music (Box 14), Folder 2 "Correspondence 1905–1909"; Undated letter signed Charles Sprague Smith.

20. The hopes for saving the theater was expressed in an article in *New York Times* —"Hope for Parisi of the Marionettes," 21 April 1908, 6.

21. "Where Puppet Knights Battle Gloriously As Lurid Tale Is Told," *New York Herald*, 20 February 1910, III:8.

22. Gleason also weighs in on prizefights in relation to the marionette culture in his *Collier's* article and especially the spectators' engagement with respective "medium." Writes Gleason: "The beast-like yells that come from the spectators at a prize-fight when the blood begins to spurt or a bone snaps are of less benefit as a form of self-expression than the naïve approval of the vendors in the rear rows as the Christian triumphs gloriously over Pagan foes." (p. 16)

23. "Marionettes Back, Speaking English," *New York Times*, 22 May 1910, 7.

24. Raymond Williams, *Marxism and Literature* (New York: Oxford University Press, 1977), Chapter entitled "Dominant, Residual and Emergent," 121–127. It seems as if Parisi's theater in its Italian language register closed somewhat later than December 1909 given a feature article from a show published in *New York Herald* on February 20, 1910. The hiatus before opening in English was therefore somewhat shorter even if the *Times* claimed that the theater had shut down six months ago.

25. "Marionettes and Moving Pictures," *New York Evening World*, 15 December 1909, 18.

26. Elisabeth Irwin, "Where the Players Are Marionettes and the Age of Chivalry Is Born Again in a Little Theater in Mulberry Street," *Craftsman*, Vol. 12, No. 6 (September 1907): 667–669; quotation from p. 669.

27. *Evening Sun* (New York), 16 December 1909, 10.

28. John Corbin, "How the Other Half Laughs," *Harper's New Monthly Magazine*, Vol. 98, (December 1898): 30–48; quotation from p. 36.

29. The translation comes from Giorgio Bertellini's doctoral dissertation, 620–623. Giovanni De Rosalia, "Scene Sicilane: Lu Cinematografu," *Follia di New York*, 7 November 1909, 4.

30. Herman Scheffauer, "The Last Refuge of 'Romance,' " *Lippincott's Monthly Magazine*, Vol. 91, No. 594 (January 1913): 120–122; quotation from p. 121.

31. For an authoritative analysis, see Miriam Hansen, *Babel and Babylon. Spectatorship in American Silent Film.* Cambridge, MA: Harvard University Press, 1991.

32. "The Old Puppet Show Is to Be Restored to Favor," *New York Times*, 4 May 1913, SM5.

CHAPTER 2

"A RED-BLOODED ROMANCE"; OR, AMERICANIZING EARLY MULTI-REEL FEATURE CINEMA: THE CASE OF THE *SPOILERS*

JOEL FRYKHOLM

THE FIRST PUBLIC presentation of *The Spoilers* (Selig, 1914) took place on March 25th, 1914, at Orchestra Hall in Chicago before a specially invited audience. Harry Ennis of the *New York Clipper* enthusiastically declared that "[a] truly American subject, has been carried out by American artists, under the direction of a wonderfully astute American producer, and the results are altogether remarkable."[1] Ennis also previewed the April 11th opening of the Strand Theatre in New York City, suggesting that *The Spoilers* was a perfect pick as the opening feature film: "[The film is chosen] not alone for its quality, but also to be in keeping with the occasion—an American story by an American author, produced in America for the premier of the greatest American photodrama theatre, which was also built by Americans, with American capital."[2]

From a scholarly perspective, *The Spoilers* offers an exciting entry point to a range of themes, topics, and discourses of relevance for our understanding of what has often been referred to as "transitional" cinema.[3] The Americanizing of the early multi-reel feature film market in the U.S.—and of movies and film culture in general we might add—is one such topic. Another relates to how the multi-reel feature film—through a complex interplay between localized diversity and homogenizing tendencies, between local strategies of exhibition and centrally tailored marketing schemes—came to be the central film industrial commodity as well as the dominant format for film artistic expression.[4]

This article explores both these areas in relation to *The Spoilers*. Drawing on various intertexts, on sources relating to Rex Beach's public persona, and on critical and advertising discourses in the newspaper press of selected cities across the United States where the film was screened, the following is as an attempt to at least initiate a reconstruction of the conditions for the historical reception of *The Spoilers*.[5]

FIGURE 1: Rex Beach, date undetermined (George Grantham Bain Collection, Library of Congress, Photographs and Prints Division).

THE BACKGROUND

Rex Ellingwood Beach's novel *The Spoilers* was published by Harper and Brothers in late 1905.[6] It had first appeared in serialized form in *Everybody's Magazine* in 1905, and was inspired by the author's own experiences of Alaskan life in the years 1897–1902, during which Beach undertook numerous failed attempts to strike Alaskan gold. The novel's plot revolves around a conspiracy "to pillage Alaska," by removing ownership and control of the lucrative gold mines from the hands of the miners and into the hands of a group of crooked Washington, D.C. politicians and lawyers.[7] In addition, a web of love stories is spun, most crucially involving the struggle between Glenister (co-owner of the Midas mine and the hero of the story, played by William Farnum in the film) and Alex MacNamara (chief among the conspirators, played by Tom Santschi) over the love of Helen Chester (played by Bessie Eyton). Glenister's desire for Helen clashes with the maintaining of his northern way of life and character—manifested by his possession of the Midas mine but also, and more abstractly, by his virility—and this central dilemma works to intertwine the two main plot lines, i.e. the conspiracy and the love stories.

The Spoilers was the eighth best selling book of 1906.[8] Possibly encouraged by the novel's success, Beach developed a script for a stage version of *The Spoilers* in 1906 together with James McArthur. By and large, the theatrical script followed the novel faithfully. No major alterations or additions were made with regard to plot structure, theme or dramatis personae.[9] An early staging (possibly the first) of *The Spoilers* was presented at the New Theatre in Chicago, premiering November 5, 1906, reportedly bringing forth "frequent applause from a large audience."[10] As a matter of fact, *The Spoilers* was the only profit-making production at the New Theatre during its brief existence, perhaps explained by the commercial character of the play (atypical for the venue) and the events that preceded the premiere. Allegedly, the theater's artistic director Victor Mapes and Rex Beach, who had been brought in to supervise the rehearsals, had clashed with each other over the featuring of the "hammerlock" in one of the fight scenes. Mapes demanded—in the name of art—that the "hammerlock" be omitted, while Beach refused any tampering with his scenes. *The Spoilers* was cancelled, replaced by another production, but soon reinstated in its original form. Interest in the play escalated on account of the quarrel, and the play drew full houses for two weeks. Soon after the successful premiere and following generally favorable reviews, it was made known that the hammerlock dispute had been a publicity stunt.[11]

Other presentations followed. Daniel Frohman's production premiered at the Academy of Music in Baltimore in January 1907, and although I have not been able to verify whether they were carried out, younger brother Charles Frohman had plans for a New York premiere later the same year.[12] The Spooner Stock Company in Brooklyn staged the "drama of Alaskan gold fields in four acts" the week commencing October 19, 1908.[13] In 1909, the play was presented at the Victory Theatre in San Jose, the same venue where the film version would have its first San Jose screenings in September 1914.[14] A 1912 staging of the play in Salt Lake City was launched within a web of tie-ins. A contest asking readers to cast the play (by matching the list of characters with the stock company actors) was arranged by the theater in co-operation with the local newspaper the *Salt Lake Telegram*, which presented a perfect opportunity for the *Telegram* to simultaneously advertise their forthcoming serialization of Rex Beach's *The Net*.[15] Salt Lake City playgoers were offered a stage version of *The Spoilers* as late as April 1917, at the Wilkes Theatre.[16]

According to Beach's own version, his venture into the film business was delayed by difficulties finding a producer that would agree to his demands. First of all, Beach would not agree to sell all his work in bulk. Secondly, he was seeking royalties rather than a one-off fee. Following the failed attempts of at least two different film production companies to furnish a satisfactory offer, William N. Selig intervened and presented a deal meeting Beach's demands. The Selig deal was strictly royalty based (the exact details are however murky) and only involved the motion picture rights to two stories—*The Spoilers* and *The Ne'er Do Well*. As Beach explained, he deemed it wise to await further developments, as prices could only be expected to rise. Hence, he firmly recommended other writers not to accept the first offer, and not to sell all their work lock, stock and barrel.[17]

An interview in fan monthly *Motion Picture Magazine* indicates that Beach possessed a certain astuteness when it came to the pecuniary aspects of his authorship. In fact, a considerable part of the interview seems to have revolved around issues of royalties and economic deal-making, and Beach did not fail to mention that he had recently secured a lucrative contract with Hearst magazines and that he received significant income from first, second and third rights to his books (all of which were at this point first published by Harper and Brothers).[18] There were other indications that Beach had been making good for some time. In 1912, the Associated Newspapers paid Beach $15,000 for the serialization of *The Net* in selected newspapers, and this figure was apparently regarded as spectacular enough to be included in the advertising for the serial.[19] From a distance, then, one can get the impression that Beach was in it for the money, but we should instead view Beach's entrepreneurial skills within the context of a free enterprise system that prompted authors and creators to, in the words of William Klein II, pull themselves up by their own bootstraps.[20] Klein II argues that this was accomplished to a large extent by the formation of various advocacy organizations created for the purpose of protecting and advancing the rights of creators and authors. By the beginning of the twentieth century this development was in its embryonic stages. As a result, when Beach began his career, he was left to his own devices to secure more money and better working conditions, which might explain his emphasis on economics.

I have been unable to disclose the figures involved in the deal struck between Selig and Beach, or the extent to which Beach was involved in various phases of pre-production and production of the film version of *The Spoilers*. We do know that Beach replied by letter to William Selig in June 1913, upon request by someone at the Selig Polyscope Company (possibly Lanier Bartlett, who was credited as the film's scenarist), to clarify certain points in the narrative. These issues, readily clarified by Beach in his letter to Selig, concerned the detailed content of the papers brought to Nome by Helen Chester, why she took the risk of transporting the papers and why it was crucial the papers reached Nome within a certain time. Beach also expressed that he was "glad to hear" that William Farnum had been engaged in the role of Glenister, and asked Selig to advise him if he could assist in any way with the scenario or anything else.[21] In November 1913, Beach again wrote to Selig, excited by rumors that the company "must have done wonderful things" with the production, but anxious to hear how everything was proceeding, as he had not received a reply to his last letter. Also, Beach inquired about the possibility of Selig sending him some stills from the production:

My dear Mr. Selig:
During the late summer I wrote you for information regarding The Spoilers, but have received no reply. Will you kindly advise me what your plans are as to date of release, etc. William Farnum is enthusiastic about the

production and, judging from a few still pictures which Mr. Pribyl sent me, I judge you must have done wonderful things.

I am deeply interested in this experiment and wonder if it will be possible to secure a set of the still pictures you took during the production. I would like to save these for comparison with the photographs of the stage version, and will be glad to pay any costs of development, etc.

With kindest regards and all the best wishes,

Sincerely yours,

Rex Beach[22]

Meanwhile, reports about the production of *The Spoilers* began to crop up in the trade as well as newspaper press. Already on August 20, 1913, the *New York Dramatic Mirror* had stated that the film was within a week of completion, and at this point, several motifs that would reappear in future coverage, reviews and promotion were touched upon. One was the great expense of the production due to the long script, stellar cast and elaborate settings. Another revolved around the "realistic" manner in which director Colin Campbell had visualized the story. A third focused on the cast, especially the fact that the film featured the first appearance in movies by the renowned theatrical actor William Farnum. All in all, the *Mirror*'s reporter had no doubt that *The Spoilers* would turn out to be an "eight-reel masterpiece."[23] The *Mirror* also made note of the relatively unusual fact that the "daily papers [were] following the many 'big' scenes with special write-ups."[24]

Three such "write-ups" were published in the *Los Angeles Times* between July and September 1913. The first one covered the scene depicting the "dynamitation of the Midas gold mine," shot in San Fernando on July 17 (most scenes were shot in Selig's Edendale studios) under Col. Selig's personal supervision. Harry C. Carr, the *LA Times* reporter, described how four different cameras were utilized to capture all angles of the explosions, and went on to offer some general remarks about the production. Several comments concerned the impressive size and scope of the film; it would take several weeks to produce, the cost resembling the value of the national bank; and that to watch it would take a whole evening.[25] Another item, appearing on August 6th discussed more general aspects of the production, for instance, how devices such as "cut-backs" and "close-ups" were used to heighten tension and further the action. The same article shared the fascination with size previously expressed by

Harry C. Carr, assuring that *The Spoilers* was the "biggest film ever made."[26] Bonnie Glessner's article from September 9th followed similar lines, reporting that "the first eight-reel photo drama to be produced in America" was now complete. Glessner's account stated that it had taken eight weeks to shoot, had cost $10,000 and consisted of four hundred scenes, all of which confirmed that this was the biggest Selig project ever undertaken. As to the results, Glessner could not recall having seen a film as clear and realistic as *The Spoilers*, much thanks to the able work of "Collins [*sic*] Campbell, the director."[27]

THE CHICAGO SNEAK PREVIEW AND THE NEW YORK CITY STRAND THEATRE PREMIERE

The first presentation of *The Spoilers* took place at the Orchestra Hall in Chicago before a specially invited audience. Some argued that this was the "most distinguished" audience ever assembled for a film screening, consisting of the "most prominent" people in the business and in Chicago, such as George Kleine, George Spoor, Chicago Mayor Carter T. Harrison, representatives of all the Chicago newspapers, and so on.[28] Colonel Selig himself was at home ill, but the "2,400 friends" of his that did attend the sneak preview appreciated the show, several of them so much that they "flooded [Selig] with appreciative letters."[29] The final version of the film, and the one presumably shown on this occasion, measured nine reels divided into three acts and a prologue. For the Chicago Orchestra Hall screening, a local organist named Robert Stronach supplied "proper music," but looking forward to the official premiere at the Strand Theatre in New York City, the *Mirror* revealed that manager Rothapfel had engaged an orchestra, "which will be fully rehearsed with the film beforehand."[30]

The Strand Theatre, located on Broadway and 47th street in New York City and managed by Samuel L. "Roxy" Rothapfel, opened on Saturday April 11th, 1914 to an invited audience. It seated about 3,500 patrons, which according to some reports made it the largest house in the country devoted to motion pictures,[31] and caused others to label it the "largest and most elaborate moving picture house in New York."[32] *The Spoilers* was chosen as the premiere feature film, an unquestionable triumph for the producers and a sign of prestige that could later be used to help propel the film toward further success, commercially and critically. The *Mirror*'s report from the opening night gives an idea of the immediate context in which the main feature film appeared. First of all, music was provided by means of a large organ but also an orchestra of twenty-seven. The program opened with the orchestra playing the national anthem while an Edison Star-Spangled Banner film was projected on the screen. After a series of additional musical intros, which included an illustrated song, more orchestral music and songs by the Strand Quartet, an episode of *Our Mutual Girl* followed. A Keystone comedy ended the first part of the show, and the second part was devoted to *The Spoilers*.[33]

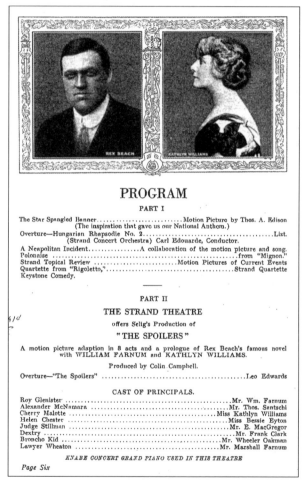

PROGRAM

PART I

The Star Spangled Banner.........................Motion Picture by Thos. A. Edison
        (The inspiration that gave us our National Anthem.)
Overture—Hungarian Rhapsodie No. 2...Liszt.
        (Strand Concert Orchestra) Carl Edouarde, Conductor.
A Neapolitan Incident................A collaboration of the motion picture and song.
Polonaise ....from "Mignon."
Strand Topical Review ....Motion Pictures of Current Events
Quartette from "Rigoletto,"......................................Strand Quartette
Keystone Comedy.

PART II

THE STRAND THEATRE

offers Selig's Production of

"THE SPOILERS"

A motion picture adaption in 8 acts and a prologue of Rex Beach's famous novel
    with WILLIAM FARNUM and KATHLYN WILLIAMS.

Produced by Colin Campbell.

Overture—"The Spoilers" ....Leo Edwards

CAST OF PRINCIPALS.

Roy Glenister ....Mr. Wm. Farnum
Alexander McNamara ....Mr. Thos. Santschi
Cherry Malotte ....Miss Kathlyn Williams
Helen Chester ....Miss Bessie Eyton
Judge Stillman ....Mr. E. MacGregor
Dextry ....Mr. Frank Clark
Broncho Kid ....Mr. Wheeler Oakman
Lawyer Wheaton ....Mr. Marshall Farnum

KNABE CONCERT GRAND PIANO USED IN THIS THEATRE

Page Six

FIGURE 2: Page from the program leaflet from the opening of the Strand Theatre (*The Spoilers* clipping file, New York Public Library for the Performing Arts).

The extensive coverage and comment awarded the opening of the Strand Theatre is evidence of its unusual significance. It was almost immediately perceived as something of a watershed event in the history of motion picture exhibition. One aspect of this was basically architectural, as indicated by the *New York Times* remark that the vast seating capacity of the Strand "marks the rapid growth from the rebuilt store moving picture theatres."[34] Another aspect, alluded to by many, among them Harry Ennis at the *Clipper*, was the notion that a "million dollar playhouse" such as the Strand would also attract a new (and implicitly, a more refined and wealthy) audience.[35] Accordingly, the initial viewing context of *The Spoilers* linked the film, at least implicitly, to the project of cinema's cultural uplift, which in turn may have influenced the critical reception of the film in a positive direction.

Reviews of *The Spoilers* in the leading trade papers were generally favorable. James McQuade of *Moving Picture World* found it to be a "great story," well directed and full of action. He complimented Colin Campbell on the selection and direction of actors and devoted considerable attention and appreciative comments to the principal characters and the actors playing them. A few of the more spectacular scenes were discussed in some detail, in particular the scene featuring the fist-fight between Glenister and McNamara, but also the scenes from the dance hall and gambling den, and the struggle between Helen Chester and Struve toward the end of the film. Thematically, McQuade mainly focused on the clash between Washington law and the self-made law of the miners.[36]

Variety's reviewer lauded the cast, complaining that only eight of the actors were "carded" (i.e. credited), as "there were others in the cast as essential and who did some great work." He also praised the film's realism and its many thrills, paying tribute to both Colin Campbell and Rex Beach for these achievements. In a conclusion of sorts, the review asserted that "[a]s a movie production, it beats the book."[37]

The *New York Clipper* review which appeared on April 25th was among the most appreciative, concluding that "[i]n every respect 'The Spoilers' as a photoplay is entitled to entrance in the 'wonder class.' " For corroboration, the reviewer offered observation and commentary concerning a variety of the film's assets. First of all, there was plenty of action throughout the nine reels, and the story was "tense" and "gripping." In terms of genre, the reviewer labeled the film "melodrama," but was quick to notice that even as such it was suspenseful, "highly interesting" and consistent. The cast was praised, and said to be of "superlative ability." The use of "well chosen scenic backgrounds," the attention to detail in the directing, a "peculiar softness" to the photography and the "pleasing tints" were other features that added to the quality. Because of the overall excellence of the film, the reviewer admitted to having a hard time singling out specific scenes, but one that had "never been surpassed" was the fight scene between Glenister and McNamara.[38]

THE SPOILERS ON THE ROAD

Although Selig was one of the production companies tied to the Motion Picture Patents Company and the General Film Company, *The Spoilers* was not released through General Film's regular or special feature service. Instead, it was distributed on the basis of road showing and state rights. This meant that the film premiered in different cities and parts of the country at different times. A major reason for Selig to defect from the standard policies of the Trust (exactly how this was negotiated is an interesting question, however, unfortunately uncommented on in the sources I have accessed) must have been precisely the economic rewards of prolonging the lifetime of the film. It is outside the scope of this particular case study to track down the deals struck with various local and regional distributors, but trade press sources and the study of the exhibition and reception of the film in the cities I have selected for this case study still generates an idea of its distribution path throughout the United States.

As we already know, the first official theatrical presentation of *The Spoilers* took place on April 11th, 1914 at the Strand Theatre in New York City, where the film ran for two weeks. This had been preceded by a private preview of the film at the Orchestra Hall in Chicago. The "real" Chicago premiere took place at the Studebaker Theatre on April 20th, where the film was booked for an indefinite run.[39] The Studebaker was owned by Charles Frohman and Klaw & Erlanger, who denied the rumors that this theater, normally dedicated to a dramatic and musical policy, would be turned into a motion picture house. They did, however, announce that they would book "high-class motion pictures" from April 20th to September 21st, beginning with *The Spoilers*.[40] As reported by *Motography*, the Studebaker summer policy aligned with that of a number of legitimate theaters in the Chicago Loop, all of which decided to turn to feature film exhibition during the summer months. Whether these other venues changed their programs more frequently I do not know, but at the Studebaker, *The Spoilers* entered its third month in late June. It was reported to do "enormous business" and was arranged to be shown for at least an additional three weeks.[41] Around the same time, *The Spoilers* had its first Chicago screening outside the Loop, at the Wilson Avenue Theatre.[42]

It appears one of the more notable patrons at one (or possibly several) of the Studebaker screenings was the wife of Mayor Carter T. Harrison, Edith Ogden Harrison, herself a well-known author. In a letter addressed to Sam Lederer, manager of the Studebaker, dated May 11th, 1914, Mrs. Harrison expressed the immense enjoyment she had got out of a presentation of the film:

> My dear Mr. Lederer: The performance of 'The Spoilers' in photoplay I witnessed at the Studebaker is 'just splendid.'
>
> It held my attention from start to finish.
>
> The acting is superb and so true, that one can almost read the words from the mute lips.
>
> It is the best entertainment of this sort I ever saw.
>
> Sincerely yours,
>
> [signed] Edith Ogden Harrison[43]

The letter was later used in the marketing of the film, quoted in selected advertisements,[44] and it is possible that the letter was induced by Selig for promotional purposes. The fact that it ended up in the William Selig Papers at the Academy of Motion Picture Arts and Sciences, in Beverly Hills although it was addressed to the Studebaker could indicate as much, and perhaps also the circumstance that it is likely that Mrs. Harrison was present at the sneak preview at the Orchestra Hall in March, while there is no evidence (except for the letter itself) that she visited the Studebaker in April or May.

The Western premiere took place in Denver, at the Taber Grand Opera House on April 26th,[45] but I have not found sources that provide specific information on this event, or the subsequent Denver run. By May 17th, *The Spoilers* had reached Duluth, Minnesota, where it made its debut at the Orpheum Theatre.[46] The Los Angeles premiere took place at Clune's Auditorium on May 25th, 1914, and sometime in late May (I am unable to confirm the exact date), the film was also shown in Kansas City, Missouri, at the Orpheum Theatre.[47] My next findings are from September, when *The Spoilers* appeared in Salt Lake City, playing at the Salt Lake Theatre early in the month; in Boise, Idaho, where it was shown at the Isis Theatre for three days starting on the Thursday, September 17th; and in San Jose, California, where the Victory Theatre screened it for five consecutive days (from September 20th to 24th).[48] Meanwhile, Philadelphia as well as Boston had to wait until November before the film premiered there. In Philadelphia, the Chestnut Street Opera House held the first screening in the city on November 9th, and in Boston, the film made its debut at the National Theatre on November 23rd.[49] The following month, residents of Columbus, Georgia as well as Olympia, Washington enjoyed the film. In Columbus, Georgia, it was first put on for one night (December 10th) at the Grand Theatre, and then for two additional days at the American Theatre.[50] In Olympia, Washington, practically as far to the northwest as one could travel from Georgia without leaving the country, the Ray Theater hosted screenings of *The Spoilers* during the final two days of the year.[51] In an advertisement appearing in the *Philadelphia Inquirer* on March 23rd, 1920, *The Spoilers* is announced to be playing at Nixon's Colonial in Germantown.[52] This is the last evidence of a public screening of the film during the period studied and in the cities included in this study.

AUTHORSHIP AND AMERICANISM: *THE SPOILERS* IN DULUTH, MINNESOTA

It seems likely that residents of Duluth were familiar not only with the novel, but also the stage version of *The Spoilers*, as the first mention of the upcoming film in the *Duluth News Tribune* promised that the screen version would be even more vividly presented than on stage.[53] The first "review" appearing in the *Tribune* labeled the film Beach's "great American romance,"[54] which signals (a) how Beach's authorship was at least partially relocated to apply to the film itself, or, more important, how Beach was seen and/or promoted as the film's creator; and (b) the need of reviewers and/or promoters to frame *The Spoilers* as somehow peculiarly and distinctly American. The same *Duluth Tribune* reporter admitted that *The Spoilers* offered a thrilling story, but also suggested that it was an important story in the sense that it captured a crucial phase of history.[55] This insistence on historical significance applied to the story itself, and not specifically to the film, but may be seen as corresponding to the widely promoted notion that film must fulfill some educational and morally up-lifting purpose. When it came to more detailed aspects of the film, the reporter did not elaborate, but he did stress its authenticity, especially as demonstrated by the marine scenes.

A lengthier article appeared in the *Tribune* on May 22nd,[56] but I would suggest that this was probably a direct transcript of publicity material put out by the marketing department of the Selig Polyscope Company. The reason for this will become clearer later, but some corroboration should be presented here. Firstly, there was a reference to the film as a "virile and [...] red-blooded story," perhaps the most frequently occurring catch-phrase connected to *The Spoilers*, and one that was most definitely pro-mulgated through the PR apparatus. Moreover, the article did not fail to mention the impressive runs at the famous New York and Chicago the-aters, another strategy inspired by central promoters.

THE OLD WEST DISPLACED TO NOME?
THE SPOILERS IN LOS ANGELES

Between May 1914 and February 1915, *The Spoilers* made four separate ap-pearances in Los Angeles, at two different theaters. As we have already seen, it premiered at Clune's Auditorium on May 25th. The high-point of this first two-week run at Clune's was surely the June 4th presentation, which was preceded by a live appearance by the cast members.[57] A second engagement at Clune's Auditorium commenced on August 17th and last-ed the week.[58] On October 5th, the film returned to the same venue for a third run.[59] In February 1915, it was shown at the Woodley Theatre.[60]

The day before the first showing at Clune's, the *LA Times*, as was the praxis of most daily newspapers that devoted space to moving pictures at this time, presented the coming attraction. It is (this too a common char-acteristic of the newspaper discourse on film) difficult to immediately as-sess the level of journalistic independence, but in the case of the *LA Times* we know that the column presenting coming attractions was wholly based on promotional material. Nonetheless, the *LA Times* preview on May 24th diverged from most items on *The Spoilers*, by identifying Bessie Eyton, in the part of Helen Chester, as playing the leading role. The article also noted the presence of Kathlyn Williams in the role of "the most appealing [...] figure" (Cherry Malotte), and that William Farnum's portrayal of Glenister was his "first venture into film dramatic art."[61] Besides highlighting the cast, focus was placed on the typical American character of the film, something we are familiar with from the Duluth context. In the *LA Times* account, this trope was located specifically to the figure of Glenister, described as a "head-strong young miner, permeated with elemental Americanism and not overburdened with the refining influences of society."[62] The last clause implies another observation about the film's narrative, i.e. the identification of a clash between Washington law and the Alaskan miner's concept of justice as a major theme. This, as well as the references to Americanism, was not unique to the *LA Times*, but in spite of the apparent promotional pick-ups (including a predictable characterization of the story as "red-blooded"), there was a peculiarity to the particular linking between Americanism, the West and the theme. Framing the film as "saturated through and through with the spirit of the old West—the West of the forty-niners, transplanted to Nome in late years" while simultaneously ascribing to the hero an "elemental Americanism" involved a move to equate the two, i.e. the West and Americanism. This point was underscored by the assertion that the moral of Beach's story was to show how the "sense of elemental justice" fostered in this milieu (the West displaced to Nome) and within such men (true American heroes) won out against the violations of this justice by Washington politicians.

DISSEMINATING TAGLINES:
THE SPOILERS IN KANSAS CITY

In Kansas City, Missouri, *The Spoilers* appeared on three different occasions at three different theaters between May 1914 and May 1915. Of the first we know very little, as the only evidence is a small and uninformative advertisement for the two last nights of screenings at the Orpheum.[63] When the film returned to Kansas City in December 1914 for screenings at the Willis Wood Theater, the shows were heavily advertised. The most significant detail about the massive advertisement that appeared in the *Kansas City Star* on December 14th was that it consisted almost exclusively of a collage of repetitions of the various catchphrases and taglines that had been furnished by the promoters of the film and disseminated through various brochures, posters and publicity sheets.

FIGURE 3: Advertisement for the Willis Wood Theatre, *Kansas City Star*, 14 December 1914.

An illustration of Glenister and Helen Chester in each other's arms (drawn from the film's closing shot) occupies the central section of the advertisement. Above the image, various headers disclose the name of the theater and the title of the film, and on either side of the image, there is column for textual information. The left column informs us: "This picturesque rugged romance of Alaska has a love story with splendid imagination that grips and holds the sympathies. 'The Spoilers' presents the most stubborn, strenuous and exciting fight ever pictured—the acme of realism. See a whole town dynamited! A volcanic earthquake extraordinary! A wonderful drawing power! Thrilling, Powerful and Picturesque. A Virile Masterpiece. The Most Wonderful Story Ever Filmed."[64] The

76

description as well as the taglines all occur in the exact same words in four-page publicity folder issued by the Selig Polyscope Company, although not in the exact order, and accompanied by a wider assortment of images.[65] The same holds true for most of the right-hand column: "Big, moving, masterful and wholesome in its human interests, thrilling in incident, absorbing in situation, powerful in progression from start to finish. 'The Spoilers' is a thrilling, red blooded story of strong men battling for supremacy, with all their power of mind and muscle—alert for every cast of chance. The picture with the punch powerful!" The essence of the text at the bottom of the right-hand column is also gathered from the centrally produced publicity material, but updated to apply to the present situation. Whereas the centrally produced version states that the film comes "[f]resh from a fortnight run on Broadway, New York City; and an eight weeks record-breaking engagement at the Studebaker in Chicago," the *Kansas City Star* advertisement modifies and adds, resulting in the following: "Fresh from an extended run on Broadway, New York City; a 16-weeks record-breaking engagement in the Studebaker, Chicago. A 6-weeks' capacity engagement in Los Angeles. And 8 weeks in San Francisco." Below the central image and the catchphrase columns, the advertisement reiterates the contents of the letter sent from the wife of Chicago's Mayor to the manager of the Studebaker (previously cited). " 'The best I ever saw!' Says Mrs. Carter H. Harrison," a header exclaims, which is followed by the information that Mrs. Harrison is a "Famed Authoress and Wife of Chicago's Mayor." The letter is then cited in its entirety, and for authenticity, Mrs. Harrison's signature is included in the advertisement.

The foot of the advertisement offers a summary of the crucial selling points: "Thousands have seen this thrilling, marvelous picture, and indorsed it as the greatest. You should see it. A story that appeals to every red-blooded American." These formulations are variations on the centrally produced promotional themes, whereas the advertisement's next, and concluding statement, may be an original Kansas City selling point: "The book sold for $1.50. Best seats for the Play cost $1.50. Those who read the book, saw the play and witnessed the picture proclaim the picture superior to both book and play." Appropriately, the admission prices— ranging from 10¢ to 25¢—are stated below this declaration of the film's superiority.

This nearly exhaustive account of the contents of this particular advertisement (a reiteration of a reiteration if you will) helps us identify an assortment of promotional arguments that were launched by centrally located publicity personnel. It is not at all surprising that this material does turn up in advertisements in various local newspapers, although instances of word by word reproduction of nationally circulated taglines could indicate a diminishing relevance of localized marketing in general, or at least that the multi-reel feature film market was furnished along new, and increasingly centralized lines.

When *The Spoilers* returned to Kansas City in May 1915 for a third run, this time at the Empress, the advertising was more modest, plain and simply designated the film "The World's Greatest Motion Picture."[66]

"GIVING 'THE SPOILERS' THE 'ONCE OVER' ": *THE SPOILERS* IN SALT LAKE CITY

In Salt Lake City, *The Spoilers* was booked for screenings at the Salt Lake Theatre on two separate occasions in September 1914, and the film returned for a third stint in July 1915 at the Rex Theatre.[67] As we know, the stage version presented by the Mack-Rambeau stock company at the Colonial Theatre in 1912 received much attention and was part of a web of tie-ins, so many Salt Lakers were likely to have been familiar with the story. The film version, too, received considerable treatment in the press, by means of large as well as small advertisements, captioned productions stills and various appreciative comments.[68]

The most original item was a comic strip published on September 9, 1914, under the header "Giving 'The Spoilers' at the Salt Lake Theatre the 'Once Over.' "[69] The cartoon sets out to render the story of *The Spoilers* in a series of succinct lines, each one summarizing a major narrative event, and each one accompanied by a pictorial reaction to each event. Fourteen frames are devoted to this undertaking, offering the following condensed version of the story: "The heroine dives in the river. She's rescued! They reach Alaska. She's almost killed!!! Drinking in the dance hall. She turns down the hero. The villain steals the mines. The hero's goin' to shoot the villain. But he don't!! The hero robs the mines. He blows 'em up—bang!!! After a desperate battle he licks the villain. The heroine says she loves him. They kiss!!!—End—." The last two frames depict the happy viewer leaving the movie theater and encourages the readers to go see for themselves. To some degree, the cartoon spotlights the film slightly differently than the marketing material, emphasizing action (as signaled by heavy reliance on verbs), the most thrilling scenes, the struggle between hero and villain and the love story, while leaving aspects of Americanism, famous authors and stars without comment.

FIGURE 4: "Giving 'The Spoilers' at the Salt Lake Theatre the 'Once Over,' "
Salt Lake Telegram, 9 September 1914.

In contrast to the originality of the comic strip, an item inserted immediately below it turns out to be a promotional text disguised as belonging to the paper's editorial material ("editorial" here in the sense of news, information and comment as opposed to advertising). This piece begins with the remark that "[i]t has been the fashion of late to picturize the work of famous authors, and Selig has advanced this as a fine art in 'The Spoilers,' from the book of Rex Beach, in most spirited and vital fashion."[70] This can be compared to the opening paragraph of an item that had appeared in the *Duluth New Tribune* a few months previously: "It has been the fashion of late to picturize the work of famous authors, and Selig has advanced this as a fine art in 'The Spoilers' from the book of Rex Beach, which is being shown this week at the Orpheum, in most spirited and vital fashion."[71] Apparently (a comparison of the two texts offer additional similar examples), the same centrally penned wording has been used in both cases, albeit slightly altered to better cater to a local audience.

As elsewhere, the "red-blooded" trope appeared on numerous occasions. The item cited asserted that " 'The Spoilers' is as virile and as red blooded a romance as any that has appeared in the Americana class during the decade."[72] An advertisement dubbed the film "The Real Red-Blooded Picture of the Year."[73] Finally, an alleged report from a screening during the film's second stint at the Salt Lake Theatre assured that the "audience that witnessed the running of the film last night was held spellbound by this gripping story of red blooded human beings."[74]

PLENTY OF MEAT FOR YOUR MONEY: *THE SPOILERS* IN SAN JOSE, CALIFORNIA

The first trace in the *San Jose Mercury News* of a local screening of *The Spoilers* did not disclose much about the film, but instead served the important purpose of letting the reader know that the Victory Theatre, where the film was shown for five days starting September 20, 1914, could be "[r]eached by all city cars transfer connections."[75]

The review appearing the following day is one of comparatively few newspaper items that I have read in which none of the standard catchphrases turn up. The opening paragraph is indicative of a higher than normal degree of critical independence:

> You get a lot of excitement for your ten-twent-thirt at the Victory this week. 'Cabiria's' pagan pageant and 'Neptune's Daughter's' poetical prettiness are superseded by 'The Spoilers,' which will prove entertaining to the people who like raw meat, the smell of the earth and unbridled passion.[76]

The reviewer moves on to compare the film with the stage version that was presented in 1909 (also at the Victory), concluding that the play "did not make much of an impression, owing to the narrow confines of the stage, while "[a]s a 'movie', with all out-of-doors for a stage setting, the story seems more plausible." He/she also makes a decent attempt to summarize the twists and turns of the plot in an alluring manner: "It is chock full of sensations, running from small-pox to dynamite and from dance halls to gambling halls to midnight suppers and mine robberies, and then back and round again to stolen papers, a death-dealing hand-to-hand encounter and a Take-me-Love-I-am-Yours for the final wind-up." In conclusion, and having left no doubt that it is primarily about action and thrills: "[P]eople who like a play in which there is 'something doing' every moment of the time will get their money's worth at 'The Spoilers.'"

When the film returned to San Jose for two days of shows ("by special request") at the Liberty Theatre, the *Mercury* succumbed to describing the film relying on a collection of, by now, familiar phrasings:

> 'The Spoilers' is a thrilling, red-blooded story of strong men battling for supremacy, with all their power of mind and muscle alert for any cast of chance. A picturesque, rugged romance of Alaska and has a love story with splendid imagination that grips and holds the sympathies. 'The Spoilers' presents the most stubborn, strenuous and exciting fight ever pictures—the acme of realism.[77]

Amazingly, the very same phrases appeared in the *Mercury News* again a few days later.[78] We know that the text was a product of Selig's publicity department, and if its word-by-word reappearance in the advertisement in the *Kansas City Star* offered a clear representation of the successful dissemination of centrally produced copy, the unabridged intrusion of the theatrical columns of the *San Jose Mercury News* represented a full promotional impact that is all the more unsettling. For film historians, the consequence is that one cannot merely browse through the daily papers to neatly collect the findings, one also has to acquire tools to distinguish between the editorial and the promotional elements of the newspapers' amusements sections. Without taking a wide range of material into account, this can be easier said than done, and as this case study demonstrates, with regard to film coverage around this time, it is often safest to assume that journalistic independence was small or non-existent.

81

"THRILLING PICTURE REALISM" AND A RECORD-BREAKING RUN: *THE SPOILERS* IN PHILADELPHIA

At Philadelphia's Chestnut Street Opera House, *The Spoilers* had a significantly longer uninterrupted run than in all other cities included in the case study, playing for a total of seven weeks to what appears to have been capacity audiences. This is perhaps to be expected considering the size of the city and taking into account that protracted runs of multi-reel feature films such as *Traffic in Souls* and *Cabiria* in Philadelphia had paved the way for *The Spoilers*. It is more surprising that Philadelphians had to wait until November 9th until the film premiered there. One hypothesis is that crucial segments of the audience habitually traveled to New York and Atlantic City (still something of a theatrical center at this point, at least during summer) for business as well as for pleasure, thereby leaving Philadelphia having to settle for being something of a second-run city.

Just over a week before the premiere at the Chestnut Street Opera House, two newspapers published previews of the film, both placing the emphasis on the realism of the pictures and the authenticity of the story —two tropes that sometimes merged but that should perhaps be distinguished from one another. The *Inquirer* set out to claim (incorrectly) that the film was "made at the actual places described." Moreover, it was assured that the story was a "rescript of actual occurrences" rather than a pure work of fiction, the ultimate proof of which was provided by the fact that Beach had actually been on the scene in the early days, i.e. he had lived many of the episodes later recounted in the book.[79] The *Philadelphia Record* also made note of the fact that Beach had been present in the Alaskan gold fields back in the day, and thereby knew what he was talking about, but differed from the *Inquirer* in their framing of the realistic settings. The *Record* recognized that the film was not shot on location, but was content with what was perceived as a very convincing "enactment" of the actual places. To substantiate this, it was put forth that the reconstruction of Nome Main Street was guided by the authenticity offered by old photographs.[80] Another item in the *Record*, appearing a week later (on November 8th), expressed further and more fervent admiration for the "wonderful fidelity" with regard to locale, and once again brought up the reconstruction of Nome Main Street as a perfect example. The method for producing "rainstorm pictures" and the employment of what was perceived to be historically authentic vessels were also identified as adding greatly to the realism. This particular review also demonstrates that size and spectacle mattered; the sheer amount of vessels employed impressed the reviewer as did the spectacular thrill of certain scenes (the explosions, Helen's escape, the fistfight) and more generally his/her belief that director Colin Campbell had spent money "without stint" in order to achieve the desired effects.[81] Interestingly, the item appearing in the *Inquirer* on the same day was very similar in its essentials (also calling attention to the "realistic rainstorm pictures," the great number of vessels employed, and so on), indicating that at this point, the two papers might both have aligned their coverage with centrally produced slogans and selling points.[82] The reference to "Rex Beach's red-blooded story of the early days of gold hunting in Nome" in the *Inquirer* article signals as much. Further substantiating this hunch, the report from the Chestnut Street Opera House published on the day after the premiere mentioned the exact same scenes as those highlighted in the advertisement that had appeared two days earlier. In addition, yet another description of the film as a "red-blooded tale" slipped in, which seems unlikely to have been coincidental.[83]

In contrast, the reviewer at the *North American* seems to have done a better job steering clear of prefabricated phrases. He/she made an effort

FIGURE 5: Advertisement for the Chestnut Street Opera House, *Philadelphia Inquirer*, 15 November 1914.

to measure *The Spoilers* against the general standard of multi-reel feature films at the time, arguing that *The Spoilers* fared very well in such a comparison: "The average feature nowadays is tiresome in the extreme, and padding is frequent." Such problems did not seem to mar this particular film, however, as "[n]one of the situations is overdone, and there is a laudable absence of interpolated thrills which have little connection with the plot, a common fault among most directors."[84]

The *North American* reviewer's essential point can be seen as a slightly more sophisticated formulation of an appreciative comment often made about *The Spoilers*, viz. that although it was a film of remarkable length, it somehow managed to rivet the attention of the audience throughout the full nine reels. Arguably, this quality appeared to be essential in explaining the film's success. Or, as a *Record* reporter put it with respect to the run at the Chestnut Street Opera House, during which people were supposedly turned away at every screening: "The unusual spectacle of theatre-goers standing through two and a half hours of a photo drama may be witnessed nightly at this famous playhouse."[85]

A $200 BOOKING: *THE SPOILERS* IN COLUMBUS, GEORGIA

In the *Columbus Daily Inquirer* on December 13, 1914, two different items on *The Spoilers* appeared side by side in the paper's "At the Movies" column. One reported from screenings of the film at the Grand Theatre a few nights earlier, noting that the film "attracted crowded houses." It was further stated that the filming of "this American novel from the pen of Rex Beach" took more than three months to complete, but that the results, especially with regard to "real action," would be difficult to rival. Compliments to the cast were issued, as were references to the remarkable runs at the Strand in New York and at the Chestnut Street Opera House in Philadelphia.[86] The other item, previewing the upcoming shows at the American Theatre adhered more closely to the nationally circulated taglines; to be sure, "powerful and picturesque," "wholesome in its human interests," "gripping red-blooded story of strong men," and "rugged romance of Alaska" all made their way into the piece, most of which could also be found in the accompanying advertisement.[87] Both the article and the advertisement, however, featured one element of localized promotion that I have not seen anywhere else, viz. the stating of a figure of how much it had cost the theater to book the film: "The cost of the picture alone is $200 [for a two-day rental] and as this theater is always on the lookout for their patrons, it will be seen to be appreciated."[88] In the advertisement, perspective to this figure was provided my means of comparison: "This picture cost alone $200.00 to show it here, which is more than five times as much as any other 5, 6, or 7 reel picture ever shown in Columbus."[89]

The Spoilers made a third, and probably last appearance in Columbus at the Bonita—"the little house with the big show"—in late December 1915.[90]

"AN IDEAL GLENISTER": *THE SPOILERS*
IN OLYMPIA, WASHINGTON

When *The Spoilers* arrived in Olympia for a two-day engagement at the Ray Theater, a major concern appears to have been how faithfully the picture version represented the novel. In particular, as "few readers of fiction" according to the *Morning Olympian* had not read the bestselling novel, and as "all readers have admired the strong characters," visitors to the Ray could be expected to demand an apt portrayal of the gallery of characters. Luckily, the *Olympian* announced there was no cause for alarm: "As an assurance that the novelist will have his characters properly portrayed, Selig, the producer of the pictures, has selected an all-star cast."[91] A belief in certain markers of authenticity might explain the seemingly odd remark that "Kathryn [sic] Williams was born and raised in Butte, Montana, a typical mining town in its early days."[92]

The next day, following the first actual Olympia screening of the film (the above was a preview), the *Olympian* returned a verdict in unquestionable favor of the cast. The players' work was claimed to follow "so close to the ideas formed over of the different characters in the novel, that the slides, and the striking scenes, from the familiar slip at Seattle to the rough mining town of Alaska, vie with the clever company in earning the praise of those who have been entertained in the reading of the novel."[93]

Among the many recurring promotional features that we have seen utilized in different places, different advertisements and different exhibition contexts, acknowledgement of Rex Beach's role and the prominence of the cast are the two most predictable and persistent. Practically all advertisements, as well as a majority of other texts appearing in the newspapers, referred to the film as "Rex Beach's The Spoilers" or "The Spoilers by Rex Beach." Similarly, a great majority of the sources stressed the presence in the film of William Farnum and Kathlyn Williams, in addition to a "great cast." The discourse surrounding the Olympia screenings, however, entailed a somewhat different and original take on the issues of authorship as well as acting. A cause for this is to be found in the insistence on the importance of fidelity to the literary source. A faithful and "proper" adaptation was, of course, deemed a desirable quality elsewhere, but within the Olympia context, to digress too greatly from the source was also to violate the rights of the film's author and true originator: Rex Beach. Moreover, the heart and soul of the original story was projected onto its clearest manifestation—the characters—and this, in turn, seems to have fostered the idea that the actors' main task was to guarantee fidelity to the literary source. In that spirit and in contrast to most reviews and promotional texts content to issue a standard phrase of praise concerning the cast, the *Morning Olympian* review of the screenings at the Ray offered a fuller treatment of the characters and of the actors' work. Aside from alluring comments upon the film's savagery versus civilization theme, the bulk of the text zoomed in on acting:

> William Farnum makes an ideal Glenister, the handsome giant who was educated for a lawyer but became a savage of the North through environment; Kathlyn Williams, whose fearlessness has been often witnessed in the Selig animal plays, fills the character of the beautiful dance hall girl, cold and distant with the ordinary habitués but womanly and touching where her sympathies are aroused; Helen Chester, the sweet gentle girl who is made an innocent participator in the terrible crime against justice, but who ends by taming the savage Glenister, is cleverly handled by Bessie Eyton; Thomas Santschi, selected for the strong but thankless character of McNamara, 'the most notorious crook in Washington,' vies with Farnum in personal attractions, being handsome and tall, but haughty and overbearing in his confidence in his physical strength and his mental superiority, and his final struggle with Glenister makes a fitting climax to this stirring conflict between these brainy and brawny giants; Even Slap

Jack, the long lean, lankey [*sic*], bald-pated man with the unique vocabulary is readily recognized in the perfect makeup of Jack McDonald. And all of the other characters, Dextry, Bronco Kid, Judge Stillman and others fit into the scenery which is a reproduction of Nome in early days, making the entire production one of the most remarkable and interesting ever produced on the screen.[94]

STILL AS GOOD AS NEW: *THE SPOILERS* IN CHARLOTTE, SOUTH CAROLINA

Of the cities included in this case study, Charlotte, South Carolina was the last to see *The Spoilers* premiere at a local movie theater. The first Charlotte shows were hosted by the Academy of Music from April 17th to April 19th, 1916, more than two years after the first public presentations of the film and about two months after the release of a twelve-reel reissue. The Academy of Music in Charlotte screened the original version, however, and seemingly used the original publicity material as the film was billed here, too, as "the most wonderful story ever filmed" and as "thrilling, powerful, picturesque."[95] More surprising than the reliance on the established catch-phrases is the fact that the *Charlotte Observer* conveyed the impression that this was a fairly new feature film: "Theatergoers, booklovers and movie patrons have long been awaiting their opportunity of seeing the world-famed novel, 'The Spoilers,' by Rex Beach made into a big photoplay. Now that it has been accomplished and will be presented in this city for three days [...] it is expected that the local playhouse will be crowded at every performance."[96] Then again, after the first day of screenings at the Academy of Music, the *Observer* instead shifted into historical gear, as indicated by the suggestive description of the most memorable scene according to the reviewer, i.e. the climactic struggle between Glenister and McNamara: "The fight between these two players has become history in photoplay annals as one of the most realistic fistic encounters that was ever staged as a part of a dramatic entertainment."[97] Sadly, however, the reviewer proved to have had some difficulty in getting the historical record straight, and went on to announce that the film had been made "under the joint direction of Rex Beach and Mr. Santschi."

"A RED-BLOODED ROMANCE": AMERICANIZING EARLY MULTI-REEL FEATURE CINEMA

We have recurrently noticed that the "red-blooded" trope was an emblematic marker of the tricky conflations of marketing and reviewing that defined the newspaper discourse on *The Spoilers* and the newspaper discourse on film in general at this juncture.

It is important to recognize that the "red-blooded" label materialized not only at the interface between promotional material and newspaper discourse. For example, some trade press reviews of *The Spoilers* made good use of the trope: James McQuade at *Moving Picture World* made reference to a "red-blooded story" in his review, and *New York Clipper*'s Harry Ennis proclaimed that "[t]his virile red-blooded romance is a remarkable volume Americana."[98] The last comment spotlights two meanings of the trope that seem to be fundamental in relation to *The Spoilers*: "virile" and "American." The first aligns with a lexical definition and may, therefore, be seen as the trope's primary meaning (or denotation if you will), while the other is derived from an assumed metonymical relationship between various lexical meanings and "American."[99] Both qualities were attributed to the persona of Rex Beach and his work, before as well as after the premiere of the film version of *The Spoilers*, and on occasion by reference to precisely the term in focus here. For example, when the *Salt Lake Telegram* announced the winners of "The Spoilers Cast Contest" in August 1912, the paper concluded that one could not doubt the "popularity here of Rex Beach as a teller of red blooded stories."[100] Similarly, the publishing of Beach's *The Iron Trail* in 1913 caused at least one reviewer to argue that "Rex Beach has written a tale as virile as 'The Spoilers,'" and that the new novel's hero "represents a larger conception of Manhood."[101] A few years later, the film version of Beach's *The Barrier* (Rex Beach Pictures Company, 1917) also rendered comparisons, one commentator noting that like *The Spoilers*, *The Barrier* was a "red-blooded" story of the Alaskan fields.[102] Thus, Beach's reputation as a writer of "red-blooded" fiction and a promoter of a decidedly masculine and virile Americana, originated already by the publishing of *The Spoilers* in 1905, and was reaffirmed thanks to a consistent circulation of this formula concerning his subsequent work. By 1914, Beach had earned the epithet "Red Blood King of Fiction,"[103] and accordingly, promotion of the film version of *The Spoilers* did not start out from a *tabula rasa*, but could take advantage of Beach's established history, readily available for spinning.

These processes did not only involve a particular promotional and critical framing of Beach's oeuvre of books and short stories and their various adaptations, but also the staging of a fitting biographical legend, or public persona. This appears to have been part of a self-promotional endeavor, evident in interviews in the trade press around the time Beach ventured into the film industry. Speaking to the *World*'s James McQuade shortly before the Chicago sneak preview of *The Spoilers*, Beach made a point of serving up his own background as the best guarantee of the authenticity and realism of the film, suggesting that a man has to go through the mill to see how hard it grinds.[104] About a year later, in an interview published in the monthly fan publication *Motion Picture Magazine*, Beach's macho identity, habitually ascribed to the alleged real-life experiences as a rugged adventurer that gave his work its stamp of authenticity, was even more pronounced. Here the interviewer, waiting for the author to finish some pressing business, recounts how the floors of Beach's New York residence are covered by "splendid skins of animals killed by Beach."[105] At this time, Beach's persona was long since pigeonholed and/or intentionally self-advertised to represent the most virile, vigorous and masculine facets of the American character. A case in point is a newspaper advertisement for Tuxedo Tobacco in which Beach appeared in 1913, alongside with John Philip Sousa ("the March King"), George Randolph Chester ("famous author"), V. Stefansson ("the famous explorer"), Geo. M. Cohan ("actor, author, composer, manager"), Zane Grey ("famous sportsman, explorer and writer"), Malcolm Strauss ("noted portrayer of girl types in pen and ink") and Christy Mathewson ("famous pitcher of the New York Giants"). This gallery featured an encircled illustration of each celebrity accompanied by their respective signed endorsing, underwriting the claim that "The Greatest Men in America Endorse Tuxedo Tobacco." Identifying a common ground for endorsing the product, the advertisement states that "[t]he live, virile men who make this country what it is, recognize relaxation from nervous and mental strain, the *restfulness*—that comes from smoking Tuxedo Tobacco." Rex Beach is presented as "famous author, playwright, sportsman, author of 'The Spoilers,' 'The Barrier,' 'The Silver Horde,' " His endorsement states: "I have smoked Tuxedo in sub-Arctic Alaska, at Panama and everywhere—would not smoke another kind."[106]

FIGURE 6: Advertisement for Tuxedo Tobacco,
Philadelphia Inquirer, 28 August 1913.

Against this background of alpha-male experiences, the significance of Beach's shift from books to movies may be read along lines where gender, the burgeoning feature market and various transformations of the scenario-writing field intersect. As multi-reel features grew more common, there was a growing uncertainty concerning exactly where story material for present and forthcoming mammoth productions would come from. One camp predicted that famous and experienced authors would soon have a field day thanks to the new market situation.[107] Others argued that the future of the feature lay with those who would seize the opportunity to learn to write original scenarios directly for the screen.[108] For some, the latter stance hinged on a belief that (a) the scenario field was undergoing processes of professionalization and division of labor demanding trained scenarists rather than "big writers," and that (b) "literary" qualities did not automatically translate into a successful scenario. Interestingly, however, at least one supporter of this view admitted that authors like Rex Beach, who "write virile action," could nonetheless possibly make it in movies.[109] Another issue is exactly how the perceived virility of Beach and his work should be related to the ever-increasing presence of women within the scenario field.[110]

We may also read the significance of Beach's entry into the film business as primarily being related to the tropes of Americanism and Americanization. In fact, the "red-blooded" trope, so crucial in navigating the reception of *The Spoilers*, resonates with a wider change affecting American culture at the turn of the last century which Richard Abel argues can be seen as prescriptive for American cinema. This change involved a new hierarchal order of visual representations that valued notions of realism, verisimilitude and authenticity while debasing notions of romanticism and imitation. Abel links this to how "Pathé's foreign subjects provided one of the principal 'others' against which to construct an American difference" in the trade press around 1908–1909. On occasion, as in the case of the *New York Dramatic Mirror*, this discourse was permeated by masculinism and racism. The relevant background which Abel derives from Richard Slotkin was the developing of a *"virilist* realism" in American culture. Within the realm of literary fiction, one expression of this was the embracing by some of the "red-blooded realism" of writers such as Owen Wister and Frank Norris.[111] A cinematic counterpart, Abel convincingly shows, was the western, a genre in which the mythical frontier served as an imaginary space for testing the virility of the "American character." Hereby, cinema was taking part in a discourse of Americanization that (Abel draws on Robert Rydell here) asserted "white male supremacy as the core of a new national identity."[112]

It is remarkable how well this framework translates to the case of *The Spoilers*. Set in the old West displaced to Nome, featuring "strong men battling for supremacy, with all their power of mind and muscle" (as one advertisement put it), marketed as a "red-blooded" story and penned by an author whose biographical legend was long since defined by a masculinized ideal of the "American character," *The Spoilers* was an early feature film highpoint in cinematic displays of Americanism. As such, it played its part in the Americanizing of feature cinema, a process that also involved fending off the threat posed by the European multi-reelers that had dominated the field until this point. The film's marketing as well as its formal qualities, not least the allegiance to the genre of action, were crucial aspects of this, as was the fact *The Spoilers* was chosen as the opening feature film of the perhaps most high-profile motion picture palace in the country—The Strand in New York City. Thought of in hindsight as a signpost event, the premiere of *The Spoilers* here in April 1914 seems to offer a missing link between the influx and initial triumphs of European features such as *Quo Vadis?* (Cines, 1912), and a trend of Americanizing within the feature field that would reach an early climax with *The Birth of a Nation* (D. W. Griffith Corp./Epoch Producing Corp., 1915). Thereby, *The Spoilers* also points our attention toward the subsequent historical trajectory along which the American feature would travel to capture the domestic as well as global film market.

ENDNOTES

1. Harry Ennis, "Success Prefaces 'The Spoilers,' " Motion Picture Department, *New York Clipper*, Vol. 62, No. 9 (11 April 1914): 14
2. Harry Ennis, "Strand, New York's Newest Playhouse, Opens Saturday, April 11," Doings in Filmdom, *New York Clipper*, Vol. 62, No. 9 (11 April 1914): 14.
3. The notion of a "transitional period" emanates from Bordwell, Staiger, and Thompson, and can somewhat simplified be said to encompass the years subsequent to the "Cinema of Attractions" but preceding the period of the "Classical Hollywood Cinema," which means that a supposed "transitional period" began sometime between 1906 and 1909 and ended sometime between 1913 and 1917. The clearest manifestation of the attempts to establish institutionalized research programs and agendas based on the notion is a volume edited by Charlie Keil and Shelley Stamp, published in 2004. Several scholars have called into question the meaning and relevance of the notion—a critical summary of some of these debates are offered in my PhD dissertation. David Bordwell, Janet Staiger and Kristin Thompson, *The Classical*

Hollywood Cinema: Film Style and Mode of Production to 1960 (New York: Columbia University Press, 1985), especially chapter 14 ("From Primitive to Classical"); Charlie Keil and Shelley Stamp, eds., *American Cinema's Transitional Era: Audiences, Institutions, Practices* (Berkeley: University of California Press, 2004); and Joel Frykholm, *Framing the Feature Film: Multi-Reel Feature Film and American Film Culture in the 1910s*, PhD diss., Stockholm University, 2009 (Stockholm: Acta Universitatis Stockholmiensis, 2009, distribution eddy.se), 24–27.

4. The breakthrough of the multi-reel feature film in the United States is addressed at length and from a variety of perspectives in my PhD dissertation. Frykholm, *Framing the Feature Film*.

5. The focus on the historical reception of *The Spoilers* is inspired by two books by Janet Staiger. It should, however, be acknowledged that as sympathetic to Staiger's project as I am, some problems remain, most crucially how to design case studies that will get us from fairly general statements about the conditions of reception to the actual experiences of real life viewers. Janet Staiger, *Interpreting Films: Studies in the Historical Reception of American Cinema* (Princeton: Princeton University Press, 1992); and Janet Staiger, *Perverse Spectators: The Practices of Film Reception* (New York: New York University Press, 2000).

6. Unless otherwise stated, all biographical information is drawn from the Rex Beach Archive website, http://tars.rollins.edu/olin /archives/150EBEACH.htm (accessed 25 May 2009). All information on serializations, publications and editions of Beach's work referred to in this section and the next is taken from The Bestsellers Database set up by the Graduate School of Library and Information Science at the University of Illinois at Urbana-Champaign, http://www3.isrl.illinois.edu/~unsworth/courses/ best sellers/ (accessed 25 May 2009).

7. James Belpedio's 1995 dissertation explores the links between *The Spoilers* and the real-life conspiracy on which this part of the story was based. James R. Belpedio, "Fact, Fiction, Film: Rex Beach and *The Spoilers*" (PhD diss., University of North Dakota, 1995).

8. Publisher's Weekly's list of bestselling fiction hardcover books for 1906, provided by Cader Books, http://www.caderbooks.com /best00.html (accessed 26 May 2009).

9. Rex Beach and James McArthur, *The Spoilers: A Play in Four Acts*, Stage Play Manuscript, the William Selig Papers, Margaret Herrick Library, Academy of Motion Picture Arts and Sciences.

10. " 'The Spoilers' Produced," *New York Times*, 6 November 1909, 9.

11. "The Spoilers Spoiled," News of the Theaters, *Chicago Tribune*, 31 October

1906, 8; and "The Spoilers," News of the Theaters, *Chicago Tribune*, 6 November 1906, 8. See also J. Dennis Rich and Kevin L. Seligman, "The New Theatre of Chicago, 1906–1907," *Educational Theatre Journal*, Vol. 26, No. 1 (March 1974): 61–62; and Kathy L. Privatt, "The New Theater of Chicago: Democracy 1; Aristocracy 0," *Theatre History Studies*, Vol. 24 (June 2004): 103.

12. " 'The Spoilers' Produced: Daniel Frohman's Presentation of the Dramatization of Beach's Novel," *New York Times*, 29 January 1907, 9; and Privatt, "The New Theater of Chicago: Democracy 1; Aristocracy 0," 103.

13. Playbill/Program of the Park Theatre in Brooklyn for the week commencing Monday 19 October 1908, the William Selig Papers.

14. "A 'Thriller' Movie at the Victory: Rex Beach's 'Spoilers' Filmed with William Farnum in the Lead," *San Jose Mercury News*, 21 September 1914, 3.

15. "Do You Think That You Would Be a Competent Stage Director? Cast the Willard Mack-Marjorie Rambeau Players for The Spoilers and Earn Tickets," *Salt Lake Telegram*, 22 August 1912, 10; "What Part Do You Want to See Your Favorite Stock Actor Play?" *Salt Lake Telegram*, 23 August 1912, 12; "Telegram Readers Cast Characters in 'The Spoilers': Many Join Contest for Rex Beach's Dramatized Story," *Salt Lake Telegram*, 24 August 1912, 10; and "Winners of 'The Spoilers' Cast Contest," *Salt Lake Telegram*, 26 August 1912, 10.

16. "Rex Beach's Gripping Drama Opens at Wilkes Tonight," *Salt Lake Telegram*, 15 April 1917, 12.

17. Henry Albert Phillips, "How I Came to Write For the Motion Pictures: The Interesting Facts Brought to Light for the First Time in an Interview with Rex Beach," *Motion Picture Magazine*, Vol. 9, No. 4 (May 1915): 95–98.

18. Ibid.

19. Advertisement for the serial publication of Rex Beach's *The Net*, *Kansas City Star*, 1 September 1912, 11.

20. William Klein II, "Authors and Creators: Up by Their Own Bootstraps," *Communications and the Law*, Vol. 14, No. 3 (September 1992): 41–72. Klein II describes the situation facing authors and creators around the beginning of the twentieth century as follows: "Book and magazine publishers, play producers, motion-picture companies—all included among their number those who (a) paid a pittance for an outright sale; (b) retained the copyright in the United States and throughout the world in their own name; (c) held on to manuscripts indefinitely without paying a penny; (d) agreed to pay piddling royalties, but then never paid them; (e) often rewrote the author's work, making it unrecognizable; ad infinitum." Klein II, "Authors and Creators," 46–47.

21. Rex Beach to William Selig, 9 June 1913, the William Selig Papers.

22. Rex Beach to William Selig, 28 November 1913, the William Selig Papers.

23. W. E. Wing, "Interest in 'Spoilers': High Expectations for Film Adaptation of Rex Beach's Story," *New York Dramatic Mirror,* Vol. 70, No. 1809 (20 August 1913): 28.

24. Ibid.

25. Harry C. Carr, "Blowing Up Movie Town: Wonderful Moving Picture Reel Played; A Complete Placer Mine Dynamited; Rex Beach's Novel, 'The Spoilers,' " *Los Angeles Times*, 18 July 1913, III:1.

26. " 'The Spoilers' Is Thrilling," *Los Angeles Times*, 6 August 1913, III:2.

27. Bonnie Glessner, " 'The Spoilers' in Eight Reels," *Los Angeles Times*, 9 September 1913, II:6.

28. "First Showing of 'Spoilers;' Selig Company Host to Distinguished Audience at Orchestra Hall—Film Pleases," *New York Dramatic Mirror* Vol. 71, No. 1841 (1 April 1914): 22.

29. Harry Ennis, "Success Prefaces 'The Spoilers,' " 14.

30. "First Showing of 'Spoilers,' " 22.

31. " 'Spoilers' to Open. Selig Production Will Be Opening Attraction at the Strand Theater," *New York Dramatic Mirror*, Vol. 71, No. 1840 (25 March 1914): 30.

32. "New Strand Opens: Biggest of Movies; Handsome Theatre at Broadway and 47th Street Seats Almost 3,500 People," *New York Times*, 12 April 1914, 15.

33. "Strand Theater Opens. In Blaze of Glory Selig's 'The Spoilers' is Well Received at Opening of Large Theater," *New York Dramatic Mirror*, Vol. 71, No. 1843 (15 April 1914): 31. The *Mirror*'s report matches the program as outlined in the twelve-page program leaflet from the opening of the Strand. Aside from presenting the program, this leaflet included an introduction to the Strand Theatre and its many amenities, a synopsis of *The Spoilers* ("The Story of the Play"), and some preview information about *The Sea Wolf*, the feature that would supplant *The Spoilers* two weeks later. Program Leaflet from the Opening of the Strand Theatre, *The Spoilers* clipping file, New York Public Library for the Performing Arts. See also and "New Strand Opens," *New York Times*, 12 April 1914, 15.

34. "New Strand Opens," *New York Times*, 12 April 1914, 15.

35. Ennis, "Strand, New York's Newest Playhouse," 14.

36. James McQuade, "The Spoilers," *Moving Picture World*, Vol. 20, No. 2 (11 April 1914): 186–87.

37. "The Spoilers," *Variety,* Vol. 34, No. 7 (17 April 1914): 22.

38. Quizz [pseud.], " 'The Spoilers' (Selig) Nine Reels," Current Film Events, *New York Clipper*, Vol. 62, No. 11 (25 April 1914): 16.

39. Harry Ennis, "Selig's Great Picture," Motion Picture Department, *New York Clipper*, Vol. 62, No. 10 (18 April 1914): 8.

40. James McQuade, "Studebaker to Be Opened by 'The Spoilers,' " Chicago Letter, *Moving Picture World*, Vol. 20, No. 4 (25 April 1914): 520.

41. G. P. Von Harleman, "Chicago Letter," *Moving Picture World*, Vol. 20, No. 13 (27 June 1914): 1812.

42. Ibid.

43. Edith Ogden Harrison to Sam Lederer, manager of the Studebaker Theatre Chicago, 11 May 1914, the William Selig Papers.

44. See, for example, advertisement for the Willis Wood Theater in Kansas City, *Kansas City Star*, 14 December 1914, 9.

45. Ennis, "Selig's Great Picture," 8.

46. "Orpheum," *Duluth New Tribune*, 16 May 1914, 6.

47. "Clune's Auditorium," Dramatic Reviews, *Los Angeles Times*, 24 May 1914, III:3; and advertisement for the Orpheum Theatre in Kansas City, *Kansas City Star*, 30 May 1914, 3.

48. "Scene from Rex Beach's Play to Be Shown at the Salt Lake," *Salt Lake Telegram*, 5 September 1914, 5; advertisement for the Salt Lake Theatre, *Salt Lake Telegram*, 5 September 1914, 5; advertisement for the Isis Theatre in Boise, Idaho, *Idaho Statesman*, 14 September 1914, 10; and "A 'Thriller' Movie at the Victory: Rex Beach's 'Spoilers' Filmed with William Farnum in the Lead," *San Jose Mercury News*, 21 September 1914, 3.

49. "Thrilling Picture Realism," *Philadelphia Inquirer,* 1 November 1914, 14; and "Boston Reopens with Film Play," *Boston Journal*, 21 November 1914, 5; and advertisement for the Boston Theatre, *Boston Journal*, 21 November 1914, 5.

50. "Great Crowd Attends 'Spoilers' at Grand," At the Movies, *Columbus Daily Inquirer*, 13 December 1914, 2; " 'The Spoilers' at the American," At the Movies, *Columbus Daily Inquirer*, 13 December 1914, 2; and advertisement for the American Theatre in Columbus, Georgia, *Columbus Daily Inquirer*, 13 December 1914, 2.

51. "Rex Beach's 'The Spoilers' at Ray," *Morning Olympian*, 30 December 1914, 4; and advertisement for the Ray Theater in Olympia, Washington, *Morning Olympian*, 30 December 1914, 4.

52. Advertisement for Nixon's Colonial, *Philadelphia Inquirer,* 23 March 1920, 3.

53. "Orpheum," *Duluth News Tribune*, 16 May 1914, 6.

54. Ibid., *Duluth News Tribune*, 21 May 1914, 6.

55. Ibid.

56. "Orpheum," Amusements, *Duluth News Tribune*, 22 May 1914, 5.

57. Jan Olsson, *Los Angeles Before Hollywood: Journalism and American Film Culture, 1905–1915* (Stockholm: National Library, 2008, distribution Wallflower Press, London), 130.

58. Ibid., 131.

59. "Rex Beach's 'The Spoilers' Returns to Clune's," *Los Angeles Times*, 4 October 1914, III:1.

60. "The Woodley," *Los Angeles Times*, 7 February 1915, III:3; and "The Woodley," *Los Angeles Times*, 11 February 1915, II:6.

61. "Clune's Auditorium," Dramatic Reviews, *Los Angeles Times*, 24 May 1914, III:3.

62. Ibid.

63. Advertisement for the Orpheum Theatre in Kansas City, *Kansas City Star*, 30 May 1914, 3.

64. Advertisement for the Willis Wood Theater in Kansas City, *Kansas City Star*, 14 December 1914, 9.

65. Selig Polyscope Co., "Selig's 'The Spoilers,' " four-page publicity brochure, the William Selig Papers.

66. Advertisements for the Empress Theater, *Kansas City Star*, 29 May 29 1915, 3; and *Kansas City Star*, 30 May 1915, 15.

67. Advertisement for the Salt Lake Theatre, *Salt Lake Telegram*, 5 September 1914, 15; "At the Theatres," *Salt Lake Telegram*, 29 September 1914, 3; advertisement for the Rex Theatre, *Salt Lake Telegram*, 1 July 1915, 10; and advertisement for the Rex Theatre, *Salt Lake Telegram*, 2 July 1915, 8.

68. Advertisement for the Salt Lake Theatre, *Salt Lake Telegram*, 5 September 1914, 15; advertisement for the Salt Lake Theatre, *Salt Lake Telegram*, 7 September 1914, 6; "Scene from Rex Beach's Play to be Shown at the Salt Lake," *Salt Lake Telegram*, 5 September 1914, 15; and "At the Theatres," *Salt Lake Telegram*, 10 September 1914, 3.

69. Casey, "Giving 'The Spoilers' at the Salt Lake Theatre the 'Once Over,' " Cartoon, *Salt Lake Telegram*, 9 September 1914, 2.

70. "Vitalizing a Romance," *Salt Lake Telegram*, 9 September 1914, 2.

71. "Orpheum," Amusements, *Duluth News Tribune*, 22 May 1914, 5.

72. "Vitalizing a Romance," 2.

73. Advertisement for the Salt Lake Theatre, *Salt Lake Telegram*, 12 September 1914, 31.

74. "At the Theatres," *Salt Lake Telegram*, 29 September 1914, 3.

75. "Important Events of the Week: When, Where and How to Get There," *San Jose Mercury News*, 20 September 1914, 8.

97

76. "A 'Thriller' Movie at the Victory: Rex Beach's 'Spoilers' Filmed with William Farnum in the Lead," *San Jose Mercury News*, 21 September 1914, 3.

77. " 'The Spoilers.' " At the Theatres, *San Jose Mercury News*, 17 January 1915, 14.

78. " 'The Spoilers' at the Liberty Theatre Today: Wonderful Film Story Is Romance of Alaska," *San Jose Mercury News*, 20 January 1915, 8.

79. "Thrilling Picture Realism," *Philadelphia Inquirer,* 1 November 1914, 14.

80. "Rescript from Life: 'The Spoilers' Told a Story that Had Been Enacted in Alaska," *Philadelphia Record*, 1 November 1914, 7.

81. "Opera House—'The Spoilers,' " *Philadelphia Record*, 8 November 1914, 7.

82. "Opera House," The Film Drama, *Philadelphia Inquirer,* 8 November 1914, II:15.

83. " 'The Spoilers': Rex Beach's Novel Seen in Films at Chestnut Street Opera House," *Philadelphia Inquirer,* 10 November 1914, 13; and advertisement for the Chestnut Street Opera House, *Philadelphia Inquirer,* 8 November 1914, II:16.

84. "Film of 'The Spoilers' Is Good Movie Drama: Nine-Thousand Feet of Pictures Give Fine Version of Rex Beach's Novel; Action Is Sustained," *North American*, 10 November 1914, 14. For a survey of discourses on padding and the early multi-reel feature film, see Frykholm, *Framing the Feature Film*, 41–44.

85. "Opera House—'The Spoilers,' " *Philadelphia Record*, 2 November 1914, 6.

86. Great Crowds Attend 'Spoilers' at Grand," At the Movies, *Columbus Daily Inquirer*, 13 December 1914: 2.

87. " 'The Spoilers' at the American," At the Movies, *Columbus Daily Inquirer*, 13 December 1914: 2; and advertisement for the American Theatre, *Columbus Daily Inquirer*, 13 December 1914: 2.

88. " 'The Spoilers' at the American," At the Movies, *Columbus Daily Inquirer*, 13 December 1914: 2.

89. Advertisement for the American Theatre, *Columbus Daily Inquirer*, 13 December 1914, 2. It should be made clear that the film was booked for Monday and Tuesday, and perhaps also that a rental price of $200 for two days for this particular town and theater, of course, does not allow for any generalizations of rental price in other cases, considering how this specific film was distributed as well as the possible price variations (for instance in accordance to order of run and location) that any given film might have been subject to at this time.

90. Advertisement for the Bonita Theatre, *Columbus Daily Inquirer*, 28 December 1915, 6.

91. "Rex Beach's 'The Spoilers' at Ray," *Morning Olympian*, 30 December 1914, 4.

92. Ibid.

93. " 'The Spoilers' Pack the Ray," *Morning Olympian*, 31 December 1914, 4.

94. Ibid.

95. Advertisement for the Academy of Music, *Charlotte Observer*, 15 April 1916, 5.

96. " 'The Spoilers,' " Amusements, *Charlotte Observer*, 17 April 1916: 5.

97. " 'The Spoilers' Fine Production," *Charlotte Observer*, 18 April 1916: 8.

98. McQuade, "The Spoilers," 186; and Ennis, "Selig's Great Picture," 8.

99. The Oxford English Dictionary Online defines "red-blooded" as "virile, vigorous, full of life, spirited." The Merriam-Webster Online Dictionary suggests "vigorous, lusty." Webster's Online Dictionary offers "endowed with or exhibiting great bodily or mental health."

100. "Winners of 'The Spoilers' Cast Contest," *Salt Lake Telegram*, 26 August 1912, 10.

101. Review of *The Iron Trail* by Rex Beach (published by Harper's), Book Review, *Duluth News Tribune*, 21 September 1913, 5.

102. " 'The Barrier' in Film," *Philadelphia Inquirer,* 18 February 1917, 11.

103. Advertisements for the Sunday's Tribune, *Chicago Tribune*, 5 December 1914, 15; and 20 December 1914, 9.

104. James McQuade, "Rex E. Beach: Author of the Spoilers Sees Filmed Story Passed by Chicago Censors, and Gives an Interesting Interview to World Representatives," *Moving Picture World*, Vol. 19, No. 12 (21 March 1914): 1506.

105. Phillips, "How I Came to Write For the Motion Pictures," 95.

106. Advertisement for Tuxedo Tobacco, *Philadelphia Inquirer*, 28 August 1913, 5.

107. See, for example, John Stuart Blackton, "Literature and the Motion Picture—A Message," introduction to Robert Grau, *Theatre of Science: A Volume of Progress and Achievement in the Motion Picture Art* (New York: Broadway Publishing Company, 1914), xxvii; and Frank E. Woods, "What Are We Coming To?" *Moving Picture World*, Vol. 21, No. 3 (18 July 1914): 443.

108. See, for example, Oliver Morosco, "Tomorrow—The Future of the Photoplay," *Motography*, Vol. 15, No. 1 (1 January 1916): 9; and Frederick James Smith, "The Evolution of the Motion Picture. IV. From the Standpoint of the Scenario Editor. An Interview with Lawrence S. McCloskey, Scenario Editor of the Lubin Manufacturing Company," *New York Dramatic Mirror*, Vol. 69, No. 1798 (4 June 1913): 25, cont. on 32.

109. Smith, "The Evolution of the Motion Picture. IV," 25, cont. on 32.

110. The gendering of the scenario writing field is addressed by Anne Morey, " 'Would You Be Ashamed to Let Them See What You Have Written?' The Gendering of Photoplaywrights, 1913–1923," *Tulsa Studies in Women's Literature*, Vol. 17, No. 1 (Spring 1998): 83–99.

111. Richard Abel, *The Red Rooster Scare: Making Cinema American, 1900–1910* (Berkeley: University of California Press, 1999), 122–26.

112. Ibid., 159–164. Abel revisits the significance of the western for processes of Americanization and for Americanizing the movies in Richard Abel, *Americanizing the Movies and "Movie-Mad" Audiences, 1910–1914* (Berkeley: University of California Press, 2006), 61–82; 105–123.

CHAPTER 3

SONG OF THE SONIC BODY: NOISE, THE AUDIENCE AND EARLY AMERICAN MOVING PICTURE CULTURE

MEREDITH C. WARD

SITTING IN THE dark, he watched as the flickering images played across the screen and he waited for the sounds he felt sure would accompany them. The images that the Lumière brothers had captured—of card players throwing down silent cards, a train pulling into the station without the clatter of the wheels along the rails, a laughing face with no gurgle issuing from its mute throat, even as the muscles contracted visibly within it—took their places in silence: without, as the author notes, "a single note of the intricate symphony that always accompanies the movements of people."[1] He writes that the "mute, grey life"[2] onscreen was the result of the Cinematograph playing "Merlin's trick," subjecting them to a strange half-life.[3] There was an uncanny quality to the life playing over the screen, existing, as it did, without the natural noises that were its birthright. The scene, unfolding so silently, almost as if it were "condemned to eternal silence," "begins to disturb and depress you."[4] The silent events so disorient the writer that he states, "You are forgetting where you are...your consciousness begins to wane and grow dim".[5] The silent world onscreen pulled him directly out of the dark place where he sat watching.

CINEMA AS BROTHEL

These words come from Russian novelist and dramatist Maxim Gorky's 1896 account of attending the first Russian exhibition of moving pictures at the All-Russian Fair of Industry at Nizhny-Novogorod. He was, by his own account, appalled by their silence. He was repulsed by what he terms the spectral images onscreen, calling them "The Kingdom of Shadows," or a world of insubstantial phantoms. The scene, indeed, plays out like his description of a nightmare. He is awakened from his "silent" hypnosis halfway through his account. Significantly, however, it is not by the sounds he seeks. It is not the laughter of the mute onscreen face that he sees contorting, the face that taunts him with its silence. Another laugh interrupts his thought process. He writes, instead, "But suddenly, along-side of you, a gay chatter a provoking laughter of a woman is heard [. . .] and you remember that you are at Aumont's, Charles Aumont's."[6]

French-Algerian entrepreneur Charles Aumont's Moscow establish-ment played two different roles in Russia at the time: first, it was a legit-imate theater house, and second, it was a brothel. It was the practice of the working girls to meet patrons in the theater by pre-arrangement.[7] The woman sitting at Gorky's elbow, whose laughter interrupts his rev-erie, was, very likely, a prostitute. Gorky, then, saw silent moving pictures in the sonic context of a brothel. The sounds associated with the Cine-matograph's images were not the sounds of the world pictured on the sil-ver screen. Rather, they were the sounds of the commerce of the body.

The prostitute's presence in Gorky's 1896 account establishes a very early explicit connection between the prostitute and the cinema. Here I will discuss a nexus of connections, exploring the links between prostitution, the working-class female body, and noise that formed during the earliest days of moving picture exhibition. The connection between cinema and prostitution in Russia was explicit; as Yuri Tsivian notes in *Early Cinema in Russia and its Cultural Reception*, "The image of the prostitute seems to be as immanently connected with film reception as that of Lumière's train."[8] The two are neatly folded together in Gorky's description. As Tsivian writes, early visitors to both Aumont's café-chantant and the moving picture screenings closely associated the cinema with prostitution.[9]

The prostitute also stood in as a metonym for the entire movie-going audience, and she was always mentioned when early accounts of movie-going described whom, precisely, was sitting in the theater. Consistently, she was sitting up in front with her "rouged cheeks."[10] Charles Aumont's carnal approach to entertainment entailed the girls' presence in the auditorium, circulating through the audience during motion picture screenings.[11] The girls, then, were undeniably part of the cinema scene, an attraction of their own among the cinematic attractions.[12] The cinema grew literally out of the brothel. The silence of the images was backed by a carnal discourse, the call-and-response of the commerce of the body that took place within the theater.

SEXUAL NOISE

In the United States in the early period, this connection was not so literally apparent. However, the connections made at the heart of Gorky's anecdote definitely apply: there was, in the U.S. as well, a potent connection between cinema, noise, and female sexuality at the turn of the century. If the cinema started quite literally in the brothel in Russia, then it began in a manner more metaphorically "promiscuous" in the U.S. In the U.S., cinema began with the carnival, with what Tom Gunning has influentially called the "cinema of attractions," or alternatively, a "carnival of the cinema."[13] These recreation sites were associated with the sounds of promiscuity in very real ways as well that need to be explored.

The sounds made in darkened movie theaters were, from the first, affiliated with the erotic. The prostitute's laughter, when it enters Gorky's account, utterly derails it, sending him on a new mental track. At this point, a nightmare vision of the future of the Cinematograph begins to form. He envisions that the infant art midwifed by Aumont's, where "the victims of social needs," meet with "the loafers who here buy their kisses," would be true to its birthplace. He envisions, from that night on, that a "blue" cinema would be created in which patrons would pay for the privilege of seeing women perform burlesque in films like, "As She Undresses." The cinema itself takes on the character of a harlot, or to quote another one of his imagined film titles, "A Woman in Stockings," after the prostitute's giggle enters his account. He imagines it to be a whore that, contrary to the scientific value of the Lumière's discovery and the Cinematograph's birth, has decided to sell herself. Significantly, the sound is colored deeply by the fact that he heard it in a room "full of women, wine, music, and vice."[14]

Beginning with the laughter of the prostitute, we can begin to trace a crisis that lasted some years in early American motion picture culture. Situating ourselves with this anecdote, we can discuss how an ongoing social concern was expressed via noise as it was heard in motion picture theaters from 1895 to about 1913. Noise itself, then, requires a definition. "Noise" is generally defined in terms of its excess beyond what is desired, as "unwanted sound." Noise is defined negatively, as what one does *not* desire to hear. As Jacques Attali writes in *Noise: The Political Economy of Music*, noise, when properly listened to, can be a site of history, a way of thinking about social and economic relations.[15]

While Gorky might not have heard a train's wheels like he desired, or the appropriate sound for the image, he heard a very inappropriate sound for the image: the discourse of the female, working-class body sitting in the audience. The commercial entertainment, with its silent figures, took its place in an already sonic scene: one animated by the sounds of the whorehouse. Here, I elucidate the connection between noise, eroticism, and the working-class woman that the trade journal *Moving Picture World* (*MPW*) created.

Second, I trace how the *MPW*'s suggestions for how to control this noise were instrumental in creating a new model of cinema spectatorship. In doing this, I will focus on two main associations, then: first, that of noise and promiscuity and secondly, that of control and harmony. The two terms—"promiscuity" and "harmony"—were bandied about with great frequency by *MPW* in the years 1907–1913, during which two major shifts occurred: a unified model of sound-image accompaniment became concrete and the model of the silent spectator arose. Noise, with the prostitute's laughter, would be woven into a historical soundscape— this soundscape would include the noises of carnal, working-class bodies, the cries of the middle-class reformers who sought to clean up the cinema, and the eventual "harmony" of the cinemas that resulted from the conflict. The way that the noise of the prostitute's laughter gives way to "harmonic" music tells us a great deal about moving picture culture at this transition. To understand why film turned to silence, however, we must first understand the meanings of noise.

In *Noise*, Attali discusses the power of noise. It can, he writes, be considered a site at which struggles over power manifest. He refers to sound as a site on which battles are waged. Noise, specifically, as sound that has not yet been harnessed or controlled to any particular purpose, is, as

Attali asserts, powerful because it is raw. He writes that because the control of noise is inextricable from the exercise of power, therefore, "any theory of power [...] must include a theory of the localization of noise and its endowment with form."[16]

Noise took two forms in the debates I outline here: first, the accompaniment to moving pictures was labeled "noise" by the trade press, for which *MPW* serves as metonymy for the purpose of this essay. Second, the audience was a site of disturbing noise in itself. The struggle during these transitional years to quiet these noises played out in moving picture culture. Both kinds of noise had to be quashed, the first in the name of musical "harmony" and the second in the name of attentiveness to the film, or its own kind of "harmony." Attali writes that, "since noise is the source of power, power has always listened to it with fascination."[17] Noise, as a form of erotic distraction, was attended to with great fascination by the *MPW*'s critics so that it could be controlled. Moving picture culture was, I argue, dealing with a crisis of promiscuity. This promiscuity was both musical and social.

PROMISCUITY AND THE CARNIVAL OF ATTRACTIONS

Two "promiscuities" were effectively brought together in discourse on early American motion picture venues. First, literally, the sounds of early cinema were many and varied. They were "promiscuous" in their variety, as Rick Altman's detailed work in *Silent Film Sound* has made clear. They were promiscuous in the sense of promiscuity's definition of heterogeneity, being "grouped or massed together without order; of mixed and disorderly composition or character."[18] They could hardly be classified under the single category of "music". First there was the noise that beckoned to passers-by out on the streets, the "ballyhoo" horn. Literally borrowed from a carnival tradition by motion picture exhibitors who sought to get bodies in the seats, the fluted horn already had a history at Coney Island; it was designed to lure patrons from long distances, rather like a musical barker. It enticed them like a siren song into the commercial entertainments.[19] Noise became a major attraction in moving picture theaters themselves as well, a distracting spectacle. *MPW* printed full-page ads for a myriad of sound devices, or professional "playthings," including "bells, chimes, forks, and traps"[20] making everything from the sound of a squalling baby or the quacking of a duck to a pipe that "makes noise like a rotten egg for punky films."[21]

Within this sonic "carnival of attractions," sound technicians were charged with a significant task. It fell to them to make appropriate sonic choices from the promiscuity of options, to match their sound performances to the images presented by any given film. The sound effects men and the girl pianists, however, often chose to exercise their own (slightly misaligned) standards of appropriateness to their craft. They often showcased a shocking lack of discretion when accompanying the motion pictures. Sound choices often undermined the film.[22] They were "promiscuous" in its second definition of being indiscriminate: "That is without discrimination or method; done or applied without respect for kind [or] order."[23]

A noise could be paired with an extremely inappropriate visual. Writers for *MPW* often objected to such inappropriate sound-image matches. For example, one *MPW* writer despairs, "At Coney Island while the poverty scene of 'Tim Mahoney, the Scab' (Vitagraph) was upon the screen, the band was vigorously playing up the 'Star Spangled Banner.' "[24] Or equally bad: "a wretched picture depicted the beheading of Charles II of England to the tune of a lively dance."[25] The writer, despite his disgust, does not seem surprised by the unholy sound-image match-ups. This, he everywhere implies, is because they occur at Coney Island. He writes that, at Coney Island, "it is only to be expected that dance music should accompany a murder." The writer makes, I believe, a surprising and highly significant connection here. He creates a link between vice, an amusement venue, and promiscuous sonic practice.

Another *MPW* writer fills in this picture of Coney Island as immoral and sonically discordant in a review called "At Coney Island" in July 1911. He begins, "In the Economopoly picture resort, discord was rampant," adding significantly, "Everyone knows that the ethics of Coney Island will not permit the blending of harmonies; it is the one place of all others where extremes must meet; in this respect, they are masters unto perfection."[26] He ends the review with "Grand Coney Island! Anything goes there—but the good." The writer connects a failure of ethics and sonic dissonance all in one assertion here. Coney Island is noisy, and Coney Island is immoral. In a place where "anything goes," neither sonic nor moral harmony can exist. What goes wrong at Coney Island is twofold: first in the failure to achieve musical harmony and secondly in its failure to achieve "harmonic" or satisfactory ethics. Discord was "rampant" at Coney Island. The sound-image matches felt arbitrary, one image as likely to be paired with a sound as another—forming an essentially promiscuous soundscape in which any visual could pair with any sound—a soundscape without discretion or restraint. Sonic practice and vice were repeatedly linked in the pages of *MPW*. The ideal of "harmony," then, had both a sonic and a moral valence.

CHEAP THRILLS AND CHEAP DATES

The multiplicity of sound-image pairings at Coney Island seems, I believe, to mirror another kind of multiplicity of couplings possible at the entertainment site. Coney Island, as a turn-of-the-century popular amusement, had well-advertised and literal ties with promiscuity. This refers to its most common, and most charged, definition, as a lack of sexual discrimination.[27] Social historian Kathy Peiss explores the connection between working-class leisure culture, gender, and sexuality in an influential study, *Cheap Amusements: Working Women and Leisure in Turn-of-the-Century New York*. Peiss argues that working-class women of the turn of the twentieth century articulated their gender through participation in these commercial amusements. The social history of women's participation in these entertainments can be read for clues as to how reformers and the middle class worked through issues of gender and sexuality as they related to traditions of male and female sociability, and social freedom as each of these categories changed in turn-of-the-century culture.

Amusement owners actively promoted the participation of young, single, working-class women. The mixed-sex character of modern amusements changed the nature of social engagement deemed appropriate in public for these young consumers and challenged conventional norms. This was one of these amusements' primary characteristics that drew both comment and concern. Peiss asserts: "leisure entrepreneurs consciously encouraged their participation in mixed-sex amusements, altering traditional patterns of sociability."[28] Commercial entertainments that thrived in urban centers at the turn of the century opened up a new social arena, particularly for single female city-dwellers.

These venues enabled the free and easy heterosocial mixing that, occurring outside of the domestic sphere and traditional courtship practices, held the seeds for a new culture of dating. Commercial culture was, as

Peiss asserts, also definitively heterosocial culture.[29] This link was its danger to a middle class that still prided itself on a notion of separation of the genders. Shelley Stamp convincingly also links middle-class reformers' anxieties about turn-of-the-century amusements to the role these sites played as hotbeds for the new dating culture. According to Stamp, social critics like Richard Henry Edwards conclusively linked "the amusement problem" and the "vice problem," writing that the "easygoing familiarity" of these environments allowed a "promiscuous sociability" in which "a more or less general promiscuity of relationships may emerge."[30]

This heterosocial environment had several new social practices associated with it. Working women, Peiss states, earned below a living wage; in practice, this meant that a working girl of 1910 was able to bring home less than nine or ten dollars per week.[31] When a ride on the trolley-car entailed skipping a meal during the week, the possibility of financing one's own evening of entertainment was only very faint.[32] Social conditions such as these contributed to creating a system of what was generally termed "treating" for young single women. As social worker Belle Linder noted in her 1909 study, it was common that "one of a [young woman's] partners of the evening may exact tribute for a standing treat."[33]

Stamp confirms Linder's implication: "Within this turn-of-the-century dating culture it became acceptable for working-class women to offer sexual 'favors' of one degree or another in exchange for being treated at amusement sites."[34] Connecting the sounds of the Coney Island nickelodeon with the laughter of Gorky's prostitute is, then, a very possible connection. Prostitution was a concern when, as *Collier's* magazine wrote, a girl's "chastity is entrusted to her young eager self for safe-keeping or for bartering."[35] Entering into commercial culture, then, meant entering into a sexual barter system that was close to, if certainly not the same thing as, prostitution. The siren song of the ballyhoo horn, calling spectators in from the street, certainly did invite them into an erotic milieu. The noise of the nickelodeon was, then, associated with two kinds of commerce: that of the cheap commercial attractions, and an illicit commerce associated with the working-class female body.

The noise of the nickelodeons' audiences was remarkable. The spectatorial practices of working-class audiences differed, in this period, a great deal from those of the middle-class. The working class was often seen as boisterous and rowdy when it was unacceptable. A tradition of conversation existed between participants in the audience. As *MPW* described, spectators at the motion picture show often spoke loudly to one another, commenting on the action. They also often spoke to the screen itself, offering commentary on the show. Viewers at the motion picture show left their seats and visited their friends and acquaintances up and down the aisles of the theater. In a period in which "familiarity" was quite explicitly linked to flirting and to overtly familiar relations between the sexes, as Peiss puts it, "Others feared 'the likelihood that the much more easy conversational relations among spectators will lead to improvised and clandestine acquaintance with men.' "[36] As it was a common practice to meet men and make dates *at* the theater itself, the chit-chat that accompanied working-class practices of watching a film carried with it the knowledge that new connections were being forged.

Such an erotic connection can also, I argue, be found in the noises of these commercial entertainments themselves. That is, the noises of the accompaniment to moving pictures very often suggested the erotic. *MPW* writer Frank H. Madison complained that at the "Springfield, Ill. Picture Shows," the show featured "an exchange of kisses blown from the finger-tips" with which "the interpreter of martial music kept tally with the tom-tom."[37] As Stephen Bottomore has noted about sound effects in early cinema, viewers in the auditorium were often encouraged to make their own smacking, wet kissing noises for onscreen kisses.[38] This constitutes a funny sort of in-joke among young single audience members who were well aware of the erotic quality of movie-going. A young female accompanist, for her part, writes disgustedly to *MPW*'s "Letters" section that, "The manager wanted *me* to imitate the kiss."[39] Despite her disgust, she apparently did so. In each situation, the noises of the commercial amusement evoked the promiscuous exchange of erotic favors.

In his 1911 article on "Jackass Music," Louis Reeves Harrison of the *MPW* picks up two promiscuous practices (the first musical and the second social) and incorporates them into one female caricature. Writing about the nickelodeon girl pianist "Lily Limpwrist," Harrison first attacks her amateur musicianship by noting her Coney Island tendency to mismatch sound and image. He writes, "Lily is all right at home, when her mother importunes her to 'play something and don't wait to be teased,' or still better as a summer-eve girl on a Coney Island boat".[40] He continues, connecting her poor musicianship to Coney Island's bad reputation in the realm of the moral: "but no man will ever marry a girl who plays a dance while the pictured man is in a death struggle;" and significantly adds, "she would probably be *at* one when the real one was in trouble." The girl, he implies, was promiscuous sonically, with her inability to match sound and image, and socially, blithely jumping from man to man in the new dating culture that enabled such behavior. What he calls Lily's "I-seen-you-glances" directed at the "box of candy young man in the first row" also marked her participation in the sexual exchange associated with working-class women in commercial entertainment.[41]

FIGURE 1: Louis Reeves Harrison, "Jackass Music,"
MPW, Vol. 8, No. 3 (21 January 1911): 124–5. Sketches by H.F. Hoffman.

FIGURE 2: Staff Writer, "The Picture Show Singer,"
MPW, Vol. 3, No. 24 (12 December 1908): 472.

With such a connection between noise and vice suggested, there needed to be both a sonic and a moral solution to the problem of noise. To fully appreciate this shift, however, we must understand the rise of silence as a reaction to what noise meant. Here, I have argued that "noise" encapsulated the *MPW*'s problem of distraction. "Harmony," I will argue, would become its suggested solution. Middle-class reformers sought to solve two problems. They sought to create a more pleasing and satisfying Soundscape, and they sought to change the nature of the film spectator's behavior. The discourse popularized by the trade press distinguished "good" spectators from "bad" observers.

The two were effectively differentiated on the pages of *MPW*. The anxieties of middle-class culture of the turn of the century seem everywhere apparent in the discourse that was invoked in order to discipline the spectator. The middle class was eager to separate its public behaviors from those of the working class. Peiss states that, "In the nineteenth century, as a distinct middle class developed in American society, the emergent class found ways to distinguish itself culturally from working-class immigrants," as well as the wealthy.[42] "The bourgeois world," Peiss argues, counterposed bourgeois ideals with the activity of the working class. In contrast to the undisciplined working class, middle-class ideology valorized "such values as sobriety and domesticity against the dissipation and promiscuity of those higher and lower in social rank."[43] Harmony was integrally tied to these virtues.

HARMONY AND THE GOOD SPECTATOR

Next, then, I will trace out how ideals of "Harmony" were woven, threadlike, throughout the middle-class approach to silence in the movie theater. The injunction against noise that appears in turn-of-the-century motion picture culture did not come, culturally, from nowhere; rather, the injunction was very much in keeping with a middle-class worldview that saw Harmony as an ideal. There is a nexus of beliefs and social practices from which the transition to audience silence in American motion picture theaters appeared.

First, let's address the question of musical accompaniment. Tim Anderson points to this shift toward harmony in moving picture accompaniment in his article on "Reforming 'Jackass Music.' " There was a move toward standardizing the sound-image relationship, concurrent with film culture's exit from the nickelodeon. [44] Sound began to serve the themes present in the narrative of any given film. This was done through actions of the *MPW*, who published scene-by-scene outlines complete with suitable musical selections for all pictures currently in distribution.[45] Light and popular songs were recommended for family scenes or playful sequences. Foreboding music was recommended for the scenes that involved danger.

As Anderson writes, the moves the *MPW* made "positioned [it] as a de facto clearinghouse for the matching of musical selection with features, scenarios, and narrative types."[46] A single sound-image pairing became the sanctioned match for film exhibition. "Suitable" music was presented as a legitimate answer to the haphazard quality of previous sound-image pairings. The *MPW*, then, arranged suitable marriages between sounds and images to create a union that was sanctified by "harmony." The sonic aesthetic reproduced the socially sanctioned relationships of the moral code of the middle class.

The aesthetics of the show's sonic pairing was just one aspect that needed reforming. However well the individual components of film exhibition ran in tandem, the new method of exhibition would "harmonize" only with a very different sort of audience than the one that had populated the nickelodeon. Reporters for *MPW* described nickelodeon spectators in sharp distinction from the type of patron they would seek to cultivate. As Miriam Hansen details in *Babel and Babylon*, one of the most significant shifts that occurred with the rise of the feature film was the reconfiguration of the spectator-film relationship.[47] Tom Gunning has asserted that it was during this period in the early 1910s that film's address to the spectator changed materially, with the end of the "cinema of attractions" beginning by roughly 1907 and the rise of the feature film by 1912–1913.[48]

The end of the more conversational movie-viewing environment, then, can be seen to naturally come to an end with the rise of feature film exhibition. Feature films required a spectator's unbroken concentration and absorption for the length of the film's screen time. It has indeed been argued frequently and convincingly by film historians that the rise of feature film is the single most influential factor determining the shift in spectator relations during the period. It was a natural consequence of narrative development and increased complexity within film form that the spectator should need to more overtly pay attention to the screen, to the exclusion of other extra-filmic areas of interest. This is, of course, helpful to creating a clear historical understanding of cinema-spectator relations in the late 1900s and early 1910s. I would like to suggest, however, that there is a significant additional area of the discussion to be explored.

THE SCIENCE OF ATTENTION

There is, I believe, another piece of the puzzle we could explore: the role of attention itself as a guiding concept. Attention, as a well-known and widespread scientific discourse of the early twentieth century, ran in ideological parallel with Harmony. The rise of silent film spectatorship can be connected to a constellation of cultural beliefs about the nature of attention during this historical moment. The descriptions of spectators from the middle class that appeared on the pages of trade publications during these years could not be more different from earlier ones that described "the noisy unwashed and uncombed,"[49] the "morbid, listless types" who "stamp their feet" in appreciation for "violent love" and "blood and thunder" spectacle[50] at the "mixed amusement temples."[51]

Neither were they the kinds of spectators described even in 1911: "the giggling slip of a girl" that distracts others by canoodling with her "escort," the girl pianist sneaking glimpses at her boyfriend in the first row, the "noisy, unwashed boy,"[52] or the "impressionable woman whose 'Ahs' and 'Ohs' punctuate the silence."[53] Rather, in 1911, *MPW* published "The Picture the Audience Likes." Here we have our first introduction to a "good" spectator. The audience depicted was much less interactive. It was a great deal more focused on the film. Here, the "World Reviewer" asserts:

> The attitude of the audience is much like that of most persons after finishing a book or looking at some picture. They do not lay down the book, or turn away from the picture with vigorous hand-clapping. They are in a more thoughtful mood, and their enjoyment and appreciation cannot be translated into applause. It goes deeper than that, and is more pleasurable than which causes a noisy demonstration of appreciation.[54]

113

The new audience was silent and attentive, or so the *MPW* asserted. They were drawn in contradistinction to earlier working-class audiences. W. Stephen Bush, whose position as a lecturer gave him a rare viewpoint on the audience, asserted in "Facing an Audience": "Audiences of this kind are by no means demonstrative."[55] However, he asserted, this did not mean they were not engaged. Rather, he writes, their attention was turned silently toward the film. They controlled their own response to be in "harmony" with the goal of attending the cinema: to see the film itself. He describes them raptly watching:

> When the lights are turned up you may see that they are thinking about what they have just seen, for the intensity of expression, so plainly visible in their faces, relaxes but slowly, showing how deeply they have been impressed with what their eyes have seen.[56]

Exhibitors were consciously encouraged by *MPW* to advertise for "the New Patron," whom they differentiated from the current audience.[57] He was the patron who, according to *MPW*, "does not yet come often to the cinema," but behaved himself appropriately when he did. His new, purified focus was encouraged by the perfection of the apparatus itself, the *MPW* argued. The moving picture offered the spectator a new means by which to train his attentive capacities. The discourse of the *MPW* here stemmed from a set of class-based assumptions: specifically, those of the middle class. Contrasting the middle-class spectator's mindset with that of the working-class denizen, then, was utmost in *MPW*'s mind. During these years, they also published articles like "Brains," "Using the Brains," and "The Cinematograph a Stimulus to the Brain." Here, they asserted that moving pictures would, indeed, *train* the spectator to achieve greater focus and self-control. The results of one writer's amateur experiments, he wrote, were "extraordinary," proving that the Cinematograph "concentrates the faculties," and calling for its recognition as a "marvel in its powers of concentration."[58] The Cinematograph, as a machine, was supposed to enhance the viewer's power of concentration on a particular object.

The spectator to which *MPW* aspired had a few distinguishing characteristics. He was young, and was modeled as a schoolboy. The experimenter who supposedly penned "The Cinematograph a Stimulus to the Brain" performed his cinema experiments on schoolboys of his acquaintance. *MPW* seems to hold a vision of a pedagogical future for the device. The writer states, "With what joy the teacher will hail any power which... concentrates the faculties and makes indelible impressions upon the memory" like the Cinematograph.[59] The Cinematograph plays the role of the tutor who helps to form the upright young scholar; it trains young minds for lives of concentrated study. The "concentration of the faculties" led to the training of rigorous mental discipline. This, of course, was a middle-class fantasy. This particular fantasy was not, however, needless, nor was it arbitrary. This hope belied certain realities of motion picture exhibition, which we will discuss here.

NINETEENTH-CENTURY THEATER AND GALLERY GODS

The fantasy of pure focus denies certain social and historical realities of motion picture exhibition at the time. Nowhere can this be clearer than in the legacy of the legitimate theater spectator to the motion picture spectator's protocols of behavior. Here, we find a model of male spectatorship that travels in a direct line of influence from the legitimate theater of the nineteenth century to the nickelodeons and the picture palaces of the early twentieth. The *MPW* may, in fact, have had this troubling legacy in mind when making its argument for the Cinematograph's ability to stimulate the exercise of discipline. Nineteenth-century American theaters had already experienced a significant mixture of noise, working-class misbehavior, and eroticism. Again, here, we return to the figure of the prostitute.

In cities all over the U.S., major and minor legitimate theaters were equipped with a "gallery." This was the "guilty third tier" balcony that held the cheapest seats in the house.[60] This was the home of the theater's prostitutes. As theater historian Claudia Johnson writes in "That Guilty Third Tier: Prostitution in Nineteenth-Century American Theaters," the third tier was an established tradition in major American cities like New York, Boston, Philadelphia, Chicago, New Orleans, Cincinnati, Mobile, and others by the 1830s and 1840s.[61] Houses of prostitution were often self-consciously situated within an easy walk from the theater. In the 1850s, more than half (53%) of all brothels were conveniently located within 2.5 blocks of a theater.[62]

Many theaters consciously appealed to this trade, offering prostitutes discounted tickets.[63] In addition to the higher-class prostitutes who sat among the theatergoers (à la Gorky's anecdote) there were the low-class, more "boisterous" prostitutes of the gallery who interacted with their Johns, the "Gallery Gods." "The house of the harlot," where she "holds her court" was charged with boisterous noise of sexual misbehavior, and the antics of the third tier often rang out and disrupted the rest of the relatively well-behaved house.[64] The Gallery was home to the "ill-behaved, the boisterous, [and] the indecent."[65] Noise and sexual misbehavior were again linked in the theater's convention of the Gallery. Due to the antics of this tier, the entire theater was, in some accounts, called "a temple devoted to the harlot."[66] The gallery was, in most instances where it existed, the most lucrative aspect of a theater's business.[67]

Prostitution was banned in the legitimate theater only at the end of the nineteenth century, when theater sought legitimization by courting middle-class, family audiences.[68] When the gallery did close at the turn of the century, it was with great trepidation that exhibitors allowed it; they were convinced these actions would damage business, since as one critic wrote, "that class of persons know that it [the theater] is a favorite amusement of those who are most easily tempted to sin."[69] Indeed, historians note that many gallery gods did abandon the theater at this point in time.[70]

This movement of the gallery gods away from the theater was concurrent with the arrival of the commercial amusements of the turn of the century, including cinema. And the cinema, according to *MPW*'s own accounts, is indeed the entertainment to which the gallery gods went. An *MPW* writer showcases charming naiveté in an article, "The Lost Gallery," when he asserts with pride that the " 'gallery god' has been lured from his accustomed haunts in the top balcony of the legitimate theater by the motion picture".[71] He gloats over the windfall the "The Lost Gallery" presents, comparing them to "the fabulous treasures of the 'Lost Galleons of the Spanish Main.' " He then proudly explains that "the gallery god…has been enticed from the 'legit' " because they, like all patrons go "wherever suitable arrangements for their comfort are provided."[72] He ends with the assertion that cinema has earned the "allegiance of the 'gallery god' by giving him the sort of entertainment his discriminating soul craved at a price that suited his purse".[73] Here, this writer rather accidentally asserts that cinema as a medium, and as a social milieu, per-

116

fectly served the gallery god's needs, at only a nickel a pop. Either the *MPW* writer failed to realize his mistake, or we must deem the article to be the most subtle of winks at his readership. Regardless, the connection between cinema and the perpetrators of sexual misbehavior is explicit.

SELF-MASTERY AND SPECTATORSHIP

It was this, I argue, that the *MPW* would have fought against when it adopted a more attentive model for the silent male film spectator. Moving picture critics would have been aware of the "dark, guilty, terrible third tier".[74] The rhetoric of *MPW*'s ideal spectator offers, I argue, a defiant counter-formation to this concept of the "gods of Paradise" as film spectators entering the cinema in large numbers.

Scientific discourse offered one way of understanding the problem of attention. Indeed, it seems particularly relevant in consideration of the brain mania that the *MPW* suffered in the early 1910s, when it asserted that the Cinematograph could be considered a mechanical aid to the cultivation of the mental faculties. It offered a model that suggested a way to resist temptation. Attention exploded as an area of scientific research from the 1870s throughout the late nineteenth century in America and Western Europe.[75]

Psychological researchers including Gustav Fechner, Wilhelm Wundt, Edward Titchener, and William James all worked to describe what Jonathan Crary, in *Suspensions of Perception*, calls the, "empirical and epistemological status of attentiveness."[76] The pathology of failures to attend properly was similarly a key component of the work of French researchers like J.M. Charcot, Alfred Binet, and Theodule Ribot.[77] The thesis of Crary's book is tightly related to this quote drawn from *Suspensions of Perception*, that: "attention has continued to be a disciplinary immobilization as well as an accommodation of the subject to change and novelty—as long as the consumption of novelty is subsumed within repetitive forms."[78] This, I argue, is the case in a specific way in cinema culture. Spectators were expected to participate in an immobilization that produced attention. The only "out" available to them was that of the film's novelty.

Spectator attentiveness became a way in which the spectator was disciplined to a state of concentration that was designed for the screen alone, to the exclusion of all other possible stimuli. Attention gave the early 20th century reform movement a scientific model for what it wished to enact in spectacular culture. The scientific discourse gave way to a shift from a range of cinematic attractions to a focus on the film alone as the viewer's natural object of attention. There was a great deal of work done on the varying descriptions of attention, from the purely physical to the abstract. One specific subcategory in the large area of scientific research was *voluntary* attention. As opposed to the larger concept of attention, which was a pure and simple function of the brain, voluntary attention, as scientific researcher Theodule Ribot wrote, was "a discipline and a habit."[79]

Attention was then, according to scientific researchers, a "decisive, *voluntary* activity of the subject."[80] As such, it was often conflated in scientific theories of the 1880s and 1890s with theories of the will. Ribot actually listed pathological failures of attention in his book *Diseases of the Will*.[81] Ribot writes in *The Psychology of Attention* (1898) that voluntary attention (as opposed to attention) "is a sociological phenomenon."[82] Indeed, the models that arose from this research generally placed the will as a force that allowed the subject to "pay attention" above and beyond the desires of the body. Attention was posed by Wundt as a faculty of the most evolved area of the brain, designed to exercise watchful control over the body. William B. Carpenter stated that attention was absolutely necessary for "the control of the Passions...and the regulation of the Conduct."[83] Many of these models also explicitly addressed the issue of physical desire; philosopher Arthur Schopenhauer, for example, posited the body as a welter of conflicting forces, some of which were sexual. The will managed the conflicting forces of the passions, creating a "purified perception" that would temporarily suspend the body's "desirous economy."[84]

For Schopenhauer, Crary asserts, the will was "directly experienced" as control over "one's own body." This provided turn-of-the-century middle-class culture with a way of *understanding* the will. It was, Crary argues, this welter of sexual impulses that posited, for Schopenhauer, the necessity of postulating "the possibility of a looking," a "purified" perception "that would be a suspension from time and the body's economy."[85]

Science, then, offered a model for cinema spectatorship that answered the needs of the historical moment. Schopenhauer's model appears with striking force in motion picture culture. This "suspension" becomes quite familiar to us when we read accounts of film spectatorship. Stephen Bush's viewers in "Facing an Audience" seem to be in a state of physical suspension. The representation on the screen became an all-absorbing presence to the exclusion of other stimuli within the theater. "Paying attention," Crary writes, meant "disengagement from a broad field of attraction[s] [...] for the sake of isolating and focusing on a reduced number of stimuli." Or better, James A. Angell's quotation from *Psychology: an Introductory Study of the Structure and Function of Human Consciousness*: "Attention is always an effort to conquer our own impulses [...] in the interest of the end to which we are attempting to attend."[86] This is an apt description of the ideal spectators described by Bush, who had to shake themselves awake after a show. Following the "cinema of attractions," they had to learn how to reduce the stimuli that still constituted an environment of physical "attractions."

Learning to conquer his own impulses toward distraction as a natural reaction to the theater environment could be considered an act of will on the part of the spectator. This act of will brought the spectator in line with cultural expectations of respectability. Crary writes that "the emergence of a specific model of behavior with a historical structure—behavior that was articulated in terms of socially determined norms and was part of the formation of a modern technological milieu" was the notable shift in understanding of perception in the late nineteenth century.[87] This was true in a particular sense in the spectacular culture of moviegoing, when the Cinematograph, it was argued, helped the spectator to focus in a distracting welter of sensory stimuli that came along with the milieu.

HARMONY AND THE ELIMINATION OF NOISE

Silencing the audience, then, was one part of the creation of a culture that took pride in self-control that was embodied in practices that produced silence and enforced "Harmonic" ideals. Scientific research and middle-class common decency formed a dynamic composition and created a model for the attentive cinemagoer. Becoming a sexually suspended, physically controlled, silent, and attentive individual made one an ideal cinematic spectator with the end of the "cinema of attractions." This was the "New Patron" that the *MPW* was cultivating.

As Crary writes, a normative 19th century observer was conceptualized "not only in terms of the objects of attention but also in terms of what is not perceived, of the distractions, fringes, and peripheries that are excluded or shut out of a perceptual field."[88] Cinema began with the sounds of promiscuity ringing clear through the air; this was, of course, unacceptable to the moral and social criteria set by the rising middle class. Solutions to the problem of erotic distraction had to be created. When these sounds were quieted, the viewer became a site of suspended desire. The middle-class cinemagoer, it seems, bound himself to the mast of middle-class morality as it related to physical matters.

When Gorky sat in Aumont's and watched the silent images spilling from the Cinematograph, he stepped into the "The Kingdom of Shadows," entering a state of suspension that took him far from the milieu in which he watched. This was, however, a delicate suspension. The milieu of Aumont's broke it. The whore's giggle distracted him, reminding him of the many attractions of the "Paradise" in which he watched, with its splendid commerce. The body had the eruptive potential to break the suspension of the spectator.

The suspensions proposed thereafter, by the *MPW* and others were, I argue, a defensive formation against this power. As Attali writes in *Noise*: "Since noise is the source of power, power has always listened to it with fascination." So it was that the needs of the middle-class reform movement began to turn to the sounds of working-class women. We, too, should listen to the accounts of bygone and forgotten sounds. If we listen closely, we can still hear the boisterous laughter that so discomfited Maxim Gorky. And we can begin to hear what cinema culture repressed when it chose to suspend the desires it had expressed in sound.

ENDNOTES

1. Maxim Gorky, "Lumière." In Jay Leyda, *Kino: A History of the Russian and Soviet Film*, translated by Leda Swan (Princeton, N.J.: Princeton University Press, 1983 [1960]), 407–409.
2. Ibid., 407.
3. Ibid., 408.
4. Ibid.
5. Ibid.
6. Ibid.
7. Yuri Tsivian, *Early Cinema in Russia and its Cultural Reception*, trans. Alan Bodger (New York: Routledge, 1994), 36.
8. Ibid.

9. Ibid.

10. Ibid.

11. Ibid.

12. In a short story he published in the same newspaper as "Lumière" just a week later, entitled "Revenge," Gorky's main character is a fictional girl of the café-chantant who, after viewing the Lumière film *Baby's Breakfast*, kills herself from shame.

13. Tom Gunning, "The Cinema of Attractions: Early Film, Its Spectator, and the Avant-Garde," *Wide Angle*, Vol. 8, No. 3-4 (1986): 63–70. Reprinted in Thomas Elsaesser and Alan Barker, eds., *Early Cinema: Space, Frame, Narrative* (London: British Film Institute, 1990), 61.

14. Gorky, "Lumière," 407.

15. Jacques Attali, *Noise: The Political Economy of Music*, translated by Brian Massumi (Minneapolis: University of Minnesota Press, 1989), 4.

16. Ibid., 6.

17. Ibid., 7.

18. "Promiscuous: 1a." *Oxford English Online Dictionary*. 2007. www.oed.com (6 June 2007).

19. *MPW*, "Plucky (Akron) Exhibitor Wins His Case: Ch. 1: To Prison in Wagon." Vol. 1, No. 9 (6 April 1907): 113.

20. Such ads were commonplace up until 1910. One example from 3 December 1910 shows these devices with a mention of a larger catalogue of "All Moving Picture Show Effects." *MPW*, Vol. 7, No. 25, 1303.

21. In a cartoon by H.F. Hoffman, "What They Want for Christmas," *MPW*, Vol. 7, No. 26 (24 December 1910): 1482.

22. An extreme example of this scenario can be found in Mary Carbine's excellent article on sound accompaniment in south side Chicago movie theaters, "The Finest Outside the Loop: Motion Picture Exhibition in Chicago's Black Metropolis, 1905–1928," *Camera Obscura* 23 (May 1990): 9–41.

23. Promiscuous: b." *Oxford English Online Dictionary*. 2007. www.oed.com (6 June 2007).

24. Martin, "Working the Sound Effects," *MPW*, Vol. 9, No. 11 (23 September 1911): 873.

25. Ibid.

26. Staff Writer, "At Coney Island," *MPW*, Vol. 8, No. 27 (8 July 1911): 1571.

27. "Promiscuous: c." *Oxford English Dictionary*. 2007. www.oed.com (6 June 2007).

28. Kathy Peiss, *Cheap Amusements: Working Women and Leisure in Turn-of-the-Century New York* (Philadelphia: Temple University Press, 1986), 186.

29. Ibid., 10.

30. Shelley Stamp, *Movie-Struck Girls: Women and Motion Picture Culture After the Nickelodeon* (Princeton, N.J.: Princeton University Press, 2000), 50.

31. Peiss, 52.

32. Ibid.

33. Linder's study is quoted on Stamp's *Movie-Struck Girls*, 49.

34. Stamp, 49

35. Quoted in Stamp, 49

36. Ibid., 151.

37. Frank H. Madison, "Springfield, Ill. Picture Shows," *MPW*, Vol. 7, No. 25 (17 December 1910): 1420.

38. Stephen Bottomore, "The Story of Percy Peashaker: Debates About Sound Effects in the Early Cinema." In Richard Abel and Rick Altman, eds., *The Sounds of Early Cinema* (Bloomington: Indiana University Press, 2001), 134–142.

39. "Hazel B's" letter to Clarence E. Sinn, the "Cue Music Man," "Music for the Picture," *MPW*, Vol. 8, No. 7 (18 February 1911): 353.

40. Louis Reeves Harrison, "Jackass Music," *MPW*, Vol. 8, No. 3 (21 January 1911): 124–5. Sketches by H.F. Hoffman.

41. Ibid.

42. Peiss, 186.

43. Ibid.

44. Tim Anderson, "Reforming 'Jackass Music': The Problematic Aesthetics of Early American Film Music Accompaniment," Cinema Journal, Vol. 37, No. 1 (1997): 3–22.

45. Anderson, 10.

46. Ibid.

47. Miriam Hansen, *Babel and Babylon: Spectatorship in American Silent Film* (Cambridge, MA: Harvard University Press, 1991), 2.

48. Gunning, "The Cinema of Attractions," 60.

49. Louis Reeves Harrison, "Managerial Stupidity," *MPW*, Vol. 7, No. 24 (10 December 1910), 1400.

50. Staff Writer, "In the Educational Field," *MPW*, Vol. 8, No. 11 (10 March 1911): 584.

51. Staff Writer, "Facts and Comments," *MPW*, Vol. 10, No. 1 (7 October 1911): 20.

52. Staff Writer, "Facts and Comments," *MPW*, Vol. 9, No. 8 (2 September 1911): 604.

53. Staff Writer, "An Original Critique," *MPW*, Vol. 9, No. 9 (9 September 1911): 705.

54. The 'World Reviewer,' "The Picture the Audience Likes," *MPW*, Vol. 8, No. 6 (11 February 1911): 310.

55. W. Stephen Bush, "Facing an Audience," *MPW*, Vol. 9, No. 10 (16 September 1911): 389.

56. Ibid.

57. Epes Winthrop Sargent, "Advertising for Exhibitors," *MPW*, Vol. 9, No. 11 (23 September 1911): 876.

58. Staff Writer, In the Educational Field: "BRAINS"—"Using the Brains"—"The Cinematograph a Stimulus to the Brain," *MPW*, Vol. 8, No. 7 (18 February 1911): 352.

59. Ibid.

60. Claudia D. Johnson, "That Guilty Third Tier: Prostitution in Nineteenth-Century American Theaters," *American Quarterly*, Special Issue on "Victorian Culture in America," Vol. 27, No. 5 (December 1975): 575–584.

61 John Murtaugh and Sarah Harris, *Cast the First Stone* (New York: McGraw-Hill, 1957), 203–205. Cited in Claudia D. Johnson.

62. Statistics originally appear in Timothy J. Gilfoyle, "City of Eros: New York City, Prostitution, and the Commercialization of Sex," (Ph.D. dissertation, Columbia University, 1987), 22–3. Quoted in Rosemarie K. Bank, *Theatre Culture in America, 1825-1860* (Cambridge, UK: Cambridge University Press, 1997), 136.

63. Johnson, "That Guilty Third Tier," 581.

64. David H. Agnew, *Theatrical Amusements* (Philadelphia, 1857), 8, 20.

65. Thomas DeWitt Talmadge, *Sports That Kill* (New York: Funk and Wagnall, 1875), 20–22. Quoted in Johnson.

66. Letter writer to the *New York Herald*, 1 and 2 November 1842. Quoted in Johnson, 579.

67. *Commercial Advertiser*, 15 March 1833, quoted in Bank, *Theatre Culture in America*, 241.

68. Johnson, 583.

69. Reverend Robert Turnbull, *The Theatre* (Hartford, 1837), 82–87.

70. Johnson, 583.

71. Staff Writer, "The Lost Gallery," *MPW*, Vol. 9, No. 3 (29 July 1911): 397.

72. Ibid.

73. Ibid.

74. Johnson, "That Guilty Third Tier," 580.

75. Jonathan Crary, *Suspensions of Perception: Attention, Spectacle, and Modern Culture* (Cambridge, MA: MIT Press, 2001), 23.

76. Ibid.

77. Ibid.

78. Ibid., 33.

79. Theodule Ribot, *Psychologie de l'attention* (Paris: F. Alcan, 1889). English trans. as *The Psychology of Attention* (Chicago: The Open Court Publishing Company, 1896).

80. Crary, *Suspensions of Perception*, 42.

81. Ibid., 47.

82. Ribot, *The Psychology of Attention*, 39.

83. William B. Carpenter, *Principles of Mental Physiology*, 4th ed. (London Kegan Paul, 1896), 130–131.

84. Crary, *Suspensions of Perception*, 57.

85. Ibid.

86. James A. Angell, *Psychology: An Introductory Study of the Structure and Function of Human Consciousness* (New York: Henry Holt, 1904), 75–76.

87. Crary, *Suspensions of Perception*, 29.

88. Ibid., 57.

CHAPTER 4

CONSTRUCTING THE GLOBAL VERNACULAR: AMERICAN ENGLISH AND THE MEDIA

KINGSLEY BOLTON

IN RECENT YEARS, English scholars and others have begun to investigate the part that the modern mass media, including film, television, and the Internet have played in spreading particular languages or varieties of a language within societies. For many commentators worldwide, it has been evident that the rapid spread of American English worldwide in recent decades has been partly due to the ubiquity of American films, television, popular music, and new media in so many countries around the globe. As Henry Luce himself noted "American jazz, Hollywood movies, American slang, American machines and patented products, are in fact the only things that every community in the world, from Zanzibar to Hamburg, recognizes in common."[1] More recently, Anchimbe, in a discussion of "world Englishes" has commented that:

> The pride and prestige of the American tongue vehicled by an easily available American culture—pop music Hollywood cinema, cable television, VOA broadcasts, Peace Corps, American Language Centres—is a great attraction for L2 users of English. This is why [...] regional and national models [...] will submerge their distinctiveness in the sweeping current of the American tongue. [2]

This essay sets out to explore the role that media have played in the formation of contemporary American English, and, more widely, to consider the ways in which the language of media (notably in radio, film and television) might begin to be investigated by language scholars. One reason for this is simply the apparent dearth of previous work in this field. While—within cinema studies at least—a great deal has been written on "the language of film," from a the perspective of cinematography, semiotics, and visual communication, very little research, to my knowledge, has been carried out on "language *in* film," with reference to the ways in which various varieties of language, not least American English, have been used and represented in motion pictures. The paper that follows is thus exploratory and speculative in its ambitions and scope, as it aims to illuminate a range of possible research issues related to language and media in the U.S., as well as considering the construction of the American vernacular in the global context.

AMERICAN ENGLISH MYTHOLOGIES

Given the daily exposure to the U.S. variety of English in so many societies worldwide, it would seem self-apparent that the media have played—and continue to play—a major role in the spread of the spoken and written forms of the American English, and that this in turn provides substantial *a priori* evidence of the powerful influence of mass media in initiating and or propelling language change, as a linguistic process. For many linguists, however, the link between media and language change is by no means self-evident. As Jack Chambers, a leading Canadian linguist explains:

> Most people assume that television and other media change the way we speak, but linguists have searched in vain for supporting evidence. [...] There is zero evidence for television or the other popular media disseminating or influencing sound changes or grammatical innovations. [...] A [...] common assumption is that the media leads language changes. In fact, it belatedly reflects the changes.[3]

In asserting that the media do not lead language change, Chambers' stance reflects the orthodox position held by many linguists in the field of dialectology and "sociolinguistics," the branch of linguistics dealing with language and society. A similar judgment on this issue was expressed some years ago by the British sociolinguist Peter Trudgill, when he asserted that:

> [T]he electronic media are not very instrumental in the diffusion of linguistic innovations, in spite of widespread popular notions to the contrary. The point about the TV set is that people, however, much they watch and listen to it, do not talk to it. [...] Face-to-face interaction is necessary before diffusion takes place, precisely because it is only during face-to-face interaction that accommodation occurs.[4]

For a number of linguists, therefore, the notion that the media play a major role in effecting linguistic change is a "myth." This belief is as misconceived, we are told, as a second not-unrelated myth concerning "Standard American English," which is a non-regional form of English that is taught to foreign learners, and that serves as a model for the language in books on the subject. Again, professional linguists demur that such a beast exists. For example, Falk (1978) has claimed that "In the United States there is no one regional dialect that serves as the model. [...] Each region of the country has its own standard."[5] Similarly, one of the most widely-used university linguistics textbooks in use at U.S. universities states that:

> SAE [Standard American English] is an idealization. Nobody speaks this dialect; and if somebody did, we wouldn't know it because SAE is not defined precisely. Several years ago there actually was an entire conference devoted to one subject: a precise definition of SAE. This convocation of scholars did not succeed in satisfying everyone as to what SAE should be. The best hint we can give you is to listen to national broadcasters (though nowadays some of these people may speak a regional dialect).[6]

While the views of serious linguists on the subject must be given some credence, these are not totally unproblematic. While it may be true, for example, that, in previous generations, the role of media may have played only a secondary role in language change, the impact of electronic media on language in the twenty-first century—given the now pervasive presence of film, television, computers, the Internet, and other new media—may not be so easily dismissed. At the same time, it is also argued that the Standard American question might also need re-assessing, not least in the light of recent scholarship that highlights the role of radio and cinema in the 1920s and 1930s in contributing to stereotypical representations of what that norm might be. A third theme that is also discussed here is that an adequate and full sociolinguistic exploration of this issue must include not only linguistic aspects of the question but also the relevant cultural, historical, and social dimensions as well. In this view, languages are not just linguistic systems—typically the prime focus of the professional linguist—but also important cultural systems. In this context, the American "vernacular", a term valorized in a number of senses by the U.S. founder of sociolinguistics, William Labov, might be reconceptualized to include its embedding in the cultural and historical experience of both the domestic past and the global present.[7]

BONFIGLIO AND THE RISE OF STANDARD AMERICAN

One of the most insightful studies of American English in recent years has been Thomas P. Bonfiglio's *Race and the Rise of Standard American* (2002), which provides a socio-historical explanation of "Standard American" through the careful examination of U.S. linguistic ideologies in historical perspective, with particular reference to issues of race and racial insecurity. The middle section of this essay will attempt to provide a concise summary of Bonfiglio's arguments.

FIGURE 1: Benjamin Franklin (1706–1790). Getty Images.

FIGURE 2: Noah Webster (1758–1843). Getty Images.

In his core historical argument, Bonfiglio demonstrates how beliefs about race and racial kinship found expression in American language debates from colonial times onwards. For example, as early as 1750, Benjamin Franklin speculated that German would become the language of Pennsylvania, and that "[i]nstead of their Learning our Language, we must learn their's [sic] or live as in a foreign Country."[8] A year later, Franklin returned to the same topic, catenating his remarks with racial fears of a broader kind:

> Why should Pennsylvania, founded by the *English*, become a Colony of Aliens, who will shortly be so numerous as to Germanize us instead of our Anglifying them, and will never adopt our Language or Customs, any more than they can acquire our Complexion. [. . .] Which leads me to add one Remark: That the Number of purely white People in the World is proportionably very small. All *Africa* is black or tawny. *Asia* chiefly tawny. *America* (exclusive of the new Comers) wholly so. And in *Europe*, the *Spaniards, Italians, French, Russians* and *Swedes*, are generally of what we call a swarthy Complexion; as are the *Germans* also, the *Saxons* only excepted, who with the *English*, make the principal Body of White People on the Face of the Earth. I could wish their Numbers were increased.[9]

The notion that the English language was the possession and birthright of Anglo-Saxons was also voiced by Noah Webster some thirty years later, who observed that "the peculiar structure of our language is Saxon, and that its principles can be discovered only in its Teutonic original, it has been my business, as far as the materials in my possession would permit, to compare the English with the other branches of the same stock, particularly the German and the Danish."[10]

A century or so later, linguistic complaints in the same tradition bemoaned the deterioration of the language occasioned by the mass immigration of the late nineteenth century, as in Theodore Mead's tract on *Mother Tongue* in 1890, which argued that "happy indeed are we of the Anglo-Saxon stock in the possession of our mother-tongue, for among the great languages of the world, whether dead or living, she undoubtedly stands in the front rank."[11] At this time, Mead looked to Britain as the guardian of the language, and conceded that Americans "have a different, and, on the whole, an inferior manner of speaking." A particular concern, at this time, was the deleterious effect of Irish immigration, and Mead argued that "the great Irish immigration" had led to speech of "Hibernian nurses and servants" intruding into good American households.[12]

Indeed, by the end of the nineteenth century, concerns about the effects of immigration were entering the popular discourses of the day. From the 1870s until 1910, the U.S. experienced massive immigration from Europe, including approximately 5 million Germans (1840s–50s), 1.3 million Scandinavians (1870s), 4.1 million Irish (1830s–40s), as well as around 3 million Central Europeans (1880s–1910).[13] Mass immigration drew a number of responses, and Bonfiglio usefully surveys a range of racist policies that were implemented at this time, including educational policies towards Native American children, and the imposition of a series of Chinese (and Asian) Exclusion Acts from the 1850s onwards. Such policies were paralleled by the growing influence of race theory during this period the period, including the writings of the journalist Burton J. Hendrick (1871–1949), the lawyer and popular anthropologist Madison Grant (1865–1937), and the historian Stephen Graham (1884–1975), who were particularly concerned about the deleterious effects of recent—particularly Jewish—immigration on both the citizenry and the language of the U.S.[14]

Around the same time, an awareness of the distinctiveness of American—as opposed to British—speech was made explicit in the work of Alexander Melville Bell (1819–1905), the Scottish phonetician and elocution teacher and father of Alexander Graham Bell, asserted that "the leading Americanism of Articulation is associated with the letter R," whose omission, he noted, contributed to a form of white "nigger speech."[15] Despite Bell's enthusiasm for this most American of sounds, however, in the late nineteenth century a number of other authorities still favored a non-r-full (i.e. non-rhotic) model of pronunciation based on the cultured speech of speakers from New England and New York.

A decade or two later, H. L. Mencken published his monumental *The American Language*, which, while criticized by linguists, still represents a linguistic declaration of independence, which set a "anti-British" tone to much of the discussion that would follow. As Bonfiglio shows, the pronunciation of the language had a particular significance for Mencken, who sought to discredit earlier accounts of standard speech that leant towards New England and New York, with their British associations. One adversary that Mencken pilloried as an "anglomaniac" was Professor Brander Matthews of Columbia University, who advocated a vision of linguistic commonality based on the shared Anglo-Saxon essence of the United States and Great Britain. At the level of pronunciation, Matthews advocated a "supra-national standard" based on "English, pure and simple."[16] For his part, Mencken advocated a "general American" accent, characterized by "the flat *a* and the clearly sounded *r*."[17] As Bonfiglio makes clear, however, Mencken's linguistic beliefs were somewhat sullied by their associations with a range of racist attitudes that were readily expressed against such minority groups as African-Americans and Jews.

FIGURE 3: Henry Louis Mencken (1880–1956). Getty Images.

THE AMERICAN *R* AND THE NETWORK STANDARD

The articulation of *r* before consonants or in word-final position (in what linguists call a "rhotic" accent) had become a marker of certain American pronunciations by the late nineteenth century. Indeed, from early on, this had had some salience in the American variety of English, and Noah Webster had even disparaged its absence in the speech of "[s]ome of the southern people", and describing this feature as "a habit contracted by carelessness."[18]

By the 1930s, the age of radio entertainment had been established in the U.S., and the radio networks were soon faced with the task of choosing suitable announcers who spoke an acceptable form of English. In the early 1930s, Francis H. Vizetelly became Dean of the Columbia Announcer's School of Pronunciation, and published a volume on *How to Speak English Effectively* (1933), which was aimed at announcers employed by the Columbia Broadcasting System (CBS). In this, Vizetelly argued for a standardized form of American speech that communicated "purity" and "vitality" and best served the American people, and here Vizetelly also emphasized the importance of articulating *r*, claiming that "[i]t is

FIGURE 4: Legendary radio broadcaster Edward R. Murrow at CBS. Getty Images.

well known that races which habitually pronounce their *r*'s are easily heard, while races that habitually do not pronounce their *r*'s are inaudible."[19] Specifically, Vizetelly warned against the imitation of British accents, as among "who ape the so-called Oxford accent" as "They cannot ask you to dinner; they ask you to 'dinnah.' They do not come to a lecture; they come to a 'lectchah.' "[20]

Throughout the 1930s and 1940s, CBS recruited a generation or two of radio announcers whose speech met the desired criteria. These initially included such figures as Edward R. Murrow, who in turn later recruited announcers such as Walter Cronkite, Mike Wallace, Dan Rather and many others. By the 1940s, the National Broadcasting Corporation had also employed its own speech trainers, including James F. Bender, who published the *NBC Handbook of Pronunciation* in 1943, which again favored the propagation of a rhotic "General American" pronunciation.[21]

HARVARD GOES WEST

Bonfiglio's third strand of explanation of the rise of Standard American concerned the academy. The racial tensions that had influenced language debates in the late nineteenth and early twentieth century also found expression at the most prestigious American universities. In 1922, the President of Harvard University, Abott Lawrence Lowell, announced that the university had a "Jewish problem," as the Jewish enrollment had risen from six percent in 1908 to twenty-two percent by 1922.[22] In June 1922, Harvard University set up a committee to deal with admissions, chaired by the philologist Charles H. Grandgent. In its report, the committee recommended increasing recruitment from the West and South of the country, and to raise the percentage of admissions from rural areas. As Bonfiglio explains, the university then turned away from New York and Boston in the attempt to recruit "the Nordic Christian (mid) western country boy as the savior of its heritage."[23]

Significantly, Grandgent had also been the author of a 1920 paper on American pronunciation, where he had valorized the Midwestern pronunciation of *r*, reporting that "our enterprising middle West [...] has developed and cherished an r-substitute, homely, to be sure, but vigorous and aggressive."[24] For Bonfiglio, then, it was no mere coincidence that the crucial shift in Harvard admissions policies occurred when it did. Later, he argues, the shift in attitudes that gave increased prestige to western norms of Americanness and American language would also underpin the popularity of such movie icons as Will Rogers and John Wayne, both of whom, in overlapping eras, came to epitomize the virtues of the male, Nordic westerner, who "speaks American" and "walks American."[25] The frontier may have been closed, but such cinema stars as Rogers and Wayne spoke to essential, and very white, American virtues, evocative of the Midwest and western states far from the contaminated and corrupt eastern cities. By the late 1930s, the speech of New York City with its limited rhoticity—and other deviations from the General American norm—had become unrepresentative of the American heartland.

FIGURE 5: John Wayne (1907–1979). "He speaks American. He walks American." Getty Images.

Finally, Bonfiglio concludes that the standardization of American English followed its own special trajectory, involving "a consciousness of race and ethnicity [...] which escalated to an outright xenophobia in the twentieth century;" the emergence of a norm associated with rural areas in the Midwest and west, "a region that acquired the meanings of *heartland*;" and the standard that had "a natural, even populist appearance," with "a transparent, seemingly non-ideological form" all of which made it seemingly "resistant to criticism."[26] In this context, Standard American was not defined positively in terms of the features of an identifiable dialect of U.S. English, but somewhat negatively by reference to the absence of those features that would characterize a variety of markedly regional speech.[27]

AMERICAN MEDIA REVISITED

While Bonfiglio's account of race and Standard American offers a number of crucial insights into the creation and promotion of standard forms of English in the U.S., the role of media in the formation and dissemination of language change remains unclear. Bonfiglio's explanation of the history of the network standard—coupled with the popularity of western films of the 1930s-50s—provides some evidence of the impact of radio and cinema during this era, but the issue of causality in language change is still open to challenge. Linguists such as Chambers are not convinced that the media has a direct impact on language change:

> The fact that certain language changes are spreading at the same time in history that mass media are going global should not be confused with cause and effect. It may be that the media fosters tolerance of other accents and dialects. [...] But there is no question: Changes themselves must be conveyed in face-to-face interactions among peers. [...] The talking heads on our mass media may sometimes catch our attention, but it's a one-way street: They never engage us in dialogue [...] it takes real people to make an impression.[28]

In a recent book, entitled *Do You Speak American?*, which accompanies a PBS television series of the same name, the authors, Robert MacNeil and William Cran—broadcasters and writers rather than academic linguists —refer to this debate on language in the media when they report that a number of pronunciation changes currently in progress "do not push the language toward pronunciations that fit within broadcast-media norms" and that some move radically away from them." Deferring to the opinions of expert linguists, they then explain that:

> All this evidence contradicts the popular assumption that the mass media are homogenizing American English and causing its treasured local varieties to disappear. The linguists we interviewed believe that the media can be useful in spreading vocabulary and causing innovations to be picked up and spread faster. Media saturation may also provide what Dennis Baron called a "passive lingua franca." We all understand what we hear on the radio or see on TV, giving us a passive vocabulary, but that doesn't mean that we use that vocabulary actively in writing or speaking. Similarly, we can understand accents different from our own, but few people change their accents because of it.[29]

However, despite this general stance, MacNeil and Cran change their position when considering particular examples of the influence of mass media on linguistic innovation and change. The first such example is the 1995 teen film, *Clueless*, which was set in a Los Angeles high school, and consciously drew on the slang and speech styles of privileged teenage girls for its authenticity and comedic effect.

FIGURE 6: Alicia Silverstone, star of the 1995 film, *Clueless*.

Of all the films of the 1990s, *Clueless* depicted a style of speech that drew on teenage California attitudes, fashion and slang that have apparently made their influence felt not only across the U.S. but also throughout teenage culture worldwide. The slang the director, Amy Heckerling, injected into her script included such superlatives as *coolio, funky, keen, kicking, rad, stella, sweet,* and *wicked,* which were matched by such expressions of negative attitude as *bogus, chickenshit, messed,* and *wack.* Verbal put-downs included such phrases as *As if! Not even!,* and the now-almost-global *Whatever!* At the grammatical level, the so-called *like* quotative, also featured in the film, as in:

> But it's *like,* when I had this garden party for my father's birthday right? I said R.S.V.P. because it was a sit-down dinner. But people came that *like,* did not R.S.V.P. so I was *like,* totally buggin'. [...] but by the end of the day it was *like,* the more the merrier!

At the level of accent, there is also evidence that the California dialect is a source of innovation in U.S. English pronunciation, with particular reference to the kind of rising intonation sometimes referred to as *uptalk,* which is also audible in the speech of the *Clueless* cast. In their discussion of this film, MacNeil and Cran seem to shift their position dramatically, conceding that while "linguists believe that movies and television do not change people's language [...] the *Clueless* film and the TV series it spawned may be exceptions."[30] In the case of the *like* quotative, they further comment that "[s]ome of these uses of *like* have spread widely, noted among people a generation older in New York and among teenagers in London," ultimately concluding that there is a body of compelling evidence that "California English is becoming one of the most influential dialects, not only in the United States but throughout the English-speaking world."[31]

A second example of contemporary media impact on language may be found in the hip-hop music that has spread from the U.S. through youth culture worldwide, with verbal expressions allegedly original to the hip-hop culture entering the mainstream of the language, as in *check it out, chill out, fresh* and *wassup?* MacNeil and Cran quote the linguist H. Samy Alim, on the crossover influence of hip-hop on white teenagers, where: "Many hip hop artists know that white suburban fans are attracted to those artists that maintain a core Black urban au-

FIGURE 7: Curtis James Jackson III, hip-hop performer,
otherwise known as "50 Cent."

dience," adding that, "In a sense many whites play 'cultural catch-up,'
letting the Black masses dictate what is in vogue and authentic."[32]
What seems at stake, here, however, is not simply argot or slang, but
an attitude and style that goes far beyond the verbal, so that:

> The urban black male represents someone who knows how to pick up
> women, who knows how to handle himself on the street, who perhaps
> knows how to handle a weapon and can take care of himself, and so for
> the white suburban male these kinds of symbols, this kind of way of walk-
> ing or talking or dressing, can give one the trappings of a masculinity that
> doesn't perhaps exist in the safe white suburbs.[33]

Elsewhere, Geneva Smitherman comments on Hip Hop Nation language
(HHNL), and Hip Hop Linguistics (HHLx), highlighting the global
reach of hip-hop culture:

HHLx agenda focuses on Hip Hop language practices in global context
[...] What do we make of South African rappers who spit heat in five languages (Xhosa, Zulu, Tsotsi-Taal, Sotho, and a HHNL-inspired English),
or the codeswitching and codemixing that take place in Canada when
Haitian, Dominican, and African immigrants practice Hip Hop as a critical site of identification with Black Americans and the development of
hybrid identities? [...] HHLx is clearly an international enterprise and
heads are needed from every corner of the Hip Hop globe to study the
HHN's expressive richness and diversity.[34]

If Samy Alim and Smitherman are accurate in their assessment of hip-
hop language as an example of an authentic African American vernacular
that has spread to white youth across the U.S. and has then gone global,
it would again appear difficult to maintain a linguistic stance that gives
limited credence to the power of the electronic media (including film,
music, television, video and the Internet) in influencing linguistic change.
To rephrase the words of a musician from a very different generation, this
may well be an instance where something may be happening but Mr.
Jones is at a loss to explain.

AMERICA'S IRRESISTIBLE VERNACULAR

The spread of American English is largely of very recent origin. Despite
the domestic debates on the autonomy of U.S. English throughout the
twentieth century, it was not until the latter part of the twentieth century that American English gained in prestige in regions as Europe, and
in many societies in Asia. A glance back to the very recent past reveals the
account penned by U.S. professor visiting Europe in 1957, and his bewil-
derment at the reception he received:

[W]e are now a prime target for caricature and lampoon [...] Almost everywhere American films are the object of criticism and, not infrequently,
scorn. They are commonly characterized as blatant, cheap, and vulgar.
[...] That our movies are having a decided impact on the spoken English
of England and the Continent needs little elaboration. [...]. Whatever
our linguistic shortcomings, the remedy does not lie merely in feeling or
feigning to feel embarrassed about them. [...] All the world knows that

we are better housed and more abundantly fed, that we drive much longer automobiles, and that we have far more gadgets to simplify and complicate our lives.[35]

By the end of the century, the situation had changed dramatically, and, today, the prestige of American English has risen in many European societies, according to many recent commentaries, including that of Hoffmann:

> In most European countries [today] the kind of English which is most influential, because of its widespread presence, is American English. [...] After World War II the American occupying forces had a much greater impact on people in Germany and Austria than did the British, and this was soon reinforced by the increasingly dominant economic, political and scientific position of the United States in world affairs. Today Europeans are exposed mainly to American English in the many spheres where English is used, [...] one could even argue that in many instances 'internationalisation' or 'globalisation,' or even 'modernisation,' are terms which could just as well be read as meaning 'Americanisation.'[36]

The growing use of American English has not been welcomed by everyone, and, in the European academy particularly, there has been palpable resistance to what is perceived as the cultural and linguistic imperialism of the U.S.:

> U.S. expansionism is no longer territorial. [...] Occupation is by economic, technological, and material means, and is increasingly ensured through mental and electronic control, through the barrage of advertising and Hollywood products, and the networks of political and scholarly collaboration that uphold an exploitative economic structure. [...] Building on this diagnosis of American empire, we can see global English as the capitalist neoimperial language that serves the interests of the corporate world and the governments that it influences so as to consolidate state and empire worldwide.[37]

Despite the opposition of those who are dismayed at the Americanization of European societies, there is little doubt that contemporary European popular culture owes much to the cultural and media products of the

United States, that this has occurred largely without military and political coercion, and that processes associated with the "Americanization" of European daily life have been adopted collaboratively—and often enthusiastically—by European citizenry.

The U.S. historian Victoria de Grazia's (2005) volume *Irresistible Empire: America's Advance through Twentieth-Century Europe* provides a detailed contemporary historical account of the adoption of U.S. business, manufacturing, marketing and media practices to post-war Europe from the late 1940s to the present. De Grazia's argument is that what the U.S. offered to Europe after 1945 were the keys to a consumer society. Consumerism was delivered by the U.S.'s "Market Empire," which deployed such tools of production and distribution as mass production, mass marketing, brand goods, chain stores, Hollywood films, labor-saving devices, higher standards of living, the service ethic, and supermarkets. De Grazia asserts that the growth of U.S. business and commercial influence in post-war Europe effected a peaceful revolution, on an unprecedented scale:

> For the Europe entrenched in the bourgeois regime of consumption down to the 1940s and for the Europe of the Soviet bloc that until 1989 was dominated by the failures of planned consumption, the consumer revolution arrived in the shape of a 'passive revolution.' [...] By the 1970s the outcome was indeed a New Europe, but a close ally of the Market Empire rather than the exact image of the United States. Forming a 'White Atlantic', with its American partner, it had as its most conspicuous feature the striving for the satisfaction, of consumers' every desire, the most basic being the comfort and convenience offered by the kitchen, the porcelain whiteness of its new material civilization all the brighter as it was viewed against the darkness of Third World poverty and the dinginess of state socialism.[38]

Viewed from the perspective of many European societies today, the term "American vernacular" refers not only (and not necessarily primarily) to the speech styles, lexis, grammar and pronunciation of contemporary U.S. English, but to a much wider swathe of social attitudes and social behaviors. Perhaps one way to move forward language debates in this context is to identify the need to embed descriptions of language change —not least in their global context—in discussions of the social and historical detail that accompany them. One exemplary case in point was the "youth culture" of 1950s rock 'n' roll, where virtually every European society had its own local Elvis (Johnny Halliday in France, Adriano Celentano in Italy, Jerry Williams in Sweden, Cliff Richard in the U.K.). For European Elvises, who often sang in their own national languages, the U.S. vernacular purveyed was not essentially verbal in substance, but typically relied on a combination of attitude, gesture, stance and fashion, not least the quiffed hair, the check shirt and Levi jeans, or the drape jacket and suede shoes.[39]

A generation or two later, European youth consume a wide range of U.S. products, including Apple, Dell, and Microsoft computer products, Nike sportswear, Coca-Cola, McDonald's, as well as computer games, DVDs, films, television programmes, and much else. Currently around 70–80 per cent of all television dramas shown on European television are from the U.S., so that "American movies, American TV and the American lifestyle for the populations of the world and Europe at large have become the lingua franca of globalization, the closest we get to a visual world culture."[40] In Sweden, downloading U.S. films and television programmes has become something of a national past-time, as Swedish file-sharing sites such as PirateBay provide access to almost all the popular U.S. TV series of the day, including such shows (often only hours after their U.S. showing) as *24, Californication, CSI, Desperate Housewives, Dexter, Grey's Anatomy, Lost, The Simpsons,* and *South Park.* Swedish children grow up playing computer games, watching *YouTube,* surfing the Internet, often weaned on a diet with a large dose of American media, and, partly as a consequence, growing up speaking English as a second language, with a "Mid-Atlantic" accent.[41] In other European societies, as in Germany, dubbing and translation may provide a firewall against some forms of media language, but the American vernacular finds expression in other ways.

FROM AMERICAN TO "GLOBISH"

Some three decades ago, Steiner summed up the impact of the U.S. on English worldwide in the following terms:

> English acted as the vulgate of American power and of Anglo-American technology and finance. [...] English and American English seem to em-

body for men and women throughout the world and particularly for the young the 'feel' of hope, of material advance, of scientific and empirical procedures. The entire world-image of mass consumption, of international exchange, of the popular arts, of generational conflict, of technocracy, is permeated by American English and English citations and speech habits.[42]

On the global stage, the importance of American English in the post-war era arose directly out of the pre-eminence of the U.S., as the world's major economic, military and political power, as well as America's close involvement and engagement with such international organizations as the United Nations, World Health Organization, the International Monetary Fund, and the World Trade Organization. With the fall of communism in 1989, U.S. political power grew throughout the 1990s, before it became enmeshed in two wars in Iraq and Afghanistan.

The English teaching efforts of Britain and the U.S. in the post-war period initially involved a division of educational labor. Traditional areas of U.S. influence in English language education have included Central and South America, and—for varying reasons—such U.S. Asian allies as Japan, the Philippines (the U.S.'s most important former overseas colony), South Korea, and Taiwan. The UK, by contrast, has had more influence in former British colonies in West, South, and East Africa, and in such Asian regions and societies as South Asia, Hong Kong, Malaysia, and Singapore. In very recent years, there has been at least anecdotal evidence that the borders of such spheres of influence have become blurred, with frequent reports of the growing popularity of American English among young people in many parts of the world.

At the same time as an apparent increase in the prestige and power of U.S. English in Asia, however, there are also distinctly local styles of English in use in such societies. It is now commonplace to refer to such varieties as Hong Kong English, Indian English, Malaysian English, Philippine English, and Singapore English. In the educational systems of former British colonies—as in India and Singapore—a variety of influences may now contribute to the linguistic experiences of young people, through school textbooks in British English, electronic media with American English, as well as the daily exposure to formal and informal varieties of localized English within the society.

In recent years, with the growth of the Internet, it has also been sug-

143

gested that English has begun to lose some of its imperialist connotations, at least according to McCrum (2010) whose recent advocacy of Globish ("Global English") paints a rosy picture of English in the contemporary age:

> With the spread of new information technology, [...] and the emergence of new, popular regimes with Anglophone inclinations, the English language began to lose its colonial connotations. Now, in keeping with its long history, English began to morph into a supranational means of global communication at the approach of the new millennium. [43]

In McCrum's brave new world of the twenty-first century, companies such as Apple, Dell, Hewlett-Packard, IBM, Lenovo, and Microsoft provide the hardware and software that connect the world, and, in this context, the language takes on a new meaning:

> Globish becomes more than just an essential means of communication: it embodies a contemporary aspiration, one that expresses a willingness to innovate, to adapt old uses and to enfranchise new people. Language is intrinsically neutral. The history of the world's English, however, puts it on the side of the individual confronting a demanding new challenge about his or her place in society. [...] Chinese, Indians, Mexicans and Poles who are ambitious to succeed in the 'flat' world will acquire the language skills necessary to achieve their goals. [44]

Today, McCrum argues, the spread of English is no longer a sign of Anglo-American linguistic hegemony, but instead the mark of a new age of a "neutral and intelligible" world language, a claim that many linguists would reject as laughable and naive at best. [45] For Robert Phillipson and many others concerned with the politics of language, globalization is synonymous with U.S. corporate power and military might:

> Globalization has economic, technological, cultural and linguistic strands to it. The globalization of English in diverse contexts, post-colonial, post-communist and western European, is one such interconnected strand in asymmetrical flows of products, ideas and discourses. Thus we live in a world in which 80% of films shown in western Europe are of Californian origin, whereas 2% of films shown in North America are of European or-

igin [...]. The trend towards the creation of the impression of a global culture through production for global markets, so that products and information aim at creating 'global customers that want global services by global suppliers' can be termed McDonaldization.[46]

Phillipson clarifies that McDonaldization entails "aggressive round-the-clock marketing, the controlled information flows that do not confront people with the long-term effects of an ecologically detrimental lifestyle, the competitive advantage against local cultural providers, the obstruction of local initiative, [which] all converge into a reduction of local cultural space."[47] Later, Phillipson goes on to quote Bourdieu to the effect that "globalization means Americanization."[48]

Support for Phillipson's take on this issue can be found in the pronouncements of former Kissinger and Clinton advisor David Rothkopf, who provides his view of U.S. foreign policy on English quite clearly:

> It is in the economic and political interest of the United States to ensure that if the world is moving toward a common language, it be English; that if the world is moving toward common telecommunications, safety, and quality standards, they be American; and that if common values are being developed, they be values with which Americans are comfortable. These are not idle aspirations. English is linking the world.[49]

CONCLUSION: AMERICANIZATION THEN AND NOW

Americanization in the early 1900s referred to the processes by which millions of newly-arrived immigrants joined mainstream U.S. society, and were made to feel American, rather than Jewish, Irish, or Italian. In the words of a commentator of the time:

> 'Americanization' is assimilation in the United States. It is that process by which immigrants are transformed into Americans. It is not the mere adoption of American citizenship, but the actual raising of the immigrant to the American economic, social and moral standard of life. Then has an immigrant been Americanized only when his mind and will have been united, with the mind and will of the American so that the two act and think together. The American of to-day is, therefore, not the American of

yesterday. He is the result of the assimilation of all the different nationalities of the United States which have been united so as to think and act
together.[50]

Americanization during that era was facilitated through a variety of
means, including the school, trade unions, the "physical environment
and the presence of American life," the Church, politics, and a range of
other forces including the press, books and libraries, private immigrant
aid societies, public playgrounds, boys' clubs, and even "American slang
and the street life," which "all act as assimilators."[51] Public schools were
the most important teachers of English, although the author, Grover G.
Huebner, reports that while "the English language is essential for Americanization in the city [...] in the country it is quite plain that the English
language is not necessary in order to secure a very considerable degree of
Americanization," noting that in the Midwest there were numerous set-
tlements of Bohemians, Germans and Scandinavians "who cannot speak
English, but they are Americans in practically every other sense."[52]

What then of the role of media in this early project of Americanization? As we saw at the beginning of this essay, the turn of the twentieth
century in the U.S. was marked by a good deal of linguistic insecurity.
The thousands of immigrants entering through Ellis Island—with varying abilities in English, if any—were entering not only the crowded tene-
ments of Lower Manhattan, but also a linguistically alien and totally new
society at the peak of early industrial and social modernity. Huebner was
writing in 1906, at a time when Antonio Parisi's marionette theater was
still holding performances on 418 E. 11th Street and his immigrant audience had not yet deserted him for the pleasures of the picture theater,
which they might later visit to learn about U.S. society, as well as to learn
the language of their new homeland through the inter-titles of silent
films (Olsson, this volume).

To return to the central issue of this essay, what now does one make
of the role of the media in the formation of American English domestically, within the U.S.? The arguments set out earlier indicate a range of
possible areas for future research. From Bonfiglio's discussion of race and
the rise of Standard American, it seems reasonable to conclude—from the
wealth of information he presents—that both the radio and the cinema
played at least some role in contributing to the formation of an *r*-full
norm, free of marked regional variations, by the mid-twentieth century.

It also seems clear that social motivation for such an idealized standard was of a very different order to that which had emerged in Britain (race not class, in brief). Despite such evidence, however, many linguists remain resistant to giving serious consideration to the role of media in language change. Walt Wolfram, another leading American linguist, again supports the orthodox view when he states that:

> It is sometimes assumed that the language of the media is homogenizing English. After all, everyone watches the same television networks, in which a dialectally neutral English has become the norm. Doesn't this common exposure affect language change and the level of dialect differences? [...] Although TV shows have clearly contributed some words to the vocabulary and facilitated the rapid spread of some popular expressions [...] media influence is greatly exaggerated because people do not model their everyday speech after media personalities with whom they have no interpersonal interaction. [...] In ordinary, everyday conversation, most people want to talk like their friends and acquaintances.[53]

Wolfram's main concern, like Chambers, is with the micro-analysis of the language systems of particular dialects and other varieties in the U.S., and much less with a consideration of the ways in which the increasingly intrusive and increasingly ubiquitous electronic media may be re-shaping the ways in which we interact with technology and interact with language (see Ch'ien, this volume).

Indeed, when it comes to the spread of English across the globe, there is at least frequent anecdotal testimony from linguists and others that the proliferation of American films, television and other media has facilitated the spread of American forms of the language. Nevertheless, despite this, many linguists still appear reluctant to engage with research on the role of popular media in promoting American English worldwide.

Americanization in the early 2000s now refers to the spread of U.S. cultural, economic, and political power around the world, partly through the attractiveness of U.S. products, and the hard and soft power of U.S. corporations. The soft power of de Grazia's "irresistible empire," discussed above, is backed up by military strength. By the early 2000s, the U.S. had more than 750 military bases located in some 130 countries, with major installations in Germany, Japan, South Korea, Kosovo, and even Kyrgyzstan. In addition, the U.S. now has around 94,000 troops in

Afghanistan and 92,000 in Iraq. American military dominance far surpasses that of any other power on the planet, with the U.S. currently accounting for 40-45 per cent of the entire defense spending of the world's 189 nations.[54]

Coming to terms with Americanization in the context of this new Anglophone Empire requires a very different sensibility than that which pertained a hundred years earlier. In the view of the historian Niall Ferguson, the U.S. is the pre-eminent imperial power of our time, in many senses a modern Rome that has spread that has spread its language and culture across the globe:

Like the Roman Empire, it has a system of citizenship, that is remarkably open: Purple Hearts and U.S. citizenship were conferred simultaneously on a number of the soldiers serving in Iraq last year, just as service in the legions was once a route to becoming a *civis romanus*. Indeed, with the classical architecture of its capital and the republican structure of its constitution, the United States is perhaps more like a "new Rome" than any previous empire [...] in its capacity for spreading its own language and culture —at once monotheistic and mathematical—the United States also shares features of the Abbasid caliphate erected by the heirs of Muhammad.[55]

Ferguson also notes that "[i]n terms of both production and consumption, the United States is already a vastly wealthier empire than Britain ever was," and today the world economy is dominated by such multinational U.S. firms as Coca-Cola, Exxon Mobil, General Motors, Microsoft, and Time Warner, concluding that "in terms of economic resources as well as of military capability the United States not only resembles but in some respects exceeds the last great Anglophone empire."[56]

Whereas previous empires relied on schools and education to provide opportunities to learn the imperial language (and access to such instruction varied greatly), the U.S. now has a global entertainment industry based on film and television, as well computers, the Internet and a range of new media. Linguists are perhaps only now coming to terms with the fact that people are now interacting with electronic media in ways not thought possible two decades ago. Customers of airlines, banks and other services regularly interact with computerized interactive voice systems on the telephone, back office and customer inquiries from the UK and U.S. are handled by call center agents in Bangalore and Manila, while teenage European kids make their own skateboard videos to be posted on the global bulletin board that is *Youtube*. The claim that people only watch and listen to electronic media, but do not talk to them, or engage in ways that facilitate linguistic accommodation may be outdated.

The thrust of this chapter has been both exploratory and speculative, and a range of overlapping and partly contradictory arguments have been explored, and remain unresolved. This essay has challenged the notion that media have had a minimal impact on language change, but does not claim that such effects are direct and uncomplicated. The argument that the impact of media on language is exaggerated (particularly by non-linguists) may be well founded from a traditional sociolinguistic perspective, as there is strong evidence that the major vector of linguistic innovation and change over time has been population flow and interpersonal contact. Evidence provided by the growing global popularity of American speech as a second or foreign language, moreover, is of a very different order than that relating to the speech of first-language speakers of English in the U.S. or elsewhere, as such "native" speech forms are often shaped by crucial family, group, and geographical loyalties. Nevertheless, as I have attempted to suggest, there are connections that may be drawn between the domestic and international spread of American English. At the very least, it appears that prestige accents were supported by radio and the cinema from the 1930s onwards, and that in more recent decades certain features of speech associated with youth culture may well have been propagated by film, television, and other media across the U.S., and elsewhere. Simultaneously, at another level, American English has evidently spread rapidly as a target norm for second language learners in Europe, Asia, and many other parts of the world, projected at least partly by U.S. global media. All of which, I would argue, indicates a range of research lacunae, too diverse and complex to cover here, which might be explored with fresh eyes in future research endeavors.

Looking back to the earlier era of U.S. cinema in the interwar period, de Grazia quotes the description of the speech of Elsie, a British housemaid, drawn from a 1936 novel: "Like most of her generation and locality [...] was trilingual. She talked BBC English to her employer, Cinema American to her contemporaries and Yorkshire dialect to the old milkmen." For audiences in the 1930s, de Grazia claims, "Cinema vernacular was literally a language," and, today, in a very different era, embedded in the standard television fare of much of the world, in U.S. feature films, popular music and new media, the American vernacular continues to redefine and reshape itself, as well as the linguistic worlds we inhabit.[57]

ENDNOTES

1. Henry R. Luce, "The American Century," *Life*, Vol. 10, No. 7 (17 February 1941): 61–65. Reprinted in *Diplomatic History*, Vol. 23, No. 2 (Spring 1999): 159–171.

2. Eric A. Anchimbe, "World Englishes and the American Tongue," *English Today* 88, Vol. 22, No. 4, (2006): 3.

3. Jack Chambers, "Talk the Talk?"2010, http://www.pbs.org/speak/ahead/mediapower/media/, accessed on 9 June 2010.

4. Peter Trudgill, *Dialects in Contact* (Oxford: Basil Blackwell, 1986), 40.

5. Julia S. Falk, *Linguistics and Language: A Survey of Basic Concepts and Implications* (New York: Wiley, 1978), 289.

6. Victoria Fromkin and Robert Rodman, *An Introduction to Language*, 5th ed. (New York: Holt, Rinehart & Winston, 1993), 251.

7. William Labov, *Sociolinguistic Patterns* (Philadelphia: University of Pennsylvania Press, 1972).

8. Letter from Benjamin Franklin, "Securing the Friendship of the Indians," (1750), http://www.historycarper.com/resources/twobf2/letter 12.htm, accessed on 9 June 2010.

9. Benjamin Franklin (1751), cited by Thomas Paul Bonfiglio, *Race and the Rise of Standard American*, (Berlin/New York: Mouton de Gruyter, 2002), 76.

10. Noah Webster, *Dissertations on the English Language*, (Boston: Isaiah Thomas, 1789), 62.

11. Theodore H. Mead, *Our Mother Tongue* (New York: Dodd, Mead and Company, 1890), 2.

12. Ibid., 31.

13. Robert McCrum, William Cran and Robert MacNeil, *The Story of English* (London: Faber & Faber, BBC publications, 1986).

14. Bonfiglio, 116.

15. Alexander Melville Bell, *Elocutionary Manual: The Principles of Elocution, with Exercises and Notations for Pronunciation, Intonation, Emphasis, Gesture, and Emotional* Expression (Washington: John C. Parker, 1878), 66.

16. Brander Matthews, "A Standard of Spoken English." In Brander Matthews, *Essays on English* (New York: Charles Scribner's Sons, 1921), 222.

17. H. L. Mencken, *American Language. An Inquiry into the Development of English in the United States*, Supplement II (New York: Alfred A. Knopf, 1948), 15.

18. Webster, 110.

19. Francis H. Vizetelly, *How to Speak English Effectively* (New York: Funk and Wagnall's, 1933), 31.

20. Ibid., 32.

21. James F. Bender, *NBC Handbook of Pronunciation* (New York, Thomas Y. Crowell, 1943).

22. Bonfiglio, 182.

23. Ibid., 186.

24. Charles H. Grandgent, "The Dog's Letter." In *Old and New Sundry Papers* (Cambridge, MA: Harvard University Press, 1920), 56.

25. Randy Roberts and James S. Olson, *John Wayne: American* (New York: The Free Press, 1995), 648.

26. Bonfiglio, 227–228.

27. The British sociolinguist Lesley Milroy comments thus: "People find it easier to specify what is not standard than what is; in a sense, the standard of popular perception is what is left behind when all the non-standard varieties spoken by disparaged persons such as Valley Girls, Hill-billies, Southerners, New Yorkers, African Americans, Asians, Mexican Americans, Cubans and Puerto Ricans are set aside." Lesley Milroy, "Standard English and Language Ideology in Britain and the United States." In Tony Bex and Richard J. Watts, eds., *Standard English: The Widening Debate* (London and New York: Routledge, 1999), 174.

28. Chambers.

29. Robert MacNeil and William Cran, *Do You Speak American?* (New York: Doubleday, 2005), 47.

30. MacNeil and Cran, 157.

31. Ibid., 169, 177.

32. H. Samy Alim in MacNeil and Cran, 144

33. Cecilia Cutler in MacNeil and Cran, 146.

34. Geneva Smitherman, "Foreword." In H. Samy Alim, *Roc the Mic Right: The Language of Hip Hop Culture* (New York: Routledge, 2006), ix.

35. Norman E. Eliason, "American English in Europe," *American Speech*, Vol. 32, No. 3 (October 1957): 166–169.

36. Charlotte Hoffmann, "The Spread of English and the Growth of Multilin-

gualism with English in Europe." In Jasone Cenoz and Ulrike Jessner, eds., *English in Europe: The Acquisition of a Third Language* (Clevedon: Multilingual Matters, 2000), 7.

37. Robert Phillipson, *Linguistic Imperialism Continued* (London and New York: Routledge, 2009), 33, 38.

38. Victoria de Grazia, *Irresistible Empire: America's Advance through Twentieth-Century Europe* (Cambridge, MA: The Belknap Press of Harvard University Press, 2005), 11.

39. I am grateful to Gregory Lee for providing such insights in his lecture, "From America to Amérique," at Stockholm University, 25 September, 2008.

40. Ib Bondebjerg, "Culture, Media and Globalisation." In *Humanities: Essential Research for Europe* (Copenhagen: Danish Research Council for the Humanities), 79.

41. Mats Mobärg, "Media Exposure vs. Educational Prescription: The Case of British and American English in Sweden." In Hans Lindquist, Staffan Klintborg, Magnus Levin and Maria Estling, eds., *The Major Varieties of English: Papers from MAVEN97, Växjö 20–22 November 1997* (Växjö University: Acta Wexionensia, 1998), 241–248.

42. G. Steiner, *After Babel: Aspects of Language and Translation* (Oxford: Oxford University Press, 1975), 469.

43. Robert McCrum, *Globish* (London, New York: Penguin Viking, 2010), 217.

44. Ibid., 225.

45. The term "Globish" was not originally coined by McCrum, but by a French former IBM executive, Jean-Paul Nerrière.

46. Phillipson, 30.

47. Cees Hamelink, *Trends in World Communication: On Disempowerment and Self-Empowerment* (Penang: Southbound, and Third World Network, 1994), 112.

48. Philipson, 125.

49. David Rothkopf, "In Praise of Cultural Imperialism," *Foreign Policy*, No. 107 (Summer 1997): 45.

50. Grover G. Huebner, "The Americanization of the Immigrant," *Annals of the American Academy of Political and Social Science*, Vol. 27, The Improvement of Labor Conditions in the United States (May 1906):191.

51. Ibid., 208, 212.

52. Ibid., 196.

53. Walt Wolfram, "Do You Speak American? Language Change: The Truth About Change," 2010, http://www.pbs.org/speak/ahead/change/change/, accessed on 9 June 2010.

54. Niall Ferguson, *Colossus: The Rise and Fall of the American Empire* (New York: Penguin Books, 2004), 16.

55. Ibid., 14.

56. Ibid., 18, 19.

57. de Grazia, 302.

PART 2

AMERICANS AT THE MARGINS

YOU ONLY LIVE ONCE: REPETITIONS OF CRIME AS DESIRE IN THE FILMS OF SYLVIA SIDNEY, 1930–1937

ESTHER SONNET

IN 1937, SYLVIA SIDNEY co-starred with Henry Fonda in a film that clearly alluded to a profound and prolonged popular fascination with the mythological aspects of the gangster banditry of the thirties Depression outlaw gangster couple Clyde Barrow and Bonnie Parker. In 1934, the Parker/Barrow gang's criminal spree of kidnapping, bank robbing and murder had been brought to a spectacularly bloody and salutary end with Barrow and Parker being violently shot to death in their car by law enforcement officers after a lengthy period in which they had eluded the pursuit of criminal justice agencies. *You Only Live Once*, directed by Fritz Lang, produced by Walter Wanger with an original screenplay by prolific Hollywood writers Gene Towne and C. Graham Baker, narrates the story of Joan Graham Taylor (Sylvia Sidney), a young and loyal public defender's secretary, whose life is tragically intertwined with her "three-time loser" lover and then husband Eddie (Henry Fonda).

From being wrongly accused of robbery to mistaken imprisonment for murder, Eddie's intentions of leading a respectable law-abiding life with Joan are continually frustrated and the couple are forced to take to the road to escape the agencies of justice that seem bent on destroying their chance of happiness together. During a jailbreak, Eddie shoots a priest sent into the prison to bring him news of a pardon for the wrong-

FIGURE 1: Promotional poster for *You Only Live Once* 1937;
Walter Wanger Productions ©United Artists Corp.

ful conviction he had tried to contest, the couple are forced to move around the country, and Jo has their baby which she gives to her sister for care while their erroneously exaggerated reputation as bandit robbers increases through national newspaper coverage. After futile attempts to evade capture, the couple are destroyed when Joan and Eddie are shot by police, with questions of their fundamental guilt or innocence left ambiguously unresolved.

CRIMINAL COUPLES AS DOOMED LOVERS

The film's depiction of the criminal couple as doomed lovers is a poignant indication of the unprecedented ideological transformations in articulations of crime that the Depression period had wrought by the mid-1930s. In the same year as *You Only Live Once* was released, Edward Anderson published his fictionalized version of a Parker/Barrow crime partnership in the novel *Thieves Like Us*, which similarly captured mass cultural interest in criminal violence in the context of the romantic couple. As Clare Bond Potter has cogently argued, widespread fascination with celebrity criminal personalities and construction of both urban gangster and rural bandit as agents of political defiance at this time indicate contradictory impulses in Depression-era conceptions of crime. Alongside the romanticization of putatively anti-authoritarian criminals in newspapers, radio, film and magazines, and responding directly to the political vacuum opened by the structural crisis of American capitalism, Potter identifies the "federalization" process by which a huge expansion of national policing permanently extended national (rather than local and/or state) jurisdiction in the "War on Crime." The financial and political consolidation of Edgar Hoover's FBI and G-Men through the early to mid-1930s clearly marks out the representations of crime as a site of considerable cultural contestation: in this context, "social banditry is virtually a counter-politics, acted out by politicized selves produced through an audience at particular moments of expanding state authority and/or nation building."[1] Given the film's social topicality and close proximity to the specifically complex cultural formations that characterized shifts in the social construction of crime in America of the 1930s, *You Only Live Once* is significant for its use of the story of the damned couple condemned by social forces and its social commentary on the cultural conditions that conspire against them. It is, essentially, a film made in the 1930s that articulates—however incoherently—a response to contradictions in prevailing ideologies of the individual, the state and the limits of personal responsibility for criminality.

Yet in many critical accounts *You Only Live Once* is often displaced from its origins in the socio-cultural politics of crime, celebrity and punishment in the 1930s. Below are some examples of critical and popular responses to the film that illustrate this tendency to locate the film within the parameters of a different narrative of American crime film history:

> It's difficult to think of Lang or *You Only Live Once* without thinking of film noir. [...] As with many noirs, the nightmare of war explodes on American streets, as bank robbers use tear gas, machine guns, and grenades to sack an armoured car. In the fog, the bank robber, with his gas mask and stealthy movements, resembles a monster, a common conception of the organised criminal in 30s and 40s America. Lang's expressionistic touches also appear throughout, most notably in the striking scene where Eddie waits in his cell for his execution.[2]

157

The point is that the best ingredients of film noir are present in a film made ten years before film noir's peak [...] that's how far ahead Fritz Lang's vision was [...] sure he went on to make 'The Big Heat' and 'Scarlet Street' among others [...] but 'You Only Live Once' is his starkest glimpse at man's small place in a vast, oppressive society where good intentions are powerless in a black universe. [...] This gritty drama is an early example of film noir.[3]

You Only Live Once is a 1937 crime film starring Sylvia Sidney and Henry Fonda. Considered an early film noir, the film was directed by Fritz Lang in America. At least 15 minutes were trimmed from the original 100-minute version of the film due to its then unprecedented realistic violence. Despite the absence of such scenes, the film was initially successful and is an early film noir classic.[4]

Bringing to the screen an obsessive and fatalistic world populated by a rogues' gallery of strange and twisted characters, Lang staked out a uniquely hostile corner of the cinematic universe; despair, isolation, helplessness, all found refuge in the shadows of his work. A product of German Expressionist thought, he explored humanity at its lowest ebb, with a distinctively rich and bold visual sensibility, which virtually defined film-noir long before the term was even coined.[5]

Lang himself emigrated to Hollywood in the mid-1930s, directing *Fury*, a wrong-man thriller, in 1936, and *You Only Live Once*, the original couple-on-the-run noir, in 1937. And from that point forward noir was a permanent part of the celluloid landscape. [6]

FILM HISTORY AND *FILM NOIR*

It is evident that the writing of film history is always dependent on epistemological assumptions that work to frame what might be said of an individual film or cycle of films. In this case, *You Only Live Once* is made significant—not as a historically specific production of Depression-era film in the 1930s—but as the precursor of what is given as the dominant form of American crime film in the 40s and 50s: *film noir*. In order to establish the serious consequences that such incorporation of 30s films within the narrative of *film noir* has had for writing American crime film history, I wish to use the case of the crime film career of Sylvia Sidney to illuminate how the concept of *film noir* (as demonstrated by accounts of *You Only Live Once*) profoundly limits and distorts our understanding of her appearance in crime films of the 1930s. This article, then, seeks to rethink approaches to American crime cinema in order to arrive at a more nuanced framework for thinking about film historically: that is, to restore to 1930s films the cinematic, historical and ideological specificities of genre, narrative, gender, audience and the Hollywood star system in cultural discourses of crime. To challenge the critical dominance of the term *film noir* and its taken-for granted assumptions about American crime, detective and gangster films, I shall explore further the conceptual foundation that underpins the notion of an "early film noir classic" or a "fatalistic proto-noir film."

FIGURE 2: *You Only Live Once* (1937) as Film Noir. Still images ©DVD release 2003.

In a remarkably dense and provocative article "Film Noir on the Edge of Doom" (collected in the 1993 edited volume *Shades of Noir*), Marc Vernet offered a trenchant critique of the underpinning assumptions that have established *film noir* as the paradigmatic category for defining post-war American crime cinema of the late 1940s and 1950s. His thesis is that the specific circumstances of the French invention of the concept of *film noir* have long been obscured in favor of its development in film history as an a-historical and generic category that has "no real validity" and is "without any foundation but a rhetorical one." [7] For Vernet, the critical dominance of the term has utterly distorted the conditions upon which a properly historical investigation of the American crime film might be made and demonstrates, from its origins in a limited and partial culture of cine-criticism, the deleterious consequences for film history when *film noir* comes instead to be "erected as an historical object."

The term *film noir* initially emerged from a context of reception defined by Parisian cine-critics newly exposed to American detective films after an enforced hiatus in their distribution caused by the Second World War: the concept of *film noir*, as forged by Borde and Chaumeton, encompasses aesthetic judgments made of unfamiliar but shared visual and narrative features identified in certain Hollywood detective/crime films of the 40's.[8] Vernet emphasizes the highly politicized post war-conditions that determined that reception of Hollywood films were profoundly ambivalent, especially by those of French Communist and Left sympathies. Construed as products of imperialist capitalist culture, Hollywood films were seen to undermine French cultural supremacy as did threats to "replace red wine with whiskey, Marcel Proust with the dime detective novel and, and 'Le Temps Cerise' with jazz."[9] Conservative moralists also condemned the "new" American crime cinema for its moral deviance, for the "fetishism of the black gloves, the flagellations, the disturbed perversions of a whore and a homosexual that the Hollywood Code of Decency guarantees in *Gilda*."[10] In this context, Vernet contends, French socialist intellectual fascination with post-war Hollywood crime film required a political justification (other than outright rejection). In order for its cinephiles to justify their continued fascination with American crime film, a position that they might not otherwise be able to own ideologically, French Leftist critics secured an argument by which specific films defined as *film noir* were those perceived to offer a "critique of the American system." Thus championed as "progressive," the political value of film noir cinema was seemingly ensured for its Leftist analysts because it "bears witness to the faultiness of capitalism."[11] Depicting contemporary American capitalist society as empty, corrupt and nihilistic in films "with an appearance of poverty in which the optimistic and moral lesson could not always easily be discerned,"[12] *film noir* offered to contradict the global self-presentation of a nation whose military, political and economic power was unrivalled. In Vernet's terms, the critical construction of *film noir* was therefore born out of the contradictions of French cultural politics, created as "a love-object of those that want to hate the United States but love its cinema."[13]

By affirming that *film noir* is a harsh critique of American capitalism, by explaining the importance of European directors and cinematographers, by emphasising the membership of Dashiell Hammett, presented as father of the hard-boiled novel and thus of the genre, in the American Communist Party, film critics [...] gave themselves a means to justify a love that was forbidden—whether it was the war (the impossibility of seeing the films), the Communist Party (whether one was a member or an opponent of it), or the supporters of a morality of hardship (often the same), if not all three, that forbade it.[14]

Correctly situated in this way within its historical moment, the conception of *film noir* in post-war French cultural criticism is revealed as both ideological and epistemological. Vernet critically dissects the processes by which the term—from within geographically and historically specific French circumstances—has subsequently "consolidated" through an extraordinary proliferation of both scholastic and popular discourses in which this historically specific context has been effaced; *film noir* has subsequently been endlessly taken up within Anglo-American film criticism but its true value as a historically situated definition of film genre, production history and cinema periodization has remained largely unquestioned.

By "taking up without any contestation its basic arguments," *film noir* scholarship has worked only to further entrench the terms of the founding insights in a cinematic archetype through which any crime film between 1945–55 must be examined, measured and categorized. Vernet shows that while rare or marginal film titles may be argued by scholars for inclusion as neglected or "lost" examples of *noir,* simply lengthening the list of such examples does not critically engage with the founding precepts. In this sense, *film noir* is a "cinephilic ready-made"[15] in which a few recurrent *topoi* are "regularly put back into circulation": the femme fatale, the shining pavement of the deserted street, unexpected violence, fatalism, pessimism and social anxiety, the private detective, émigré directors importing German "Expressionist" lighting/camera angles, complex narrative structure and a putative relation to "hard-boiled" fiction. In short, *film noir* presents a "fine example of cinema history and aesthetic reflection that is founded on distribution (in France at a certain point in time) and critical discourse, and not on production (in the United States during several decades), in a complete ignorance of the larger cultural context."[16] The result is "a sort of imaginary enclosure in which [...] the resulting critical work ends up occulting the films themselves and their production."[17]

It is, then, precisely this very lack of rootedness in the historical reality of production of Hollywood detective (and crime/gangster films more generally) in the period that drives Vernet to argue forcefully against the subsequent "valorization" and "unexamined adoption" of the concept of *film noir* that has dominated Anglo-American accounts. Vernet's analysis astutely reveals the epistemological limitations that permit the term "film noir" to dominate histories of American film production: "speaking about *film noir* consists, from the beginning, in being installed in repetition, in taking up the unanalysed discourse of those predecessors, with pre-established definitions [...] that are impossible to criticise."[18] Film history in this context is an essentially encyclopedic project that underpins the classification of post-war crime films according to a few topoi that are used to validate films for inclusion/exclusion within the *noir* category. The role of the *noir* historian is thus confined to a project of reiteration and extension, in which privileged film texts continue to be reinforced as canonical while claims are made for the inclusion of overlooked minor examples: in either sense, "complacent repetition is more or less general."[19]

My understanding is that the *film noir* framework is also teleological and I want now to argue that much of the distortion of crime film history wrought by the *noir* project is directly attributable to its epistemological dependence on that. Teleology is a highly influential but rarely examined philosophical and theological construction of time and causality that conceives of the process of history as the movement towards some pre-defined end-point. Historical process is understood in terms of a purposeful movement towards the fulfillment of a pure state or telos (variously: salvation, Enlightenment, war, communism, Progress, political emancipation). In this conceptual schema, historical forms, ideas or periods previous to the achievement of the telos are gauged according to their contribution to the achievement of that end-point. Historical meaning, then, lies in a retrospective attribution of significance, according to which earlier forms are regarded as manifestations of what will come to be in the future.

TELEOLOGY AND THE HISTORY OF *FILM NOIR*

Teleological thinking is rarely recognized for the epistemological construction that it is, passing instead as the "common-sense" way to understand history; as a model for connecting ideas about time, causality and the relations of influence in historical process, teleology is a paradigmatic given for a huge range of critical analyses that rely on its fundamental tenet that "what comes before" is significant only because of "what comes later." Postmodernist historiographers such as Jean-François Lyotard have convincingly demonstrated that modern fields of knowledge are predominantly organized by "meta-narratives," by *grand recits* that structure historical relations between events, people and time in order to tell a predetermined "story."[20] This is explicitly the case of the epistemological project of *film noir* scholarship: the meta-narrative of teleology effectively underpins in its tendency to conceive of what "comes before" (film productions of the 1930s) according to its imperfect yet identifiable manifestation of what will "come later." The term "proto-noir" is highly condensed signifier of a conception of history in which the significance of earlier crime films lies in what they might be said to anticipate of the topoi defining *film noir* of the 40s/50s. Hence the frequent description of 1920s/30s crime films such as *You Only Live Once*—for example, *Underworld* (1927), *The Racket* (1928), *The Public Enemy* (1931), *The Glass Key* (1935), *Bullets or Ballots* (1936), *Racket Busters* (1938) or *Blind Alley* (1939)—as "early noir" or "proto-noir," "proto-typical noir," or even just "prenoir." The notion of *noir* having "precursors" marks a deterministic film history that ensures that films of the 1930s are accounted for only within the retrospective developmental narrative of *film noir*: historical relations between films are thus understood as connected in one direction and that direction is not only linear, but also teleologically predetermined.

In this schema, the *noir* credentials of *You Only Live Once* are easily established: Fritz Lang is an émigré German director of later canonical "classic" *noir* films such as *The Woman in the Window* (1944), *Scarlet Street* (1945), *Secret Beyond the Door* (1948), *The Blue Gardenia* (1953), *The Big Heat* (1953), *Human Desire* (1954), *While The City Sleeps* (1956) and *Beyond a Reasonable Doubt* (1956);[21] there is evidence of an "Expressionist" visual ethos in lighting, camera movement, mise en scene and frame composition; the fugitive criminal figures Bonnie Parker & Clyde Barrow provide the film with a "hard-boiled" source, while the theme of futile escape and doomed entrapment, and the critique of "freedom" offered as a nihilistic commentary on compromised individualism, anticipate the dominant tenor of "classic" *noir* e.g. *Farewell My Lovely* (1944), *Double Indemnity* (1944), *The Killers* (1946), *The Postman Always Rings Twice* (1946), *Out of the Past* (1947), *Night and the City* (1950), *The Big Combo* (1955) and *Kiss Me Deadly* (1955). However, I would argue that the underpinning structure of teleology that extends the *film noir* category backwards to include crime films of the 1930s on these terms testifies to a profound lack of real engagement with the history of crime cinema from the early years of the Depression to the onset of American engagement in WW II. Vernet offers cogent reasons to support this view as his own appraisal argues strongly against the facile inclusion of any 1930s film simply because it might be said to exhibit some "noir" features. Simply identifying examples of the "uncriticized list of heterogeneous criteria" in order to recoup them into a critical discourse that privileges *film noir* stands resolutely against the historical specificity of the production of crime, thriller and gangster films in the period. *You Only Live Once* belongs with many other crime films such as *The Big Gamble* (1931), *Two Seconds* (1932) or *Private Detective 62* (1933) that feature Expressionistic low-key lighting, themes of anxiety, social disillusionment and alienation. Why, then, if these features are present in films "before noir," are they features which define *film noir* as qualitatively different from what came before? In what, after all, does the specificity of *noir* lie if previous films already exhibit its "heterogeneous criteria"? The encyclopedic drive towards extension of the *noir* category to account for their presence in earlier films (inclusion on the basis of their prior manifestation of "*noir*-ness") inadvertently works to destroy any historical integrity that the concept of *film noir* might ever have had in describing a specific epoch in Hollywood crime filmproduction.[22]

RETHINKING CRIME FILM HISTORY

Vernet's statement that "history strongly" resists the definitions that have hitherto been imposed on it is a polemical call to dispense with the meta-narrative of *film noir* as the primary way to account for crime films of the 1930s.[23] My own research into crime film production cycles of Hollywood at this time argues firmly for the need to rethink crime film history outside of the a priori givens of *film noir*. This would be to challenge radically the a-historical, archetypal criticism that has long stood as adequate to the discursive complexities of the 1930s crime film. It is, I contend, the precondition upon which much more nuanced and responsive understandings of the discursive construction of crime in Hollywood film in this period might be attempted. *You Only Live Once* is better approached not, then, as an "early noir" but as a later development of cinematic trends and themes already established in the decade of the Depression that lie wholly outside of that characterization.

If the preceding sections have been at pains to question the value and ultimately reject the use of *film noir*, it is because for the feminist film historian of the 1930s there are exceptionally substantial issues that are occluded by it. Primarily, it is the constriction of critical interest in the representation of women in *film noir* to the archetypal figure of the *femme fatale* that requires further scrutiny.

Women in Film Noir (1978) was a seminal collection of articles written by feminist film analysts who wished to engage with the relations between Hollywood *film noir* and gendered power relation in wider culture: "[. . .] film noir stands out as a phase in the development of the gangster/thriller of particular interest to feminist film criticism, which seeks to make progressive or subversive readings of Hollywood genre films."[24] For Janey Place, the central characteristic its representation of women is that "film noir is a male fantasy, as is most of our art. Thus woman is defined by her sexuality: the dark lady has access to it and the virgin does not."[25] The *femme fatale* is created as a figure of duplicity who uses sexual attraction to entrap an unguarded male into committing self-interested acts of criminal wrong-doing on her behalf: she exists "as a crucial feature within the dangerous criminal world which the hero struggles with in the course of his investigation, and as often as not becomes the object of the hero's investigation."[26] Highly eroticized and sexually active, the *femme fatale* offers considerable psycho-sexual threat to patriarchal demands for active male control of sexuality and for female submissiveness. Accordingly, setting, lighting, camera movement and narrative investigations in *film noir* are typified by their concern to conspire towards the consolation of masculine spectators, staging crime narratives that demand both erotic interest in, then destruction and punishment of, the *femme fatale*. For "female sexuality is also juxtaposed within the investigative structure to the law and the voice of male judgement"[27] so that the "ideological operation of the myth (the absolute necessity of controlling the strong, sexual woman) is thus achieved by first demonstrating her dangerous power and its frightening results, then destroying it."[28] However, while it is evidently the case that a small range of films such as *Murder, My Sweet* (1944), *The Postman Always Rings Twice* (1946), *The Big Heat* (1953), *The Maltese Falcon* (1941), *Gilda* (1946), and, paradigmatically, *Double Indemnity* (1944) exhibit the operation of the *femme fatale*, it is not useful to extend this insight to measure crime films of the 1930s in terms of a later coalescence of gender ideology, narrative and film style—as the recuperation of films as "early noir" precursors is wont to do. Simply marking the absence or presence of a *femme fatale*—the measure of "noirness"—in previous film productions is crude and largely self-justifying.

The retrospective limitation of the analysis of representations of women in crime film to the *femme fatale* has had a seriously distorting effect on the writing of film history. This is by no means the fault of the feminist critics collected in *Women in Film Noir* since most are careful to confine their observations to the historically specific period of film production under review. Yet, sophisticated feminist critique aimed at disclosing the operations of patriarchal misogyny nonetheless contributed to the hegemonic hold of *film noir* over studies of women in crime film. The over-riding impression has been forged: that women in crime film *per se* are inextricable from the spider women and treacherous dames of *film noir*. In that, a male-defined critical construction secures its hegemonic function in obscuring other histories of women's representation in crime films. Such critical displacement is a substantial consequence of *noir* annexation of prior American crime film, and of the epistemological dominance of archetype over historical production.

Yet there is a small space in feminist readings in which to consider what is utterly marginalized in accounts of both *noir* and *femme fatales*—the female spectator. Place recognized that for non-masculine spectators of *film noir, femme fatale* figures are highly ambivalent, offering contradictory pleasures:

> Film noir is hardly 'progressive'—it does not present us with role models who defy their fate and triumph. But it does give us one of the few periods of film in which women are active, not static symbols, are intelligent and powerful, if destructively so, and derive power, not weakness, from their sexuality.[29]

However, I would argue that this is a minor compensatory justification; while acknowledging the putative presence of a female audience, it is still enclosed within the same masculinist/misogynist terms that first worked to cut film history to the measure of *film noir*. The representation of women within the criminal world of *noir* is polarized: as Place notes in passing:

> The opposite female archetype is also found in film noir: woman as re-deemer. She offers the possibility of integration for the alienated, lost man into the stable world of secure values, roles and identities. She gives love, understanding (or at least forgiveness), asks very little in return (just that he come back to her) and is generally visually passive and static.[30]

My central argument is this—if these are the terms of *noir* feminist analy-sis, they are wholly inadequate to the complex configurations of women's roles in crime narratives of the 1930s. Again, they may be entirely accu-rate in critically evaluating a small range of historically located *femme fatale* crime films but Place's assertion that these reveal "one of the few periods in which women are active" testifies only to the effectiveness of the process by which *noir* has supplanted historical record.

How might the contours of a study of women in crime film history appear without *film noir's* presuppositions? The ready answer would, of course, be to look instead to the gangster genre to account for the condi-tions under which women appear in the 1930s crime film. However, here again accepted understanding of the narrative, iconographic and themat-ic concerns of the gangster film in the 1930s is underpinned by an equal-ly masculinist epistemology. Robert Warshow's "rise and fall" theory of the "gangster as tragic hero" is paradigmatic in the sense that successive gangster genre theorizing has stayed largely within the terms of his ana-lysis of the Big Three: *Little Caesar* (1931), *The Public Enemy* (1931) and *Scarface: Shame of a Nation* (1932).[31] Here, the male gangster is alienated from bourgeois values such as marriage and romance: even when aligned to a "moll," it is a financial and sexual arrangement that precludes senti-ment or affection. Women's sexuality in this version of the gangster film is therefore as border-line prostitute or "kept" woman, with molls add-ing only to the symbolic qualities of the gangster's "rise." But my re-search has found that these life-stories of individual gangsters were actu-ally atypical at the time. Rather than representing a "pure" inauguration of gangster pictures, the Big Three sit within film production cycles of immense hybridity in which gangster figures were deployed by Holly-wood in a multiplicity of narrative forms that do not obey the strictures of archetypal gangster genre theory. As with *film noir*, concentration on a few examples of gangster films has severely diminished what might be understood of the presence of women in crime films of the 1930s.

THE GANGSTER AND ITS FEMALE AUDIENCE

In constructing the history of the gangster film through a diachronic suc-cession of films that fulfill the archetype's requirements, what is "lost" or marginalized is the synchronic context of production and with it—the centrality of the female audience in shaping crime narratives in which gangsters figured. This is the foundation of a project of historical recla-mation which should have profound consequences for the figuration of women in crime film of the 1930s, the kind of film narratives that were actually produced and for recognition of the spectatorial pleasures of-fered to female audiences through their identification with women in dangerously close contact with the criminal male. The sheer wealth of films from which a female audience can be inferred in this period focuses attention on what lies outside both *film noir* and gangster genres: women —in representation on screens, in the audience and as historically absent participants in the cultural configuration of crime discourse through American cinema. This is a radical reframing that requires a major shift in thinking of 1930s crime film history to properly accommodate the his-torical fact of female audiences. Hollywood did not make pictures for male-only audiences, not even crime films: the challenge is to construe the historical presence of women from extant films, newspapers, maga-zines, reviews, production and censorship records.

In the case of *You Only Live Once,* the "precursor" status that confines it within the paradigm of *film noir* is historically negligible when the film is brought within the anterior context that I am indicating here: instead, *You Only Live Once* is a better seen as a repetition of themes that situate their female protagonists within narratives of crime as desire.

This is not simply to make claims for the canonical status of films ig-nored by male theorists, nor is to supplement either canon with counter-examples. Instead, with film star Sylvia Sidney as a thread of continuity, I want to use three films *City Streets* (1931), *Ladies of the Big House* and

FIGURE 3: *You Only Live Once* as Romance Addressed to a Female Cinema
Audience. Promotional poster 1937; Walter Wanger Productions
©United Artists Corp.

Mary Burns, Fugitive (1935) to demonstrate: a) the significance of a specific female star in crime film of the 1930s, b) the recognition of female
audiences made in discourses on the titles, and c) the subsequent necessity of relocating what a crime/gangster film was onto the terrain of
melodrama and romance.

Born Sophie Soklow in the Bronx, New York in 1910, Sylvia Sidney's
film career began with a courtroom drama *Thru Different Eyes* aka (*Guilty/
Public Opinion*) in 1929 and before *You Only Live Once* in 1937 she starred
in a range of Hollywood films including film adaptations of Theodore
Dreiser's bestselling and scandalous novels *An American Tragedy* (1931)
and *Jennie Gerhardt* (1933).

A close working association with Fritz Lang was forged through her starring roles, with Spencer Tracy in *Fury* (1936) and with George Raft in *You and Me* (1938). With leading roles in *Confessions of a Co-ed* (1931), *Street Scene* (1931), *The Miracle Man* (1932), *Merrily We Go to Hell* (1932), *Madame Butterfly* (1932) and *Thirty Day Princess* (1934), Sidney was an enormously popular actor whose star persona was forged as the "Face of the Depression." Actively engaged with Jewish New York left-wing theatre and politics, Sidney worked across a range of films where little else but her performances binds them together. Notable roles in crime films of the period included *City Streets* (1931), *Ladies of the Big House* (1931), *Pick-Up* (1933), *Mary Burns, Fugitive* (1935), Hitchcock's *Sabotage* (1936) and *Dead End* aka *Dead End: Cradle of Crime* (1937). As Richard Dyer argues, star images are both inter-textual and culturally determined constructions, forged out of a network of discourses outside of the films themselves and dependent upon specific historical circumstances for their meaning.[32] The "meaning" of a star is accrued over time including previous film roles hence the importance of not separating films according to predefined genres or themes but instead to situate Sidney's crime films within the particular qualities of her star "persona." Sidney was frequently cast to play young women abruptly confronted by unforeseen circumstances that reach the limits of their physical and emotional strength; often emotionally tested, betrayed, abused and disillusioned, her persona was developed to exhibit a compensating strength of character: vulnerability and resilience, exploitation and determination, female weakness and personal fortitude. It is difficult to determine exactly what this combination of qualities should be termed—it fits neither with the noir *femme fatale*, not the redemptive women nor the moll of the gangster. It is a combination of honest sentiment and a specifically feminine bravery in the face of adversity: it is perhaps the quintessence of melodrama, in which "tears" are the primary signifier of emotional devastation but also of resolution to action.

Sylvia Sidney perfected a look of utter devastation, often held in close-up shots, that registered the full impact of her recognition that circumstances had conspired to provide no alternative sphere for action. It is a "look" used to punctuate emotional intensities of the narrative and can be found in all of Sidney's performances, whether as wealthy heiress in *Merrily We Go to Hell*, as the dishonored Cho-Cho San in *Madame Butterfly* or the tenement drama of *Street Scene*. This suggests that Sidney's popularity was due to her delicate yet complex figuration of a mode of femininity that appealed to Depression-era audiences. An emblematic model of female strenght, Sidney's star persona accrued the qualities of stoicism in her characterization, of patience and endurance in the face of adversity. Yet, as the three films below should confirm, it is a form of stoicism that is not passive but capable of action when situations compel it. As such, it contrasts markedly with the modes of "Depression" female stardom embodied by figures such as Ruby Keeler, Glenda Farrell, Joan Blondell, Mae West, Carole Lombard, Miriam Hopkins, Constance Bennett, Claudette Colbert or Janet Gaynor. Sylvia Sidney's special star appeal lay in combining an affecting openness with the recognition of the inevitability of harsh realities in life, emotional vulnerability with a bitter determination to fight for what she sets as her own standards. In *City Streets* these qualities are only nascent but it does provide an exemplary instance of the manner in which Sidney's star persona carried these emotional qualities, and that these were required in order for a gangster film to be propelled by a female protagonist. Without wanting to suggest a purely binary set of spectatorial pleasures organized absolutely along gendered lines for the audience, nonetheless the presence of Sidney in crime/gangster films signaled a significantly female-addressed aspect through expectations of romantic melodrama. Sidney's persona was, then, particularly well developed to anchor films that acknowledged its female audience through hybrid narratives that took crime stories as the occasion to rehearse the pain and the pleasures of desire.

CITY STREETS (1931)

In 1930, Dashiell Hammett's commission from Paramount to write "originals" or screen outlines was offered in the hope of drawing to the studio and its stars some of the "hardboiled" qualities for which Hammett was celebrated as a writer of detective fiction.[33] One result was "After Hours," the story of a young couple—a gangster's daughter and a sharp shooter at the gallery—whose lives are brought together in Prohibition beer-running and inter-gang warfare. Nan (Sylvia Sidney) goes to prison after hiding a murder weapon for her father and, believing her lover The Kid (Gary Cooper) has been corrupted into the racketeering business by her father, decides to offer herself to the rival gang-chief to prevent the death of The Kid. After gun battles and high-speed car drives,

FIGURE 4: Publicity poster for *City Streets* 1931 © Paramount Pictures.

the couple is reunited after quitting the gangster scene. Films requiring a release certificate needed to pass on pre-production scripts through the offices of the Production Code Administration for advice on how to avoid post-production censorship. A November 14th 1930 letter from Richard H Dix Jr. to Colonel Jason Joy noted: "On July 7th I talked with you over the telephone about 'After Hours' a short story by Dashiell Hammett. At that time you thought the story could be made into a motion picture, but that we would have to be careful with the handling of the gun angles and the tarts." [34]

FIGURE 5: Studio portrait of Sylvia Sidney in *City Streets* circa 1931
©Paramount Pictures. Scanned postcard.

A later memo from June 18th 1931 from Jason Joy records the process of modification and stresses how the generic provenance of the film should be conceived: "through careful re-editing the aspect of bootlegging and crime was toned down, so that the story comes more in the category of love and jealousy, and crime instigated by jealousy."[35] The *New York Evening Post's* review published on the release of the picture makes clear Sidney's role in securing a female-directed address for the film:

> *City Streets* differs from most of the film dramas of the school in the fact that it handles the subject from the point of view of the gangster's girls rather than purely from the masculine attitude. That, incidentally, is perhaps a trifle surprising coming from Mr Hammett, the most masculine of the current novelists. In the leading role—once to have been played by Clara Bow—Miss Sylvia Sidney plays with resource, earnestness and moving honesty, while Gary Cooper is pleasant as the simple two-gun man from the circus, who joins the beer mob when he believes his girl has had him framed by the police.[36]

Similarly, a *Variety* review of April 22nd 1931 recognizes the importance of dual audience address in terms of box office appeal to both men and to women:

> Probably the first sophisticated treatment of a gangster picture. Art flourishes here and the settings are costly. For small town reaction these phases may balance each other out. Film looks to be moderate big spots with the heavy name cast helping. The story is the usual love-redeeming tale of two kids caught in a gangster vortex. Picture is lifted from mediocrity through attendant acting and the appeal of Sylvia Sidney. This legit girl makes her first screen appearance here as co-star with Gary Cooper. From a histrionic standpoint she's the whole works, and that's not detracting from the others who perform ably. She's not so well known inland but Cooper and other names in the cast compensate. She won't be unknown long.

Interestingly, as early as 1931 there are indications that Hollywood had been engaged with gangster film for some time before its supposed emergence with *Little Caesar* and *The Public Enemy*:

One false spot in the story is where the girl, permitted to take a prison rap for a shooting her father did, returns to the latter when freed from jail. If gangsters are meant to be brutal, slow-witted and phoney braves this picture almost shows that. Not entirely though. Gang chieftain is shown controlling everything from his henchman's women to his sidekicks' lives. He doesn't control his own life, though, and a jealous girl sends him low when he tries to shelve her for Babe. Final has Babe and her boyfriend make the heights of decency when they trick three badmen executioners, trailing them, into a long and speedy ride through the great outdoors. This ride will thrill but lacks essential dramatic warmth of the finish. The bad boys won't shoot because they fear destroying themselves in a car that's tearing along at seventy. The story treatment suffers audibly from a platitudinous attempt to artify but beyond a desirable limit. Camera angles are piled on thick. Most of the time these shots serve to slow up the film and to confuse. But for chronic fandom, the picture's personalities will probably overshadow story weakness. Whether the public sentiment which forced films into beer-racket pictures has changed can't be figured except at the box office. Theatres have been demonstrating that good gangster pictures pay.[37]

The reason for the "platitudinous attempt to artify" can be placed firmly with the director of *City Streets*. As the *New York Times* of April 18th 1931 suggested:

> Another gangster film, called 'City Streets,' is holding the fort at Paramount. It was directed by Robert Mamoulian, who staged several plays with the Theatre Guild and who was responsible for the picturization of 'Applause.' In this new work, Mamoulian reveals some clever cinematic ideas, but more often than not he loses his interest in the story and dialogue through his zealousness for unusual camera stunts and angles. This production, however, is quite entertaining [...]

The *New York Evening Post* also indicated a degree of irritation with Mamoulian's Expressionistic style:

> Having decided in solemn sales conference that gangster pictures are outmoded, Paramount is presenting a gangster picture all decked out in camera angles and symbolism arranged by the Theatre Guild's Mamoulian.

175

There is reason for suspecting that Mr Mamoulian's preoccupation with his camera and his unceasing concern with photographic imagery add a note of pretentiousness and ostentation to the production that is not altogether justified by the worth of the story. A simple and straightforward melodrama about gunmen and their girls no doubt loses as well as gains something when presented as its director felt it possessed some subtle cosmic significance. In addition, there are moments in which the constant use of pictorial symbols, or surf or statuary or anything else available for the camera, with the hint that they possess some profound import, results in unintentional amusement rather than impressiveness. Dark brooding photography takes away the vigor, brings style, individuality etc. Then, a melodramatic incident at the end of the picture which turns the conventional 'take him for a ride' into a genuinely exciting incident of recent cinema. Even with Dashiell Hammett, Oliver HP Garrett and Max Marcin involved, the script is less than epoch making.[38]

It is small wonder that Mamoulian's *auteur* excess now qualifies the film for "noir" precursor status.[39]

Figured from the point of view of thwarted lovers in which crime is the impediment to closure, *City Streets* claims social redemption for the protagonists through a legitimated heterosexual union. Though profoundly concerned with murder and violence, gang organization, gun battles with the law and inter-gang power struggles as should warrant the "gangster film" label, it has proved too nearly a romance, too near to feminine desire and to feminine inflections of popular melodrama and romance to qualify with the contemporaneous Big Three.

It is worth noting in this context Tom Milne's rejection of *City Streets* for its lack of generic purity:

Although *City Streets* tells a typical gangster tale of bootlegging, hijacking and mob rule, it is not strictly speaking a gangster film. For one thing Big Fella Maskal, the gang boss, has really more in common with George Bancroft's strutting, vainglorious Bull Weed in Sternberg's *Underworld* (made in 1927) than with the characters immortalised by Cagney, Edward G. Robinson, Paul Muni, et al. The conventions of the gangster film, with their defiant heroes taking on the whole world and spraying the streets with machine gun bullets, were yet to be defined, on the basis of *Little Caesar* (1930), by *Public Enemy* (1931) and *Scarface* (1932). Instead *City Streets* is first and foremost a love story, looking back to *Underworld* in its relationships and its stylised view of gangsterdom, and forward (though less doom-ladenly) to Lang's *You Only Live Once* in its story of young love at odd with society.[40]

I would argue that it is the motor force of heterosexual desire and longing for reunion regardless of social consequence that make a more direct case for the lineage taking *City Streets* to *You Only Live Once*, and that Sidney's star persona provides a dynamic semantic continuity between them.

LADIES OF THE BIG HOUSE (1931)

As I have argued elsewhere, gangster figures located within scenarios of romance and melodrama act as potent symbolizations of an active female desire. In this sense, the spectatorial pleasures offered to women in the audience can be found in the libidinal disturbance of the dominant register of heterosexuality that romance/melodrama crime films encourage; though worked out to necessarily conventional ends, the principal narrative drive of gangster romances is to offer vicarious pleasure to women confined within heterosexual normativity:

> The dangerous, exciting and coercive gangster provided an imaginary space into which transgressive fantasies of female desire could be projected: powerful enough to 'force' women into sexual compliance, the gangster was constructed as a perilous seduction and catalyst in narratives that explored the boundaries of 'decent' or 'legitimate' female sexuality.[41]

In *Ladies of the Big House* Sylvia Sidney is cast as Kathleen Storm who meets and falls in love with "Mac" McNeil at a dance hall.

Having previously been involved with vicious gangster leader Kid Athens, the plot details Athens' revenge on Kathleen for spurning him in favor of her new beau. In collusion with a corrupt Assistant DA, Athens manages to plant false evidence of murder that convicts them both: Kathleen is sentenced to life imprisonment in a women's prison and Mac sent to Death Row for hanging. The main part of the film centers on Kathleen's experience in the women's prison where she meets a range of female prisoners—a black women committed for the murder of her hus-

177

band, an abandoned pregnant Mexican woman frightened to give birth in prison and a spiteful moll Susie who had previously been jilted by Athens for Kathleen.

Unable to persuade the authorities of their innocence while her husband has only 48 hours until execution and supported by other women in the prison, Kathleen joins a jailbreak only to be retaken by the police. However, Susie's vengeful disenchantment with her gangster ex-lover drives her to inform the authorities of the source of the false evidence and corruption that exonerates the couple in time for Mac to be reprieved.

Based on a play by reformed criminal Ernest Booth (who while in Folsom Prison serving a life sentence for armed robbery also wrote a play that the film *Ladies of the Mob* (1928) adapted), *Ladies of the Big House* presents a women's view of imprisonment and escape, a female-centered narrative though similar to other films in an extensive cycle of prison films including *Fast Life* (1929), *The Bad One* (1931), *The Big House* (1930), *The Criminal Code* (1931), *The Lawyer's Secret* (1931) and *20000 Years in Sing Sing* (1932). The women's penal institution in which Kathleen is incarcerated is not especially harsh but presented as a place of female solidarity where prisoners support each other and share the gendered conditions of their crimes—crimes committed by wronged mothers, lovers and wives. The *New York Times* somewhat scornfully noted the film's "ingenuity in giving an intimate domestic touch to the prison" and "frequently picturesque way of exhibiting pride, jealousy, vanity and other untrammelled feminine emotions."[42] Similarly, a Memo to Colonel Jason Joy at the PCA noted a "vast difference between penal institutions for men and those for women. Paul Garnett (adviser on Metros's The Big House) says that women's prisons are far, far ahead of the others, better personnel, entirely different atmosphere, etc." However, the matter of verisimilitude is secondary to the way in which *Ladies in the Big House* allow a prison film to be driven by a subjugated female protagonist spurred into action to redeem her wronged lover and overcome the invidious grip of her gangster tormentor. From the point of view of romantic melodrama, the overall trajectory of the film offers its female protagonist an active expression of her desire, using the narrative of criminal events, wrongful incarceration and gangster violence to facilitate legitimation of the appropriate heterosexual union. A repetition of this theme underpins Sylvia Sidney's next crime film, again with extended prison scenes, *Mary Burns, Fugitive* (1935).

MARY BURNS, FUGITIVE (1935)

The story begins with an honest young woman Mary Burns (Sylvia Sidney) pouring coffee in a small diner; her place within a protective rural community is established in an Arcadian scene where children play safely with puppies and the church social defines the boundaries of social life. Into this simple scene comes Don "Babe" Wilson, a killer and thief who has come back to her country diner to retrieve stolen bonds he had hidden there. Unbeknownst to Mary, Babe is a wanted gangster—she believes her boyfriend is away for long periods because he is an oilman. Mary is coerced into marrying him immediately over the border in Canada; Mary is unaware that they are being pursued by the authorities and that she will soon be arrested when her husband shoots dead a policeman and escapes. Sent to the penitentiary for fifteen years for aiding, abetting and harboring a criminal and unable to win her appeal for wrongful conviction, Mary is befriended by ex-moll turned informant,Goldie Gordon, who sets up a prison-break, as Mary believes it will allow her to find evidence to establish her innocence. Goldie, however, has entered into a deal with the police to help them trap Babe through his continued obsession with Mary. In the meantime Mary takes a job as a nurse under the assumed name of Alice Brown and, though her romantic illusions are shattered, falls in love with a patient, snow-blinded explorer Barton Powell. Barton comes to know her real identity but is convinced of her innocent character. With Babe still pursuing her, Mary is obliged by the police to co-operate in engineering a showdown at an isolated log cabin where the still-blinded Barton has installed her as his private nurse and amanuensis. Barton's sight is restored and he sees Mary/Alice for the first time; having previously declared "I don't care if you have got a face like a mud pie," there follows an intense moment of romantic recognition—"Is that Mary Burns? I have never seen her in my life." Immediately, psychotic Babe breaks in and attempts to kill Barton. In the ensuing struggle, Mary turns the gun on Wilson and kills him. Mary secures her pardon and is reunited with Barton, freed to join him on his world explorations.

Mary Burns, Fugitive emerged in the context of a shift away from crime figures to cinematic glorification of Government agents in 1935–6: *G-Men, Let 'Em Have It, Men Without Names, Public Hero Number One* and *Counterfeit*. Here, Mary Burns is recruited to act on behalf of the G-Men and as a woman is recruited to play an active role in the re-establishment of law and order, as in *Public Enemy's Wife* (1936). Like the prison scenes in *Ladies of the Big House*, the representation of Mary's incarceration offers an occasion to comment on the ideological problematic position of women in prison. A voice-over comments that women's prisons "denied everything that they were put on the earth for [...] homes, children" and signals the view of the un-naturalness of women in prison as they "caged up like wild animals." Again, the causes of their crimes are directly attributable to the effects of patriarchy: that "men have been kicking women around since time began—nearly every one of 'em here because of a man like Wilson." The film makes very significant play with the discrepancy between respectable feminine identity and that of the moll. In one scene, a montage of newspaper headlines document the previously unassuming Mary Burns into a media-constructed gangster's moll. Confronting "herself" in the paper under a banner headline "Gun Moll Won't Talk," the newspaper photograph is shown to come to life, supposedly heavily rouged and lip-sticked. When a junior journalist points out to his senior colleague that "she wasn't rouged and she didn't say anything," he is told, "you're paid to write what the public want to read."

In *Mary Burns, Fugitive* the competing modes of masculinity that fight for Mary provide the basis of a romantic melodrama: on one side, a deranged, violent maniac with an obsessive, predatory sexual desire and, on the other, a ruggedly physical, authoritarian and educated man who falls in love with her voice and nurturing kindness. Mary's intensely romantic desire to protect Barton drives her to shoot Babe and repel the threat of unrestrained libidinal excess that he posed to the "normal" standards of bourgeois marital sexuality.

The hybrid melodrama-romance-crime film of the 1930s that takes crime scenarios to stage the ideological mediation of female desire might be read as a narrative form that personalizes broadly abstract notions of crime, punishment and justice. That such abstract notions might be concretized around matters of gender, heterosexuality, family, relationships, sex and desire must be extended to studies of the American crime film of the 1930s in order to appreciate that film narratives articulate ideologies of crime in forms that are recognizable and pleasurable for all the cinema's audiences. Reviewing some of the crime films that Sylvia Sidney had appeared in before *You Only Live Once* offers fertile material for appreciating the star "meanings" and audience expectations that would have preceded her role as an unassuming public defender's secretary whose romantic expectations are smashed in the course of the couple's inevitable destruction. At the centre of each of these films is a staging of heterosexual desire through scenarios of crime; their core message, despite their often conventional terms of resolution, is that abiding love and sexual attraction must be tested against the boundaries of law—in *You Only Live Once*, the fugitive couple who die together rather than live apart, shot to death by the police and hounded by a censorious justice they cannot escape. As later "outlaw couple" films—*They Live By Night* (1948), *Gun Crazy* (1950), *Bonnie & Clyde* (1969), *The Getaway* (1972), *Badlands* (1973), *Thieves Like Us* (1974) and *Natural Born Killers* (1994)—submit, the criminality of events are largely lost to the spectacle of pursuit of the couple towards/of normative heterosexuality. It is this conflation of compulsive attraction and the defiance of conventional law through crime that is the veritable essence of romance itself.

ENDNOTES

1. Claire Bond Potter, *War on Crime: Bandits, G-Men, and the Politics of Mass Culture* (New York: Rutgers University Press, 1998), 85.
2. http://archive.sensesofcinema.com/contents/cteq/08/48/you-only-live-once.html
3. The Internet Movie Database: http://www.imdb.com/title/tt0029808/user-comments
4. *http://en.wikipedia.org/wiki/You_Only_Live_Once_%28film%29*
5. http://www.theauteurs.com/films/3557
6. C. Jerry Kutner, "Beyond the Golden Age: Film Noir Since the '50s" at http://www.brightlightsfilm.com/54/noirgolden
7. Marc Vernet, "Film Noir on the Edge of Doom." In Joan Copjec, ed., *Shades of Noir* (London: Verso 1993), 1–32; quotation from p. 2.
8. Raymond Borde & Etienne Chaumeton, *Panorama du film noir americain* (Paris: les Editions de Minuit 1955; trans. Paul Hammond, *A Panorama of American Film Noir, 1941–1953* (San Francisco: City Lights Books. 2002 [1955]). Critical works on film noir is voluminous: key collections of writing on *noir* are *The Film Noir Encyclopaedia*, edited by Alain Silver, Elizabeth Ward, James Ursini and Robert Porfiro; *Film Noir Reader* Vol. I, eds., Silver & Ursini (New York: Limelight Editions, 1996); *Film Noir Reader* Vol. II, eds., Silver & Ursini, (New York: Limelight Editions, 1999), and *Film Noir Reader* Vol III,

eds., Silver, Ursini & Porfiro New York: Limelight Editions, 2002. See also James Naremore, *More Than Night: Film Noir and Its Contexts* (Berkeley: University of California Press, 1998), Frank Krutnik, *In a Lonely Street: Film Noir, Genre, Masculinity* (London: Routledge, 1991), and Arthur Lyons, *Death on the Cheap: The Lost B Movies of Film Noir* (New York: Da Capo Press, 2000).

9. Vernet, 5.

10. Ibid.

11. Vernet, 6.

12. Vernet, 5.

13. Vernet, 6. The mutual advantage of this is patent: "if French criticism finds an advantage in inventing *film noir,* Anglo-American criticism, by taking up without any contestation of its basic arguments, gives American cinema a cultural label and a critical force validated by Europe."

14. Vernet, 6.

15. Vernet, 2.

16. Vernet, 26.

17. Ibid.

18. Vernet, 2.

19. Ibid.

20. Jean-Francois Lyotard, *The Postmodern Condition: A Report on Knowledge,* trans. Geoff Bennington and Brian Massumi (Manchester: Manchester University Press, 1984). See also Keith Jenkins, ed., *The Postmodern History Reader* (London: Routledge, 1997).

21. See Tom Gunning, *The Films of Fritz Lang: Allegories of Vision and Modernity* (London: BFI, 2000).

22. In Vernet's words "what is completely strange in discourse on *film noir* is that the more elements of definition are advanced, the more objections and counter-examples are raised, the more precision is desired, the fuzzier the results become; the closer the object is approached, the more diluted it becomes." 4.

23. Vernet, 14.

24. Christine Gledhill, "Klute I: a contemporary film noir and feminist criticism." In E. Ann Kaplan, ed., *Women in Film Noir* (London: BFI, 1980), 6–21; the quotation is from p. 13.

25. Janey Place, "Women in Film Noir." In *Women in Film Noir,* 35–67; the quotation is from p.35.

26. Gledhill, ibid., 15.

27. Ibid.

28. Place, ibid., 45.

29. Ibid., 35.

30. Ibid., 50.

31. Robert Warshow, "The Gangster as a Tragic Hero" (original date of publication 1948), in *The Immediate Experience: Movies, Comics, Theatre & Other Aspects of Popular Culture* (Cambridge, MA./London: Harvard University Press, 2001), 85–88.

32. Richard Dyer, *Heavenly Bodies: Film Stars and Society*, (London: Routledge, 2003) 2nd edition, passim.

33. Even classic *noir*'s seemingly fixed connection to the "hard-boiled" school of detective writing epitomized by the 40s "rediscovery" of Hammett—*Red Harvest* (1929), *The Dain Curse* (1929), *The Maltese Falcon* (1930), *The Glass Key* (1931), *Woman In the Dark A Novel of Dangerous Romance* (1933) and *The Thin Man* (1934). For Hammett's relationship to Hollywood screenwriting, see Richard Laymen and Julie M. Rivett, eds., *Selected Letters of Dashiell Hammett 1921–1960* (Washington, DC: Counterpoint Press, 2001). Vernet is also unimpressed by the defense of the considerable time lag between the emergence of the American hard-boiled detective in the 1930s and the later *film noir* adaptations when explained by the fact that the "public was too affected by the Depression to be able to bear seeing the hard realities of existence recalled too strongly, and that it was necessary to wait for the post-war economic recovery" in order to make "sinister films." How, one might ask, could written crime and detective fictions have been so copiously produced, yet not filmed? Further, why have some film adaptations of hard-boiled novels made during the 1930s "been occulted [...] just as other detective films that could easily enter into the frame of the definition of film noir have been": "numerous films are swept under the rug in order to attempt to maintain an artificial purity, going against simple common sense, whereas the examination of anterior novels and films could be enlightening." Vernet, 14.

34. Production Code Administration, *City Streets file*: AMPAS: Margaret Herrick Library, Beverly Hills.

35. Ibid.

36. *New York Evening Post*, 1931, no date given: in *City Streets* press file: AMPAS, Margaret Herrick Library, Beverly Hills.

37. *Variety*, 22 April 1931.

38. *New York Evening Post*, 1931, no date given: in *City Streets* press file: AMPAS, Margaret Herrick Library, Beverly Hills.

39. The Internet Movie Database: *City Streets* http://www.imdb.com/title/tt0021750/

40. Tom Milne, *Mamoulian,* (London: BFI, 1969), 29.

41. See Esther Sonnet, "Ladies Love Brutes: Reclaiming Female Pleasures in the Lost History of Hollywood Gangster Cycles 1929–31." In Lee Grieveson, Esther Sonnet, and Peter Stanfield, eds., *Mob Culture: Hidden Histories of the American Gangster Film* (New Brunswick, N.J.: Rutgers University Press, 2005), 93–119; quotation from p. 94.

42. *New York Times*, 25 February 1931, undated clipping, AMPAS.

CHAPTER 6

PUNKS! TOPICALITY AND THE 1950s GANGSTER BIO-PIC CYCLE

PETER STANFIELD

"This is a re-creation of an era.
An era of jazz
Jalopies
Prohibition
And Trigger-Happy Punks."
— Baby Face Nelson

THIS ESSAY EXAMINES a distinctive and coherent cycle of films, produced in the late 1950s and early 1960s, which exploited the notoriety of Prohibition-era gangsters such as Baby Face Nelson, Al Capone, Bonnie Parker, Ma Barker, Mad Dog Coll, Pretty Boy Floyd, Machine Gun Kelly, John Dillinger, and Legs Diamond. Despite the historical specificity of the gangsters portrayed in these "bio-pics," the films each display a marked interest in relating their exploits to contemporary topical concerns. Not the least of these was a desire to exploit headline-grabbing, sensational stories of delinquent youth in the 1950s and to link these to equally sensational stories of punk hoodlums from 1920s and 1930s. In the following pages, some of the crossovers and overlaps between cycles of juvenile delinquency films and gangster bio-pics will be critically evaluated. At the centre of analysis is the manner in which many of the films in the 1950s bio-pic gangster cycle present only a passing interest in period verisimilitude; producing a display of complex alignments between the historical and the contemporary.

DELINQUENTS, GANGSTERS, AND PUNKS

In the 1950s, the representation of gangsters and of juvenile delinquents shared a common concern with explaining deviancy in terms of a rudimentary psychology, which held that criminality was fostered by psychopathic personalities. Part of the presentation of character archetype, with a basis in contemporary discourse on popular psychology, was the naming of gangsters and juvenile delinquents as "punks." This essay locates in this a shared etymology that offers connections in the meanings generated by calling deviants "punk," and observes the importance of considering the films discussed here as a distinct cycle of production, rather than examples of gangster films operating within a generic tradition.

The gangster bio-pics competed in the market place with other popular representations of Prohibition-era hoodlums including television programs, paperback books, pulp magazines, radio series, comic books, and bubblegum cards. The number of films produced between 1957 and 1961 based on the lives of gangsters was not particularly high, perhaps only twelve titles; it was, however, sufficiently concentrated and visible to spur the *Motion Picture Herald* critic to note that *Mad Dog Coll*, released toward the end of the cycle in 1961, was the latest in "a recent flurry of motion pictures dealing with the lives of gangsters of the 1920s."[1] The November 1957 release of *Baby Face Nelson* effectively began the cycle. The film was an Al Zimbalist production, distributed by United Artists, directed by Don Siegel, and starred Mickey Rooney as the titular gangster. *Variety* accurately predicted the subsequent cycle, and called *Baby Face Nelson*: "A hot exploitation picture!"[2]

Independent production companies such as AIP and Allied Artists were the principal producers of the films in this cycle. In the wake of the bio-pic of Lester Gillis, aka Baby Face Nelson, came the AIP double billed *The Bonnie Parker Story* and *Machine Gun Kelly* in 1958. Allied Artists released *Al Capone* in 1959, in January 1960, Lindsay Parsons Productions with distribution by Allied Artists released *The Purple Gang*, a story of Detroit's hoodlums. This was followed by The Le-Sac production of *Pretty Boy Floyd* and the Warner Bros. distributed *The Rise and Fall of Legs Diamond* in February, 1960. Screen Classics' production *Ma Barker's Killer Brood* opened in June, 1960, while Princess Productions' (20th Century-Fox distributed) *Murder, Inc.* was released a month later. *Murder, Inc.* followed the exploits of killers Abe "Kid Twist" Reles and Lepke Buchalter.

186

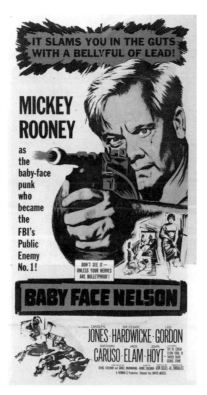

FIGURE 1: Newspaper advertisement for *Baby Face Nelson*, which markets the sensational, calls attention to the film's visceral appeal, "guts," "bellyful," and calls Rooney's character the "baby-face punk."

In 1961 Warner Bros. produced *Portrait of a Mobster*, a Dutch Schultz bio-pic and Thalia Films produced *Mad Dog Coll*, which was distributed by Columbia. Allied Artists closed out the year with *King of the Roaring 20's—The Story of Arnold Rothstein*. Other films that shared the same period setting and which also featured gangsters, but had relatively lavish production values compared to the independent pictures, included *Love Me or Leave Me*, *Pete Kelly's Blues*, both 1955, *Party Girl* (1958), and *Some Like It Hot* (1959).

This cycle of films sat alongside the contemporary exploitation of Prohibition-era hoodlums in television, which included NBC's *The Lawless Years* (1959-61) and the extraordinarily popular *The Untouchables* (Desilu Productions) which ran for four seasons during 1959-63 (the first two episodes being released theatrically as *The Scarface Mob* in Britain in

1960 and two years later in the States). The first season's attractions used most of the hoodlums also being portrayed in the film cycle.[3] The gangland subject matter of *The Untouchables* had been preceded by the television series *Gangbusters* (1952), from which the producers spun off a feature film *Gang Busters* (1955) and re-edited three episodes as *Guns Don't Argue* (1957), which was given a theatrical release. Gangland was also the setting for *The Roaring 20s* (1960–62), which ran for two seasons, and was Warner Bros. Television's attempt to share in *The Untouchables'* success in the ratings.

Paperback publishers produced numerous titles on the lives of Prohibition-era gangsters; between 1960 and 1962 Monarch Books published biographies of Baby Face Nelson, Dutch Schultz, Legs Diamond, Lucky Luciano, Frank Costello, and John Dillinger, alongside a novelization of the film *Mad Dog Coll*. Pyramid Books carried John Roberts' novelization of *Al Capone* alongside his original novel *The Mobster* (1960), while Signet published Harry Grey's fictional account of Dutch Schultz, *Portrait of a Mobster* (1958), later to be produced as a film by Warner Bros., and his 1953 novel *The Hoods* (eventually adapted by Sergio Leone as *Once Upon a Time in America*). This publishing activity, however, only scratches the surface of the paperback industry's exploitation of the nefarious doings of 1920s and 30s gangsters, which was complemented by the retelling of their stories in men's adventure magazines. [4] Arguably more important than either magazine, book, film, or even television in the contemporary proliferation and dissemination of images and stories concerned with Prohibition-era hoodlums was the comic, edited by Charles Biro and Bob Wood, *Crime Does Not Pay*, published by Lev Gleason between 1942 and 1955, and, which at its height in the 1950s, was selling a million copies a month until it was brought to a close as part of the crackdown on crime and horror comics.[5] *Crime Does Not Pay,* and its many imitators, repeatedly covered the careers of gangsters such as Baby Face Nelson, Pretty Boy Floyd and John Dillinger.[6]

In order to counter claims of glorifying the criminal and encouraging acts of imitation, the Production Code Administration (PCA) had effectively thwarted the use of the names of real-life gangsters in fiction films, but, following the 1945 release of the King Brothers production of *Dillinger*, the moratorium on the exploitation, in Will Hays' words, of an "actual criminal figure from current life," was effectively ended.[7] With the break up of the studio system, and the consequent weakening of the

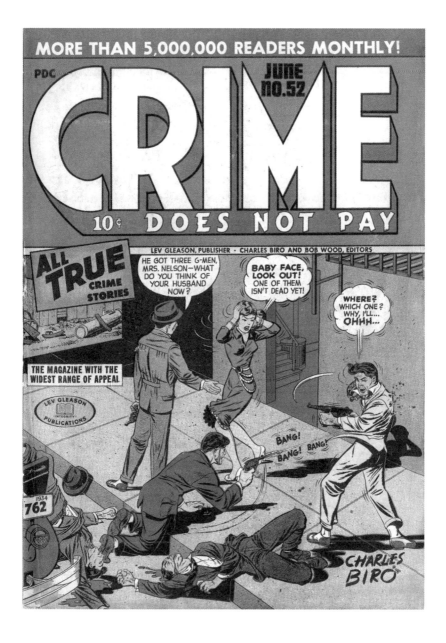

FIGURE 2: Typical cover splash for the comic book *Crime Does Not Pay*. This one features the exploits of Baby Face Nelson. Note the banner headline claiming the comic book had "more than 5,000,000 readers monthly!"

PCAs' control over film content, the new independent production companies undertook the exploitation of the public's prior knowledge of notorious gangsters with no little enthusiasm. The economic logic of this production strategy was clear to all, as *The Hollywood Reporter* remarked, *The Bonnie Parker Story* "finds exploitation in the name of a real criminal instead of an established star."[8] The exploitation of real-life hoodlums was such that in January 1958 *The Hollywood Reporter* also drew attention to an on-going attempt by Kroger Babb's Hallmark Productions to secure an injunction that would prevent Sam Katzman and Clover Productions from using the name "Pretty Boy Floyd," over which Babb claimed sole ownership. The injunction was denied.[9] A film purporting to tell Floyd's story was eventually made, but not by either Babb or Katzman. The Le-Sac Production of *Pretty Boy Floyd* was released in January 1960, just over two years after *Baby Face Nelson*.

If there was something of a rush to exclusively claim the names of better-known gangsters, the gallery of actual gangsters are represented, or are name checked, throughout the cycle regardless of who is named in a film's title. Dillinger, for example, featured in, or is referred to, in *Baby Face Nelson, Pretty Boy Floyd, Ma Barker's Killer Brood*, and *Machine Gun Kelly*. Actors also migrated from film to film in the cycle, or from film to television. Mickey Rooney in *Baby Face Nelson* and *King of the Roaring Twenties*, Dorothy Provine, who had the title role in *The Bonnie Parker Story*, reappeared as the lead in the television series *The Roaring 20s,* and Ray Danton played Legs Diamond, not only in *The Rise and Fall of Legs Diamond*, but also in *Portrait of a Mobster*. In the latter film, Vic Morrow, who played Dutch Schultz, gave a performance that was modelled on Rod Steiger's Capone in *Al Capone*.[10] Actor, character, performances all produced connections between the films in the cycle.

THE CINEMA AND TELEVISION LOOP

Bit part actors, as much as, if not more than, the stars, also created overlaps between the films. Before playing Al "Creepy" Karpis in *Ma Barker's Killer Brood*, Paul Dubov had occupied the same role in three episodes of the TV series *Gangbusters* from1952, parts of which, that included appearances by Dubov, were re-used in *Guns Don't Argue*, released in 1957. Dubov also had a bit part in *The Purple Gang*. Continuity is reinforced by the reappearances of other character actors, such as Frank De Kova who appeared in *Machine Gun Kelly, Legs Diamond, Portrait of a Mobster*, or Joseph Turkel who performed in *The Bonnie Parker Story, The Purple Gang*, and *Portrait of a Mobster*. These actors also had numerous appearances in other crime and gangster films from the period and in crime television series. De Kova and Dubov both had roles in the first episode of *The Untouchables*, and Turkel later appeared in the series on five separate occasions.

Conforming to stereotype, De Kova in *Legs* and *Portrait* played a sleazy Italian gangster, an ethnic caricature commensurate with his roles as a "red injun" or Mexican elsewhere. Turkel's pinched rodent-like features and wiry frame made him a perfect casting choice to play hoodlums who seem to have just stepped out of the pool hall, or dusted their knees following a game of craps in an alley. De Kova and Turkel are part of the period's rogues gallery—a lineup of familiar faces; landmarks on a tour of a fictional gangland, producing not only an aspect of the iconography of fictional crime, but an element of continuity that linked together individual films creating a gangster film meta-narrative.[11]

Repetition of the same found or stock footage from film to film also helped to produce this meta-narrative. According to gangster film historian, Carlos Clarens, at least a third of *Dillinger* was constructed out of stock footage, both documentary and fictional, including the armoured car heist sequence from Fritz Lang's *You Only Live Once* (1937).[12] *Al Capone* and *The Purple Gang* (both Allied Artist productions) used newsreel footage from the age of Prohibition, with a good number of overlaps between them. Montage sequences are a particularly heavy user of this type of material, little being unique to the production in which the sequence is inserted. *The Purple Gang* reused footage of storefronts being bombed, machine guns being fired, and cars crashing in its montages that earlier appeared in *Al Capone*. *Legs Diamond* presented a twist on the use of stock documentary footage by having Legs watch newsreels as he tours around Europe; a means of keeping him (and the film's audience) informed about developments in the underworld back home. *Murder, Inc.*'s montage used still, rather than moving, images; mixing documentary crime scene photographs with recreations that used the film's actors. *Portrait of a Mobster* seamlessly used period footage to provide wide shots of exterior locations before cutting to medium or close up shots of the actors on stage sets. *Mad Dog Coll* recycled both found footage of the Prohibition era and an opening shot of a burlesque marquee that is a direct steal from the opening of Samuel Fuller's *Crimson Kimono* from 1959. These were not films that made any particular claim to uniqueness or originality. What these films sold was the promise of the sensational.

Beyond the shared subject matter, these mediations on the figure of the gangster were designed for maximum impact in their appeal to an audience with a predisposition for the sensational. As the press book cover for the film *Baby Face Nelson* announced, exhibitors should "SELL IT SENSATIONALLY!" Why? Because this film portrayal of a gangster was "More Vicious Than Little Caesar! More Savage Than Scarface! More Brutal Than Dillinger!" Baby Face Nelson: "The Deadliest Killer of Them All! ... The 'Baby-Face Butcher' who lined 'em up—chopped 'em down—and terrorized a nation!" "It slams you in the guts with a bellyful of lead! ... Mickey Rooney as the baby-faced punk who became the FBI's Public Enemy No. 1!" This was the "shock-angle bally" that was to sell the film. The press book called the movie an "exploitation picture" and added that the promotional material "carries that 'extra' selling kick."[13] In its promise to deliver a "*more* vicious ... *more* savage ... *more* brutal" depiction of gangland violence than has been previously seen, the film's exploitative strategies are laid bare.

CRIME FILMS AS URBAN EXPOSÉ

In all their many guises, crime films can be seen as part of what scholar Will Straw has defined as the urban exposé, in which one finds "a variable balance between the ameliorative impulse toward documentation and the exploitational imperative to produce moments of textualized sensation."[14] This is particularly so of the cycle of crime films that paralleled the gangster bio-pics. In the *Motion Picture Herald* review of the contemporary exposé, *Inside the Mafia* (1959), there is a direct acknowledgement of the grounds upon which the film will be sold: "Exploitation, accentuating newspaper headlines, is limitless in this particular instance." The film is a late entry in the cycle that initially exploited the topicality and headline grabbing attraction of the findings of The Special Committee to Investigate Organized Crime in Interstate Commerce, popularly known as the Kefauver Hearings, which ran between May, 1950 to July, 1951.[15] Earlier films that worked a connection with the Hearings, and could claim to be as timely as today's headlines, included *711 Ocean Drive* (1950), *The Enforcer* (1951), *The Racket* (1951), *Hoodlum Empire* (1952), and *The Captive City* (1952).

As an historian of this cycle of crime films, Ronald Wilson, has noted, filmmakers' attempts "to narrate the story of organized crime produced several cyclical variants of the syndicate-film format." These included the city exposé/confidential films that Will Straw has documented, the witness protection films that Wilson touched upon, as well the rogue cop and police procedural films. Closely allied to these cycles are films about the labor rackets, including *The Mob* (1951), *On the Waterfront* (1954), *Rumble on the Docks* (1956), *Edge of the City* (1957), *The Garment Jungle* (1957), and *The Big Operator* (1959). Yet another variant was the cycle of gangster films with "turn-of-the-century" settings; films that purported to show the deep roots of the syndicates and the authorities' response to organized criminal activities, notably *The Black Hand* (1950), *Black Orchid* (1953), and *Pay or Die* (1960). These linked with syndicate films such as *Chicago Syndicate* (1955), *Never Love a Stranger* (1958) and *Underworld USA* (1961) that had contemporary settings, but which also flashback to provide an historical context for present day gangland activities. Some of the films in the bio-pic cycle also represented the development of the syndicate.

FROM THE TWENTIES TO THE FIFTIES

The opening narration for *Al Capone* tells the audience the story of Capone and the Roaring Twenties has "an important meaning for us today." And at the film's close, following the revelation of Capone's death, the voiceover narration returns: "we must continue to fight the remnants of the organization he built that still touches everyone of us today." The film's claim to topicality lies in what it has to say about the roots of contemporary organized crime. *The Rise and Fall of Legs Diamond* is the story of a maverick, an individual's rise to prominence within gangland, his fall comes when the criminal fraternity forms a "combine—a syndicate, nationwide." The film does not make an explicit claim to having contemporary relevance, but the lone gangster who is able to control an empire of crime is shown to be an historical phenomenon. Rather than end with the demise of the individual gangster, *Murder, Inc.* begins at that point. The film tells the story of Louis "Lepke" Buchalter and his marshalling of a gang of hit men led by Abe Reles (Peter Falk), which spans the historical divide between the demise of Al Capone and the contemporary era. Prohibition is over, Lepke tells Reles, "we're working now like a combination. [...] Like any sensible business." Or as the DA describes the syndicate, "a government within a government." The modern gangland is controlled by anonymous mobsters working in combination with others, films such as *Murder, Inc.*, *Al Capone* and *Legs Diamond* told the story of the origins of these combinations, which linked them with a cycle of crime films with contemporary settings that explicitly set out to expose the many arms of organized crime.

The historical setting of the bio-pic cycle would appear to contradict the idea that these films had an equally topical relevance to those films that directly exploited the Kefauver investigations. Certainly this was the position a reviewer in *The Hollywood Reporter* took with regard to *Baby Face Nelson,* which he argued "seems as much a period piece as a 19th century Western about Billy the Kid."[16] *New York Times* reviewer agreed, though thought it was the film's formulaic story that was out-of-date: "a

FIGURE 3: Publicity still: *The Bonnie Parker Story.* Bonnie (Dorothy Provine) and punk boyfriend Clyde Darrow (Jack Hogan) in an armoured car hold up.

thoroughly standard, pointless and even old fashioned picture, the kind that began going out along with the old time sedans. As a matter of fact one of the few absorbing sights in this UA release [...] is a continual procession of vintage jaloppys [*sic*] chugging in and out of the proceedings."[17] Other reviews of films in the cycle noted the historical nature of the subject but also made the point that this was recent history, such as the review in *Motion Picture Herald* which reported that *Ma Barker's Killer Brood* was "a forceful study of a not–so–long ago crimeland era."[18] Writing in *The Hollywood Reporter*, Jack Moffitt considered the historical veracity of *The Bonnie Parker Story* in his review, and added a very personal angle to its claim to verisimilitude: "Miss Provine's performance gives promise for a credible acting future. She's much better looking than the real Bonnie but, despite the accuracy of her cigar-smoking, her dialogue is monotonously on a tough key. The real Bonnie (who I knew in Kansas City) could scare you to death by smiling and saying 'pretty please.' "[19]

DRESSED TO KILL

The dialogue between past and present is particularly apparent in the costuming of the actors. *Al Capone* takes the most care with dressing its actors in fair approximations of 1920s dress styles; men's headwear included homburgs and straw boaters, rather than 1950s fedoras with low crowns and wide brims which seem to dominate elsewhere in the cycle. Spats and co-respondent (black and white) shoes are noticeable, wide lapels and double breasted suits with waistcoats are also clearly on view. Women too are dressed with some regard to 20s trends, but dresses are, however, cut too tightly into the waist, too much cleavage is shown and atypical bra straps can be seen through the rear of some costumes. The dressing of actresses in cantilevered brassieres across all the films in the cycle which, with a tucked in waist line and a tight skirt, accentuate an hour-glass figure, had little to do with either 20s or 30s female fashions, and everything to do with a 1950s idealisation of a female body shape.

Murder, Inc. is the film least concerned with maintaining specific period identity as, apart from some vintage cars and two verbal and textual declarations that the film is set in the mid-thirties, absolutely no one is dressed in 30s clothing. No homburgs, no straw boaters, and men's coats, hats, shoes are all contemporary with the film's production, which is also repeated in the female costuming. The leading actresses' blonde hair is worn long and unprocessed, completely inappropriate for women's hairstyles of the 1930s but completely in accord with styles of the early 1960s.

FIGURE 4: Publicity still: *Murder Inc.* Abe "Kid Twist" Reles (Peter Falk), right, Joey Collins (Stuart Whitman), center, and Eadie Collins (May Britt), left. The costuming and dressing, particularly the hair-styles, are all contemporary with the film's release date of 1960, yet the film is set in the 1930s.

Locations also offer moments of temporal contradiction and confusion. Much of *Murder, Inc.* is shot on stage sets, though it has some notable exterior location scenes, many shot on empty city streets. However, one short sequence uses the crowded public space of a New York train station. The scene is composed in long shot with the camera positioned high above the concourse, though not so far away that we are unable to identify Peter Falk/Abe Reles. As the gangster walks through the concourse the people surrounding him go about their business, moving past the actors playing out the scene. It is no more than a snapshot of a train station in 1960, there has been absolutely no attempt to dress the station or extras in period costumes or detail. Only the knowledge that we have been told the film is set in the "mid-thirties" and that the events portrayed are "factual and the people real" contradicts the scene's contemporaneity.

None of the films in the cycle display an obsession with period costuming and interior and exterior design that can be seen in the cycle of gangster pictures with historical settings made in the late-1980s and early 1990s, which included *The Untouchables* (1987), *Miller's Crossing* (1990),

196

Mobsters and *Bugsy* (both 1991). Anachronisms do appear in that cycle, not least, and in keeping with the 50s cycle, female undergarments, but there is nevertheless an extraordinary obsession displayed with period detail elsewhere. This is an aspect of the '90s retro gangster film that Esther Sonnet has documented; arguing that the costuming of these films is used to reinstate the image of hegemonic masculinity—"a retrenchment into outdated gender orthodoxies."[20] The 1950s gangster bio-pic cycle is not discernibly concerned with nostalgia, but, in contradistinction, by a fixation to mark the films as topical—to be seen to be of the moment, producing a distinct form of dialogue between "past" and "present."

On *Baby Face Nelson*'s fast and free approach to historical verisimilitude, Geoffrey O'Brien in a laudatory 2006 review wrote:

Some appropriate clothes and cars are provided to avoid blatant anachronism—the cars more than earning their rental fees since so much of the movie is devoted to shots of them tooling along obscure country backroads—but otherwise Baby Face Nelson feels absolutely like a movie about the mid-Fifties. In fact, with black-haired Carolyn Jones (as Rooney's faithful-unto-death girlfriend Sue) coming across as an archetypal Beat Girl, Van Alexander's jazz score pouring out large doses of West Coast Cool. [...] Baby Face Nelson taps into a mood of subcultural nihilism far more effectively than those exploitation pictures that attempted to take on the Beats directly.

FIGURE 5: Publicity still: *Baby Face Nelson*. Nelson (Mickey Rooney) and Sue (Carolyn Jones). Sue is dressed and costumed as an "archetypal Beat Girl."

Despite O'Brien's claims that *Baby Face Nelson* stands apart from the rest of the cycle in its "lack of interest in even making a gesture toward period flavor or historical perspective," all the films exhibit historical anachronisms and use automobiles as the principal means of signifying a 1930s time period. *The Bonnie Parker Story*, which could equally be said to tap into a mood of "subcultural nihilism," opened with a voyeuristic view of Bonnie undressing in a locker room. Parker's dress, undergarments, and hair, all conform to 1950s styles. An instrumental rock 'n' roll soundtrack, principally produced on an electric guitar, aurally underscores the sense of contemporaneity. At the end of the title sequence the film's setting and dateline is verbally announced and reinforced in text: "Oklahoma City —1932." The announcement undercuts the preceding visual and aural clues to the film's historical setting. The effect is to create temporal instability which allowed for a reception of the film as both historically located and yet contemporaneous with the time of the film's initial screening.

In terms straight out of a 50s JD or Beatnik movie, Bonnie wants "kicks—real kicks, big city style." The eponymous villains in *Pretty Boy Floyd* and *Mad Dog Coll* are also out for "kicks": "power and kicks," for the former, and "killing for fun and kicks" for the latter. A further link to JD and Beatnik movies is casually made toward the end of *The Bonnie Parker Story* when Guy is shown laying back in an easy chair and blowing on a saxophone. Following the ambush in which Bonnie and Guy are killed, the saxophone is seen for a second time, now lying alongside a tommy gun in the smoking wreck of the automobile—a symbol for the age, but clearly for the 1950s, not the 1930s; making the popular association of illegitimacy now extended from the 1930s gangsters to the non-productive society of JDs and Beats. Apart from incorporating the occasional 1920s jazz motif into the mix, the soundtrack to *Machine Gun Kelly* is as equally contemporaneous as that used in both *Baby Face Nelson* and *The Bonnie Parker Story*. Rather than west coast cool or rock 'n' roll, *Kelly* opens with a rhythm and blues sound of squalling saxophones. There are no Beatnik allusions in the film, but the men's haircuts are 50s styled and the suits are all off the peg, narrow lapels, cut straight at the waist, and only the occasional character wearing a newsboy flat cap suggests any interest in replicating 30s fashions.

While these films make no overt claim to topicality, *The Purple Gang* makes an explicit connection with the day's headlines. The film opens with a prologue supplied by California Congressman James Roosevelt.

He believed the same sickness that lay behind bootlegging is still present today, the symptoms have changed but the illness remained the same, and only an informed and vigilant public can provide the cure. A text crawl follows which explicitly aligned Prohibition era gangsters with juvenile delinquency. At the end of the film, Harley in a voiceover told viewers: "The times have changed yet the daily headlines remain the same." The Congressman asks for public vigilance in helping to counter delinquency, and the premise of his appeal is that *The Purple Gang* provides a history lesson from which we might better understand contemporary criminality.

FIGURE 6: Publicity still: *Mad Dog Coll*. Vincent "Mad Dog" Coll (John Davis Chandler), standing in light colored double-breasted suit, in his gang's clubhouse. Note the high-styled 1950s hair-cuts of two of his gang members.

FIGURE 7: Publicity still: *Stakeout on Dope Street*. The three young tearaways who have discovered a canister of heroin discuss what to do with their find in their clubhouse. The setting is interchangeable with the clubhouse used by the young gangsters in Mad Dog Coll.

FROM HOODLUMS TO DELINQUENTS

A number of the films in the bio-pic cycle made direct links between prewar hoodlums with post-war delinquents. The independent trade journal aimed at exhibitors, *Harrison's Reports* related the hoodlums in *The Purple Gang* openly to their later counterparts through a use of contemporary nomenclature: "A teen-age rat pack operating out of Detroit's slums and led by the psychotic Robert Blake."[21] Similarly the *Motion Picture Herald* noted the link, overtly relating the production company's exploitation of topical subjects with the film's historical dimension: "Lindsay Parsons, whose Allied Artists releases have had critical and audience acclaim for their briskness of approach and topical subjects has turned engrossing attention to Detroit's fabled Purple Gang, the Manor City juvenile mob which emerged as one of the country's most feared band of racketeers."[22] "Rat-pack terrorists" is the term used by the police Lt. Harley (Barry Sullivan) to describe Detroit's hoodlums. When the gang were still no more than a group of teen-agers running wild on Hastings Street, moving up from petty theft to shakedowns, Harley had confronted the boys' welfare worker, an earnest young woman who believed the young gangsters would respond positively to more sensitive treatment, a little "psychological readjustment." They have, she tells Harley, "grown up without love and no real feeling of security." Harley dismisses her "three syllable words." "They are just a gang of punks," he tells her. The gang later rape and murder the welfare worker.

The Purple Gang is forthright in its statement that delinquents, young and old, are best dealt with by direct and unfettered police action, supported by a civic-minded American public. Though the film rejects outright the value of psychological explanations as a means toward solving the problem of juvenile crime, it nevertheless uses popular psychology in its characterization of the principal characters, particularly the gang leader Honey Boy Willard, played by Robert Blake. Willard suffers from claustrophobia and Harley uses his knowledge of the phobia to try and get the hoodlum to crack. By the end of the film Willard is crawling around on all fours, hysterical, a broken boy/man. The psychologically fractured protagonist typifies the cycle, at the close of *Machine Gun Kelly* we are presented with the image of the abject gangster: confronted by the law he withdraws into a foetal position at the feet of the arresting officers. By the close of *Mad Dog Coll*, the gangster is completely delusional. Coll dies in a shoot out with the police in a drug store, his death crawl takes him out onto the street, his last words are "I hate . . ." At the beginning of the film the narrator had asked the question of how Coll would have turned out if his father had been a high school principal, would he have been like other kids, or was he born different? The film does not give a definitive answer, but shifts attention away from complex problems of determination by deferring attention onto the commonsensical and simplistic solution of shooting "mad dogs," which presupposes that criminal deviants are no more than animals.

The gangster bio-pic and juvenile delinquency cycles shared a general-ized concept of how to understand and explain criminality. For the most part the films in the cycle proposed that criminal careers are nurtured on urban streets, or in an environment of rural deprivation, that was very much in keeping with earlier explanatory schemes given by the movies.[23] However, social explanations for criminality are often contradicted within the films by recourse to popular psychology that explain deviancy in terms of individual complexes. The *King of the Roaring Twenties* is a good example of how the contradiction between determining factors works. Arnold Rothstein comes from an upper middle-class family, but as a juvenile he spends all of his free time on the streets. Street life forms the man and helps to explain his move into a criminal career. However, it is not the only explanation offered, as if in an echo of the *The Jazz Singer*'s Oedipal rebellion, the Jew, Rothstein, rebels against the word of his father and chooses the secular streets over respectability and ethnic tradition. In this instance it is not lack of opportunity, but a failure of character that explains the criminal. In all cases, however, the explanation given for criminal behavior, whether sociological or psychological, it is always crude and reductive; a caricature of sophisticated and complex theories.

The casting of the bio-pic cycle of films also fostered a marked overlap with juvenile delinquency movies, both the heady exploitation films produced by AIP and Allied Artists and those financed and distributed by the older studios that strove for a greater social realism. Richard Bakalyan, who was Bonnie Parker's husband in *The Bonnie Parker Story*, initially made his mark in an independent production directed by Robert Altman, *The Delinquents* (1957), and went on to become something of a JD icon; Vic Morrow who played the deranged Artie West in *Blackboard Jungle* (1955) is cast as Dutch Schultz in *Portrait of a Mobster*; John Davis Chandler who played a despicable gang member who murders a blind teenager in *The Young Savages* (1961) played Vincent Coll in *Mad Dog Coll*; and Fay Spain, who had the female lead in *Al Capone*, had previously played the leader of a female gang in *Teenage Doll* (1957) and a hot-rodder in *Dragstrip Girl* (1956). Such casting visually linked the gangster and the JD films together, but it was also designed to garner interest from a core film going constituency. As the *Motion Picture Herald* noted about the casting of the lead in *Pretty Boy Floyd*, "John Ericson, of considerable marquee weight, to the vitally important teenage film audience as well as to the post-35 age group that will patronize an appealing motion picture tops the cast of this Le-Sac [...] attraction."[24]

The casting of Mickey Rooney as Baby Face Nelson had little overtly to do with making connections between the bio-pic and JD cycles, but it was not wholly unrelated to representations of adolescence. The role helped Rooney to establish a persona far removed from his origins as a song and dance man and the boy-next-door in the Andy Hardy series. But audience memories of that wholesome juvenile must surely have informed the reception of his portrayal of a psychotic killer in *Baby Face Nelson* and his subsequent tough guy persona in two 1959 crime films, *The Last Mile* and *The Big Operator*. In the former Rooney plays "Killer" Mears, a man on death row who leads a prison riot, and in the latter his character is the labor racketeer "Little Joe" Braun.[25] *Motion Picture Herald* described Rooney's character in *Baby Face Nelson* as a "warped sadistic killer"; the actor, it reported, "proves once again his versatility as an accomplished performer [and] sinks his teeth into the role and shakes it for everything that is in it." The journal's reviewer noted that the "physical attributes of Nelson match those of Rooney, in the two respects of short stature and a round, young face, which provides even greater verisimilitude to the role."[26]

LITTLE CAESARS AND POP PSYCHOLOGY

Rooney's lack of height recalled the casting of the lead figures in the canonical gangster films: James Cagney in *Public Enemy*, Paul Muni and George Raft in *Scarface: Shame of a Nation*, Humphrey Bogart in *The Petrified Forest*, and, of course, Edward G. Robinson in the aptly named *Little Caesar*. Other films in the cycle followed *Baby Face Nelson* in using short actors in the lead, Robert Blake in *The Purple Gang*, Peter Falk in *Murder, Inc.*, and John Davis Chandler in *Mad Dog Coll*. Even the "distaff side of American crime" was portrayed as undersized. The *Motion Picture Herald* suggested that Dorothy Provine's portrayal in *The Bonnie Parker Story* may stretch some audience members' credibility who "will challenge the excess viciousness attributed to a diminutive member of the fairer sex."[27] This characterization of Parker as deviant in terms of both her criminal actions and her gender was in keeping with the other films in the cycle, regardless of whether the gangster was male or female.

The gangster portrayed as a runt underlined "common-sense" psychology's view that deficiency in height equates with an inferiority complex, and hence the resentment of and resistance to authority. *Baby Face Nelson* repeatedly emphasised Rooney's/Nelson's diminutive presence. Infantilized in both name and body, from sloshing around in a bathtub, to being picked up off a bed by a policeman as if he were a child, and when Nelson first meets John Dillinger it is at a children's playground. The gangsters sit on swings, above which a sign reads: "No Children over the age of 12." Coded messages between mobsters—"Baby—call. Daddy needs you"—that appear in newspaper advertisements further instantiates the infantilization of adult men. It is Dillinger, significantly known as "The Big Man," who names Lester Gillis "Baby Face," but it is Gillis' girl, played by Carolyn Jones, who provides her surname, Nelson, as his alias. Lester, it is suggested, is just a little too ready to lose his patrilineal privilege when he takes her name. "You've got all of me but my name. Why don't you take that too?" she offers, after cooling him down following a killing by repeatedly calling him "Baby." "Yeah, okay," replies Gillis, "any name's better than my old man's."

In terms of characterization, the figures in the film are all drawn with broad strokes, caricatures rather than nuanced and complex individuals. Dillinger—The Big Man—played by Leo Gordon contrasting with the squat Rooney, the "brain guy," played by the lanky Jack Elam offering another contrasting physical presence; the use of other undersized actors like Sir Cedric Hardwick, who plays the mob-employed doctor who tends to Baby Face's wounds and attempts to burn off the killer's fingerprints, or gang member played by Elisha Cook Jr. who Nelson knocks around. Taking a banker hostage, Nelson rides with him in the back of the getaway car. Noticing that he has an inch or two in height over the man, Nelson pulls himself higher in his seat and asks the hostage whether he has considered using lifts in his shoes. The banker replies he *is* wearing them. With caricature, size matters.

The Hollywood Reporter indirectly noted the use of caricature when it called attention to the characters' "stark presentation," which had "none of the contemporary effort to provoke and understand the how and the why. The characters are vicious but flat and never very interesting."[28] This period of film production was something of a high point in the popularization of psychoanalysis as a means of explaining character motivation. An example of this can be seen in the contemporaneous cycles of police procedurals and rogue cop movies. Will Straw has noted that in these films there was a "transformation of police characters from unde-

FIGURE 8: Publicity still: *Baby Face Nelson*. Nelson holds his tommy gun on the kidnapped banker (George E. Stone). Nelson lets the man live, because he is shorter than himself. Also sitting in the car is the equally diminutive actor Elisha Cook Jr., who plays Homer van Meter.

veloped ethnic figures of ridicule or inconsequence to fictional persona whose characterological density is the pivot around which narratives frequently turn."[29] In contrast, the gangster bio-pics resolutely reject psychological density and complexity, and, unlike the generic novelty of policemen as "bearers of class resentment or disgust at urban degradation" such as are found in *The Prowler* (1951) or *On Dangerous Ground* (1952), the bio-pic gangster is a ready-made, familiar, conventionalized and standardized figure.[30]

It was, however, precisely this very lack of psychological subtlety in American action movies and their use of the visually arresting image that would appeal to the cinephiles and cineastes in France. Jean-Luc Godard wrote in 1959 of François Truffaut's *Les 400 Coups*, then in production, that its "dialogue and gestures [would be] as caustic as those in *Baby Face Nelson*."[31] Later Anglo-American critics with a cultish appreciation of postwar American films, such as Geoffrey O'Brien, would echo Godard's sentiments: "You keep waiting for the false note—the grandiloquent symbol, the self-conscious lyrical touch, the hammy emotional explosion, the heavy-handed injection of sociology or psychology—and It never comes."[32]

The comic play with pop-Freudian explanations for the gangster's "warped sadism," undersized with an Oedipal complex, is as sophisticated as the films get to "explaining" their characters' subconscious motivations. *Mad Dog Coll* opens with the title character walking through a cemetery at night, dry ice swirling around his ankles, like a scene from a cheap horror movie. Coll stops before his father's grave and fires a machine gun at the tombstone—a fantasy that sees him obliterating the man that beat him senseless for being a mama's boy. By the film's close, Coll is completely delusional: first recalling his visit to the graveyard to "kill" his father, he then believes a member of Dutch Schultz's gang he is holding hostage is in fact his father; "killing" him once more by stabbing the gangster.

Alongside the rudimentary articulation of Oedipal complexes, visual images of emasculated men appear in all the films in the cycle. In *Machine Gun Kelly* two minor characters are used to maximum effect; one a fey man, Fandango, who Kelly uses to ferry booty from bank and kidnapping jobs, the other, Harry, who might or might not have lost the use of his right arm when mauled by a lion. Harry now runs a gas station behind which he has a small zoo stocked with caged monkeys and a mountain lion he claims he trapped himself. For dipping into the takings from a bank job, Kelly punishes Fandango by pushing him against the mountain lion's cage; he loses his left arm. Toward the end of the film Harry and Fandango are visually linked together, two matched one-armed men. Among the many instances of the signifying of impotence in the film, the most withering occurrences are built around Kelly's inability to act out a masculine vitality. His girlfriend tells Kelly that she had "mothered" him until he was able to prove he was a man, but when tested he falls short of the potent ideal she desires. Faced with images of death—an empty coffin carried in the street, a skull and crossbones tattoo on the back of a mug's hand—Kelly becomes immobilised, fear runs through him and he is exposed as being "naked yellow." His tommy gun is revealed to be just a prop to hide his lack of virility. When Federal agents at the film's close take him away they mock the cowed gangster, infantilizing him as "Popgun Kelly."

CHEAP PUNKS GOING NOWHERE

Demeaning the gangster is a key narrative strategy in this cycle, and a primary means of achieving this is in the use of the term "punk." The bio-pic gangsters are repeatedly referred to as "punks," which takes place not only in the films' dialogue, but also in publicity and marketing materials, and in reviews of the films. The *New York Times* thought Rooney's character Baby Face Nelson was "nothing more than a rotten, sadistic punk without one redeeming trait."[33] *Harrison's Reports* called the title character, in *Pretty Boy Floyd*, "a cheap punk who made it big."[34] Even Rothstein, in *King of the Roaring Twenties*, and Capone, in *Al Capone*, are called punks early in their criminal careers to signify both their youth and the lack of respect they are held in by older and more powerful figures to whom they yet pose an inchoate threat. In contemporary set *Chicago Syndicate* the mob boss takes a nostalgic tour of the neighborhood he grew up in and recalls the time when he was a "young punk." Being a "punk" was something you left behind with your youth; a measure of the distance since travelled from ghetto to penthouse, from juvenile to adult, by Capone, Rothstein, and the Chicago mobster.

When DA Burton Turkus asks police Lt. Tobin, in *Murder, Inc.*, how he would deal with the hoodlum problem, the Irish cop gives it to him straight: "play dirty. Show the neighborhood what they are—bums, punks, hoodlums." When finally cornered and spilling all he knows to the authorities, bum, punk, hoodlum, and hit-man, Abe "Kid Twist" Reles tells the DA, "any punk we hit, deserved to be hit." When Dutch Schultz in *Portrait of a Mobster* is confronted by a delegation to the Bronx of "spaghetti benders," he dismisses them and their attempt to coerce him into joining their Chicago organization. He tells the "greaseballs" that "in that town, any punk can be big." Whether determined by policeman, hoodlum, or killer, a punk is anyone considered beneath contempt. But in these films to call someone a punk is not simply to demean them socially, it also calls into question their masculinity.

In *The Bonnie Parker Story*, Bonnie is introduced waiting tables in a greasy diner, her husband Duke Jefferson (Richard Bakalyan) is serving a 175-year jail sentence, and as a wife of a convicted criminal this is the best job she can find. As she explains to the owner: "All I ever met was punks; they come from no place, going nowhere." She hooks up with Guy Darrow (Jack Hogan) who sports Elvis-like sideburns and a Brando-esque penchant for walking around in a white vest. (Guy had caught her eye when he pulled out a tommy gun with the cool intent to impress a girl such as Bonnie with the size of his weaponry—an image of potent masculinity, a virility that has been denied to her in her relationships with "punks.") Guy, though, fails to fulfill Bonnie's desire, and toward the end of the film she tells him what she really thinks of him: "you're a punk! You can stand on your head but you'd still be a punk."

FIGURE 9: Publicity still: *The Bonnie Parker Story.* In a world where the only men she meets are punks, Bonnie sleeps alone. Note the long guns propped up beside her bed.

More than anything, Ma Barker hates sissies. She wants her kids to show plenty of guts, and, in *Ma Barker's Killer Brood*, she follows gang member Al Karpis' maxim that guts are more important than brains. Surrounded by the police the old woman plays out her final hand, and for the last time attempts to beat the sissy out of one of her boys. Cajoling a cowering Fred Barker to take action, she calls him "a gutless punk, you're as yellow as your old man." Caught between a castrating mother and representatives of the law, suitably chastened and emasculated, Fred dies a punk's death in a hail of bullets. Similarly, Charles Bronson's eponymous character in *Machine Gun Kelly* is called a punk by a Ma Barker type, who has little time for his ineffectual bragging and is able to see through his virile posturing as being no more than an empty gesture.

In *Portrait of a Mobster* the female lead wants a man who can live up to the masculine ideal embodied by her recently deceased father; not a punk. She's sick of weak men, she tells her policeman husband. He, though, like Guy Darrow, fails to fulfil the masculine ideal. "Lean on me," says Dutch Schultz, who exploits her frustration and dissatisfaction with her husband. However, unbeknownst to her, Schultz is the killer of her father. Her punishment for having an illicit desire for Dutch is to become a lush, trapped in a loveless relationship. Good (whole) men are hard to find, this cycle of films contended, but emasculated infantilized punks seemed to be everywhere. The semantic work of the term "punk" thus undermined (and unmanned) upstart hoodlums.

Punk is used in the same manner in films that more explicitly exploit the hot topic of juvenile delinquency, such as *Four Boys and a Gun* (1957) or *Stakeout on Dope Street* (1958) where the JDs are called punks by an authority figure in the former, and by older hoodlums in the latter. In the 1961 musical *Westside Story*, patrolman officer Krupke confronts the street gang, called the Jets, by threatening to "run *all* you punks in!" And the Jets respond, in song:

> Dear kindly Sergeant Krupke,
> Ya gotta understand –
> It's just our bringin' upke
> That gets us outta hand.
> Our mothers all are junkies,
> Our fathers all our drunks.
> Golly Moses—natcherly we're punks!

The domestication of the word via its comic and musical inclusion in *Westside Story* was new to the movies, but not to other forms of American popular culture. The fairly common usage of "punk" as a put-down in 1930s and 1940s in newspaper comic strips, such as *Dick Tracy* and *Terry & the Pirates*, a means to verbally demean or show a marked lack of respect toward someone, suggests its use was not considered to be particularly offensive at that time, at least not in the United States, and certainly not when used to describe a caricatured underworld figure or street hoodlum.[35] The 1946 edition of Funk & Wagnall's *New Practical Standard Dictionary* gave a "young gangster" or someone who is "worthless and useless" as comparable definitions of the popular use of "punk."[36] This was certainly the dominant meaning in the word's use in Alex Raymond's widely syndicated daily strip, *Rip Kirby*, between August 1946 and April 1947. "Punk" was used in the story's dialogue on eight occasions during this period. A boy playing cops and robbers, holding his scarecrow adversary at gunpoint first uses it in the series, he exclaims: "You can't win, punk!" It is next used to describe gangsters a taxi driver is reading about in the papers. 13 strips later a policeman calls one of the gangsters a "punk." In early December, in a new story, a blackmailed band-leader hands over some money to a juvenile delinquent, who he calls a "corrupt little punk." In a January strip a card shark is called a "gamblin' punk" by a fellow member of gangland, and later he is simply called a "punk" by one of his victims and "da punk!" by another hoodlum.[37] The repeated use of the term in the strip suggests there was an accepting familiarity with it on the part of readers, particularly when used in the context of crime and underworld stories.

THE LEXICON OF PUNK

In Great Britain, "punk," alongside terms such as "shag" and "sissy" were blacklisted by film censors and hence had been excised from American films by the PCA in the years prior to the 1950s, though it makes a remarkable, but isolated, appearance in *Dillinger*, released in 1945.[38] Given its cinematic absence, the emphatic use of "punk" in gangster films in the latter years of the 1950s undoubtedly appealed in terms of its novelty value and its seemingly benign vulgarity; an authentic example of lowlife slang that carried a suggestion of indecency in its use. The etymology of "punk," however, reveals the word to be rich in meaning, and utterly indecent, not least in its sexual connotations. "Punk's" deep roots are in Elizabethan slang, in which it was used as a common term for prostitute, and more recently, in the United States, as a term for a hobo's or prison inmate's younger male sexual companion. If the term had any shared meaning in England in the 1950s, other than as a vernacular Americanism, it was conversely, given its Elizabethan meaning, now used to denote a "pimp," and hence its problematic standing with the censors.[39]

The post-40s use of "gunsel" offers a parallel to "punk" in organizing a range of meanings to do with deviancy, crime, sexuality, and power. Often understood as referring to a gunman, gunsel is in fact a slang name for a catamite. [40] The shared context of commonly recognized acts of deviancy, criminal or sexual, has helped to promote the misrecognition of the meaning of gunsel. As a prison slang term, the root meaning of "punk", like gunsel, signified the passive, often coerced, partner in homosexual acts. The way "punk" is used in the gangster bio-pic cycle there is little, if any, overt signifying of its sexual meaning. "Punk's" sexual connotations, nevertheless, lie behind all of the putdowns that seek to emasculate, diminish and infantilize the gangster.

The homosexual undertone of "punk's" meaning is never entirely absent, and certainly adds piquancy to an early prison scene in *Dillinger* when the more mature inmate, Specs Green (Edmund Lowe), explains his philosophy to the jailhouse novice Dillinger: "First society gets careless with the criminal and then the criminal gets careless. First thing to gum things up is a trigger-happy punk. Personally, I have no use for a punk. Some fellers, if you pat them on the back, they'll kill a man for you. If you treat a punk right, you can get the biggest man in the world killed." Though what he is saying is not readily apprehended by the naïve Dillinger, Green is obviously describing his young jail mate. A point confirmed to the audience almost immediately when Green introduces Dillinger to his fellow gang members, including Kirk Otto (Elisha Cook, Jr.), who spits judgmentally in his direction and, when Dillinger leaves, calls him a "fresh punk." "He'll learn," says Green. "The hard way," says another. "I think the kid has possibilities," says Green, concluding the scene. Without knowledge of the word's etymology "punk " is used in this context as little more than a means to demean Dillinger the neophyte; he has yet to earn his reputation, but if an audience has any knowledge of prison slang then the dialogue becomes overly ripe in its sexual inference, adding much to the film's tale of criminal deviancy.

The somewhat indeterminate meaning in the use of "punk" to help indicate a concealed sexual aspect of deviancy among the criminal classes can be found in other forms of popular culture. In *Rip Kirby*, for example, an effeminate underworld character, Boom Boom, who is twice referred to as a "punk," is also called a "perfumed little maggot!"[41] Similarly suggestive of sexual deviancy is the camp performance by Mark Rydell, in Don Siegel's JD pix *Crime in the Streets* (1956), who, alongside Sal Mineo, plays sidekick to John Cassavettes' street punk, and who, in the course of the film, shuns all female attention. This tacit play with "punk's" homosexual association is made explicit in a 1958 pulp paperback by William R. Cox, *Hell to Pay*, in which a gambler is caught in a war between the syndicate and a gang of punk hoodlums in leather jackets with high-combed greased hair, high on marijuana and the "Big H." "They're hopped-up punks, at war with the syndicate —and they kill, just for kicks"—is how the cover's tag line describes the story's premise. At the close, the gambler discovers that one of his errand boys, Little Skinny, has sold him out to the gang's leader. He witnesses the two punks "fawning" over each other and smelt "lavender." Little Skinny, he is "shocked" to discover, is a "deviate." With gangs of young punks going head to head with the syndicate, the gambler is a witness to a "social revolution" made up of "homosexual kids in a world of switchknives and marihuana."[42]

FIGURE 10: Cover of the Signet paperback original of William R. Cox's *Hell to Pay.* This story of juvenile delinquents and the syndicate made explicit use of "punk" as an idiom for a young homosexual.

THE GANGSTER BIO-PIC CYCLE

The shared designation of "punk" to define delinquent juveniles of the 1950s and gangster hoodlums since the 1920s, the compact of crude environmental and psychological means to explain their deviancy, the exploitation of shock and sensation to sell these films, the lack of interest in historical authenticity and verisimilitude, and the dependence upon convention in the telling of these tales produced a formulaic, standardized, product, where differences in temporal settings are little more than superficial appeals to novelty: this ensures that even in their historical guise the films, which form the gangster bio-pic cycle, are topical. Not only because they were part of a broad discursive contemporary fascination with crime, but because they were also conceived as sensational fictions tied to the exploitation of everyday headlines, albeit ostensibly reworked as history.

Mapping the repetitions, overlaps and fusions that form the associations that link the individual films within the cycle and in turn the liaisons and connections between various cycles of crime fictions in this period helps to produce a better understanding of film production trends than can be achieved by traditional genre analysis, because cycles are inherently temporal while genres tend to be conceived as a-historical. Conceiving of films in terms of genres too often means conceptualizing films as belonging to exclusive fixed groupings. The concept of cycles, however, allows for both the recognition and identification of films with shared characteristics, and also allows the scholar to see how a cycle merges and blends with other cycles. The scholar thus becomes interested in film's inherent seriality, indeed, its commonality with other films, and therefore less with any given film's apparent uniqueness. The study of cycles often reveals uniqueness to be little more than a re-articulation of existent components, a shibboleth dedicated to the myth of originality and individual creative endeavor. But the shape, form, style and content of film do change over time and documenting and analysing cycles of films while being cognizant of shifts in social and cultural contexts, and in the production, distribution, exhibition and reception of films, can help account for these changes.

ENDNOTES

1. *Motion Picture Herald*, Product Digest Section (6 May 1961): 276.
2. *Variety* quotation used in advertising copy and press book for *Baby Face Nelson* (6 November 1957): 6.
3. For a history of the television series and a episode guide, see Tise Vahimagi, *The Untouchables* (London: British film Institute, 1998).
4. See for example *Stag Magazine*, Vol. 9, No. 5 (May, 1958), which includes "THE FBI'S DEATH DUEL WITH BABY FACE NELSON," or *Amazing Detective Cases* (December, 1958) featuring "Vince 'Mad Dog' Coll. The killer who killed for kicks," "Free Love Ladies of Murder Inc.," "The Amazing Saga of a Renegade G Man," and "The Spider Spins a Noose." For an illustrated, anecdotal, history of men's magazines see, Adam Parfrey, ed., *It's A Man's*

World: Men's Adventure Magazines, the Postwar Pulps (Los Angeles: Feral House, 2003).

5. David Hadju, *The Ten-Cent Plague: The Great Comic Book Scare and How It Changed America* (New York: Farrar, Straus, Giroux, 2008).

6. Mike Benton, *The Illustrated History of Crime Comics* (Dallas: Taylor Publishing, 1993).

7. On the PCAs' attempt to distinguish between representations of legendary, historical and contemporary criminals see, Peter Stanfield, *Hollywood, Westerns and the 1930s: The Lost Trail* (Exeter: University fo Exeter Press, 2001), 183–85.

8. *The Hollywood Reporter* (3 July 1958): 3. In preproduction the film had been called *Lady with a Gun* and *Tommy Gun Connie. The Hollywood Reporter* (6 March 1958): 4.

9. *The Hollywood Reporter* (21 January 1958): 3.

10. Both play their parts by producing an over fabricated supplication in appealing for understanding or trust from others. In its excess, this pretence reveals rather than hides their true psychotic personalities.

11. For a guided tour of movie gangland's most memorable mug shots see Ian & Elizabeth Cameron, *Heavies* (London: Studio Vista, 1967).

12. Carlos Clarens, *Crime Movies: An Illustrated History* (New York: Norton, 1980), 189.

13. Even the notes on the back sleeve of the tie-in soundtrack album promoted the sensational: "A word about the picture. Mickey Rooney is 'Baby Face Nelson.' He is. But only for the film. Carolyn Jones is the 'chick.' Mmmmmmmmmmm. Sir Cedric Hardwick is the 'Doc.' Wow! The original story was written by Irving Shulman. He collaborated with Daniel Mainwaring on the screen treatment. Al Zimbalist was the producer. The picture was directed by Don Siegel. It's gutsy."

14. Will Straw, "Urban Confidential: The Lurid City of the 1950s." In David B. Clarke, ed., *The Cinematic City* (London: Routledge, 1997), 113.

15. *Motion Picture Herald*, Product Digest Section (3 October 1959): 437.

16. *The Hollywood Reporter* (6 November 1957): 3.

17. *New York Times*, 12 December 1957, 35.

18. *Motion Picture Herald*, Product Digest Section (25 June 1960): 749.

19. Jack Moffitt, *The Hollywood Reporter* (3 July 1958): 3.

20. Esther Sonnet & Peter Stanfield, " 'Good Evening, Gentleman, Can I Check Your Hats Please?': Masculinity, Dress and the Retro Gangster Cycles of the 1990s," Lee Grieveson, Esther Sonnet, & Peter Stanfield, eds., *Mob Culture: Hidden Histories of American the Gangster Film* (New York: Rutgers University Press, 2005), 182.

21. *Harrison's Reports* (9 January 1960): 6.

22. *Motion Picture Herald*, Product Digest Section (January 16, 1960): 557.

23. Richard Maltby, "Why Boys Go Wrong: Gangsters, Hoodlums, and the Natural History of Delinquent Careers." In Grieveson, et al. (2005), 41–66.

24. *Motion Picture Herald*, Product Digest Section (23 January 1960): 565.

25. "The Last Mile," *Motion Picture Herald* (31 January 1959): 433.

26. *Motion Picture Herald*, Product Digest Section, (9 November 1957): 593.

27. *Motion Picture Herald* (12 July 1958): 905.

28. *The Hollywood Reporter* (6 November 1957): 3.

29. Straw (1997), 119.

30. Ibid.

31. Jean-Luc Godard, "La Photo du mois" *Cahiers du Cinema*, No. 92 (February 1959), reprinted in translation in Jim Hillier, ed., *Cahiers du Cinema: The 1950s —Neo Realism, Hollywood, New Wave* (Cambridge, MA: Harvard, 1985), 51.

32. Geoffrey O'Brien, "In Cold Blood," *Film Comment* (May-June, 2006), 22–3.

33. *New York Times*, 12 December 1957, 35.

34. *Harrison's Reports* (30 January 1960): 18.

35. *Terry and the Pirates*, by Milton Caniff ran from 1934-46. The complete strips have been reprinted in six volumes by The Library of American Comics, published by IDW (San Diego). The same company is also reprinting the complete Dick Tracy strips.

36. The dictionary defines a "gangster" as a "member of a gang of roughs, gun-men or the like." *Funk & Wagnall's New Practical Standard Dictionary* (New York: Funk & Wagnall, 1946).

37. The strips are reproduced in Alex Raymond, *Rip Kirby 1946–1948* (San Diego: The Library of American Comics, IDW Publishing, 2009), 71, 72, 77, 100, 115, 141, 142.

38. In a November 1st, 1939 memorandum on profanity and vulgarity in films, produced by the PCA following discussions engendered by the use of "damn" in *Gone with the Wind*, a list of proscribed words is produced with an indication in which territory the word is particularly problematic. I am grateful to Richard Maltby for sharing this document with me. For a wider discussion of the British censors' influence on the PCA, see Ruth Vasey, *The World According to Hollywood, 1918-1939* (Exeter: University of Exeter Press, 1997).

39. See the *Oxford English Dictionary* for the word's etymology. The English use of punk for pimp was provided by my father-in-law, Ron Sonnet, who recalls it being used this way in Portsmouth in the 1940s and 1950s. The OED lists

"punkateroo," a vulgar compound of "punk" with the Spanish "muleteer," as a procurer of prostitutes.

40. For a revealing discussion of the confusion over the use of "gunsel" see, Gaylyn Studlar, "A Gunsel is Being Beaten: Gangster Masculinity and the Homoerotics of the Crime Film, 1941–1942." In Grieveson, et al. (2005), 120–145.

41. Raymond (2009), 110.

42. William R. Cox, *Hell to Pay* (New York: Signet, 1958), 119–21.

CHAPTER 7

IMPORTING EVIL: THE AMERICAN GANGSTER, SWEDISH CINEMA, AND ANTI-AMERICAN PROPAGANDA

ANN-KRISTIN WALLENGREN

The story in brief: On the run from his past, an American racketeer of Swedish descent, Glenn Mortensen, moves into a small town in southern Sweden together with his gang. Restless and anxious to keep his talents from rusting, he starts an evangelical crusade, a con game, a hustle with a contemporary twist. He starts a campaign in the shape of an American revival show in order to disseminate the Swedish model of democracy throughout the world. This is however only a façade, and in reality, Mortensen is a rapist and a murderer. He is reckless, vicious, and charmingly malevolent. Few can see through him, and those who do are terrified and desperate to stop him. In the end, an old communist and revolutionary and his grandson take up arms against the gangster. (This synopsis is a combination of the English and the Swedish programs published by the Sandrews production company in Sweden).

When *The Gangster Film* (*Gangsterfilmen*) premiered in Stockholm in 1974, it flopped hard at the box office, and the film was very rapidly taken out of distribution. In 1975, the film was retitled as *A Stranger Came by Train* but also failed to achieve any success. Despite this, it was designated as Sweden's entry to the Berlin Film festival in that year. The only country where the film was able to attract an audience and achieve some measure of success was Poland.[1]

216

VIOLENCE AND THE SWEDISH IDYLL

The film's director, Lars G. Thelestam, stated in several newspaper interviews that his intention in the film was to explore what might happen if violence and fascism came to Sweden, and how Swedes might react when confronting such a threat. In his film, he claimed, he also wanted to explore the issue of democracy, and to raise the question of whether a liberal democracy was strong enough to withstand the threat of totalitarianism. In interviews, one argument he voiced was that democratic methods were inadequate against the threat of fascism and violence, citing the example of Salvador Allende's Chile. He argued that it was impossible to meet violence without violence, and that the Swedish welfare state was incapable of protecting itself against the kind of ideology that Glenn Mortensson, the gangster, represented.[2] The idyllic Swedish village and its inhabitants in the film are seen as "good" people, whereas Mortenson and his gang are shown to be deceptively "evil." Thus traditional Swedish virtue is contrasted with foreign vice and malice, and this is distinctly portrayed in the scene where Mortenson arrives at the little village. Here the village band plays an emblematic Swedish rhapsody by the composer Hugo Alfvén (*A Midsummer Vigil*), which contrasts sharply with the jazz music heard so far in the film.

Film critics more or less agreed that the film was competently made, with more action than usual in Swedish films, and that the acting was generally good, but that the central conflict between good and evil was too simplistic, and that the political message was overdone. Some critics found that the film was entertaining, while one reviewer commented that the arrival of the gangsters by train to the Swedish village was like a group of Mickey Spillane gangsters arriving at Moomin Valley.[3] Another critic compared the film to a greyhound bus that had lost its way and mistakenly ended up in southern Sweden.[4] Another influential critic pointed out that it was hard to understand what kind of criminal racket Mortenson was involved in, and how he expected to make any money in Sweden.[5]

Variety wrote that the theme was an attractive idea, but that the portrayal of the gangster as a psychopath, a mere rapist, undermined this theme.[6] One Swedish left-wing newspaper panned the film, although another interpreted the gangster as a symbol for the corrupt and imperialistic economic system of the U.S.[7] Indeed, there is good reason to interpret the film as not about evil in some metaphysical sense, nor about totalitarism generally. Instead, the film reflected a then widely-held Swedish view of the evils of American cultural and political imperialism, as Thelestam himself made explicit in at least one press interview.[8] In spite of the avowed political agenda of the movie, however, very few of the critics discussed the political message in any detail. From a wider perspective, the fact that Thelestam was a socialist and one of the actors a committed communist only partly explains the anti-American propaganda of the film.[9] Rather, the film might better be seen as just one of many manifestations of anti-Americanism in Sweden, an anti-Americanism that has had a long history but nevertheless reached new heights in the 1970s during the Vietnam War.

Ironically, however, the same film also reveals a fascination with things American, not least in the explicit construction of the film as a classic western, complete with a cruel villain who terrifies a town, and a "sheriff" who tries to stand up to him.[10] However, at the same time, the film avoids glamorizing violence, and uses handheld cameras in the fight scenes.[11] All in all, Thelestam's film betrays a certain ambivalence towards American culture, an ambivalence that has had a long tradition in Sweden over the past two hundred years or so.

FEAR OF AMERICANIZATION

Swedish apprehension about the U.S. has risen and fallen over the last two centuries, in relation to Swedish perceptions of American society, and Swedish perceptions of U.S. history and development. Issues such as racial politics and the Vietnam War tended to dominate the 1960s and 1970s, but the Swedish fear of Americanization can be traced back much further, and because of the impact of Hollywood on European cinema market, film has long been regarded as one the most important channels of American cultural influence.[12] Hollywood represented, and still represents, what Swedes regard as the negative aspects of America—bad taste, commercialism, immaturity, materialism, shallowness, violence, vulgarity, etc., all of which tends to surface in *The Gangster Film*.

At the same time however, America has often held a positive allure, and the American dream has had a long history in Sweden. As a number of scholars have noted, in part, the dream originated in Enlightenment thought, and America came to be seen as a land of political freedom and

FIGURE 1: Showtime for the American gangster in Sweden.
1974 Svenska Filminstitutet/Swedish Film Institute.

opportunity.[13] America was the country of the future, and, during the nineteenth and the beginning of the twentieth century, emigrants headed for a society that was synonymous with equality, freedom, individual opportunity, industrial optimism, organization, and technology.[14]

What, then, is meant by the term "Americanization" in this context? Today, as the Swedish historian Martin Alm claims, the term implies a wide range of ideas, symbols and values, and this is how I use the term here.[15] By the end of the 1910s, the term Americanization was firmly established, denoting "a political, a commercial, an aesthetic, and a moral issue where American society and American culture became synonymous references."[16] Attitudes towards America and Americanization were strongly linked to ideas about modernization, which supposedly was characterized by "mass culture," and where thus film played a significant role. From the European perspective, the American cinema has typically been regarded as overly commercial, mass-produced, and profit-driven, and consequently as a threat to European (and Swedish) film production, which has rarely achieved the popularity of American motion pictures.

219

HOLLYWOOD MASCULINITY

The cinema as an important conduit of values and norms was a natural arena for staging popular conceptions of America, and Swedish film was not late in picking up influential iconic figures and figurations as well as emblematic images from Hollywood movies. The way the Hollywood icons are used through ninety years has been almost exclusively a male affair. When a Swede dreams about the big wide world through Hollywood icons, male identity is often at stake. These male icons have been used for different purposes: as an escape from the everyday, as a target for deconstruction, or as a mask to hide sexual identity. The issue is nevertheless male identity. It always ends the same way, however—the bubble bursts, and it becomes obvious that the Hollywood ideal is not useful for Swedish everyday culture. Still, the negotiation in Swedish cinema over these icons is a symptom of a fascination with Hollywood culture.

When Swedish cinema has used iconic or common images there has almost always been a transformation, no matter the prevailing ideological opinion. The icons and images are taken out of their proper surroundings and transformed into comic features. One Swedish film scholar explains this transformation as a procedure he called "the funny mirror." A small country is forced to transform its underdog position into a comic national virtue, as a means of balancing its relationship with the U.S.[17] This interpretation is probably true, but a further explanation might be found more precisely in the genre of comedy itself. Comedy has been seen as "serving a useful social and psychological function in that it is an arena, or provides an arena, where repressed tensions can be released in a safe manner" as Susan Hayward explains in *Cinema Studies*.[18] Discussions of race and national prejudices are common subjects for comedy, and the Swedish fascination for America has repeatedly found expression in comedy. Male icons from Hollywood may be interpreted in similar fashion. The fascination is there, but the ordinary (Swedish) man is not able to live up to the ideal, and instead turns to irony and satire as a strategy for self-defence.

Throughout the twentieth century, the gangster became an emblem of America in Swedish film, and arguably the most important Hollywood icon for the Swedish cinema. The image of the visiting American gangster in Swedish cinema is a kind of prism through which to study the shifting view or apprehension of the U.S.: from the more naïve fascination and the comic treatment in the 1930s, over the genre imitation or transformation in the 1950s to the pronounced criticism of the 1970s. Here, it is also significant that Swedish films have frequently portrayed the criminal as a "foreigner," from outside Sweden or the Nordic region. Criminals and gangsters are often associated with America, and are thus—in Swedish eyes—cultural transgressors by birth. In *The Gangster Film*, Mortenson is not only an American, but a Swedish-American, while another of his gang also comes from Sweden, and his bodyguard is African-American. In the evangelical show they stage in the village, one theme is that Glenn Mortensson has come home at last, even if he has brought an American flag with him.

GANGSTERS AND SWEDISH-AMERICA

Interestingly enough, from the 1920s to the 1960s, Swedish perceptions of the U.S. were often expressed through cinematic representations of the experiences of Swedish-Americans. In the decades before the 1920s, anti-emigration propaganda in Sweden also produced films telling of the dangers of America. Emigration to America in the late nineteenth century and early twentieth century had a major impact on Swedish society, when, over a period of eighty years, twenty per cent of the population left for America.[19] In 1907, the National Society against Emigration was founded, and several silent propaganda films were produced depicting the U.S. as dangerous place for naïve Swedish immigrants.[20] In these films, the immigrants met with misfortune, often at the hands of American criminals. Sometimes, immigrants died, sometimes they were forced to return to Sweden, and sometimes they even became criminals themselves. In the Swedish anti-emigration film *The Emigrant* (also named *The Amulet, Emigrant/Amuletten*) from 1910, a man emigrates to America. As soon as he arrives in the U.S., he is taken into a bar where crooks and prostitutes drink and play cards, Americans are thieves and bandits, African-Americans are shoe shiners and servants, and Jews are loan sharks.

The similarities to *The Gangster Film* are rather striking, despite the time span of sixty-five years. There are three men in the gang, and the African-American in *The Emigrant* is portrayed in similar fashion to his black brother in *The Gangster Film*. The 1910 movie was however never released and thus had no impact on the debate. The appeal of Hollywood in Sweden grew throughout the 1920s and 1930s. The general admiration for Hollywood film stars was still a source of concern to some critics, who argued that American films glorified crime and criminals, and that the exuberant settings of the Hollywood cinema provided a distorted view of life.[21]

American dollars occasionally appear in Swedish films, particularly in the 1930s, often with villainous Swedish-Americans delivering the money, as in the 1938 comedy, *Dollar*, where anti-Americanism reached new heights. *Dollar*, was based on renowned author Hjalmar Bergman's play of the same name, though Bergman's dystopian view of the U.S. may have been influenced by his own unsuccessful stint as a Hollywood screenwriter in the mid-20s. In other films like *Living in Clover* (*Livet på en pinne*, 1942) or *Never with My Jemmy* (*Aldrig med min kofot*, 1954), visiting criminals, or at least shady characters, from America dominate the action. These popular comedies derived their appeal from the Swedish fascination with gangsters, and through such films the gangster movie emerged as metonymic for the American culture as a whole. When the comedy film *Fun with Boccaccio* (*Lattjo med Boccaccio*, 1949) ends, it has three alternative endings, one American, one French, and one Swedish. The American ending features a scene of decadence with jazz music, men in fedoras and Stetsons, and women in revealing dresses. Everyone is drinking and smoking, and then someone breaks into the scene and starts shooting. The French and Swedish endings are equally stereotypical, with the French one featuring jealous love scene in a bedroom, and the Swedish version a folkloric ending. In the 1950s, Swedish film companies adopted the gangster film genre in the shape of detective films with a Swedish setting. Such suggestively titled films as *Hidden in the Fog* (*I dimma dold*, 1953), *The Stranger from the Sky* (*Främlingen från skyn*, 1956) and *The Lady in Black* (*Damen i svart*, 1958) tried to attract audiences, with varying levels of success.

Hollywood icons, however, continued to influence the Swedish imagination in the 1960s and 1970s, despite growing criticism of American political tendencies at that time. The Vietnam War changed the image of America in the world, and in Sweden. In the 1960s, the Swedish welfare state was at its peak, and Swedish politicians often presented themselves as the keepers of the moral conscience of the world. Several films, particularly dramas or semi-documentaries, mirrored this position, and featured mostly African-American Vietnam War deserters seeking asylum in Sweden, as well as African-American musicians preferring a life in Sweden with Swedish women to life on the frontline in the war against communism. In much of the Swedish media, America was by now regarded as a disreputable nation of crooks, racists, and spoiled consumers living in sprawling and polluted cities. This was also how some 1970s and 1980s educational programmes in Swedish public service television depicted the U.S.[22]

By the time of *The Gangster Film* in 1975, the gangster was no longer the enthralling mythic person from the big wide world or a transformed icon in a comedy. Instead, he now comes to Sweden and only spreads evil, as a number of characters in *The Gangster Film* point out. Thelestam's film thus presents a very obvious form of anti-American propaganda, which is highly characteristic of that particular period of Swedish domestic history.

GLENN MORTENSEN AS EVIL FOREIGNER

Glenn Mortensen is characterized through various signs that make him foreign, American and "gangster-like" in this Swedish film. He is flashily dressed with white shoes and sunglasses, and sports a ring on his little finger and a chain around his neck. He usually has a drink in his hand, and his violence regularly erupts abruptly.

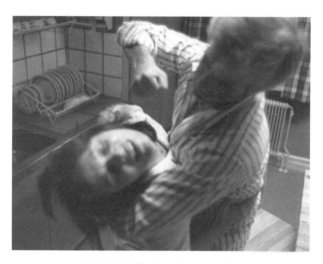

FIGURE 2: The American as rapist.
1974 Svenska Filminstitutet/Swedish Film Institute.

Glenn Mortensen is evil because he comes from America, even if the police assistant explains his violence as emanating from "homosexual tendencies," which was apparently a vice that could also be ascribed to Americans, at least from a 1970s Swedish perspective. His violence is most dramatic when manifested through rape, suggesting, symbolically and heavy-handedly, that American culture and politics threatened the rape of Swedish people and society.

Thelestam said at the time that he wanted to depict the battle be-tween good and evil, with the good apparently depicted by the Swedish people in the film. However, the "goodness" of the villagers is not entirely unproblematic, as the chief of police fails to stand up to Mortensen him-self, and finally resorts to encouraging the veteran revolutionary Carl to shoot the gangster, with the support of his grandson. No-one else puts up a fight against the gangster, and even if Thelestam himself described the ending as "improbable," he was satisfied with seeing the old revolu-tionary passing over his gun to the younger generation.[23] Thelestam also asserted that, in his view, democratic methods were not enough to stop fascism, and that violence must be met with violence. Perhaps it was a sign of the times that the Swedish Film Institute chose to support a film so heavily-laden with anti-American propaganda and an explicitly left-wing ideology.

In a press article after the completion of the film, based on an inter-view with the director Lars Thelestam and the actor Clu Gulager, who played Glenn Mortensen, the writer records the praise of director and ac-tor for each other.[24] Gulager saw Thelestam as a new Fellini, and Theles-tam compared Gulager to Dustin Hoffman. Such grandiose assessments of each other's talents were not fulfilled by subsequent events. Gulager continued his career by making 'B' movies, mostly for television, while Thelestam made only one other feature film after 1974. Nevertheless, *The Gangster Film* provided Thelestam with a singular cinematic legacy, and no Swedish films have given expression to such an explicit and obvious anti-American ideology since that time.

ENDNOTES

1. "Succé i Polen för Gangsterfilmen," *Kvällsposten,* 13 September 1975, 13.
2. For example, "En USA-gangster kom till Sverige," *Dala-Demokraten,* 28 October 1974, 6; "Samhällsdebatt utan pekpinnar—så vill Thelestam göra film," *Göteborgs-Posten,* 27 October 1974, 37.
3. "Mickey Spillane i Mumindalen...," *Svenska Dagbladet,* 29 October 1974, 13.
4. "En ovanlig regidebutant som lyckas långa stycken," *Expressen,* 29 October 1974, 28.
5. "En splittrad regidebut," *Sydsvenska Dagbladet,* 29 October 1974, 10.
6. "Gangsterfilmen (The Gangster Movie)," review, *Variety,* 1 November 1974, 9.

7. Negative review in *Arbetaren,* 22 November 1974, 10, "Gangsterfilmen." Positive review in *Arbetarbladet,* 28 November 1974, 9, "Svenska gangsterfilmen: Friskt vågat, hälften vunnet."

8. "Spännande yta djupt innehåll," *Dagens Nyheter,* 19 April 1974, 9.

9. "Roligare när jag kan komma frivilligt," *Göteborgs-Posten,* 21 April 1974, 37.

10. "Publiken ska skratta och rysa," *Expressen,* 27 October 1974, 38.

11. "Samhällsdebatt utan pekpinnar—så vill Thelestam göra film."

12. Martin Alm, *Americanitis: Amerika som sjukdom eller läkemedel: svenska berättelser om USA åren 1900–1939,* (Lund: Nordic Academic Press, 2002).

13. Birgitta Steene, "The Swedish Image of America." In Poul Houe and Sven Hakon Rossel, eds., *Images of America in Scandinavia* (Amsterdam, Atlanta, GA: Rodopi, 1998), 145–192; and Tom O'Dell, *Culture Unbound: Americanization and Everyday Life in Sweden* (Diss. Lund University, 1998).

14. Alm.

15. Ibid.

16. Steene, 174.

17. Olle Sjögren, "Det blågula stjärnbaneret. Om amerikanska smältbilder i svensk film" ["The Swedish Star-Spangled Banner: An Essay on Blended Images in Film."] In Rolf Lundén and Erik Åsard, eds., *Networks of Americanization: Aspects of the American Influence in Sweden* (Uppsala: Uppsala universitet, 1992), 130–161.

18. Susan Hayward, *Cinema Studies. The Key Concepts* (London and New York: Routledge, 2003).

19. H. Arnold Barton, "A Heritage to Celebrate: Swedes in America, 1846–1996." In *Scandinavian Review,* Vol. 84, No. 2 (Autumn 1996): 4–10.

20. Some of these films are discussed by Marina Dahlquist, "Teaching Citizenship via Celluloid", in Richard Abel, Giorgio Bertellini, and Rob King, eds., *Early Cinema and the 'National,'* (New Barnet: John Libbey Publishing, 2008), 118–132.

21. Alm.

22. Ann-Kristin Wallengren, "Samhällsbyggarnas tv-undervisning. Estetik och ideologi i utbildningsprogram för televisionen" ["Television Teaching by the Builders of Modern Society. Aesthetics and Ideology in Educational Programmes for Television."] In Ann-Kristin Wallengren and Cecilia Wadensjö, *Om tilltal, bildspråk och samhällssyn i utbildningsprogrammen* (Stockholm: Stiftelsen Etermedierna i Sverige, 2001), 19–125.

23. " 'Gangsterfilmen' fellanserad i Sverige," *Svenska Dagbladet,* 2 July 1975, 9.

24. "Gulager lanseras för gangsterfilm," *Dagens Nyheter,* 28 June 1974, 10.

PART 3

AMERICAN DREAMS/
AMERICAN NIGHTMARES

CHAPTER 8

SUN YU AND THE EARLY AMERICANIZATION OF CHINESE CINEMA

CORRADO NERI

ONE OF THE most frequent remarks made in discussions of contemporary Chinese cinema is that it is "Americanized," or "Hollywood-like." This usually implies a slight disdain for Hollywood cinema, or an over-evaluation of the supposed "originality" of Chinese cinema. Commentators tend to think that this "Americanization" is, at best, an imitation of Western models as regards narrative, structure, and aesthetics, and, at worst, a betrayal of China's most authentic "traditional" values. Of course, what is actually meant by "American" or "Hollywood" is highly debatable. For the most part, these critics are implying that recent Chinese film is commercial (which is also a highly debatable term), genre-oriented, formulaic, opulent and ostentatious, predictable, market-oriented, and a vehicle for the star system—not to mention other characteristics of the film industry that cinema historians have been describing and debating since the very beginning of cinema studies. One example is the relevance of orchestral music and its profound effects on reception, emotional impact, and ideology.

In his encyclopedic history of Japanese cinema, Tadao Sato argues that the western-style orchestral music was a characteristic of all successful movies of the silent era in Japan, when the orchestra played live in front of the screen.[1] At the same time, traditional Japanese music was considered to be vulgar, and survived only in popular festivities. This was also true in China[2], where piano and violins gradually gained more popularity than traditional music on the burgeoning middle class's entertainment scale. Formulaic rhetorical music devices still find their place in most contemporary Chinese and Japanese productions—the yearning piano solo that accompanies a parting couple, forceful violins that signal heightening emotion, and so forth. The Hollywood model (in both its mass appeal and its industrial organization) surely continues to seduce contemporary film producers and audiences in China.

Yet, it is important to remember that this is nothing new. Cinema was imported to the "Orient" as a foreign good, both as a technique and as an art, a science, as well as a window on the uncanny "West." It is amply documented that in China (and in the Far East in general), the public was eager to see western movies, particularly Hollywood films, in the first few decades of the 20th century. Citing an American study published in 1938, Laikwan Pang reports that in 1936 "among all films shown in China, only 12 percent of them were local productions, yet American films comprised more than 80 percent, and Soviet movies represented a mere 2.4 percent."[3] Popular taste was enthusiastic about and modeled by Hollywood production, often claiming disdain for local creations, dismissing them as vulgar, technically inferior, and less daring. When sympathetic with the Maoist revolution, later scholars harshly criticized the dominance of Hollywood movies and their supposed brainwashing effects on the public. Regis Bergeron, for example, condemns all American films available in China, claiming that they serve as a means to colonize the imagination of the Chinese people and to divert the revolutionary production into light entertainment. Bergeron notes, not without disdain, that China had not only produced its own versions of Laurel and Hardy, but also versions of Charlie Chaplin—as regards the latter, arguably without the disruptive energy and the harsh critique of the status quo typical of Chaplin.[4]

If on the one hand, popular taste tended to indulge in treacherous Occidentalism,[5] on the other hand, filmmakers were more ambivalent. During the 1920s and 30s, the Soviet model was popular among intellectuals in China owing to translations of Soviet theories, the screening of movies directed by Vsevolod Pudovkin and Dziga Vertov, and a much celebrated séance introducing the *Battleship Potemkin* in 1926 (Sergei Eisenstein, 1925); note that this screening was not public, but limited to a select list of cinematographers and intellectuals. While the impact of the *Battleship Potemkin*'s visual force was arguably remarkable on a few politically committed artist and journalists, the practice of Eisenstein-like montage was nevertheless seldom utilized in a context where, in the first place, left-wing parties were repressed and censored and, secondly, cinema had to depend heavily on public recognition in order to survive. Laikwan Pang has written about the contrasts between Hollywood and Soviet models in pre-1949 Chinese cinema:

> The real impact of Soviet Cinema to the Chinese one was restricted to a symbolic level. In fact, Chinese spectators at the time only watched a handful of Soviet productions, far fewer then the Hollywood films. Soviet films were not allowed to be shown in China in the 1920s because the Chinese government refused to acknowledge the Bolshevik revolution and the legitimacy of the new socialist state. [...] While Chinese spectators most of the time favor those stories full of antagonist struggles on the semantic level of plot, they enjoy continuity and clarity on the syntactic level. If [...] 'conflict' structured many Chinese films beginning in the 1930s, this notion of conflict was definitely more 'melodramatic' than 'montage,' refers more to the content than to the form. That is to say, Chinese films in the 1930s were highly aware of using conflicts, which correspond, however, more to the emotional confrontation within the story than to the Soviet montage designed for intellectual enlightenment.[6]

Chinese (or maybe Shanghainese) cinema was struggling at the time between commercial and political models. These categories, even if imprecise and overlapping, were discussed at that time by theoreticians, filmmakers, critics, journalists, audiences, and writers. By analyzing articles published in the newspapers and magazines, and more intellectual studies on the (relatively) new art form, it is evident that national cinema was trying to emulate Hollywood dominance in this field. Widespread dislike of national cinema was taken for granted—the most immediate example that comes to mind is Lu Xun 鲁迅 (1881–1936), considered to be the father of modern Chinese literature. Being a writer who was extremely concerned about the nation's future, one would expect that he would have endorsed local production. Yet, we discover from his diaries that he almost exclusively watched and enjoyed American movies.[7]

Although national cinema (a slippery term, within the context of a rapidly changing political situation like the Chinese one at the beginning of the 19th century) was not being ignored, it was sometimes difficult to differentiate between the "local" and the westernized cinematographic models; cinematographers, script writers and critics periodically argued over the necessity to endorse and sustain their national cinema in the face of the colonial cultural dominance of the western model. However, this was much more closely related to production values and content ethics than it was to form or style. Producers and investors had to survive without state subsidies (unlike post-revolution Russia); many of them found it more lucrative to speculate on fluctuations of the market, by buying and selling equipment (including the very film itself) and studio proprieties, rather than invest in the high-risk enterprise of moving pictures.

On the other hand, in the eyes of progressive filmmakers, the ultimate goal was the engagement of all citizens, a coming to consciousness that would ultimately lead to radical changes in society and politics. Thus the most "Chinese/traditional" productions (those related to popular entertainment like the *wuxiapian*/martial movies and the opera film) were loved by the public, but rejected by the intelligentsia and pioneer filmmakers as a suspicious—if not despicable—remainder from feudal times. Yet even the more leftist productions, later acclaimed by official historiography as the seeds of the new revolutionary consciousness in cinema, needed public recognition, box office response, as well as a safe way through censorship's control. The most practiced way to reach public acclaim and to spread modernist and democratic values was through melodrama. As a "new" genre, indebted to western romantic and popular literature, Ibsen's theater, Beethoven's symphonies and of course, Hollywood "Griffithiana," melodramatic cinema was—in the late twenties and thirties—already a largely global language. Many critics had argued that melodrama was one or *the* principal characteristic of Chinese cinema in general.[8] Others tried to redefine this idea using different concepts, such as the concept of the "vernacular." Zhang Zhen writes:

> In grafting cinema studies onto the social and experiential body of a modernizing vernacular culture in China, my primary concerns lie with the parallel and intertwining vernacular movement and Shanghai cinema. The latter manifests itself as a complex ramification of, contribution to, and intervention into the former. The vernacular here is configured as a cultural (linguistic, visual, sensory, and material) 'processor' that blends foreign and local, premodern and modern, high and low, cinematic and

other cultural ingredients to create a domestic product with cosmopolitan appeal. This processor—a worldly technology, a translation machine, and a cultural sensorium—allowed for different levels of mediation and forms of synthesis. It continually catered to and changed the local audiences' tastes, shaping and reshaping their worldviews. The cinema substantially fashioned China into something of a modern democratic society, and as such it imagined and configured new perceptions of the body, gender, and sexuality. These changes were exemplified by the first generation of screen actors and actresses and the cinematic renderings of the marginal heroine, the dandy, the revolutionary and the Modern Girl.[9]

What I intend to present here is a preliminary analysis on how part of the codes of Hollywood narrative cinema arrived in China and how these codes were developed to suit local standards. One of the most prominent movie makers of the golden age of Chinese cinema consciously and admittedly introduced Hollywood techniques, styles and aesthetics in national cinema, via a lyrical yet realistic, popular yet informed, consistent yet variegated cinematographic style. I am referring here to the pioneer director Sun Yu 孫瑜 (1900–1990). Zhou Binde, a professor of film studies at Fudan University in Shanghai, argues:

From a Chinese point of view, cinema is an 'imported item.' Traditional Chinese culture and cinema have no blood ties. During its one hundred years' history, Chinese cinema has always been swayed by European and American cinematographic traditions. We may argue that in China, cinema is the art form that has most prominently received European and American influx. [...] Among the various influences that have shaped Chinese cinema, the most profound and far-reaching comes from Hollywood. [...] Even if later few directors and scriptwriters were to receive a professional training like that of Hong Shen and Sun Yu, they did study playwriting and directing in the States. Therefore, for the most part, their theoretical knowledge and practical experience came from American culture, and their creative works could not completely free themselves of the unobtrusive influence of Hollywood. For example, in 1930 Sun Yu wrote and directed *Wild Flowers* for the Lianhua studio company. The film was inspired by the American film *Seventh Heaven*. Therefore, looking at the totality of Chinese cinema, we can argue that since 1920 very few movies have dealt with social problems, or reflected any progressive ideology.

However, many of them did convey a commercial awareness and an entertaining aspect because they had learned the lessons taught by the experience of the Hollywood industry. They were deeply 'Americanized.'[10]

I shall try to demonstrate by means of a textual analysis how Sun Yu contributed substantially to the globalization of this language—or "Americanization"—if we consider Hollywood a synonym for "American," and the Hollywood mode of production, a transcultural endeavor based on a collage of expertise, as well as a vertical, assembly-line production process. I argue that this director was to have a seminal influence, albeit subterranean and undeclared, on Chinese cinema to come. The main feature introduced by Sun Yu in Chinese cinema consists of a technical quality that I can only describe as "realism," vague as this may seem: a specific form of realism: poetic, ideological, revolutionary and romantic, or perhaps even "critical realism," marked by a special "fluidity."[11]

How many adjectives to define Sun's peculiar "realism"! I am very well aware that there is no one "realism." Every culture, epoch, historical moment has its own notion of realism, as David Bordwell and Kristin Thompson demonstrate:

> Notions of realism vary across cultures, through time, and even among individuals. [...] Moreover, realism has become one of the most problematic issues in the philosophy of art [...] It is better, then, to examine the *functions* of mise-en-scene than to dismiss this or that element that happens not to match our conception of realism.[12]

As an ideal reply, we may recall here the words of Laikwan Pang: "I insist that there was a specific realist approach, although the critics/filmmakers failed to define it themselves, that was adopted and evolved in this cinema [early Chinese production, during the twenties and thirties], most significantly marking the uniqueness and achievement of this cinema in aesthetic terms."[13] The uniqueness of this realism is described as follows: "This cinema often risks reason to celebrate and exploit emotions. While the classical Hollywood cinema 'created' realism by supplying causal motivation that addresses the viewer's psychology, this Chinese left-wing cinema made its own by soliciting its spectators' identification emotionally."[14]

Sun Yu is a pioneer who helped Chinese cinema "fight" Western cinema on its own ground, helping it find a large audience and develop a personal, challenging, original language, as well as its own mode or interpretation of "realism." As we have seen, the Hollywood influence on Chinese cinema was direct and well documented. I argue that this "influence" (I call it an influence for lack of a better way to put it) could also be seen as extremely positive for the development of Chinese cinema. It helped this cinema to find its own blend, its own distinctive characteristic (the definition of which is not within the scope of this essay) in a transnational, transcultural cinema culture that is also a characteristic of Hollywood itself.[15] At the same time, we have also mentioned a fighting spirit and the contradictions related to the perceived inferior position of China towards the "West." Sun Yu, as most of his colleagues, was struggling to obtain a place for Chinese cinema (and Nation), a maturity that would encourage audiences to watch local productions and engage in local struggles to empower the masses—or at the very least, its illuminated representatives. He writes:

When I was in Wisconsin, I often watched movies. But at that time, in some American films, Chinese people were all target of twisted and disqualifying misrepresentation, described as symbol of stupidity and treacherousness. To us, Chinese foreign students, this was the most difficult thing to accept. [. . .] In school, American classmates, boys and girls alike, were very intimate to me, sitting next to me and having pleasant discussions. But on the street, when I met them, especially girls classmates, due to racial discrimination, they did not find it appropriate to greet me with excessive sympathy, let alone walk with me.

我在威校讀書時也常看電影,但當時在一些美國電影裡,中國人都成了歪曲醜化的對象和陰險愚蠢的象徵,這是留美的中國學生最感難受的事了. [. . .] 在課堂里,美國男女同學和我親近雜坐交談,但在街上和他們相遇,特別是女同學,由於種族歧視的偏見,就不便過分親近地打招呼,更難得結伴同行了.

[Sun Yu, *Da lu zhi ge* 大路之歌 [Song of The Big Road], (Taibei, Yuanliu, 1990), 70–71]

Sun Yu was the only filmmaker at the time to complete his education in the States. After a period at Qinghua University in Beijing (where he studied theatre and literature), in 1923 he began his literary studies at the University of Wisconsin, where he remained for three years, and later graduated from the New York Institute of Photography. He also took evening classes at Columbia University (where he specialized in photography and film-making). Sun Yu was there during the "Roaring Twenties," when American cinema was crafting its global appeal. The influence of a solid traditional Chinese literary education, American-style filmmaking and first-hand experience in the New York of the Jazz Age mingle in his works and writings.[16] His most accomplished films include *Wild Rose* (*Ye meigui* 野玫瑰, 1932), *Daybreak* (*Tianming* 天明, 1933), *Little Toys* (*Xiao wanyi* 小玩藝, 1933), *Queen of Sports* (*Tiyu huanghou* 體育皇后, 1934), and *The Big Road* (*Da lu* 大路, 1935). Later, his famous and acclaimed *Life of Wu Xun* (*Wu Xun zhuan* 武訓傳, 1949) had the misfortune of being one of the first films to receive a direct and fierce critique from the *People's Daily*, signed by Mao Zedong himself, and which almost put an end to his career. He still managed to produce a few movies in the late fifties, but they were pale works of propaganda, lacking any creative tension. In his silent films, Sun Yu developed his own personal poetics, strongly influenced by his technical apprenticeship in the States and his practical experience as an avid moviegoer.

His was a vision, which, as the motto of the time was claiming, was able to use western techniques to express (embody) the Chinese soul. He became one of the most influential figures in Chinese cinema because despite what we may see as profoundly Americanized language, he managed to give voice to specific features and narratives of modern Chinese history. What Sun Yu brought back from New York was an idea of realism, a specific cinematic form of (historically determined) realism obtained through camera work and his direction of actors. He remained very much attracted to his country's social reality. He did not attempt to reproduce artificially the genre system—as others have before and after him, for example by creating a "Chinese horror movie,"[17] or later, a Chinese musical inspired by Broadway hits. Admittedly, Sun Yu was influenced by the works of King Vidor, F. W. Murnau, and D. W. Griffith, as he himself notes:

> When I was attending Nankai High School I became a movie fan. I watched many art films by the so-called 'father of the screen,' D.W. Griffith, like for example the subversive *Way Down East*, starring the drama star Lillian Gish; or *Broken Blossom*, that tells the story of a tragic love between a Western girl and a Chinese man; or *The Three Musketeers*, by Alexandre Dumas Père. I recall *The Four Horsemen of the Apocalypse*, about

234

the tragedy of World War 1. When I was attending Qinghua University, I subscribed by mail from the States the magazine Photoplay Writing which I read attentively after class. Since I became a 'movie fan,' I did not engage in the literary creation, as the comrade Mao Dun encouraged me to do.

我在南開中學讀書時早已迷上了電影,曾看了不少文藝性強的電影,如:號稱"美國銀之父"葛里菲斯(D.W.Griffith)導演,悲劇影星麗蓮吉許(Lilian Gish) 主演, 有反對建內容的" 賴婚" (Way Down East),中英青年愛情悲劇"殘花淚"(Broken Blossom),大仲嗎 (Alexandre Dumas Pere) 的"三劍顆" (The Three Musketeers). 還有歐戰悲劇"四騎士" (Four Horsmen of the Apocalypse, 1921) 等.在清華讀書時,我已從美國函購"電影編劇法" (Photoplay Writing)一書在課餘時鑽研學習.由於我"迷"上了電影,因此沒有走上矛盾同志鼓勵我從事文學創作的道路.

[Sun Yu, *Da lu zhi ge* 大路之歌 [Song of The Big Road], 62–63]

Besides the many evenings Sun Yu spent in cinema venues in the States, he and his colleagues also had a vast choice of Hollywood movies in China. Many sources (among which the previously cited scholarly works, as well as newspapers, novels, diaries and so on) acknowledge the release and popularity of comedies with Charlie Chaplin, Laurel and Hardy, and Buster Keaton. The movie experience was not limited to the actual screening, as it began well before and continued long after the actual showing via radio programs, advertisements, movie posters, and magazines, which all helped the public familiarize with the "western" way of life and the burgeoning star system. Regis Bergeron describes the culture shock induced by the public display of affection, particularly by the notorious "kissing scenes" that reportedly shocked the Chinese public.[18] Magazines and newspapers published enormous amounts of pictures related to the movies themselves and to the pantheon of the star system; magazines studied the mise en scène, the script and the technique of the most successful films, and translated western reviews. For example, *It Happened One Night* (Frank Capra, 1934) and *Crime and Punishment* (Joseph von Sternberg, 1935) received wide coverage in the Chinese press.[19] *Seventh Heaven* (Frank Borzage, 1927) was the direct inspiration for the classic *Street Angel* (*Malu tianshi* 馬路天使, Yuan Muzhi 袁牧之, 1937) in terms of style and especially plot. *Seventh Heaven* was also, as discussed above, the inspiration for a lost Sun Yu movie.

The Chinese urban public was exposed to Hollywood culture. Yet, arguably because of the first-hand experience and formal education he received in the States, Sun Yu developed his own particular language and went on to become one of the most influential figures in Chinese cinema. Earlier I mentioned the idea of "realism" as a personal view of sculpting time, the human body and nature, a view that managed to be deeply Americanized, and yet intensely local. By "Americanized" I am referring to some narrative techniques. These techniques (which I will discuss further on) make his plots more character-driven, readable, and engaged in a narrative form that outdistances his cinema from the "traditional Chinese narrative that favors abundant details and branch developments."[20] Sun Yu's idea of realism (I would say "poetic realism," but this term is usually used to refer to another current in French film history) remains very much attached to his homeland, to the representation of China, to China's struggle against imperialism, and to the exaltation of the beauty of the Chinese physique. What Sun Yu elaborates and develops is a specific form, which, of course, brings content along.

First, he re-creates the image of young people via an innovative use of camera work, shifting sensuously around actor's body. The realism of Sun Yu is made of great sensuality—obtained by the absence of evident artificiality. This is a paradox of cinema (often, of art in general): complexity and elaboration seem "natural." Sun Yu was one of the first directors to avoid the "grotesque" rendering of emotion, shifting away from a well-established theatrical tradition—the most evident example of which is the diva Hu Die, 胡蝶 (a.k.a. Butterfly Hu), who was indeed charming, but very much indebted to theatrical codes. Sun Yu recruited his actors not from established classical theater groups, but from dance troupes made up of marginalized and very young people. Such was the case of Wang Renmei 王人美 and Li Lili 黎莉莉 (a former dancer); but also Jin Yan 金焰, who, thanks to his roles in Sun Yu's movies, became China's leading actor and was nicknamed "the Chinese Valentino."[21]

The performance Sun Yu required from his actors was all about being spontaneous, showing inner strengths and avoiding theatrical clichés. His players are very sensual, often exposing their strong bodies and sweating faces. With a disregard for traditional modesty, the young stars present straightforward, self-assertive characters and physical presence. The images of Jin Yan and Li Lili in Sun Yu's movies are dynamic, strong, and vital. These young people have nothing in common with the "Yellow

Peril" stereotype of sickly, feeble-minded, submissive individuals. On the contrary, they are ideal vehicles of self-assertiveness, individual responsibility, moral and physical strength, and political commitment. These characters are prepared to fight the traditional pillory, as well as western (and Japanese) imperialism. The new physical body represented by Sun Yu is not sculptural (motionless), but dancing, a healthy, athletic weapon. It is a human body that runs, swims, and suffers.

This representation is indebted to the process of the Americanization of Chinese cinema, and functional to a progressive discourse that aims to enlighten the masses with "new" conceptions of hygiene and health—the most obvious and celebrated example being Sun Yu's *Queen of Sports*, where multiple sequences show the athletic physiques of young female students training for running and other sports or gymnastics. In one notable sequence, the smiling face of Li Lili is shown as she brushes her teeth. This didactic suggestion is in keeping with the political pedagogic necessity to overcome the "sickness" of China as a nation, a weak entity under the rule of colonial and imperialist power. *Mens sana in corpore sano* used to be a Confucian principle, but it apparently had been long lost. A new focus on medicine, an obsession with hygiene was sweeping through China at the beginning of the 20th century,[22] and some movie directors (above all, Sun Yu) endorsed this program, shifting away from theatrical conventions and delighting the public with images of young, healthy, semi-naked stars. Magazines were eager to publish pictures of sports queens, movie stars wearing sexy swim suits and posing in diving positions.[23] Of course, with the political program of empowerment of the national body, there was also a sexual interest in the re-discovery of the nude body.

FIGURE 1: Li Lili in *Daybreak*.

Directing techniques were one of the significant novelties introduced by Sun Yu. His actors stopped acting with their eyes, and started acting with their bodies. The other major novelty popularized by Sun Yu was unprecedented dynamic camera work. Sun Yu contributed to the spreading of complicated pan movements, tracking shots, and crane shots. At the time, these techniques were major innovations, shifting from static, theatrical representation, where the camera was at the same height and angle as the spectator's gaze in a theater, staring fixedly at the scene.

I would like to focus here on some examples of significant mobile framing in *Daybreak*, as a case study. The movie tells the story of a young couple, Lingling (Li Lili) and her cousin (Gao Zhanfei 高占非) arriving from the countryside to Shanghai.

FIGURE 2: Li Lili back home.   FIGURE 3: Li Lili in Shanghai.

They live a poor but happy life in a cramped apartment and they work in a textile factory. Sun Yu edited parallel images of a wheelbarrow unloading some raw material, with a high angle shot of the workers coming out of the factory, showing the massification of human labor (and perhaps paying homage to the very first movie ever made, which showed the workers coming out of the Lumière factories in Lyon). The contrast of the darkness of the city with the bright light of the countryside is explicit. The big city is merciless: the boy is fired by the evil capitalist, and a descent to hell starts for Lingling; she is raped and sold to prostitution. She understands, however, that the human heart is not solely responsible for her situation, but society itself has played its part, and she devotes her charm to revolutionary activity, becoming a spy for the revolution. She is discovered while hiding her former lover, turned revolutionary. Rather than sell him out, she sacrifices her own life. In the end, she is shot dead, but her example moves one of the soldiers, who then rouses his fellow soldiers to rebel against the tyrannical generals. He too is shot, but the camera rises, and, behind the wall of the execution ground, a new dawn casts its rays of hope on the martyred city.

The movie is rich in formal inventions. The following is one of the most stunning examples of Sun Yu's fluid, critical, sensual and poetic realism. We are at minute 00:34. In her obscure cramped Shanghainese room, Lingling is framed from a high angle, weeping over her lost innocence.

FIGURE 4: Cramped apartment in Shanghai.

Iris shot: Same frame, same angle, but now the girl is on a boat, still young, back in her fishermen's village. It is a flashback showing an idealized past of innocence and youth. The contrast with the present, when the character is obliged to prostitute her body to spy for the revolution, is tragic and heroic. Other differences between the two frames: in Shanghai, the light is low key; the girl is sitting in the dark. In the flashback, we are almost blinded by the light. After this symbolic contrast between the past and present, rhetorically obtained solely by the juxtaposition of two similarly framed images, Sun Yu utilizes another innovative technique —the girl is on a boat with her boyfriend, the boat is sailing, and a composite construction of a series of high-angle long shots, close-ups and slow pans follows the dawdling sliding of the boat between lotus flowers. The girl is lying down on the boat, and she is extremely sensual, but innocent at the same time. Her bare legs, her open smile, her nonchalant Lolita pose communicate great seduction, but also a realism never seen before on the Chinese screen. The high angle shot is followed by a shot/reverse shot of the subjective views of the two young people gazing at each other with frank smiles and seductive eyes. This direct representation of their bodies and desire expresses a new ideal of youth: free, emancipated, determined and strong. The spontaneity and joy with which Sun Yu represents the young bodies of his protagonists, male and female, via formal devices inspired by Hollywood "naturalism," breaks free of the constraints of previous representations anchored to theater conventions, aiming to relocate the political push to free the nation, women and youth in their own bodies. Not only women are revisited and recreated in Sun Yu's poetics, for a sensuous tracking shot accompanies the march of the bare-chested virile heroes of *The Big Road*. Here, we can find the crafting of a new ideal for Chinese men—an anticipation of the iconic Maoist martyr.

FIGURE 5: Shot of Li Lili and Jin Yan.   **FIGURE 6:** Reverse shot of Li Lili and Jin Yan.

In *The Big Road*, the young protagonists are building a road that will lead the Nationalist army to fight the Japanese invaders. Their bodies are followed by a long and sensuous tracking shot that expresses their youthful energy, as well as the idea of an entire nation marching towards independence. There is something literally stretching out towards liberation, towards emancipation, towards empowerment. The movement of the camera, the novelty of the tracking shot, the dynamism never seen before of the interaction between the camera work and the bodies of the young characters, all lend a special, "modern," blatant, energetic and fresh meaning to the ideological image of the newly constructed social class, that is, young romantic rebels in a young China. Again in *The Big Road*, we witness a spectacular 360°pan shot that films the friends all around a table talking and laughing, uniting their faces in the same sequence and, symbolically, in the same battle. Constructed camera movements collaborate to build a sense of unity that is both visual and ideological. The movie also experiments with high and low angle alternative frames and crane shots (the final massacre, coming from the enemy planes). An extremely low angle shot can be observed in the battle sequence of *Daybreak*. Partly due to the constraints of a low budget, Sun Yu does not show the armies fighting, but uses dynamic frame work to represent the fast progression of the revolutionary army. From a low angle, he shows us the soldiers running above the camera lenses, disappearing out of the picture in a fast movement conveying energy and their fighting spirit.

More use of complex mobile frame engineering is seen in *Little Toys*, where long, reflective tracking shots follow the protagonists as they walk and talk their way along the familiar, ancestral village roads. As in some films by Naruse Mikio 成瀬巳喜男, walking together is a sign of acknowledgment and the sharing of common values. And in subsequent shots depicting the war, the shifting direction of the tracking sensitively expresses the feeling of lost hopes and the despair of the characters lost in the tsunami of history.

Another Sun Yu technique that was to develop and spread in China consists of the manually operated crane-up: with a vertical movement from the lower to the upper floors of the buildings of Shanghai (we see it in *Daybreak*, *Wild Rose*, and *Queen of Sports*), Sun Yu depicts the multilayered class struggle of the big city. This was a particularly original way to envision a new modern, westernized way of filmmaking. The first occurrence in *Daybreak* takes place at minute 00:34. A young couple has just arrived in town. They take the inevitable (as the intertitles tell us) city tour, and are then welcomed to their new apartment. The crane follows the characters climbing up the stairs with a vertical movement, as they pass by different apartments. By means of this particularly dynamic and fluid movement, the audience is introduced to Shanghai's living situation, which is cramped and crowded. The verticality tells of the tall building craze in urban China at the time (and now as well, for that matter). The movement tells of the fluidity of social life and the fast-paced social transformation. The style—relying on different spaces with a fluid movement—tells of the vitality of a cinema experimenting with all kinds of new devices and the content reveals the proximity of the different family units—giving both the idea of mutual community help and the idea of big-brother-like control by means of the moralistic gaze of the neighbors. Finally, the movement suggests the possibility of rapid ascent, as well as—being a melodramatic film—the vertiginous descent awaiting the young couple.

Later, an extremely significant crane-up closes the film—starting from minute 01:37. In the final sequences of *Daybreak*, Sun Yu creates an icon for the century, in the persona of the young, rebellious, spontaneous and heroic Li Lili, elevated by sensuous mobile framing. Sun Yu was admittedly inspired by Hollywood movie stars such as Lillian Gish, Mary Pickford, and Janet Gaynor.[24] He was the first Chinese filmmaker to enjoy first-hand experience with the modern movie-going craze. However, the aura of Hollywood movies stars was shining in China too, on the screen and in the press. Anne Kerlan-Stephens and Marie-Claire Quiquemelle see in the final sequence of *Daybreak* an homage to Marlene Dietrich herself, particularly to *Dishonored* (Joseph von Sternberg, 1931). In both movies, the protagonists walk to their end—the firing squad—fiercely defying the perturbed gaze of the soldiers.[25] If Marlene brandishes her mythical cigarette, Li Lili lets her beautiful smile shine over her dark fate. Lingling accepts her destiny, she does not betray her lover, and she accepts death by the firing squad. She does this with two conditions though, both related to her image. In the first place, she wants to face death dressed in her village clothes. She refuses her evening dress, her refined but corrupted camouflage, and chooses to return to her "original" identity, which represents purity, innocence, and ultimately, the inner, original strength of the Chinese soul. Her second condition: she wants to smile. She is going to die, but she wants her death to be a symbol of future hope, of optimism, of a fighting spirit, of martyrdom. It is noteworthy that Lingling, in endorsing the revolutionary cause, understood the importance of the image, of the symbol. Thanks to her village dress and girlish smile, Lingling is not a simple individual girl, for she represents all of China's youth.

Later, the image of the martyr will become central to the poetics of Communist fiction and cinema—note for example the iconic characters of the *White-Haired Girl* and the *Red Detachment of Women*—and would be utilized in various forms (film, ballet, opera, the radio play, and the comic book) during Maoism. Recently, the figure of the female spy shot dead by collaborators has been revived by the controversial *Lust, Caution* (Si, jie色.戒 Ang Lee 李安, 2007). As noted above, *Daybreak* ends with a manually operated crane-up. The eye of the camera gazes at the young girl and the soldier shot dead. They lay in a plastic position (we can also note an error in continuity, given that in the previous shot the two bodies were in different positions). They represent the young martyrs of China, oppressed by patriarchal authority and the military, tyrannical government at the service of foreign imperialism. Then, slowly, the camera rises up, showing, behind the wall, the roofs of the city, and the sun coming up. It is the dawn cited in the title, representing future hope for China.

FIGURE 7: Final shot of *Daybreak*.

This camera movement refers to the by now classical ending of the Hollywood paradigm: an external eye, looking down upon all human misery, becoming detached from it, signifying the end of the story, and bidding farewell. Here, Sun Yu utilizes this trope, adding a moral implication: what people behind the wall cannot see—for they can see only death, defeat, foolishness—is a bright future arriving from afar. He portrays the martyr, the rebellious hero in order to signify the sufferance of China, and to demand a reaction from the crowd. This crane-up movement is a revelation—dawn is not far from coming—and a call to arms—we should rise and march towards it.

I am not suggesting here that Sun Yu was the only one to acknowledge and develop the specificities of the cinema medium, nor that the ability to use these techniques in a symbolic, poetic and effective way originated exclusively from his education in New York. Definitively, however, the familiarity with the most progressive techniques of filmmaking and the solid technical education he received in the U.S. gave him a mature vision of the new media, and helped him develop an original visual style that was both universally effective and deeply concerned with the politics of China. His works helped to create "a progressive cosmopolitanism strand of Shanghai cinema."[26] As mentioned above, along with this revolutionary and coherent use of camera movements, Sun Yu developed an innovative way of directing his actors and actresses, aiming towards "realism." Consistently, he asks them to be "natural," and, even though today this acting no longer seems "realistic," compared with more formulaic, static, expressionist performance of movie stars at the time, Sun Yu's heroes and heroines are incredibly spontaneous and generous.

This image of youth is functional to the idealist project of Sun Yu, and of numerous intellectuals of the time. It is both a calling to arms addressed to a new generation of young people, and a description that insists that Chinese youth are not weak, and shall not be. Utilizing the "western" technique of cinematography, which he apprehended in loco, Sun Yu shifts the representation of the intellectual heroes from that of a weak scholar and a submissive refined young lady to an image of strength, energy, and engagement.[27] Along the tragic path of his heroes and heroines—revolutionary martyrs, saint-like prostitutes, but also common young women who sacrifice their pride to collective honor as in the *Queen of Sports*—Sun Yu elaborates a new ideal of battling youth. His movies remain largely popular (or "vernacular") and endorse the melodramatic mode to call for public response and reaction.[28] Like other members of intellectual circles of the time (to which he was closely tied), the director called "the poet of the silver screen" rejected western and Japanese imperialism while appropriating western democratic ideals, romantic momentum, a fascination with science and social progress, and representational techniques.

His visual style, the way of filming young bodies that are leaning straight ahead towards the camera, and the idealization of the (paradoxically) realistic push towards progress and rebellion, often interrupted by war, society and religion, portray the patriotic engagement of Sun Yu, as well as an aesthetic ideal made of freedom, liberty and sensuality, an ideal for the building of a new generation that may embody the future of China itself.

FIGURES 8 & 9: The natural grace of Li Lili.

244

ENDNOTES

1. Tadao Sato, *Le Cinéma japonais* (Paris : Centre Georges Pompidou, 1997).

2. Tadao Sato, "Le cinéma japonais et le cinéma chinois face la tradition." In Marie-Claire Quiquemelle and Jean-Loup Passek, eds., *Le Cinéma chinois* (Paris : Centre George Pompidou, 1985), 77–84.

3. Laikwan Pang, *Building a New China in Cinema. The Chinese Left-Wing Cinema Movement, 1932–1937* (Boston: Rowman and Littlefield, 2002), 148.

4. Regis Bergeron, *Le Cinema chinois: 1905–1949* (Alfred Eibel editeur, 1977). For an overview of early Chinese cinema, see also Quiquemelle and Passek; Zhang Yingjin, *Chinese National Cinema* (New York and London: Routledge, 2004); Paul Clark, *Chinese Cinema: Culture and Politics Since 1949* (New York: Cambridge University Press, 1987); Jiao Xiongping焦雄屏, *Shidai xianying: Zhong Xi dianying lunshu* 時代顯影: 中西電影論述 [Historical developments: discussion of Oriental and Western cinemas] (Taibei: Yuanliu, 1998), 15–80; Poshek Fu, *Between Shanghai and Hong Kong. The Politics of Chinese Cinema* (Stanford: Stanford University Press, 2003); Cheng Jihua 程季華, *Zhongguo dianying fazhan shi* 中國電影發展史 [History of Chinese Cinema] (Beijing: Zhongguo dianying chubanshe, 1963); Dai Xiaolan戴小蘭, *Zhongguo wusheng dianying* 中國無聲電影 [Chinese silent Cinema] (Beijing: Zhongguo dianying, 1996); Chen Bo 陳播, *Zhongguo zuoyi dianying yundong* 中國左翼電影運動 [Chinese Left Wing Cinema] (Beijing: Zhongguo dianying, 1993); Xianggang Zhongguo dianying xuehui 香港中國電影學會 *Tansuo de niandai*, 探索的年代 [Origins of Chinese Cinema] (Hong Kong, Hong Kong Arts Center, 1984); Xiao Zhiwei, "Cinema cinese. Il periodo del muto 1896-1936 [Silent Chinese Cinema 1896–1936]." In Gian Piero Brunetta, ed., *Storia del cinema mondiale. Vol. 4* (Torino: Einaudi, 2001), 715–737; Li Suyuan 酈蘇元 and Hu Jubin 胡菊彬 (*Zhongggguo wusheng dianying shi* 中國無聲電影史 [History of Chinese Silent Cinema] (Beijing: Zhongguo dianying, 1997); Hu Junbin, *Projecting a Nation. Chinese National Cinema Before 1949* (Hong Kong: Hong Kong University Press, 2003).

5. Occidentalism is a very slippery notion. Chen Xiaomei, in *Occidentalism: A Theory of Counter-discourse in Post-Mao China* (New York and Oxford: Oxford University Press, 1995) underscores the positive effects of using the "Other" (here, Chen refers to some literary texts of western culture) as an inspirational force to empower the submitted; she is also well aware of the risk involved in such an intellectual enterprise. "Occidentalism" is a notion inspired by the popular concept of "orientalism" proposed by Edward W. Said (*Orientalism*,

New York, Vintage, 1979); it aims to be its complementary analytical tool. See also Ian Buruma and Avishai Marglit, *Occidentalism* (London: Atlantic, 2005).

6. Laikwan Pang, 145–148.

7. Anne Kerlan-Stephens and Marie-Claire Quiquemelle, "La compagnie cinématographique Lianhua et le cinéma progressiste chinois: 1930–1937." In *Arts Asiatiques,* No. 61 (2006): 5.

8. Nick Browne, "Society, and Subjectivity: On the Political Economy of Chinese Melodrama." In Nick Browne et al., eds., *New Chinese Cinemas. Forms, Identities, Politics* (Cambridge: Cambridge University Press, 1994), 40–56; Wimal Dissanayake, ed., *Melodrama and Asian Cinema* (Cambridge: Cambridge University Press, 1993), Stephen Teo, "Il genere *wenyi*: una esegesi del melodramma cinese" [The *wenyi* genre: the Chinese melodrama], in Festival del cinema di Pesaro, *Stanley Kwan. La via orientale al melodramma* (Roma: Il Castoro, 2000).

9. Zhang Zhen, *An Amorous History of the Silver Screen: Shanghai Cinema, 1896–1937* (Chicago & London: University of Chicago Press, 2005), 30. To be noted that since melodrama is to some degree a foreign concept, the Chinese translation is shifting. It is often rendered as *tongsu ju* 通俗剧, where *tongsu* means "popular "and *ju* "play, drama". Zhang Zhen refers to *baihua* literature. "Vernacular literature" is written as *baihua* 白话 "common language." Other possible translations of melodrama include 情节剧 *qingjie ju* "narrative drama" (as opposed to opera) and 文艺片 *wenyi pian* "literature-art films." Realism is an evasive term as well. We find both 写实主义 *xieshi zhuyi* "writing the real, concrete, actual" and 现实主义 *xianshi zhuyi* "present reality." Both are ideologically burdened, since *zhuyi* stands for –ism. Chris Berry and Mary Farquhar, discussing early Chinese cinema, write: "melodramatic realism is a major strain in the Chinese cinema because its central theme of outraged innocence was often perceived as real in national, and not just personal, terms. [. . .] melodramatic realism is the mixed mode of the national" in *China on Screen. Cinema and Nation* (New York: Columbia University Press, 2006), 82.

10. 對於中國來說,電影則是"舶來品",中國傳統文化與電影並無直接的血緣關系。中國電影百年來的生命歷程,不斷受到歐風美雨的吹拂浸染,可謂是受歐美文化影響最深的文藝樣式。(. . .)　在中國電影所受到的外來影響中,美國好萊塢電影文化的影響最為深遠。(. . .)即使后來某些科班出身的編導,如洪深、孫瑜等,也是在美國學習的戲劇和電影,他們關於電影的理論知識和創作經驗,也較多的來自於美國的電影文化,所以其創作也無法完全擺脫好萊塢電影潛移默化的影響。例如, 1930年孫瑜在聯華影業公司編導的影片《野草閑花》, 就是受到了美國影片《七重天》的啟發和影響而創作的。故

246

而，從20年代中國電影的總體創作情況來看，盡管也有少數影片觸\u21450及社會現實問題，表現出進步的思想意識，但大多數影片凸現了電影的商業性和娛樂性，往往是對好萊塢電影簡單的借鑒和模仿，"美"化傾向十\u20998分嚴重。Zhou Binde周斌德 "百年中國電影與中外文化" (One hundred years of Chinese cinema and its relation to foreign cultures", in *Theory People*, http://theory.people.com.cn/BIG5/49167/ 3855547.html, 25/06/09. Unfortunately, *Wild Flowers* (*Yecao xianhua*, 1931) is considered to have been lost.

11. Thus defined by scholar Linda Lai on her very creative web site: Linda Lai, "Big Road, an Eclectic Text", *Linda Lai Floating Site*, http://www.lindalai-floatingsite.com/contents /writings/Bg/ index.html (27/06/09). It is note-worthy that in the Chinese version of the same text, the notion of "critical realism" is rendered as "社會良心的鏡子shehui liangxin de jingzi," its literary translation being "mirror of social conscience." It appears that in the Chinese language context it is even harder to use the concept/term of "realism" than in an English language context.

12. David Bordwell and Kristin Thompson, *Film Art: An Introduction* (New York: McGraw-Hill, 2001), 157. See also Julia Hallam and Margaret Marshment, *Realism and Popular Cinema* (Manchester: Manchester University Press, 2000).

13. Laikwan Pang, 200.

14. Laikwan Pang, 200; Zhang Zhen also talks about a "growing popular 'taste for reality' " when discussing long narrative films and the cinema boom of the early 1920s. Zhang Zhen, 38.

15. It might be useful to mention briefly that even if Hollywood is often per-ceived today as a monolithic force imposing its dominion on the imagination of the global audience, it does and did have a plurality of souls and, what is more important here, it was created thanks to the meeting of different, het-erogeneous narrative and visual traditions.

16. It may be a common stereotype, but Chinese culture loves its cuisine: Sun Yu defines its cinema (and, indirectly, himself) as *zasui* 杂碎 or chop-suey (which brings to mind the famous self-definition of Ozu Yasujiro 小津 安二郎 as a tofu-maker). See Sun Yu 孫瑜, *Yinhai fanzhou—huiyi wo de yisheng* 銀海泛舟- 回憶我的一生 [Floating on the screen. Memories of my Life], Shanghai, Shang-hai Wenyi chubanshe, 1987; and Sun Yu, *Da lu zhi ge* 大路之歌 [Song of *The Big Road*] (Taibei: Yuanliu, 1990). Note that the "traditional" chop-suey dish is not traditional at all, but instead a "construction" of the Chinese diaspora; see Gregory B. Lee, *Chinas Unlimited: Making the Imaginaries of China and Chi-neseness* Honolulu: University of Hawai'i Press, 2003).

17. I make reference here to the famous *Song of Midnight* (*Yeban gesheng* 夜半歌聲,

Maxu Weibang馬徐維邦, 1937), allegedly the first Chinese horror flick, a passionate mélange of *Frankenstein* (James Whale, 1931), *The Phantom of the Opera* (Rupert Julian, 1925) and local revolutionary epic melodrama.

18. Bergeron, 69–72.

19. Kerlan-Stephens and Quiquemelle, 11.

20. Pang, 148.

21. It should be mentioned that one of the first Chinese male movie stars was of Korean origin. Like "Americanization," "Pan-Asiatism" also played a part in influencing Chinese cinema from the very beginning. On Jin Yan, see Richard J. Meyer, *Jin Yan: the Rudolph Valentino of Shanghai* (Hong Kong: Hong Kong University Press, 2009).

22. Frank Dikötter, *Sex, Culture and Modernity in China* (London: Hurst & Company, 1995).

23. Which reminds us of the fascination with the modern "sirens" expressed by the Japanese writer Tanizaki Jun'ichiro 谷崎 潤一郎 in his novels and screenplays.

24. Sun Yu 孫瑜, *Yinhai fanzhou—huiyi wo de yisheng* 銀海泛舟- 回憶我的一生 [Floating on the screen. Memories of my Life], (Shanghai : Shanghai Wenyi chubanshe, 1987), 30.

25. Kerlan-Stephens and Quiquemelle, 11.

26. Zhen, 289.

27. A traditional model: Song Geng, *The Fragile Scholar. Power and Masculinity in Chinese Culture* (Hong Kong: Hong Kong University Press, 2004); Stephen Teo, *Hong Kong. The Extra Dimensions* (London: BFI Publishing, 1997).

28. "Sun's commitment to both social progress and cinematic innovation led him to create a particular film language that may be called 'unofficial/popular discourse,' which for my purpose, may be reformulated as 'vernacular' discourse"; Zhang Zhen, 296–297.

CHAPTER 9

IF AMERICA WERE REALLY CHINA OR HOW CHRISTOPHER COLUMBUS DISCOVERED ASIA

GREGORY LEE

"They have not yet realized, that time having manufactured time,
that we have finally become them."
— Raphaël Confiant *Case à Chine*[1]

THE CHINESE FIRST populated America three millennia ago, and have been going there regularly ever since. Chinese American author Shawn Wong's hero in *Homebase* gets this story from an old Native American encountered on Angel Island in San Francisco Bay. Angel Island was the "back door" Ellis Island, a detention centre where would-be Chinese immigrants were held in the early twentieth-century, while their family affiliations and right to immigrate were verified; "normal" immigration procedures for Chinese were suspended by the 1882 Exclusion Law. The legislation denied right of entry and American citizenship to all Chinese except those who were close relatives of existing American citizens. When the hero of Wong's novel visits the detention centre on the island in the 1970s it is abandoned, derelict and about to be demolished.

'You know people say I look Chinese.' [said the old Indian]
…
'People say I look Chinese,' he repeated.
I looked at him in the dim light. He did look Chinese.
'Where are you from,?' I asked.
'Acoma'.
'Lots of Chinese in New Mexico?'

He started laughing and lit up another cigarette. 'Where are you from?'
'Berkeley.'
'Where are you from originally?'
'Berkeley.'
'How long you been here?'
'Three days.'
'No. How long you been in the United States?'
'All my life.'
'You mean you ain't born in China.'
'What do you mean? Don't I look like I come from Gallup?'
'You ain't Navajo. You Chinese. You like me.'
'You ain't Chinese, though.'
'My ancestors came from China thirty thousand years ago and settled in Acoma Pueblo.'
'Is that why you look Chinese?'
'Naw, my grandfather was Chinese.'
'Your grandfather was Chinese?…'
'He wandered into New Mexico and married a widow before anyone knew he was Chinese.' [2]

An old "Indian," a "native" American, Chinese because his ancestors immigrated tens of thousands years ago, but also Chinese and "native" because his grandfather in the nineteenth-century immigrated to California and married a "native" American.

In between the two migratory moments, according to a Chinese seventeenth century history book, America was "re-discovered," and named Fusang 扶桑, the equivalent, in the pre-modern Chinese world-vision of the lost continent of Atlantis. The Chinese Buddhist missionary Hui Shen 慧深 (in Japanese, Kei-shin) around the year 500 had set sail from China's eastern seaboard and hit land 10,000 kilometres east of China.[3] Once he had returned to China Hui Shen made a report of his discovery to the Emperor who reacted with some indifference to the news.[4] What interested the supreme rulers of China more than finding a continent, was finding the substance that would give them longevity, if not eternal life, and indeed in the third century before our era numerous maritime missions had been dispatched in the vain search for plants that would enhance life expectancy. Of what interest was Fusang, yet to be named America, if it could not provide this? Almost a thousand years after Hui

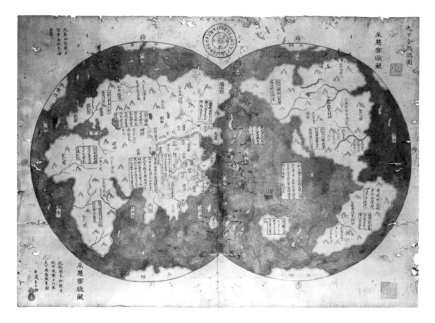

FIGURE 1: A 1763 Chinese map of the world, claiming to be a reproduction of a 1418 map after descriptions of Zheng He's voyages.

Shen's voyage, Chinese ships again arrived in America, beating Columbus to the post by a number of decades. The Chinese explorer was Zheng He, an imperial eunuch appointed admiral of the fleet by the Ming Emperor Zhu Di. However, once again the Chinese sailed away, and that is why there is today no United States of Fusang, and also why the capital is not Zhu Di City, District of Zhenghe, but rather Washington, District of Columbia, USA.

It was in the mid-to-late nineteenth century that the dream of America, of California, of the Gold Rush, that gave us the Chinese translation of San Francisco—Old Gold Mountain 舊金山—became immensely attractive to a southern Chinese population devastated by the economically ruinous impact of British imperialist encroachment. The opium trade which Britain and other powers had forced upon China, waging the Opium Wars in order to prise open its ports and hinterland, literally impoverished southern China and led millions to seek economic refuge overseas.[5] Many were tempted by contracts which left them virtually enslaved as coolies in foreign lands. Their preferred destination was America, country of the *Fakei/Huaqi* 花棋 "flowery flag," as the Stars and Stripes were called by the Chinese. The United States were also known as *Meiguo* 美國 "the beautiful country," or again simply as America, transliterated as *A-mei-lei-ga* 亞美利加 in Cantonese.[6] It was a land, particularly after the Rush following the mid-nineteenth-century discovery of the precious metal in California, where the streets were reputed to be paved with gold. For the Chinese, America was not a utopian refuge from persecution as it was for many European immigrants, but rather a temporary detour made necessary by economic hard times in China, as the straightforward lyrics from a nineteenth-century Cantonese folk song illustrate:

爸爸去金山
快快要寄銀
全家靠住你
有銀好寄回

Father has gone to Gold Mountain
Hurry up and send money
The whole family is counting on you
When you have money send it back quick.[7]

But the Chinese need to find alternative sources of income and wealth by emigrating to California also coincided with mid-nineteenth century America's need to rebuild itself as a nation-state.

When Baudrillard declares in his *Amérique* (America) that twentieth-century America has no problem of identity, and that it does not "cultivate origins and mythic authenticity," he neglects the ideological work of the nineteenth-century that inscribed the myth of America as the land of refuge welcoming those seeking justice and liberty.[8] The historical reality is that that myth of America as a generous haven for all the world's downtrodden which is so much a part of its modern identity, and is even inscribed in the form of the words of Emma Lazarus on the base of the Statue of Liberty, is founded on a lack of memory, not to say a lie. America had to re-imagine and reconstruct itself: to institute the imaginary America that Walt Whitman had mapped out in verse. In order to do so post-bellum America, now settled within its new northern and southern borders, and which had now "pacified the Far West" by practically annihilating the indigenous population, was in need of another vision of alterity against which to construct itself. This Other was to be found

FIGURE 2: The Statue of Liberty welcomed millions of passengers to the New World
while the Chinese were juridically excluded from America.

across the "American lake," across the Pacific, in the form of the Celestial
Empire, China.

Thus, China was imagined and represented as decadent, old, decrepit,
a faded civilization ill-adapted to the new industrial and scientific world
of which America would become the herald and the embodiment. But if
China was decadent and backward so must be its people. So how was it
possible to denigrate China without denigrating its people, and indeed
its emigrants? And what place could such degenerate "untouchables"
have in the new consolidated United States of America? And so over a
period of several decades propagandists and politicians militated for the
legal and actual exclusion of Chinese from America. The project to
exclude Chinese people from America, from citizenship, and from simply
being American, started around 1850, was partly accomplished by 1870,
with the Naturalization Act which denied the right of naturalization to
Chinese, and was formally concluded with the adopting of the Exclusion
Act of 1882.[9]

253

Furthermore, so as to protect Americans and Americaness in China, a legal and jurisdictional cocoon was constructed. In 1844 the United States became the first nation to demand and obtain extra-territorial rights for its citizens in China; a situation which ensured their immunity from Chinese law. Americans thus removed themselves from Chinese jurisdiction. Juridically Americans when in China were in America. By the same token, the Chinese were excluded even in their own country. By the turn of the century so naturalized and legitimate had this system of extraterritoriality become that Congress, in 1906, established the United States District Court for China.[10] Academia made its contribution in the person of Andrew D. White, president of Cornell University, who lent his support to Senator Sargent, the prime advocate of the exclusionists in Congress. According to the 1877 congressional record, White expressed a "deep-seated dread of this influx of Asiatics of a type which it seems to me can never form any hopeful element in this nation."

In 1882, the Chinese Exclusion Act passed the House of Representatives with 201 votes in favour and a mere 37 against the measure. It thus became practically impossible for new Chinese immigrants to enter the country. After the 1882 Exclusion Act had been passed, there followed a second set of measures aimed at maintaining American "purity": almost every state in the union passed anti-miscegenation laws preventing the marriage of whites with non-whites. As for the Chinese Exclusion Act, it was not finally repealed until 1943, and not until 1967 did the U.S. Supreme Court declare anti-miscegenation laws unconstitutional.

In the late nineteenth-century, for the millions legally excluded from the United States, the dream of America was displaced onto other regions in need of cheap labour: Australia, Canada, South Africa. But all of these would eventually put up barriers too. And then there were those Chinese who naively and unwittingly signed contracts which promised them America, but which in reality took them to European colonies off the coast of the Americas where in the wake of the abolition of slavery Chinese and Indian coolies were used to replace the former African slaves.

The story of the exclusion of the Chinese is now well-known to those taking introductory courses in Asian American history in U.S. universities which over the past thirty years have developed ethnic American studies departments. They would also study that other history that is increasingly included in such courses: that of the unjust, and even illegal, internment of Japanese Americans during the World War II in concentration camps in the American desert. While Americans whose forbears hailed from other belligerent states such as Germany and Italy did not suffer such a fate, Japanese Americans were not only denied their liberty but had to wait forty years for an apology from the American government. That these narratives should be part of "mainstream" American studies today seems self-evident, but they are not. And what was the fate of those attracted to but yet spurned by the dreamland that was America?

THE CARRIBEAN ROAD TO NEW YORK

"Martinique is a part of America. You just need to find the road to New York and walk straight ahead, I tell you."
— Raphaël Confiant, *Case à Chine*[11]

Raphaël Confiant has recently told the story of the Chinese coolie in the French Caribbean, the Chinese coolie who had "signed up" for America but found himself imprisoned on an island. Raphaël Confiant spent the first half of his literary career crafting a literary language out of the spoken language of the people of Martinique—a language shared by the descendants of white colonials, black slaves, the half-black bourgeoisie, and the descendants of Indian and Chinese migrant laborers.

Confiant now writes in French so as to reach a wider public, but still weaves Creole into his narratives. His latest work tells the story of the Chinese presence in Martinique, the story of the desperate economic and political conditions of mid to late nineteenth-century China that led many Chinese to leave for what they thought was America. The book is called *Case à Chine* (Chinese shack), in Creole: "Kay Chine." At the outset the young hero, Chen Sang, who, like a character in the fiction of magic realist Garcia Marquez, lives to a venerable old age of around a hundred years, is obliged to leave southern China and finds himself, having crossed three oceans, on Martinique. As Chen Sang's grandson is told in the narrative:

You should know young man [...] that in our race the men have always dreamed of returning to their homeland, whereas the women, being more realistic, have preferred to confront the real world. There are those, like

255

your grandfather who went even further in his fantasies, since it is told that *he* actually tried to get to New York. New York no less! It's true, of course, that in Canton and Shanghai the [coolie] traders had seduced our ancestors with the word 'America.' My mother often said that many emigrants had accepted to sign a contract because the word sounded sweet to their ears. Laughable, isn't it? [12]

Like his fellow immigrants, Chen Sang had indeed signed a contract as an indentured laborer for a period of five years after which time he would theoretically be free to go back to China, almost no-one ever did. Side by side with his Indian counterparts, he cut the sugar cane that used to be cut by the African slaves, before the abolition of slavery.

Chinese and Indians were brought to numerous destinations in the Caribbean. The British, needless to say, brought in coolies to Jamaica and Trinidad, but also, as the dominant maritime power of the moment, to Cuba. In 1858, the *London Illustrated News* reported:

Between November, 1854, and September, 1855 [...] nearly 11,000 embarked for Cuba [...] and amongst them the mortality before they got to the end of their voyage was 14 ¾ per cent. Our laws, though well intended, could not cover the whole case, and it is somewhat remarkable that the mortality on board British vessels engaged in this traffic was greater than the mortality in other vessels. When we find legislation attains very imperfectly the objects it aims at more immediately within its scope, we cannot be surprised that it should not be successful in dealing with things so strange and so remote as the emigration of crowds of Chinamen. [...] The mode, too, in which they are sometimes collected is not creditable. Chinese passage-brokers residing at Hong-Kong, often men of straw, dispatch agents to the mainland, who seem to find plenty of persons desirous to emigrate, or whom they tempt to emigrate, and who buy of them, at five dollars a piece, a bargain-ticket signed by the broker. The emigrants then repair to Hong-Kong, where they receive, on paying the balance, a passage-ticket for California or Australia. The brokers thus collect a great number of emigrants; and, having got their money, do not always provide the passage, or they take up any old ship that offers. Our Government, in spite of its many precautions, seems sometimes to be made instrumental in helping the brokers to impose on the emigrants. As it can scarcely prevent all abuses, it seems doubtful whether the

Legislature should not withdraw from the attempt to regulate and organise the emigration of the Chinese.

The novel *Monkey Hunting* by Cristina Garcia tells a similar story to Confiant's about Chinese immigration to Cuba:

The men [having arrived in Havana] were ordered to peel off their filthy rags and were given fresh clothes to present themselves to the Cubans. But there was no mistaking their wretchedness: bones jutted from their cheeks; sores cankered their flesh. Not even a strict regimen of foxglove could have improved their appearance. The recruits were rounded up in groups of sixty-wood haulers and barbers, shoemakers, fishermen, farmers—then parceled out in smaller groups to the waiting landowners. A dozen Cubans on horseback, armed with whips, led the men like a herd of cattle to the barracón to be sold. Inside, Chen Pan was forced to strip and be examined for strength, like horses or oxen that were for sale in the country districts of China. Chen Pan burned red with shame, but he didn't complain. Here he could no longer rely on the known ways. Who was he now without his country?

One hundred fifty pesos was the going rate for a healthy chino. A Spanish landowner paid two hundred for him, probably on account of his height. His father had taught him that if you knew the name of a demon, it had no power to harm you. Quickly, Chen Pan asked one of the riders for the name of his buyer. Don Urbano Bruzón de Peñalves. How [in the world] would he ever remember that? [...] Now there was no question of his purpose in Cuba. He was there to cut sugar cane. All of them were. Chinos. Asiáticos. Culís. Later, there would be other jobs working on the railroads or in the copper mines of El Cobre, five hundred miles away. But for now what the Cubans wanted most were strong backs for their fields.[13]

Chinese immigration to Cuba left its traces not only in Cuba but also in the Cuban émigré population in the United States; in New York for instance the Cuban-Chinese hybrid restaurant has been for decades a major feature of Manhattan's multicultural landscape. In Confiant's story the Chinese *never* get to New York. Sino-Caribbean hybridity remains Sino-French, Sino-Creole, Sino-Martiniquais, finally just Martiniquais.

The Chinese coolie in Confiant's story, Chen Sang eventually runs

away from the sugar plantation having slaughtered an intolerable over-
seer. Refusing to believe that he is on an island, still seeking his America,
his utopia like a character in a frenetic and ex-centric version of *The Wizard of Oz*, he treks its length and breadth of the Caribbean island looking
for the (yellow brick) road to America.

> Chen Sang had roamed all over the southern part of the land, moving
> only by night and living off roots he found along the borders of the plan-
> tations. He almost gave in to despair when he realized that everywhere
> the sea presented an obstacle to his dreams. [. . .] So this land was a an is-
> land after all, as the cane-cutters beside whom he had laboured so many
> years had always maintained. [. . .] The Chinese had not believed them.
> [Chen Sang would tell them:] 'You are talking rubbish! Martinique is a
> part of America. You just need to find the road to New York and walk
> straight ahead, I tell you.'
>
> And there all he was doing was repeating what the recruiters heralded
> in the slum quarters of Canton they haunted offering to all who would
> listen lashings of rice wine. [. . .] [All this was confirmed] by the famous
> Captain Morton. At the height of the storm which threatened to send the
> good ship Galileo to depths of the ocean, the British officer had endlessly
> harangued his crew and the emigrants:
>
> 'Courage! Once we get through this, the gateway to the New World
> will open wide to you!'
>
> And didn't the labor contract of the young Chen Sang not stipulate
> that he was emigrating to 'America' for five years, at the end of which the
> company was meant to repatriate him? [. . .] [But try as he might he could
> not obtain from the locals the slightest clue as to how to find the road
> out.] New York, then, remained a big dream. He had been constrained to
> sign a new contract since he did not have the wherewithal to pay his debts
> at the plantation shop.[14]

If the story of Chen Sang can be encompassed by the metadiscipline of
American studies, and I suggest that it can, the question becomes one of
its boundaries. Should they be spatial, physical? Or temporal? For surely
implied in the question "Who is America," is embedded the question
"When was America?" Or should they also relate to the imaginary, to the
realm of desire, including unfulfilled desire? Is America not also the imaginary that drove, and still drives so many, to risk their lives to reach it?

Is America not also the little Americas that those who cannot physically attain America construct themselves, with the aid of Hollywood and globalized consumption practices, in Asia, in Africa, in Europe ? Is America not rather the Americas, and its margins?

Chen Sang, exhausted, hunted and starving is saved by a black woman who is full of character and with whom he goes on to found a hybrid dynasty. Finally, generations later, it falls to Raphaël, the namesake of the author, to tell the story of the Chinese on the island. Raphaël feels Chinese but also Martiniquais. The multiplicity, the singularity, the complexity of this mixed, intertwined ethno-linguistic community is foregrounded towards the end of the book when Raphaël tells the part of the story that takes place in the latter half of the twentieth century.

> The mystery of sounds, or more precisely, the relationship between sounds and the meaning of words, intrigued me greatly. Having always heard three languages at home—Creole, French and Chinese—having become used to Spanish and English thanks to transistor radios that brought us the rumba and calypso all day long, having witnessed the arguments in Arabic between the Syrian shopkeepers along François-Argo Street as well as the prayers spoken to Hindu gods in Tamil in the Au-Béraud district, having heard all this had taught me the singularity of each, not in each, but in us. I mean to say that when my great grandfather hinted, *in Chinese*, that I should pay more attention to what he said, I who usually only half-listened to what he was saying, he was not the same person as when he told me the same thing in his hesitant and sometimes jumbled French. As for Man Fideline [his very old black great grandmother], her incessant jabbering during our walks downtown, in Creole and in Banana-French, paralleled my grandfather's case. I was certain that changing language was equal to changing personality or inhabiting another part of oneself. Myself, in Creole, I was the little negro-Chinese bastard, a born vagabond, who took advantage of the absence of his teachers to explore, in a gang, the forbidden quarters of the neighbourhood. On the other hand in French, I became the good little boy who politely greeted the adults and obeyed without complaint their commands. And the few words of Chinese I could muster had the effect of transforming me into a warrior. What would my grandfather have said had he known that I would dream at night of being the sidekick of the legendary Chinese bandit [he had fled during his youth], that warlord of Yunnan he so cursed.[15]

Chineseness for Confiant is part of a larger composite universe that has coalesced in this officially French dominion, in this fictional, yet real, corner of France separated from Paris by an ocean and 8,000 kilometres.

Confiant, describing the way in which the Chinese community is now part of the general, now hybrid, community that is Martinique, tells us:

> When they [the majority] name us and nickname us all 'China'—Mrs. China, China-Chinese, China, Dr. China and so on—they believe they are consigning us to what is indistinct, and of our lives, all they retain is what they believe is our eternal passivity. [...] They have not yet realized, that time having manufactured time, that we have finally become them. Not the them they were before we landed in this land, this stump of earth that forms part of this arc that constitutes such a pretty eyelash for America, but a new 'Us.' [...] Our blood is mixed with theirs, against their will as much as in line with their desire, our voices blend in gradually with their songs, with their laughing. [...] Because the rotten luck is still there [...] Because we have to get over the mourning for the Land Before This One, Because living together while being so different is such a challenge, Because to finally carry on one's back the improbability of the whole world, is no simple game, by God! [16]

Case à Chine focusses on the Chineseness of Martinique's community. But Confiant's universe is much larger, taking in France, Britain, European, Asian and African cultures in general. But his Europe and his France and his Africa and Asia are recounted spaces that are interweaved with strands of Chineseness, jumbled, left-behind, dislocated, an image of the history of the nineteenth and twentieth-centuries, the modernity of which colonialism was an intrinsic component whether in Havana, in Fort-de-France, or in Shanghai.

Yet was this very mixedness that late nineteenth-century scientific racism, which bolstered and justified colonialist practices, held responsible for the non-white peoples' supposed incapacity to govern themselves and to be intellectually productive. Legendre, for example, as late as 1925 was still profoundly attached to the scientific hierarchisation of races which accounted for racial degeneracy in terms of the "impregnation" by the non-white of pure racial national bodies. Thus, Chinese or "yellow" civilization can be discounted, and Chinese intelligence with it:

> There is, and there has never been, a yellow civilization, no more than there has been a negro civilization. The white race alone, constituted of Aryans and Semites, has been, in the history of peoples, a ferment of intelligence and activity. [...] The Yellow is only a métis of conquering whites and negroids.[17]

The Chinese people's alleged mental weakness was also due to this wanton mixing of "races":

> To what then should this deficiency in the Chinese brain be attributed? Without doubt to the catastrophic reaction of this mass of negroids and métis—the Yellow—forming the majority of the population and whose blood, by dint of a widely practiced polygamy, impregnated the elite, originally of white race.[18]

But the fact that this very mixedness, this membrane of practices resulting from forced hybrid cultural matrices, whether individual or communal, have been a central constituent in the new writing of the late twentieth century is evident from the corpus of twentieth-century literature that starts with Joyce. That it may constitute the acknowledged vector of writing and representation of the twenty-first century depends on our capacity constantly to remember, to re-memorize, and to re-fashion its lessons in a constantly changing globalized socio-cultural environment.

A FILM YET TO BE MADE:
THE STORY OF CHAN/CHEN

I have made little reference to film so far, not because there have not been filmic representations of Chinese in America or of Chinese Americans, but because the film that would comprehensively relate the complexity of the story of Chinese (in) America has not been and perhaps could not be made. One Chinese American film in particular pointed to this probable impossibility: The film *Chan is Missing*, a mystery set in San Francisco's Chinatown, told the allegorical story of a Chinese cab driver who went missing with a large sum of money.[19] The film recounts and represents the fruitless search of two of his fellow taxi drivers, and business partners, for Chan Hung. The representation of the quest provides the opportunity to show aspects of Chinatown daily life that were, and for most remain, unknown to the American movie spectator. In American studies, and in American cultural production, Chan is still missing. S/he is still missing because "mainstream" America, and American studies while making a place for non-white America, for ethnic Studies departments and Asian American studies programs, is still, despite the rhetoric of tolerance and multiculturalism, incapable of *integrating* Chinese American writing and history and film into its logic and its consciousness. What is more, the text below indicates, if the earlier racist discourse is now sublimated in the public media, there persists an exotic marginalizing vision of Chineseness in America indicative of an incapacity to see that what is at stake is not just minority history but a history that interrogates and calls for a revision of the story of the totality that would be American history were it written.

In Canton Chan had bought a ticket for California, but they had transported him to this overgrown island, a fact he did not understand until many years later having marched through the desert from Melbourne to Durban without finding the Old Gold Mountain, a much larger undertaking than circumscribing Martinique.[20]

Chan would played rugby in Australia, which was somewhat ironic since he had been banned and barred from the whites-only colony several times. Chan was playing a modern-day enforcer's role now, "physical presence combined with skill," said the sports paper, which was once again ironic since in previous decades not only was Chan classified a weakling but was also described as degenerate, unbalanced, demented and generally mentally deficient. A diet of Australian dairy food and organic barbecued tofu had evidently resulted in fortifying Chan's physique and in changing his mind. But what had changed the white Australian's mind? Never mind. The sports report described Chan as "a late bloomer." Very late in fact since he had not been allowed into the game for more than a century. "But this was not a gentleman's game." And Chan was still waiting to take a wicket.

The restaurant that Chan opened in Minnesota got mixed reviews— well, Chan had never been near a wok before arriving in America. "I've been three times and have had so-so to bad experiences. First time I had the 3 seafood combo. It was delicately flavoured, i.e., a little dull. Last time I had beef with Chinese broccoli. But the beef was a bit tough and flavourless. Am I ordering the wrong things?"

"Oh no! Sorry to hear this as I was looking forward to trying Chan's."

Chan was not cut out for catering. An illustrious moment in Chan's career came with the winning of a local foundation arts prize. Chan was acclaimed, mostly by family and friends, "a major Napa Valley poet and visual artist." Of course, Chan could not survive by poetry alone and had a day job as a visiting professor at the Hospitality Management Faculty of the Culinary Institute of America, Santa Barbara.

Despite not being a wizard with the wok, Chan was capable of making real fresh noodles from plain flour and water, just like grandfather had shown him. Flapping the elongated dough into longer and longer strips, he had looked like he was performing some elaborate kungfu exercise in the dimly lit scullery in the old Edwardian house which had once been a seaman's café for Chinese mariners who, legally obliged by British and American laws, had manned the transatlantic convoys during World War II. But the café had closed when all its clientèle was deported back to China in 1946 for having dared to demand equal wages with white seamen during the war. The Blue Funnel shipping company collaborated with Britain's MI5 rounding up Chinese sailors in night raids and leaving thousands of white women to rear their children alone. That was why Chan was now penniless and why his grandchild watched mesmerised as the noodles took shape. But Americans wanted real noodles, yellow noodles out of a packet.

"I'm not suggesting that Chan's is going downhill. It's probably that I'm ordering the wrong things."

"The key is not to expect too much or head to Vancouver or Toronto for the real deal."

Chan indeed had frequented Canadian Chinatowns as early as the end of the nineteenth century. In 1883, Chan's Canton-San Francisco passage ticket had been converted without his knowing into a Vancouver passage after the passing of the 1882 U.S. Exclusion Law rendered the landing of new immigrants impossible. Chan was later joined by other Chans. With great loss of face, since Louis, had not made good, they were obliged to work for Mr. Sin at number 7 Douglas St. They are all listed in the 1901 census:

08/19/14 CHAN, LOUIS, m, lodger, s, May 10th, 1858, 42, CHN, to Can: 1884, Conf, Laundry hand.

08/19/15 CHAN, LONG, m, lodger, s, December 4th, 1878, 22, CHN, to Can: 1899, Conf, Laundry hand.

08/19/16 CHAN, FOO, m, lodger, m, May 5th, 1864, 36, CHN, to Can: 1899, Conf, Laundry hand.
08/19/17 CHAN, TONG, m, lodger, s, March 1st, 1879, 22, CHN, to Can: 1899, Conf, Laundry hand.
08/19/18 CHAN, GING, m, lodger, s, January 2nd 1877, 24, CHN, to Can: 1899, Conf, Laundry hand.

Chan was averse to laundering and found it as humiliating as the intellectual Chinese poet Wen Yiduo who would construct one of his better known "patriotic" poems around the shame of China reduced to a laundry service for Americans. Moreover, Chan had already been the object of a hate-campaign in England, in 1906. Chan's laundry—accused of using Moonlight soap—was threatening English laundries that claimed that whites washed whiter.

"No laundry today," said the chorus girl to Detective Chan. "So I notice," retorted Chan, nodding towards the chorus girl's scanty costume.

"I want to punch Charlie Chan in his too pregnant stomach that bellies out his white linen maternity suit."

Chan went missing with the cab fare. And what a cab fare: $4,000!

"Nice set-up, but ultimately disappointing, but there were marvelous views of Chinese San Francisco."

Chan was no peasant. He had studied for the Chinese civil service examinations, but found himself stymied by their abolition in 1905. He studied accountancy but found there was no post for a Chinese bank clerk in British Hong Kong. He had mastered English and even learnt French before shipping out. But somehow as hero of the Honolulu Police his linguistic skills disappeared to leave Chan talking like a fortune cookie (a great American invention, just like the chop suey roll):

'Dog afraid of losing job if make mistake, often fail to see tiger approach of not instructed to watch for tiger.'

'Old fashioned detective have own poor methods.'

In Hawaii, Chan also spent two years in gaol for laundering. Money that is. Chan had run a gambling operation from his back kitchen between 1987 and 1993. But Chan had been obliged to resort to such measures. Chan had been left penniless in California, all possessions having been lost when the family house had been burnt down in the arson attack on Santa Clara Chinatown during the late nineteenth-century Anti-Chinese Exclusion Campaign. But undaunted Chan moved back to California. By 1997 things seemed to have changed for the better and Chan was elected California State Assemblywoman, even becoming Democratic Majority Leader in 2002.

There was the scenario. But the film has not yet been made.

*

I have thus far discussed different kinds of yearnings for America, of those seeking utopia, and of those searching simply for temporary economic relief. For some the desire for America was consummated but then disappointment followed as they were subjected to racist exclusion or marginalization. For others the desire was frustrated as their voyage led them not to America but to substitute Americas.

There is one further category of migration to America I should like to mention, it is an emigration that is perhaps the most pervasive in the modern world: armchair migration, or immobile migration. Elsewhere in this volume the importance of American cinematic production and the impact of its processes on Chinese cinematic production has been discussed. Here I refer not simply to dubbed American movies that have encroached on, not to say dominated, world cinematographic and televisual consumption around the globe. In 2009, the Fall of the Berlin Wall was commemorated. In late 1989 the population of Eastern Europe suddenly had access to a way of life they had not experienced directly before. But what they had experienced, and what perhaps fired their imagination physically to enjoy more of it, was the access to the televisual representation of Western consumerism and in particular of the American Dream. East Germans had since the late 1950s watched what their western compatriots watched.

In China, where the Wall did not fall, the American model had been equally pervasive. Almost everything Western, including French critical theory that played an important part in the intellectual debate of the late 1980s, was filtered through America. And the tragic end to the democracy movement showed spectacularly the degree to which Chinese urban intellectual youth was wedded to the American ideology of liberty that was supposed to accompany capitalistic liberalization. When the Goddess of Democracy, a crude replica of the Statue of Liberty was, rolled into Tiananmen Square in late May, it was in ignorance of the historical context of China's relationship with America: the sad irony being that as the Statue of Liberty began her reign over New York's Ellis Island immigration station and welcomed the "huddled masses" of Europe, the Chinese had just been legally excluded from immigrating and from being American. On the other side of the continent, would-be Chinese immigrants were greeted not by Liberty but by the detention camp on Angel Island in San Francisco Bay.

Yet even after the the débâcle of June 1989, America remained the model of reference with which China's authorities would inspire and chivy on the country's citizens to enter into the spirit of market capitalism. While the dissemination of the Hollywood cinematic product was still strictly controlled, the authorities allowed superficially ambiguous representations of the American way of life to be screened. While seemingly warning about the negative effects of American culture on Chinese values, the mini-series *A Beijinger in New York* simultaneously introduced the early 1990s Chinese spectator to the wonders of American capitalist life.

The mini-series soap *A Beijinger in New York* (*Beijingren zai Niuyue*) showed the early 1990s Chinese television spectator besuited professional white men sipping diet Coke, and chain smoking 555s, a brand of American cigarette which was particularly popular in China.

Soft drinks and cigarettes were the entry point of the Chinese consumer, as early as the beginning of the 1980s, to the American-style consumer utopia to which the Chinese authorities wished their people to aspire. The domestic television soap opera *Beijingren zai Niuyue* (*A Beijinger in New York*), a twenty-one part television series, aired on Chinese television in the autumn and winter of 1993 was a Dallas-type soap opera, a text through which Chinese viewers could mediate their own popular ideology, which then was a collage of pre-Maoist "values" and remnants of post-1949 official Communist-promoted nationalist ideology. Then as today the officially inspired populist ideology emphasized, as had pre-revolutionary era Confucianism, the family unit.

In the mid-1980s, when American televisual products were still invisible on Chinese TV screens, Latin American *telenovelas* dubbed into Chinese were screened two or three episodes back to back, and proved extremely popular with Chinese television audiences. The soaps, in which the action took place principally indoors, lay great stress on apparent social mobility, the illusion of choice and practices of consumption, and, beyond the superficial ideological message, these were the very concerns that Feng Xiaogang's *Beijingren* represented and mediated. Ien Ang, noted how "personal life" provided the "ideological problematic" of the soap opera, the inner world, the family being "regarded as the ideal cradle for human happiness."[21] The external world, society, was what threatened the ideal.

Dallas, the classic TV soap, was exceedingly popular with British audiences in the 1980s, because the British TV spectator then possessed little knowledge of the reality of American life. Just as the Hollywood movies of the 1930s–1950s had successfully accompanied the spectators of Britain's cinemas through the Great Depression and the World War II, *Beijingren* would nourish the secret yearnings of the long materially-deprived Chinese television viewer. Despite the ruin that his family and dreams of being a symphony cellist had become, the protagonist Wang Qiming's two-storey spacious modern home in the New York suburbs represented an attractive and powerful vision for the Chinese urban dweller inhabiting a small and frugal apartment. American manners and customs were also explained and introduced to the then naive Chinese viewer. For instance, when Wang Qiming asked his white American competitor in the clothing business why his friend the buyer had not offered help when he was facing bankruptcy, Wang is given a lesson in the American way: "When you are in trouble you are on your own."

Wang's personal life also fell foul of American customs so alien to the early 1990s Chinese intellectual that he was. It was the love of his family that led him to give up his motherland and sacrifice his personal ambitions (his desire to become a professional cellist). But Wang Qiming lost his wife to his American business competitor, saw his daughter seduced by a young white high school student, and later become engaged to be married to the same student's father. However, while the TV series was necessarily set in New York, Chinese capitalism, the message seemed to be, *will* be different. Despite this, as China lurched into wild capitalist practices in the late 1990s the effects of Chinese capitalism did not prove to be different, least of all for women. In capitalist China woman again became a commodity object as feudal attitudes towards women crept back into the male social imaginary.

Now, a decade and half after *Beijingren* was screened, there is no longer any need to show the American capitalist model for it has already long since become the Chinese model. No matter now whether the supermarket be French-, American- or Chinese-owned, the model and the practices of consumption are those invented by America. Fifteen hundred years after Hui Shen's ship sailed to America, Chinese ships queue up in America's ports to deliver the myriad consumer goods manufactured in China to satisfy the American consumer. Has America now Americanized China or is America simply becoming the China it has Americanized?

ENDNOTES

1. Paris: Mercure de France, 2007, 279.
2. Shawn Wong, *Homebase* (New York: Penguin Books, 1993), 82–83.
3. The French orientalist Joseph de Guignes in his *Recherches sur les navigations des Chinois du côté de l'Amérique, et sur quelques peuples situés à l'extrémité orientale de l'Asie* (Paris: Académie des inscriptions et belles-lettres, 1761) was the first to evoke this "discovery," but later European sinologists were to discredit and denigrate his findings. However, twentieth-century specialists such as Joseph Needham accredited the theory of visits and migrations to the Americas by Asians over a sustained period of time lasting two millenia starting in the the 3rd century before our era. Needham also supports the theory that earlier migrations from Asia to the Americas had taken place some millenia before; see Joseph Needham, *Science and Civilization in China*, IV:3, 548–549 (Cambridge: Cambridge University Press, 1971) and see also the study in Chinese by Wei Junxian, *Zhongguoren faxian Meizhou chu kao* (Taibei: Shshi chuban gongsi, 1975). Thus Gavin Menzies' book *1421: The Year China Discovered the World* (New York: Harper Collins, 2002) is just the latest in a long series of texts recounting the prowess of Chinese mariners and promoting the claim that "the Chinese discovered America."
4. Why do we talk of Chinese emperors and of a Chinese Empire? Quite simply because the West decided to imagine China that way. Before the modern West imposed its epistemology on China those inhabiting and ruling the space

now called the Chinese Empire, called it simply *tianxia*, meaning literally "what is under the sky," in other words "the world," the known world.

5. See Gregory Lee, *Chinas Unlimited: Making the Imaginaries of China and Chineseness* (Honolulu: Hawai'i University Press, 2003), passim.

6. Since most contacts with China before the twentieth century occurred via the Cantonese-speaking ports of the south, Canton, Macau, Hong Kong, many Western names and terms were transliterated into Cantonese, when these were subsequently pronounced in Mandarin the sounds were frequently quite distant from the sounds of the original European language and their Cantonese transliteration. For instance, America, A-mei-lei-ga in Cantonese, becomes Ya-mei-li-jia in Mandarin or "modern standard Chinese."

7. Cited in Marlon K. Hom, *Songs of Gold Mountain: Cantonese Rhymes from San Francisco Chinatown* (Berkeley: University of California Press, 1987), 41.

8. Jean Baudrillard, *Amérique* (Paris: Grasset, 1986), 76.

9. See Gregory Lee, *Troubadours, Trumpeters, Troubled Makers: Lyricism, Nationalism and Hybridity in China and Its Others* (Durham, NC: Duke University Press, 1996), chapter 7.

10. There also existed a "US Postal Agency Shanghai China" which issued stamps sold in local currency. The stamps were valid for mail dispatched to the United States.

11. 102

12. Confiant, 344.

13. (New York: Alfred Knopf, 2003), 20–21.

14. Confiant, 102-103.

15. Confiant, 403.

16. Confiant, 279.

17. A.-F. Legendre, *L'Illustration: Journal Universel*, 26 December 1925.

18. Ibid.

19. Wayne Wang directed the, first Chinese American, feature film *Chan Is Missing* in 1981. Chan is the Cantonese reading of the surname 陳, and Chen its pronunciation in *putonghua* or modern standard Chinese.

20. A notorious color bar excluded would-be immigrants of color from Australia for several decades in the twentieth-century, and the Chinese in particular had known this fate as early as the nineteenth century. See Brian Castro's *Birds of Passage* (North Ryde, NSW: Angus & Robertson, 1989).

21. Ien Ang, *Watching Dallas: Soap Opera and the Melodramatic Imagination* (London: Routledge, 1985), 68.

CHAPTER 10

CIVIL RIGHTS ON THE SCREEN

MICHAEL RENOV

THE INSPIRATION FOR this essay is Barack Obama's 2008 presidential campaign and election and the enthusiastic response those events generated in the United States and around the world. One possible measure of the tidal wave of reaction stirred by Obama's election is the sheer volume of clips posted on YouTube devoted to the man. Put "Obama" in the You-Tube search box in March 2009 and you'll find there are 453,000 items. One such piece is a rather brief and not terribly popular video (with a few more than 2,000 hits and only a handful of responses posted). Entitled "Obama and Martin Luther King Speech—I Have a Dream," this brief clip (one minute twenty-seven seconds in length) is, in many ways, exemplary of much of the populist reaction sparked by the ascent to power of the first African American elected to the presidency: hyperbolic, iconoclastic, and decidedly ahistorical.

What we see is familiar enough: Obama on the campaign trail, delivering a speech, one of thousands delivered over the course of months, to what appears to be an arena of supporters. He gesticulates forcefully, microphone in hand, eventually sharing a hug with wife Michelle and superstar pal Oprah Winfrey. The power of the piece, though, lies in the blending of these rather unremarkable visuals with a soundtrack that almost (but not quite) synchs up with it, composed of carefully edited excerpts from what, by the title of the piece ("Obama and Martin Luther King Speech—I Have a Dream"), one might assume to be the seventeen and a half-minute "I Have a Dream" speech given by Martin Luther King, Jr. on the steps of the Lincoln Memorial on August 28th, 1963 during the March on Washington for Jobs and Freedom. Delivered to a live audience numbering in the hundreds of thousands, shown live on all three major television networks, "I Have a Dream" is among the most celebrated speeches of the 20th century. Barack Obama was barely two years old when King spoke of a dream he had, "that one day on the red hills of Georgia the sons of former slaves and the sons of former slave owners will be able to sit down together at the table of brotherhood." Though the match of sound and image is far from perfect and the historical mapping disparate by decades, the point is made effortlessly. For the present purposes, the clip is a noteworthy instance of semiosis, one that will allow us to ask some questions about the character and mutability of the sign itself.

FROM KING TO OBAMA

Our discussion of that mutability begins with the clip's title which promises to link the words of King's most visionary speech with its eventual culmination through the political ascendancy of a black man to the presidency. In fact, the audio is taken from another speech entirely, one given the night before King's murder on August 4th, 1968 in Memphis, Tennessee. Known as the "I've Been to the Mountaintop" speech, it was delivered at Mason Temple, the Church of God in Christ headquarters in Memphis. The chilling words delivered at the close of that speech have of course Biblical echoes (Moses allowed to view Canaan from atop Mount Nebo but not to enter it), but King had come to town to add his ethical weight to a labor struggle, that of Memphis sanitation workers—almost exclusively African Americans—out on strike, in search of a fair contract. He was there to encourage the people of Memphis to rally around their brothers in need, to remain mindful of their strength through solidarity. Yet the concluding moments of the oration are what survive, seeming harbingers of the darkness on the horizon: "Well, I don't know what will happen now. We've got some difficult days ahead. But it really doesn't matter with me now, because I've been to the mountaintop. And I don't mind ... And so I'm happy, tonight. I'm not worried about anything. I'm not fearing any man! Mine eyes have seen the glory of the coming of the Lord!!" The dramatic conclusion reaches a messianic peak that the You-Tube author no doubt hoped to channel. Yet the gap between title and content—the concatenation of King speeches in a piece that I've characterized as hyperbolic, iconoclastic and decidedly ahistorical—I take to be symptomatic of much current political rhetoric and popular culture in ways that I shall outline.

FROM CIVIL RIGHTS TO THE WHITE HOUSE

The ideological bottom line proposed by this YouTube clip or rather "produced" through the magic of cinema (a play of sound/image relations orchestrating multiple temporalities) is a commonly held notion of Barack Obama as the apotheosis of more than fifty years of struggle for racial equality in the United States dating to the 1955 Montgomery (Alabama) Bus Boycott, a year-long effort to end the segregation of public buses in the Alabama state capital that brought to the world stage Rosa Parks and a very young Martin Luther King, Jr. Exemplars of passive resistance—non-violent civil disobedience in the tradition of Mahatma Gandhi—Parks and King were but the public faces of an army of dedicated volunteers, shock troops committed to bringing down racial segregation in the American south. Soon they were to be joined by countless others— the college students, beginning in February 1960, who "sat-in" at lunch counters from Greensboro, North Carolina to Nashville, Tennessee and were carted off to jail, the Mississippi Freedom Riders who, in May 1961 left Washington, D.C. on a chartered bus to test the limits of desegregation in the darkest corners of the south, and the marchers in Birmingham, Alabama on April 2nd, 1963 who, under order from Police Chief Bull Connor, were attacked by police dogs and, subsequently, had their images splashed on the pages of newspapers and magazines around the world.

But these are only the first chapters of a long engagement during which the Civil Rights movement was transformed—radically and in a few short years—in part through the assassinations of Medgar Evers, Malcolm X, and King (in 1963, 1965 and 1968 respectively) and the heightened militancy of the late 1960s. What I want to argue is that the elision of the darker and more militant phases of struggle effected by the merger of Obama 2008 and King 1963 works, through its shorthand, to draw the newly elected president back toward the consensual middle while sidestepping vast chunks of the historical record. It proposes a direct lineage, an unbroken and idealized succession of inspirational leadership for those engaged in the struggle for racial equality.

Let me be clear. I make no accusations or cast aspersions. For it is the very nature of semiosis to engender slippage, a malleability of meaning, even abject appropriation. The question is the cost to deeper critical and historical understanding. In this essay, I want to return to the historical record by way of the documentary film, to see through recourse to a series of documentary instances how the sounds and images of struggle played out on the screens of America. In that process we will discover the power and flexibility of these signs to inspire and energize contemporaneous audiences as well as those of subsequent times who had no personal memory of the events to which they refer.

SEMIOSIS AND THE DOCUMENTARY

As I've stated, this is a study of semiosis. As a documentary scholar, I have on occasion written of the special *indexical bond* of the documentary film by which I mean the physical linkage between sign and referent, the guarantee that what one sees on the screen stands as a verifiable trace of what once stood before the lens. The light rays that bounce off the object placed before the lens are registered on photosensitive material leaving an imprint. The photograph, writes Roland Barthes, offers "an immediate presence to the world—a co-presence [...] Every photograph is a certificate of presence."[1] The images of an orating Barack Obama hard at work on the campaign trail inspire belief that what we see is precisely what existed before the camera's lens. In fact, the claim of indexicality insists in all the photographic arts. It is the status to which André Bazin refers in his famous essay on "The Ontological Status of the Photographic Image": "Only a photographic lens can give us the kind of image of the object that is capable of satisfying the deep need man has to substitute for it something more than a mere approximation, a kind of decal or transfer. The photographic image is the object itself, the object freed from the conditions of time and space that govern it."[2] The documentary's power as a vehicle of preservation and revivification depends upon its indexicality, its physical tie to a preexistent social field.

But it was Peter Wollen, in his ground-breaking 1969 book, *Signs and Meanings in the Cinema*, who, despite the prevailing preference for the works of Ferdinand de Saussure, suggested that film studies had need of the insights of Charles Sanders Peirce, an American philosopher and historian of science who had posited the three-fold character of the sign. According to Peirce, there were indexical, iconic and symbolic signs. As we have seen, the index draws its force from physical linkage or connection (e.g., the footprint in the sand), while the icon pivots on similarity or resemblance, and the symbol establishes meaning through convention ("the relationship between a symbolic sign and the object it represents is conventional, functioning on the basis of an interpretative habit agreed to by consensus")[3].

But if we turn to the works of Peirce and his followers, we learn that signs are intrinsically dynamic. Indexical signs, for example, almost always contain elements of the other two types of sign (iconic and symbolic). "Whenever a sign enters into the semiosis, the dynamic process in which it signifies a given object and produces an interpretant, all three mechanisms—connection/ interaction, similarity and convention—help establish the meaning of the sign. Therefore the designations 'indexical,' 'iconic' and 'symbolic' simply indicate the sign's dominant, but never sole, mechanism of the standing-for relation."[4] Wollen agreed: "The great merit of Peirce's analysis of signs is that he did not see the different aspects as mutually exclusive. Unlike Saussure he did not show any particular prejudice in favour of one or the other. Indeed, he wanted a logic and a rhetoric which would be based on all three aspects. It is only by considering the interaction of the three different dimensions of the cinema that we can understand its aesthetic effect."[5]

We can see this dynamism and fluidity in the YouTube Obama/King duet. The gestural Obama now given the voice of his martyred forebear is an amalgam of index (we intuit the veridical or documentative guarantee), icon (both the image of the president-to-be and the voice of King are instantly recognizable) and symbol. It is the cinema's symbolic domain that is the most elusive and has inspired entire interpretive communities. For his part, Wollen held that the indexical and iconic aspects of the cinematic sign were far more powerful while the symbolic was "limited and secondary."[6] While this claim may hold for the cinema proper (the feature length fiction), it is not persuasive as we consider the text at hand. The Obama/King sound/image is heavily overdetermined, overflowing with meanings tinged by the symbolic. It is thus to the symbolic register that we must turn for explication of its tangled signification.

In a text entitled *Mythologies* published in France in 1957, Roland Barthes wrote persuasively of "mythic speech," by which he meant a peculiar or second-order sign system, a kind of meta-linguistic process through which a sign became a signifier for a second level of semiosis. Barthes' famous example was of a cover image from an issue of *Paris-Match* in which a young black soldier in a French uniform is shown happily saluting what is presumed to be an out-of-frame French flag. For Barthes the sign of one young man's salute is at the same time the ground for a second-order semiotic activity, the production of a mythic meaning that implies the continuing potency of the French Empire and its nationalist appeal even to the colonized, black Africans, Algerians and others, who by the late 1950s had begun to rebel.

The meaning of the sign at the first level (one young man saluting) is enveloped in and overwhelmed by the second-level imputation of a multi-cultural French beneficence: "As a total of linguistic signs, the meaning of the myth has its own value, it belongs to a history, that of the [...] Negro: in the meaning, a signification is already built, and could very well be self-sufficient if myth did not take hold of it and did not turn it suddenly into an empty, parasitical form."[7] As Barthes notes, the fundamental character of the mythical concept is to allow itself to be appropriated. "This is because myth is speech *stolen and restored*. Only, speech which is restored is no longer quite that which was stolen: when it was brought back, it was not put exactly in its place. It is this brief act of larceny, this moment taken for a surreptitious faking, which gives mythical speech its benumbed look."[8] In simplest terms, mythic utterance is frozen speech, deprived of its power to speak the past: "Myth deprives the object of which it speaks of all History. In it, history evaporates."[9]

Now I don't mean to say that our YouTube clip, act of fandom that it is, can be accused of the history-robbing sleight of hand of the infamous *Paris-Match* cover. But in its easy, 1963-to-2008 elision of a complex and volatile history of struggle for civil rights and racial equality, it renders mute the struggles, the debates and most of all the inelegant radicalism of and reactionary violence against those who served and sacrificed.

275

What I propose to do here is to offer, by way of recovery and resurrection, some of the documentary sounds and images of the intervening decades as an antidote to mythic speech, a road back through the history of the movement. In doing so, I hope to rediscover the power of these signs and to note their dynamism, fluidity, and malleability.

THE DOCUMENTARY ANTIDOTE TO "MYTHIC SPEECH"

The first of these reclaimed scenes comes from a remarkable film entitled *Sit-In*, first broadcast on December 20th, 1960 as the second installment of NBC's "White Paper" series. Created as a "flagship" documentary series to be anchored by Chet Huntley and as a rival to "CBS Reports" which, under the guidance of Fred Friendly and Edward R. Murrow, had the year before begun to produce ambitious exposes and public affairs programming,[10] "NBC White Paper" sought to burnish the network's reputation and help dispel the cloud that hovered over the industry in the wake of the quiz show scandals.[11] The choice to focus on the sit-in movement was a timely one. Having erupted only months earlier (the first sit-in occurred on February 1st, 1960 in Greensboro, North Carolina when black college students began spontaneous demonstrations and "sit-downs" in protest of the segregation policies of Woolworth and Kress stores), the movement was beginning to attract the attention of the nation. Boycotts of downtown businesses were demonstrating the economic clout of black America. Moreover striking images of black college students being carted off to local jails en masse while singing protest songs were beginning to affect public opinion and move local lawmakers. Here was Gandhi and King's non-violent civil disobedience in action and the drama was riveting. Cameras were capturing the stand-downs between black and white, the violent reprisals of white supremacist counter-protestors who verbally insulted and physically attacked the black youth as well as the actions of law enforcement who frequently mistreated them. In the hour-long broadcast, directed by Robert D. Young (later the writer, director or producer of a succession of socially-conscious features including *Nothing But a Man* [1964], *Alambrista!* [1977] and *The Ballad of Gregorio Cortez* [1982]), direct cinema footage of marches and confrontations alternate with interviews with the participants.

FIGURE 1: Robert D. Young's *Sit In* (NBC White Paper, 1960)
brought the Civil Rights struggles of young African American college
students to an American audience.

In her fine account of the program, Sasha Torres notes that the show in-cluded a rather unique device, the flashback. It begins at the height of the conflict—when four thousand blacks marched on City Hall—and returns to the beginnings of the struggle two months earlier. But the most re-markable insight Torres offers has to do with the continuing life and util-ity of the program long after its initial broadcast. She cites Andrew Young's memoir in which the future mayor of Atlanta, Congressman, and U.S. Ambassador to the United Nations recalls watching the broadcast with his family and realizing it was time to leave his job with the National Council of Churches in New York and return home to the front lines of battle in the south. Young was to go on to use the film as part of the curriculum of the citizenship school he helped run at the Dorchester Center in Georgia in the early 1960s. The graduates of this school and so many others like it were to become the grass-roots organizers who would fan out across the south to organize in the community, register black voters and push for so-cial change.[12] We can say with some certainty that this nationally broad-cast documentary film served a secondary audience: it was for some a training film that demonstrated how to build a non-violent movement dedicated to passive resistance, solidarity and community action.

By mid-decade, a mere five years after the making of *Sit-In*, the world had radically changed. In the wake of the assassinations of Medgar Evers and Malcolm X; the September 1963 death of four little black girls in a church bombing on a Sunday morning in Birmingham, Alabama; the dis-covery of the bodies of three young civil rights workers, Goodman, Schw-erner and Chaney, in a ditch outside Philadelphia, Mississippi in August

277

1964; Bloody Sunday (March 7th, 1965), the attack by armed police on peaceful demonstrators on the Edmund Pettus bridge in Selma, Alabama; and the eruption of violence in the Watts ghetto outside Los Angeles in August 1965, non-violent protest as the primary weapon for change was being seriously challenged. King had indeed received the Nobel Peace Prize in October 1964 but young leaders such as Stokely Carmichael of SNCC (Student Non-Violent Coordinating Committee) were beginning to ask what his organization had to offer the black community in the wake of all the violence and frustration: "For too many years," wrote Carmichael, "black Americans marched and had their heads broken and got shot [...] After years of this, we are at almost the same point—because we demonstrated from a position of weakness. We cannot be expected any longer to march and have our heads broken in order to say to whites, come on, you're nice guys. For you are not nice guys. We have found you out."[13] By 1966, the year of Carmichael's manifesto entitled "What We Want," the demand for Black Power had begun to replace "We Shall Overcome."

This is the context for the second text to be considered, Santiago Alvarez's 1965 short film, *Now!*, produced in Cuba as an act of solidarity with American blacks struggling for their rights a mere 90 miles away. A film set to a song—sung by Lena Horne to the tune of an Israeli folk tune, "Hava Nagila," with lyrics by Betty Comden and Adolph Green (the musical comedy duo better known as the creators of *On the Town*, *Singin' in the Rain*, and *The Bandwagon*)—*Now!* relied upon news footage and photojournalism appropriated from the pages of *Life* magazine. Alvarez's montage style, likened by many to that of 20's Soviet cinema, was necessitated in part by limited resources. "The North Americans," said Alvarez, "blockade us, so forcing us to improvise. For instance, the greatest inspiration in the photo-collage of American magazines in my films is the American government who have prevented me getting hold of live material."[14] The images Alvarez recycles and renders dynamic are nothing more nor less than the public record of these troubled times, a record that the assumption of a King-to-Obama direct lineage must of necessity ignore. In the United States, *Now!* has remained for more than four decades an underground classic. In the 1960s it was available for viewing only through an underground network that linked movement audiences on college campuses and in major cities. It is now distributed by New York's Third World Newsreel, the latter-day manifestation of the Newsreel collective of radical documentary filmmakers founded in 1967.

FIGURE 2: *Now!* (1965), coupling scenes of struggle with a rousing
Lena Horne vocal, was Cuban filmmaker Santiago Alvarez's
contribution to the American Civil Rights movement.

In July 1967, riots in Detroit and Newark, cities with large and isolated black populations, left sixty-nine dead. That same year, Muhammad Ali was stripped of his heavyweight boxing crown for refusing military service and 100,000 demonstrators marched on the Pentagon to protest the Vietnam War. On April 4th, 1968, Martin Luther King, Jr. was shot dead by sniper fire as he stood on a Memphis motel balcony and the nation erupted in violence.

But the life and writings of H. Rap Brown may be the best barometer of the turbulent times. The one-time chairman of SNCC, by 1968 Brown had renounced his membership and joined the Black Panther Party, eventually serving as their Minister of Justice. His was but one of many angry black voices whose words polarized America and electrified the black community. In 1969 book entitled *Die, Nigger, Die!*, Brown famously opined: "The question of violence has been cleared up. This country was born of violence. Violence is as American as cherry pie. Black people have always been violent, but our violence has always been directed toward each other. If nonviolence is to be practiced, then it should be practiced in our community and end there. Violence is a necessary part of revolutionary struggle [...] We can no longer allow threats of death to immobilize us. Death is no stranger to Black folks. We've been dying ever since we got here [...] The country has delivered an ultimatum to Black people; America says to Blacks: you either fight to live or you will live to die. I say to America, Fuck It! Freedom or Death. Power to the People."[15]

FIGURE 3: Newsreel's *Black Panther* (1969) was a paean to black militancy at the height of its power.

The film *Black Panther* was shot in 1969 in Oakland, California, headquarters of the Black Panther Party. It was the work of San Francisco Newsreel, the Bay Area counterpart to the New York collective that had months earlier produced *Columbia Revolt (Newsreel #14)*, an insider's account of the Columbia University student strike that resulted in the takeover of five university buildings and the eventual arrest of scores of students. *Columbia Revolt* included, among other things, footage of a student protestor wearing sunglasses and smoking a cigar, his feet propped up on Columbia President Grayson L. Kirk's desk in Low Library. It also included footage of black students occupying Hamilton Hall asking white students to leave. Militancy, separatism, black nationalism—such was the order of the day.

As early as 1966, the Black Panther Party, soon to suffer the death or imprisonment of many of its leaders, announced a ten-point plan which it circulated within the black community. A secondary audience was the white power elite, target of the rhetorical attacks, characterized by Black Panther Party Minister of Information Eldridge Cleaver as "the bald-headed businessmen from the Chamber of Commerce." Nonviolence, passive resistance, King's "table of brotherhood" were now despised by this most militant faction of the movement. The final demand of the ten-point plan, the Party's major political objective, was for a United Nations-supervised plebiscite to be held "throughout the black colony in which only black colonial subjects will be allowed to participate, for the purpose of determining the will of black people as to their national destiny."[16] This was nothing less than a call for black national sovereignty and separation from the United States of America, the country that would, four decades later, be led by a black man.

BLACK, PROUD AND GAY

The final proof of the malleability perhaps even fungibility of the audio-visual sign across the rich history of the civil rights movement as represented on the screen comes from Marlon Riggs' groundbreaking *Tongues Untied* (1989). This autobiographical work of much power helped launch what Bill Nichols has called the performative mode of documentary. Often fragmentary, densely textured and personal, such works perform a self, a body, construct a subjectivity within a context that is often historically precise and politically engaged.[17]

In *Tongues Untied*, Riggs sets out to extend the arena of civil rights and of black activism to a rather different community, that of the black, gay male. The claim is that the solidarity King and others long championed for the movement must be extended to those whose sexual identities and choices have resulted in their exclusion from the black mainstream and its institutions—the church, the press, the political and cultural elite. *Tongues* sought to rally, in Riggs' words, "a nationwide community of voices—some quietly poetic, some undeniably raw and angry—that together challenge our society's most deeply entrenched myths about what it means to be black, to be gay, to be a man, and above all, to be human."[18] Produced near the height of the AIDS epidemic, a moment when the slogan "Silence = death" became a rallying cry for public health advocates and gay activists alike, the film (with images of black men kissing) enraged political conservatives who called it obscene and attacked the National Endowment of the Arts and the Corporation for Public Broadcasting for their fiscal sponsorship.

But *Tongues*'s attack was aimed not only at the right. Riggs accused a homophobic black America of silent collusion with its historic foes. "The legacy of Harriet Tubman," wrote Riggs, "Sojourner Truth, James Baldwin, Bayard Rustin, and Martin Luther King, Jr., and the many thousands more who lived and died to free us all from prescribed social roles defined by a dominant majority, that legacy has come to this: black straight Americans [...] passively, silently, acquiescing as political bedmates to the likes of the Reverend Wildmon, James Kilpatrick, and Jesse Helms."[19] At *Tongues Untied*'s close, an aggressive graphic announced "BLACK MEN LOVING BLACK MEN IS *THE* REVOLUTIONARY ACT." The film sought to extend the reach of the historic civil rights movement to include those who had been excluded, silenced, and erased *within* the black community. Using a lengthy lap dissolve that binds together past and present, Riggs linked the marchers for freedom at Selma (King, Ralph Abernathy, James Lawson) with bare-chested black men marching down a Manhattan street in a 1980s gay pride parade. That intercutting and its claim for a fundamental equivalency across the two scenes has raised many an eyebrows over the years.

Like the Obama/King YouTube piece with which we began, it can be accused of hyperbole and iconoclasm but not, I would argue, ahistoricism. Instead Riggs offers something very like Eisenstein's notion of intellectual montage in which apparently disparate elements are compared and equilibrated in a forceful rhetorical gesture.

I have undertaken here a study of semiosis, of a chain of significations of a particular sort, those surrounding the movement for racial and civil rights in America that has, by some accounts, culminated in the election of Barack Obama. I have suggested that a teleology of this kind, played out in popular culture, is false because fundamentally ahistorical and in a way that stunts and diminishes our understanding. For if the King-to-Obama connection is a necessary one it is also profoundly inadequate owing to its blindness to that complex weave of social forces and actors that, in all its contradictions, constituted that movement. I have taken recourse to the public record, to the witnessing capacity of a series of documentary texts that remind us that the struggles of the past half-century have almost always been waged with cameras present, often as a tool and a weapon. What was and continues to be a social movement for change is also the basis for a semiotic activity without end.

ENDNOTES

1. Roland Barthes, *Camera Lucida: Reflections on Photography*, trans. Richard Howard (New York: Hill and Wang, 1981), 84, 87.

2. André Bazin, "The Ontology of the Photographic Image," *What Is Cinema?* trans. Hugh Gray (Berkeley: University of California Press, 1967), 14.

3. Jorgen Dines Johansen and Svend Erik Larsen, *Signs in Use: An Introduction to Semiotics*, trans. Dinda L. Gorlee and John Irons (London: Routledge, 2002), 46.

4. Ibid., 51.

5. Peter Wollen, *Signs and Meaning in the Cinema* (Bloomington, IN: Indiana University Press, 1969), 141.

6. Ibid., 140.

7. Roland Barthes, *Mythologies*, trans. Annette Lavers (New York: Hill and Wang, 1972), 117.

8. Ibid., 125.

9. Ibid., 151.

10. The best known of these long-form documentaries may be *Harvest of Shame*, an interrogation into the plight of migrant farmworkers first broadcast on 26th November 1960.

11. Sasha Torres, *Black, White and in Color: Television and Black Civil Rights* (Princeton, NJ: Princeton University Press, 2003), 36–37. Torres references Michael Curtin's *Redeeming the Wasteland: Television Documentary and Cold War Politics* (New Brunswick, NJ: Rutgers University Press).

12. Ibid., 41–44.

13. Stokely Carmichael, "What We Want." In Judith Clavir Albert and Stewart Edward Albert, eds., *The Sixties Papers: Documents of a Rebellious Decade* (New York: Praeger, 1984), 137.

14. Michael Chanan, *The Cuban Image* (London: BFI Publishing, 1985), 184.

15. H. Rap Brown, "Die, Nigger, Die!" In *The Sixties Papers*, 157, 158.

16. The Black Panther Party, "Platform and Program." In *The Sixties Papers*, 163.

17. Bill Nichols, *Blurred Boundaries* (Bloomington, IN: Indiana University Press, 1994), 92–106. See also my account of documentary subjectivity in *The Subject of Documentary* (Minneapolis: University of Minnesota Press, 2004).

18. Marlon Riggs, "Tongues Re-Tied." In Michael Renov and Erika Suderburg, eds., *Resolutions: Contemporary Video Practices* (Minneapolis: University of Minnesota Press, 1996), 185.

19. Ibid., 187.

PART 4

AMERICA GOES DIGITAL

CHAPTER 11

GOODBYE RABBIT EARS: VISUALIZING AND MAPPING THE US DIGITAL TV TRANSITION

LISA PARKS

THE SHIFT TO digital television in the U.S. was scheduled to occur on February 17th, 2009. The federal government had been preparing for the transition since the 1990s, mandating that new TV sets be manufactured with digital tuners, supporting broadcast stations as they phase out analog and phase in digital systems, and informing consumers about the imminent changes. This historic transition, compared to the inauguration of color TV, and referred to as the Digital TV or DTV transition, had been widely publicized. Though regulators, broadcasters and manufacturers had already made many of the key decisions about the future of television, technological negotiations remained for many consumer/citizens. In December 2008 there were an estimated 19 million U.S. households still using analog television sets. In technology studies we often hear of "early adopters" and we might call this group the "diehard users." Owners of analog sets had to decide how and whether they want to continue to receive a television signal and could either purchase a digital converter box or a television set with a digital tuner, or subscribe to cable or satellite television. The federal government subsidized the transition and the National Telecommunication and Information Administration (NTIA) administered a $1.5 billion coupon program to support those who wanted to retrofit their analog receivers with converter boxes.

In January 2009 the U.S. Congress decided to extend the deadline for the switchover to June 12, 2009 as a Nielsen corporation survey indicated 6.5 million U.S. homes were still not prepared for the transition.[1] Additional funding came from the Obama administration's federal stimulus package in the amount of $650 million to support the coupon converter and public outreach programs. As Senator Rockefeller who introduced the delay bill observed, "The transition is going to hit our most vulnerable citizens—the poor, the elderly, the disabled, and those with language barriers—the hardest."[2]

The Telecommunications Act of 1996 mandated the digital TV transition, and since then several players with varied interests have maneuvered to benefit from the shift. Electronics manufacturers stand to increase profits from the sale of digital TV receivers and converter boxes. Cable and satellite providers hoped to attract new subscribers and have become increasingly competitive. Consumers have upgraded their systems and have been promised that DTV will bring a "clearer and better" picture as well as new channels and services. Federal agencies hoped to effectively facilitate this nation-wide infrastructural shift and take credit for a smooth transition. Broadcasters, however, have had the most to lose since any kind of signal interruption—whether resulting from confusion on the user end or the limited range of the digital signal —could lead to a reduction in viewership and therefore a decrease in advertising revenues.

Media and communication studies scholars have been tracking the digital TV transition for over a decade, critically examining federal policies, technological changes and entertainment industry practices. Existing research tends to focus on two areas. First, several have used diffusion theory to consider issues of technological adoption focusing on the willingness of consumers to adapt to DTV.[3] Second, others have examined how the transition has impacted U.S. consumer electronics and its fledgling position in that global industry.[4] Few, if any, have engaged with the discourses of public outreach initiatives and their address to specific communities. In an effort to supplement this work, then, I explore how technical information about DTV was communicated to the public in the months leading up to the transition. Examining a variety of materials, from news reports to maps, from public service announcements to amateur videos that document the end of analog service, I consider how consumer-citizens have negotiated the digital TV transition. In the process, I highlight three issues: 1) the way fixed income and minority communities have been singled out in relation to television; 2) the uneven geographies of the transition; and 3) the way viewers and digital corporations have responded to the transition in its aftermath. What I hope to emphasize throughout is that multiple U.S. "televisions" exist, which is manifest in the variety of signal distribution systems (OTA, cable, satellite, web, mobile phone) that persist, the different social communities that engage with television technologies, and the differential geographies of its transmission.

"YOUR TV NEEDS TO BE READY
SO YOU CAN KEEP WATCHING"

Despite TV scholars' recent focus on cable, satellite, interactive and web-based TV, it is important to recognize that a significant chunk of the U.S. TV audience—roughly 15%—has continued to receive "free" over the air signals for decades. What if the moment of the digital transition led to scholarly investigations of the analog diehards rather than the technophiles that raced to join the alleged digital TV "revolution"? Given the fixation on novelty in our techno-culture and often in our field, we have much to learn from consumers who, whether by default or by choice, continue to use machines simply because *they still work*. It's too easy to equate the use of old machines with poverty or reticence alone.[5]

Many assume that analog TV viewers are elderly folks who grew up with rabbit ears, and indeed some of them are. Yet a glance at the FCC digital transition website reminds us just how diverse the U.S. analog TV audience is. Information about the transition is provided in the following languages: Amharic, Arabic, Bosnian, Cambodian, Chinese, Creole, French, Hmong, Japanese, Korean, Kurdish, Laotian, Navajo, Polish, Portuguese, Russian, Somali, Spanish, Tagalog, Vietnamese, Yupik. That this array of languages appears suggests that non-English speaking ethnic communities were particularly impacted by the transition. Indeed, some such communities have historically received local over the air programming in their own languages. One public service announcement about the digital TV transition features a Somali American woman conveying information about the transition to her community in the Twin Cities. Another features two white men demonstrating how to hook up a converter box yet the voiceover dub is in Hmong and it has English sub-titles as well. Yet another made by students participating in the American Indian Summer Institute shows the father of the home jerryrigging rabbit ears with foil to in an effort to get reception.

In 2007 Nielsen Corporation released results of a study that found that low income, elderly and Hispanic and Black viewers were the least prepared for the transition. The FCC (Federal Communications Commission) and NAB (National Association of Broadcasters) used the survey as a basis for their many public outreach programs, targeting elderly, minority and low-income communities, many of whom live on fixed incomes and cannot afford to purchase new television sets, or subscribe to cable or satellite television. The Nielsen survey has drawn attention to populations that are for the most part ignored by the commercial television industry and has been used, in effect, to foster a "no viewer left behind" policy. For decades, the interests of the elderly, the poor and a multitude of ethnic minorities have been strikingly incongruent with those of the commercial television industry. There are few, if any, primetime network TV series or major national cable channels addressed exclusively to elderly, low-income and/or ethnic minorities, except for Spanish-Language channels such as Telemundo, Univision and Galavision, and the African American cable channel, BET. With the shift from analog to digital, however, there emerged a change of tune. Suddenly broadcasters began to care about these constituencies and this was registered not in a shift in programming content, but in the major public outreach campaigns conducted by organizations such as the National Association of Broadcasters, which has desperately tried to maintain current viewership and not let anyone slip through the ratings cracks.

Indeed, national and local broadcasting organizations have gone to great lengths to communicate with viewers about the transition. As suggested already there has been an armada of public service announcements heralding the changeover. They range from the relatively high budget flashy videos of trade groups to the more homegrown ones of local community organizations. One PSA sponsored by the National Cable and Telecommunications Association that frequently aired on CNN featured a sixty-something man strolling through a barren landscape, and, as the sun sets behind him, he announces the end of analog and birth of digital TV. Another starred former FCC Chairman Kevin Martin with a direct address to TV viewers in which he proclaims, "Your TV needs to be ready so you can keep watching." Yet another presented a popcorn-munching family huddled around a suspense show that disappointingly turns into static. One, sponsored by the American Disabled Peoples Association, structured as a music video sung to the ABBA song "S.O.S.," featured several "doctors" performing surgery on their TV receivers.[6] Finally, a parody from late night TV revealed a sweet elderly woman trying to set up her converter box. After wrestling with tangled cables she asks, "Will all of this make Jack Benny come back?" She then snips a cable with her scissors and sticks her remote control in the microwave in a desperate effort to capture the digital signal.[7]

While this parody no doubt stirs a chuckle, in much press coverage of the digital TV transition senior white women have been positioned as the archetypal "neighbors who need our assistance." *The Oregonian* featured a photo of 87 year-old Bernice McNeel with the caption "no signal" and reported that after having two converter boxes installed, she was still not receiving all of the channels she used to. The article goes on to explain that reception problems are "especially common in Portland where hilly terrain complicates reception and where an unusually high proportion of people rely on over-the-air broadcasts to watch programs."[8] A *New York Times* article shows a photo of 77 year-old Vesta Clemmons who lives alone in Houston as she watches a meals-on-wheels volunteer install her converter so that she won't have to miss her favorite news show "World News with Charles Gibson."[9] Some senior men apparently had challenges with the transition as well. For instance, a 70 year -old Joplin, Missouri man was arrested and charged with unlawful discharge of a firearm when he shot his television set after trying unsuccessfully to set up his converter box.[10]

While some of the PSAs offered step-by-step instructions about how to hook up a converter box, others emphasized the superior quality of digital TV as a rational for system upgrades. This broad collection of PSAs, of which I've mentioned a tiny sliver, is important in that it registers the various ways in which the public has been encouraged to understand and negotiate the transition from analog to digital TV. Most of the PSAs emphasize the importance of keeping the television set operating and this serves divergent agendas. Broadcasters (both stations and trade organizations) have been blanketing the airwaves with PSAs not only because they are concerned about their public service mandate, but also because they do not want to lose viewers in the transition since their advertising fees are contingent upon ratings. And civil rights groups have insisted access to television is important not just as means of entertainment, but because it is the source of vital information such as weather reports (ie tornado warnings and fire evacuations), school closings and news needed by all citizens.[11] Some PSAs positioned television as a public utility, emphasizing the need to upgrade so that citizens can continue watching programming that is both personally meaningful to them and that keeps them informed about important daily developments.

A number of public education and outreach projects have been supported by civil rights and eldercare organizations. The Washington, D.C.-based Leadership Conference on Civil Rights Education Fund organized Digital TV Assistance Centers in major cities across the U.S. and provided educational materials for translation in different languages and trained volunteers. The organization partnered with local groups to help a range of communities, whether Chinese Americans in San Francisco or African Americans in Atlanta.[12] As one of the San Francisco-based volunteers points out, for many people technology is very complicated and becomes even more complicated when encountered in a foreign language. For consumers who don't speak English, she explained, it can be very difficult to know which converter box to buy at the store much less how to install it at home since instructions are typically in English.[13]

Since the DTV transition impacted a high proportion of elderly citizens living on fixed incomes, local senior citizen centers and national organizations such AARP, Elders in Action and Meals on Wheels developed education and assistance programs in an effort to help. Senior citizen centers hosted public lectures about the changeover (sometimes by FCC commissioners themselves) and distributed FCC information packets. AARP provided a DTV information hotline in English and Spanish and published a series of articles about it in their national website and magazine.[14] Meals on Wheels programs from Minneapolis to Houston coordinated and performed converter box installations for seniors who were already having hot meals delivered.[15]

Local communities also banded together to figure out ways of addressing the shortage of federal coupons for converter boxes. By December 2008 the program had run out of funding and there were an estimated 2.6 million people on the waiting list for coupons. While 44 million coupons were distributed, only 18 million had been redeemed.[16] Informal economies emerged as a result. The $40 coupons expired after 90 days of receipt, but were transferable. Thus local churches and community organizations began to collect and redistribute un-used coupons as a way of helping those on the waitlist or others who need them.[17] While major chain stores charged up to $100 for new converter boxes, some local electronics stores charged only $40, which is the value of a coupon. At its 3,400 stores retail giant Wal-Mart sold converter boxes for $9.87 with a digital coupon (for a total of $49.87).[18] Others who acquired coupons but did not plan to use them, attempted to scalp them on craigslist for $20 or best offer. Still others set out to impede the purchase of converter boxes altogether by posting a Youtube video claiming the Wal-Mart Magnavox converter box was equipped with a tiny camera and microphone and that the DTV transition was at the heart of a conspiracy to extend surveillance into the American home.[19]

Ironically, there has almost been more discussion and recognition of the interests of the poor, elderly, disabled and ethnic communities in relation to digital television than in relation to any other federal programs for education, health care or housing. While this concern for low-income, elderly and minority communities may seem on the surface to be a good thing, it also exemplifies a paternalistic posturing toward these communities that figures them as uniquely dependent upon television above all else. What this discourse conceals is how deeply dependent U.S. commercial television is upon a viewer body count. As experts have explained, a substantial loss in numbers of viewers threatens to compromise the business model of U.S. broadcasters. Since the Nielsen rating samples are randomly drawn, each and every viewer in each and every household counts.

Moreover, the cost of television upgrades came at a moment of economic crisis for many in the U.S. Though the federal government has included provisions for the DTV transition in the federal stimulus package, an economic crisis makes conditions worse for those who are already struggling. During this time the unemployment rate rose to 10% in several states and an increasing number of families were faced with the loss of their jobs and homes and tried to keep food on the table. In these conditions, the prospect of purchasing a new digital television set, converter box or antenna, or subscribing to cable or satellite television was a luxury that many could not afford. As one writer suggested, anyone on fixed incomes should immediately give up their cable or satellite subscriptions and make the necessary investment to access free digital TV. By his calculations, doing so could save the consumer $13,000 over 20 years.[20] As the Leadership Conference on Civil Rights indicates, "a successful transition from analog to digital television is vital to ensuring that those who may be on the remote edges of the economy and society, and already on the wrong side of the Digital Divide, do not suddenly also find themselves on the wrong side of a Digital Television Divide."[21]

OUT OF RANGE

Cartography is yet another way that the digital TV transition has been visualized and communicated. One detail view of a national map reveals the anticipated impact on viewer reception of the ABC network's signal. Orange dots on the map indicate areas across the states of Iowa, Missouri and Kansas that underwent signal loss with the conversion to digital TV. The FCC made a variety of such maps available to visually communicate the effects of this infrastructural change from local and national perspectives.[22] By examining such maps it is possible to observe some of the unevenness and false promises of the transition. Different areas across the U.S. have been affected in different ways. Rather than gain a sharper crisper image, many viewers have lost "free" television signals altogether. In 2009 the FCC predicted that 196 or 11% of the nation's 1,749 broadcast stations would have a signal that reaches at least 20% fewer viewers than their current analog signals. Thus just as the transition has impacted social communities in different ways, so has it effected particular locations in different ways.

Historically, U.S. broadcast coverage has taken on the form of a patchwork of systems rather than existing as a ubiquitous transmission field. These coverage maps are useful because they make this technical reality intelligible. In the national network maps of ABC, CBS, Fox and NBC the orange areas indicate signal loss, the green patches indicate signal gain. Despite the promises of glossy trade PSAs, then, these maps exposed the reality that the conversion has not occured equally for all. Many viewers on the edge of a station's coverage area lost television service. Some not only required a new converter box, but some had to purchase a different roof top antenna or booster as well. Digital signals are more finicky than analog broadcasts and topography can effect reception. It is possible for one home in a neighborhood to get great reception, while another up the block could have its clear picture obscured by a tall tree or far-off hill. This is a significant issue that was not adequately addressed in national public information campaigns.

These maps also contain information that has been used by antenna manufacturers and cable and satellite operators to target "out of range" citizen-consumers who are unable to receive free digital TV channels and consequently may want other services, whether a cable or satellite subscription or high-powered multidirectional antenna. In this way, the maps intimate the location-based or geo-economic strategies of the broadcast industry. One NAB map showed areas with a high proportion of broadcast households in need of targeting for DTV outreach. Put another way, it pinpointed areas where there are a high proportion of low-income, ethnic minority and elderly residential districts in the U.S. and revealed areas (and hence communities) targeted by the NAB and others in their efforts to keep all viewers watching. Another map showed areas that underwent the transition early, areas and communities on the other side of the DTV divide.

Such maps enabled the NAB to conduct "grass roots marketing" related to the DTV transition. For instance, the NAB sponsored project called the DTV Road Show traveling exhibit making four major routes across the U.S.[23] Beginning in November 2007 two "DTV Trekkers"—moving trucks designed to resemble giant TV sets—crisscrossed the country and targeted areas with a high proportion of broadcast-only households.[24] By mid 2009 they had ventured into 200 markets and attended 600 events nationwide including state fairs, festivals, and sporting competitions. According to group's website, "The Roadshow schedule prioritizes areas with high over-the-air (OTA) density, attending events that help us reach those most affected by the switch, including minority/non-English speaking populations, older Americans, residents of rural areas, and economically disadvantaged populations."[25] Thus while maps may make broadcasting's unique coverage patterns and signal histories intelligible, they could also be used as platforms for direct marketing campaigns as well.

Since newly "out of range" viewers needed a new antenna to receive a signal, and since others were bound to experience reception problems, the Consumer Electronics Association partnered with the NAB to offer a service that would assist viewers by recommending antennas and thereby capitalize upon the transition. Recommended by the FCC, Antenna Web, is a website sponsored by the CEA (Consumer Electronics Association) and NAB, that invites the user to enter his/her address and receive recommendations about which kind of antenna will provide the best reception of signals available in that location. After the user enters a

U.S. address the interface offers a list of stations available in that market as well as a list of which antennae will work best to receive the different signals. The website also shows a map of the location as well as optimum angles for antenna installation. Tellingly, the website not only collects consumer information, but shows the user the kind of pinpointed residence-specific information that the NAB and CEA already have! Indeed, the practices of the NAB and CEA are consistent with the kind of "interactive" media regime that uses freedom of choice as a mechanism for extensive consumer monitoring and profiling, a practice Mark Andrejevic refers to as the "digital enclosure."[26] Regardless of how such interfaces and maps are used by the industry, they serve as helpful visualizations for TV scholars because they can enable us to better comprehend and convey television's spatial and territorializing properties. Further, each PSA, website or map is an attempt to translate largely imperceptible technical processes (which we are socialized to remain naive about) into intelligible forms that can be interpreted, discussed and evaluated.

FROM SNOW TO WHITE SPACE

When the scheduled DTV transition date, February 17th, 2009, rolled around several Americans were prepared, perched at their analog sets with video cameras pointing at their TV receivers to record the last moments of the analog signal of their local station as it disappeared forever. By March 4th, 2009 there were sixty such videos posted on Youtube. These "end of analog kinescopes," as we might call them, not only document the death of various analog TV signals, but they provide an interesting glimpse into the range of ways stations and viewers have also communicated about and understood the transition. One viewer in Iowa set up six television sets and let them run simultaneously so that he could record which ones made the transition and which did not. Two of the monitors lost their signals indicating they moved to digital and others kept running in analog. While some stations across the country simply went off air (such as WEDU in Tampa Bay) and abruptly let the image turn to snow, other stations made a local news event out of the switch off and integrated it into the last analog evening new report. WGEM in Quincy, Illinois, for instance, had a reporter flip the off switch live as the station went "over to digital." WDEF in Chattanooga provided a short station history before signing off. WMTV-15 in Madison, Wisconsin played the national anthem while a flag waved at the state capitol building and signed off with a familiar test pattern. And WSRE-23 in Pensacola, Florida, which typically ended its broadcast day with a photo of the sunset, had an announcer proclaim, "It's the end of an era. From this point forward the sun will never set on our signal" and ended not only the broadcast day, but the analog era as the monitor turned to snow.

Just as analog television's inauguration was celebrated as momentous when it occurred decades ago in the 1930s and 40s so too was its termination. These videos and events are important televisual timepieces. It's an ironic coincidence that the videos were recorded similarly to that of early kinescopes. They serve as records of what appeared on the monitor during the signal's transmission and document analog TV's grand finale and its disappearance. These viewer-produced videos capture the the last moments of a system of broadcasting that operated for more than fifty years and many of them end with snow. In this sense, TV snow is an apt icon for this historic moment. Even in its obscurity and abstraction, the image of snow manages to bring a set of material conditions to the surface and evokes a consideration of certain technical, historical and economic issues.

First, and most literally, snow communicates the technical reality of a signal interruption or that a station has stopped broadcasting. Since many stations ended their broadcast day by placing a test pattern, color bars, or station identification in the frame until broadcast resumed in the morning, snow either represented a broadcasting break or system error. The second meaning is more temporal. Since snow will no longer appear on TV after the digital conversion, it will become *the* symptom of a bygone era of broadcasting. In this way, snow represents a television system that once was and serves as a kind of master shot of analog television's past. Finally, snow alludes indirectly to the open or unused bandwidth in the electromagnetic spectrum, which is sometimes referred to as "white space." Since numerous parties are interested in the future of this "white space," snow makes intelligible this part of the spectrum that is of great economic value and imminent regulatory concern.

In recent years companies such as Google, Dell, Earthlink and Intel among others have banded together to pressure the FCC to allow them to utilize this so-called "TV white space" for high-speed Internet connections.[27] Two organizations, the White Space Coalition[28] and Wireless Innovation Alliance, formed to pressure the FCC to reallocate the part of the spectrum formerly allocated for analog broadcasting (TV channels 2-51 - 54-698 MHz) for use by unlicensed (TVBDs and WiFi - wireless) devices. In 2007 Google launched a specific advocacy project called "Free the Airwaves.com." The goal of the initiative is to make this part of the spectrum available for free to unlicensed users. As Google boasts on its public policy blog "Today: TV Static, Tomorrow: Broadband."[29] Broadcasters have opposed this move because they claim such use would result in interference to licensed broadcast stations still using part of this bandwidth. Wireless corporations such as Verizon and AT&T have already paid billions of dollars for access to this part of the spectrum and have been waiting to introduce new products that rely upon it.[30] On November 4th, 2008, the FCC surprisingly voted 5-0 to approve the unlicensed use of white space, thereby silencing opposition from broadcasters.

The re-allocation of this bandwidth is a complex and important story and I cannot go into depht about it here. Suffice it to say that the interests of low-income, elderly and ethnic minority communities that were at the core of public discussions of analog television drop off the radar completely in those of the White Space. These "free airwaves," as they are referred to again and again, seem to be envisioned as a mobile multimedia playground, ostensibly accessible to anyone, but ultimately restricted to those who can afford to purchase high-end mobile devices and have the knowledge to use them. Thus while most have hailed the FCC's decision as a major victory, I am a bit more skeptical and see this decision as imbricated within the ways the politics of taste, class, race and gender are interwoven with technological innovation and change. Further, Google and other digital companies often use such initiatives in the public sphere as a way of camouflaging their profit-motives and market domination, acting as if they are merely agents of digital humanitarianism and public service. Yet Google's efforts to "open up" the white space may not be so benevolent and resonate with Siva Vaidhyanathan's provocative contention that we are undergoing the "Googlization of Everything."

CONCLUSION

We might think of the digital transition as a meta-moment in television's history in that we are confronted with various manifestations of television itself. Rarely are citizens-viewers encouraged to think so carefully about how they get their signals and how their receiver works—to think so specifically about an object that is at once so familiar and so strange. This can be a useful moment, then, in that there is an increase in the circulation of technical knowledge about television in the public sphere. And the analog diehards, in particular, are being addressed, lest they be "left behind" or remain beyond the "digital enclosure."[31] Still, several questions linger, even as new knowledge about television circulates. After the transition will citizens know not only what digital TV is, but what the FCC is and who its Chair and Commissioners are? Will they care about where their trashed analog TV sets and antennae end up? Will they insist that community television stations not die along with analog TV? And, again, what will become of the white space—that part of the spectrum left open in the wake of analog TV's termination? Finally, what does this mean for the future of television scholarship? It is my hope that we will continue our research backward and forward at once, and keep the enticing shimmer of the new—whether we call it the digital or something else—in perspective so that we can continue to explore the multifarious ways in which people in the U.S. and beyond have (re)arranged, tinkered with, hybrized and defined television technologies in the past and will continue to do so in the future whatever its standard.

Author's note: This essay was written while I was the Beaverbrook Scholar-in-Residence at McGill University in Montreal in March 2009. I am grateful for feedback I received while delivering the paper at Concordia University in Montreal, Stockholm University, and the Annenberg School at USC. I would like to thank Meredith Bak for her helpful research assistance.

ENDNOTES

1. "6.5 Million U.S. Homes Unready for Digital TV Transition," Nielsenwire, 22 January 2009, available at http://blog.nielsen.com/ nielsenwire/media_ entertainment/65-million-us-homes-unready-for-digital-tv-transition/, accessed 18 March 2009.
2. Brian Stelter, "Digital TV Delay Runs into Protest," 16 January 2009, *The New York Times*, available at http://www.nytimes.com/2009/01/17/technology/ 17digital.html, accessed 17 March 2009.

3. Jean K. Chalby and Glen Segell, "The Broadcasting Media in the Age of Risk: The Advent of Digital Television," *New Media & Society*, Vol. 1, No. 3 (1999): 351–368; and Ian Weber and Vanessa Evans, "Constructing the Meaning of Digital Television in Britain, the United States and Australia," *New Media & Society*, 2002, Vol. 4, No. 4 (2004): 435–456.

4. Mari Castaneda Paredes, "The Complicated Transition to Broadcast Digital Transition in the United States," *Television and New Media*, Vol. 8, No. 2 (2007): 91–106; Mari Castaneda Paredes, "Television Set Production at the US-Mexico Border: Trade Policy and Advanced Electronics for the Global Market." In Justin Lewis and Toby Miller, eds., *Critical Cultural Policy Studies: A Reader* (Malden, MA: Blackwell, 2003), 272-281; Jeffrey A. Hart, *Technology, Television, and Competition: The Politics of Digital TV*, (Cambridge: Cambridge University Press, 2004), 60–83.

5. For a discussion of the complexities surrounding the practices of old and new media technologies, see Charles Acland, ed., *Residual Media* (Minneapolis: University of Minnesota Press, 2007) and Lynn Spigel and Jan Olsson, eds., *TV after Television* (Durham: Duke University Press, 2004).

6. Jenna Wandres, "AAPD Releases DTV Transition Music Video," 3 December 2008, available at, http://www.civilrights.org/dtv/index.jsp?page=3, accessed 18 March 2009.

7. This aired on Fox's Talkshow with Spike Ferensten, season 3, episode 3, available at http://www.hulu.com/watch/36608/talkshow-with-spike-feresten-cable-psa#s-p1-st-i1, accessed Dec. 3, 2008.

8. Mike Rogoway, "Time Running Short to Make Digital TV Leap," *The Oregonian*, 1 November 2008, accessed 18 March 2009.

9. Jacques Steinberg, "Digital TV Beckons, but Many Miss the Call," *New York Times*, 28 January 2009, available at http://www.nytimes.com/2009/01/29/arts/television/29ears.html, accessed 18 March 2009.

10. John Eggerton, "KARE: Man Shoots TV Over Converter Confusion," *Broadcasting and Cable*, 20 February 2009, http://www.broadcastingcable.com/article/174518-KARE_Man_Shoots_TV_Over_Converter_Confusion.php. Thanks to Jeff Sconce for sending this story to me.

11. The civil rights organizer toolkit describes access to television communication as a "necessity [...] not just entertainment" since weather reports such as tornado warnings, school closings and breaking news updates need to be known by all citizens. See "Digital Television Transition Organizer Tool Kit," civilrights.org, available at www.civilrights.org/dtv/toolkit/, accessed 18 March 2009.

12. See Jenna Wandres, "LCCREF Video Tells the Story of a DTV Assistance Center at Work," 5 March 2009, available at www.civilrights.org/dtv/index. jsp?page=2, accessed 17 March 2009.

13. Another example of digital TV centers translating into different languages comes from LISTA (Latinos in Information Sciences and Technology) who organized training classes in Atlanta. See Jose Marquez, "Join LISTA on Digital Justice Day and Volunteer in ATLANTA," available at http://network.nshp.org/forum/topics/join-lista-on-digital-justice, accessed 4 November 2009.

14. "Get Ready for Digital TV," AARP.org, 8 March 2007, available at http://www.aarp.org/money/consumer/articles/digital_tv.html, accessed 18 March 2009.

15. "Keeping Seniors Connected," Meals on Wheels Association of America, available at http://www.mowaa.org/Page.aspx?pid=338, accessed 17 March 2009.

16. *Washington Post*, 30 December 2008.

17. A local newspaper/radio station in Chicago collected and redistributed them to those who needed them most.

18. "DTV Transition: Wal-Mart Selling Digital TV Converter Boxes," Broadbandinfo.com, Feb. 14, 2008, available at http:// www.broadbandinfo.com/news-archives/2008/dtv-transition-wal-mart-selling-digital-tv-converter-boxes.html, accessed 18 March 2009.

19. See video entitled "Cameras in Digital Convert Boxes! BEWARE!!!!," posted by mechanismstudios, 16 February 2009, available at http://www.youtube.com/watch?v=TQ4iIM8Eljc, accessed 18 March 2009. Also see "Camera and mic found in digital convertor box paid for by Feds," Prison Planet Forum blog, 17 February 2009, available at http://forum.prisonplanet.com/index.php?topic=87074, accessed 18 March 2009.

20. Jason Weitzel, "Pulling Free TV Signals out of Berks County's Thin Air," Reading Eagle.com (Penn.), February 2, 2009, available at http://readingeagle.com/articleprint.aspx?od=123746, accessed 18 March 2009.

21. "Transition in Trouble: Action Needed to Ensure a Successful Digital Television Transition," available at http://www.civilrights. org/publications/reports/dtv/introduction.html, accessed 17 March 2009.

22. "Updated Maps of All Full-Service Digital TV Stations Authorized by the FCC," available at http://www.fcc.gov /dtv/ markets/, accessed 17 March 2009.

23. Hired Atlanta based company Mobile Marketing Enterprises to organize it.

24. "DTV Roadshow," DTVAnswers (NAB), available at http://www.dtvanswers.com/roadshow/, accessed 17 March 2009.

25. "Summary of the DTV Roadshow," DTVAnswers (NAB), http://www.dtvanswers.com/roadshow/, accessed 17 March 2009.

26. Mark Andrejevic, *I Spy: Surveillance and Power in the Interactive Era*, (Lawrence: University Press of Kansas, 2007), 2–3.

27. "The White Open Spaces," Editorial, *Washington Post*, 16 August 2007 available at http://www.washingtonpost.com/wp-dyn/content/article/2007/08/15/AR2007081502128.html, accessed 17 March 2009.

28. The member companies include Microsoft, Google, Dell, HP, Intel, Philips, Earthlink, and Samsung Electro-Mechanics.

29. Richard Witt, "Today: TV Static. Tomorrow: Broadband," Google Public Policy Blog, 12 December 2007, available at http://googlepublicpolicy.blogspot.com/2007/12/today-tv-static-tomorrow-broadband.html, accessed 17 March 2009.

30. Brian Stelter, "Switch to Digital TV Wins a Delay to June 12," *The New York Times*, 4 February 2009, available at http://www.nytimes.com/2009/02/05/business/media/05digital.html, accessed 17 March 2009.

31. Andrejevic, 2–3.

CHAPTER 12

ARCHIVAL TRANSITIONS: SOME DIGITAL PROPOSITIONS

PELLE SNICKARS

IN MID-JULY 2009 Wikinews published an article claiming that the National Portrait Gallery in London threatened a U.S. citizen with legal action since he had allegedly breached the museum's copyright of several thousands of photographs of works of art. Apparently, the young American, Derrick Coetzee, had come up with a program that automatically downloaded high resolution imagery from the National Portrait Gallery's website, images that Coetzee as a regular contributor to Wikimedia Commons uploaded to the site. Wikimedia Commons is the database of free-to-use media that Wikipedia writers use for illustrations; today the database contains some five million photographs. The digital images that Coetzee uploaded were exact digitized reproductions of artworks, drawings and older photographs. Since the holdings of the National Portrait Gallery consisted of mostly older material, Coetzee considered the digital reproductions to belong to the public domain and thus free for public use under United States law (where he and Wikimedia Commons were based). The crux of the matter was that copyright to digital reproductions was claimed to exist in the U.K. where the museum was situated. Hence, in "a letter from [the museum's] solicitors sent to Coetzee via electronic mail, the National Portrait Gallery asserted that it holds copyright in the photographs under U.K. law."[1] They demanded that Coetzee provided undertakings to remove all of the images from Wikimedia Commons.

Derrick Coetzee uploaded the e-mail to his Wikimedia Commons account, and since Wikipedia has 330 millions of users news of the event spread quickly. BBC picked up the story—and soon the National Portrait Gallery had most of the blogosphere and numerous web commentators as its opponents. In Britain, copyright law apparently gives new copy-

FIGURE 1: Elizabeth I of England, the Armada Portrait 1588. Digital image gathered by Derrick Coetzee from the National Portrait Gallery and uploaded to Wikimedia Commons which states: "While Commons policy accepts the use of this media, one or more third parties have made copyright claims against Wikimedia Commons in relation to the work from which this is sourced or a purely mechanical reproduction thereof."

right to someone who produces an image full of public domain material, Cory Doctorow at boingboing.net sarcastically commented, "effectively creating perpetual copyright for a museum that owns the original image, since they can decide who gets to copy it and then set terms on those copies that prevent them being treated as public domain. [. . .] If you take public money to buy art, you should make that art available to the public using the best, most efficient means possible."[2] Under the heading "Who's Art Is It, Anyway?" *The Wall Street Journal* wrote that it was not hard to understand the museum's frustration. "It goes to all the trouble and expense of making accurate photographic copies [. . .] and then someone comes along with a few clicks of a mouse and appropriates thousands of images." However, copyright law tries to balance between private ownership of intellectual property and public usage decades after the work's author is dead. "If new copyrights can be attached to old works of art, the whole copyright system is thrown out of whack." According to the *The Wall Street Journal*, copyright law exists, and has existed for one purpose: to make creativity pay. Producing exact photographic copies of paintings "is no doubt valuable and involves painstaking work. But it isn't—and isn't meant to be—creative." The champions of intellectual property, the newspaper asserted, "can't afford to waste their energies trying to monopolize images that already properly belong to us all."[3]

HERITAGE INSTITUTIONS AND THE WEB

During the last decade heritage institutions across the world have been challenged by new digital technologies as well as by entrepreneurs who rapidly understood the advantages of the networks of networks characterizing the Web. The discussions and media debates following the polemics between Derrick Coetzee and the National Portrait Gallery are, hence, not only a clash between a new binary American frontier and an old European museum. The conflict also highlights how memory institutions within the so-called ALM-sector (archives, libraries, museums) have been seriously contested by unprecedented cultural players that embraced new information technology, given them as much popularity as conceptual advantage. Heritage institutions have for long been remarkably absent, and at times almost invisible on the Web. The situation is beginning to change, but during the late 1990s the absence resulted in a situation where the digital domain was largely left to the market, and various user-oriented initiatives as Wikimedia Commons. In 1995, for example, when the two major American online photographic archives were established on the Web, Corbis and Getty Images—taking advantage of the possibility of using binary code as the new interface for older stock imagery—most European heritage institutions were only beginning to think about whether or not one should upload metadata on the Web. Naturally, budgets were tighter and copyright put numerous restrictions on material, yet the conceptual understanding of digital technologies was by large absent. Of course, there were exceptions. A number of American heritage institutions for example, notably the Library of Congress, were keen on using new digital technology. Yet as the controversy above illustrates, heritage institutions across Europe are still, fifteen years later struggling with how to perceive and conceptiualize the Web.

In this article I would like to address the relation between the contemporary Web and heritage institutions in a broad sense. Various American websites and companies have during the last decade in many ways challenged the ALM-sector, not the least from a European perspective. In short, doing American studies within the memory sector simply means acknowledging that U.S. enterprises like YouTube, Flickr or Wikipedia have paved the way for completely new ways of organizing heritage material for the global user. The purpose of the article is, hence, to outline a number of archival transitions, as well as put forward and discuss some digital propositions focused on how heritage institutions could, or rather should understand and use the Internet as well as the Web. The "digital" is not a threat to archives and the ALM-sector—it is a blessing. Digital user patterns are totally different from analog ones, social tagging can produce the most amazing results, and through various forms of data mining digitized collections of heritage material can be used to deduce unprecedented knowledge structures. The networkable nature of new digital technology can also be applied to various distributed digital preservation programs—in short, file sharing as a storage model in the age of the networked archive.

In fact, the most challenging task facing heritage institutions today is how to deal with the new binary networks of networks. On the one hand, the Web needs to be thought of as both a tool for access, primarily for distributing collected heritage material, as well as distributed preservation. But on the other hand, the Web also poses numerous problems for heritage institutions, not the least in terms of collection and assemblage strategies of new digital material. Access to information is what the Web does best, and although controversial, the Google Book Search project vividly illustrates how heritage material could be accessible on a mass scale. Today more than two million books belonging to the public domain are downloadable from Google Book Search in full PDF-format, and numerous national book services providing information on titles held by university and research libraries, as for example the Swedish Libris system, uses the open APIs from Google to include links to these scanned books. An API [application programming interface] is an interface that defines ways by which an application program may request services or data from another system. Open APIs have, in short, changed the way in which private web-based companies as well as publicly funded institutions interact on the Internet by exchanging information and data using the network as a distribution channel for Web services.

GOOGLING FOR BOOKS

What the Google Book Search project has foremost taught heritage institutions is that the costs of digitizing per item can be radically cut if one digitizes in an industrial manner rather than in a traditional way based on choosing material on certain criteria. In the Google Book Search nothing is choosen; instead stack after stack is digitized, and like everything else at Google the project is based on scalability. Mass digitization, then, concerns millions of books rather than millions of pages. Even though many heritage institutions "welcome the unprecedented access to all this information, Google has also been criticized for the inferior quality of their images, the emphasis on the English language, the violation of copyright laws and the lack of attention for preservation issues," to quote the librarian Astrid Verhausen. "The question therefore arises," she writes, "can libraries do better than Google?"[4] Well, of course they can in terms of quality, and they did during the 1990s—but never ever in terms of quantity. The reason is scale, money and know-how. One of the partners in the Google Book Search project, the Bavarian State Library in Munich, will receive approximately 50 million Euros from Google, a sum most national libraries can only dream off.[5] "The digitisation of books is a Herculean task but also opens up cultural content to millions of citizens in Europe and beyond," Viviane Reding, EU Commissioner for Information Society and Media, recently stated in a press release. However, regarding Google and the U.S. lead and advantage in the digitization struggle, he also confessed that "Member States must stop envying progress made in other continents and finally do their own homework. It also shows that Europeana alone will not suffice to put Europe on the digital map of the world. We need to work better together to make Europe's copyright framework fit for the digital age."[6]

Still, the Web with its abundance of information also poses problems for heritage institutions. The legal deposit law for example doesn't work at all in the digital domain, and Web content characteristics as high dynamics and format variety makes Web archiving a real challenge. Since the Web 2.0 revolution most information seems to have dispersed into bits and bytes that are constantly changing. Preserving content that is bottom-up driven, distinguished by interactivity and a networkable nature is problematic—if not impossible. Heritage institutions should acknowledge this, not least in a situation where the cloud computing trend is transforming parts of the Web into a platform of distributed storage. The new cultural landscape of the 21th century is, hence, very different from the previous one. It is made of binary code, and we are increasingly living in a software culture, "a culture where the production, distribution, and reception of most content—and increasingly, experiences—is mediated by software."[7]

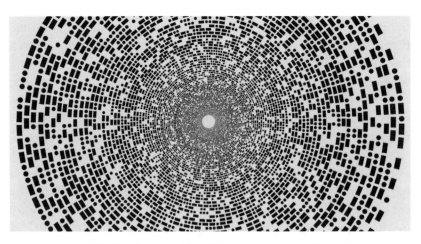

FIGURE 2: All cultural systems of modern society run on software—binary code is the invisible glue that ties everything together.

The software culture regulating the Web is ubiquitous—it is everywhere. As the frequency of updates and mash-ups increases, it is for example more and more difficult from an archival heritage perspective to pinpoint what a "digital object" actually is—even if it is conceptually perceived as the sum of its parts. When the digital object is interactive, it constantly changes, or as media theorist Lev Manovich has stated: "When a user interacts with a software application that presents cultural content [as for example Google Earth] this content often does not have definite finite boundaries. [. . .] Google Earth is an example of a new interactive 'document' which does not have its content all predefined. Its content changes and grows over time."[8]

Yet, at a time when "the digital" has become the default value of culture, most heritage institutions are still hesitant in responding to the new situation. As is well known, we are at the moment undergoing a shift in cultural production, consumption and distribution of more or less cataclysmic proportions. The lines can be drawn between what Lawrence Lessig has called the "Read-Only" and the "Read/Write cultures"—RO and RW respectively.[9] From a heritage perspective, previous analog RO media had sort of an "object" quality. In the film archive, for example, archivist could store film reels in the vault, and even though a film was often made up of several reels, they were still objects to be preserved on shelves. The matter totally changed with the introduction of binary code and the coming of digital and immaterial media. Within the contemporary Read/Write cultures, documents have begun to loose their static boundaries. Naturally, digital media for example can still be an object—a CD or DVD for example —but online RO media and the new cultural forms visible on the Web gradually resemble kind of processes. If "production" was a code word for the 20th century cultural landscape, "distribution" seems now to be the buzzword of the new software culture.

ARCHIVAL MODE OF ONLINE MEDIA

Being online, media scholar Geert Lovink has claimed, "we no longer watch films and television—we watch databases."[10] The digital archive is by nature a database, that is, a structured collection of data stored in a computer system. Database structures are organized according to various models: there are relational ones, hierarchical ones, networked ones and so on and so forth. Focusing databases, however as central for new media, is hardly a novelty; it is after all the main theme of Lev Manovich's book *The Language of New Media* written almost ten years ago.[11] Nevertheless, a consequence of the database structure of online media, which arguably wasn't too visible a decade ago, is that the differences between various media forms seem to be disappearing. Inside the media archive (or within the database), the concept of medium specificity is starting to become archaic. On the Web all media seems to be gray; or more correctly, on the Web there is on closer observation no media at all, just files in databases containing numerically coded information. Just as the 20th century media forms are converging they are replaced by surface effects of algorithms, that is, by various kinds of programmed content consisting of text, sounds and (moving) images. Filled as it is with binary files, the Internet would seem to be the only channel of communication that still remains. Access to media history and memory, hence, becomes a question where to look.

At the same time media history teaches us that new media never radically replaces older media forms. As a consequence a rather strict division between different media forms still prevails on the Web. For instance, when public service radio or television has been upgraded to digital platforms, the programs are still packaged using the respective media's special signatures, logotype etcetera. Web based television is still seen as an *extension* of conventional TV—even though this may gradually be changing within the industry. The specificity of the medium is still rooted in the analog past and not in the digital future. Naturally, there are exceptions; pod casting for example has become a distinct media-specific feature of online radio. Different from conventional radio, but similar to newspapers and magazines, pod casting allows listeners to subscribe to programs. They can be automatically downloaded to one's mobile Internet device, and like a book or newspaper used whenever.

However, a major difference between analog media and its subsequent binary online version is the latter's database structure—or its "archival mode." File clusters shared at various P2P-networks are a good example of the archival mode of online media. The Pirate Bay in Sweden (or wherever it is now located) has for years had more than one million trackers to various media files and more than 25 million unique peers. Torrents themselves also have a distinct archival character to them; the package of 200 episodes of the Sci-Fi TV series *Mystery Science Theatre 3000* contains 135 GB of data—a media archive in its own right. In fact, since approximately 50 percent of Internet traffic is made up of media files being up- and downloaded in various P2P-systems, the digital domain can be described as one giant media transfer network built upon an organic and rapidly increasing archive of cultural content. The more the online archive is used the bigger it gets; once you're downloading you are always uploading. P2P-protocols work acts exactly the other way around than HTTP-protocols. The genius of BitTorrent and the like are that while a website is loading slow if there are too many users, P2P-protocols operate in the opposite way—the more users, the faster the distribution and the more "the archive" grows.

One might, hence, argue that the archival mode of online media is apparent on at least three levels. First, there are the P2P networks (described above), secondly there are the actual media archives on the Web, and thirdly the storage mode is vivid in archival formats of media. The Internet Archive, the World Digital Library or Europeana are examples of online archives where metadata and media material are no longer separated as in analog media archives. The archival mode is, thus, apparent in the way the computer screen functions as the actual archival interface. In the fancy demo reel for the World Digital Library, for instance, the GUI, the graphical user interface is not only a window to the world, the screen is also an archival interface in time. Texts, images, maps and videos are shown side by side in a multimedia display where themes and topics are central rather than the actual media forms.

FIGURE 3: Archival interfaces—screen shot from
the concept video of World Digital Library.

Still, archival modes are perhaps most apparent in the third category of new forms of digitally upgraded media, notably television and radio. These new media forms are together with the P2P networks, probably the best examples of how the Web has changed, altered and modified these media in various archival directions. The way these new media forms are presented and promoted also testifies to the apparent storage quality of online media. The archival slogan of the BBC iPlayer for example states: "Making the Unmissable, Unmissable," and in a similar fashion the logo for the Web version of Swedish Television, the so called SVT Play notes: "More than 2.000 hours of TV—whenever you like." SVT Play is, hence, promoted as a distinct archival application, and the same basically goes for public service radio. At the Web page of Swedish Radio you can, for example, find more than 9,000 hours of radio, a neat collection of structured sound in the form of a giant database. Furthermore, music archives built up at sites like Last.fm or Spotify also relates to the same archival mode. Apparently, Last.fm's database contains millions of audio tracks, and Spotify even boasts more than 10 million tracks. The latter is a proprietary P2P and music streaming service that allows instant listening to specific tracks or albums with no buffering delay; music can be browsed by artists or albums as well as by direct searches—all in the form of online archive. In short, Last.fm and Spotify are media archival applications that take advantage of the storage abilities and networkable nature characterizing the current Web.

ACCESS 24

The most important lesson that the Web 2.0 transition has taught, is probably that people are not only connected to the Internet and the Web. They are to an even greater extent connected to each other. Napster and file sharing have paved the way for social networking sites where information is linked, shared and distributed. Worldwide Facebook is, for example, ranked as the sixth most popular site on the Web, with some 275 million regular users. Naturally, Facebook is always accessible, and with the Facebook app on Apple's iPhone a user can do just about anything even while on the move. The bigger picture, however, is that digital usage has led to completely new user patterns in relation to culture in general, and media in particular. Digital user patterns are very different from previous analog ones, not the least with regards to the heritage sector. In the mid-1990s, the film archivist Paolo Cherchi Usai wrote an article where he claimed that in traditional film archives some five to ten percent of the holdings are—and will be—used. The rest of the films will remain on their shelf; that is, some ninety percent of preserved films will never be looked at.[12]

FIGURE 4: Analog viewing patterns are very different from new digital ones. In a traditional film archive som five to ten percent of the holdings are and will be used—on the Web the opposite holds true.

It is interesting to compare Cherchi Usai's archival estimations to the latest statistics from Comscore regarding online video, figures that were released in March 2009. Almost 80 percent of the total U.S. Internet audience viewed online video, that is, four out of five of every U.S. surfer. Each of these 150 millions video viewers watched a little more than 100 videos equalling some six hours[13]—which of course still is nothing compared to similar figures for television. The point, however, is the way usage pattern changes when moving image databases and archives are accessible at any time on any computer at any place. On YouTube, for example, it is hard to find a video with less than ten views. Thus, almost all videos uploaded are seen by someone, a viewing pattern totally the opposite to traditional media archives. Basically, the same goes for any type of cultural collection of material on the Web. If users can access material—they will. Unlocking archives and using the generative potential of the Internet and its networks, as put forward in Jonathan Zittrain's book, *The Future of the Internet*, seems hence to be an urgent task for heritage institutions.[14]

The media archivist Richard Wright at BBC sometimes refers to this caricature of an archivist as someone who wishes researchers or the public wouldn't come in and disturb and damage the collections. In the digital domain, however, such an attitude is impossible—not the least from a political perspective. Of course, the role of archives is to protect content but the worst way to assure preservation is to deny access, especially at a binary time when "sharing" is a key concept on the Web. Such denial generates no value, and, as Wright has argued in various contexts leaves archives unable to afford to run preservation projects. Protecting content requires public interest—which today comes from digital access.[15]

THE DIGITAL AS DEFAULT

In the binary world everything is plenty; online there is always enough for everybody. The value of digital information is, in fact, hardly measurable, and lack is a word lacking in the digital domain where the cost of distributing information and reproducing it is neglible. As people like Chris Anderson keeps reminding us, there has never been a more competitive market than the Internet, and every day the marginal cost of digital information comes closer to nothing. According to an article in *New York Times* so called "freemium" is becoming the "most popular business model among Web start-ups."[16] In short, freemium is sort of a business model that works by offering basic services for free, while charging for advanced or special features. Slowly these ideas are also heading towards the heritage sector. Rick Prelinger's collection at Internet Archives is, for once, free to use without restrictions, and more than 2,000 film files can be downloaded from the Web. Free has in fact been Prelinger's way of making a business. The Prelinger Archive's "goal remains to collect, preserve, and facilitate access to films of historic significance that haven't been collected elsewhere. Included are films produced by and for many hundreds of important U.S. corporations, nonprofit organizations, trade associations, community and interest groups, and educational institutions."[17] Letting producers browse and look at footage for free, and then charging them for high-resolution imagery has proven to be a business model more profitable than not providing access.[18]

Within parts of the archival sector there are, however, those who are still in doubt regarding "the digital." In the age of digital reproduction an organization like FIAF for instance, the International Federation of Film Archives, hardly see binary code as the default value for archives and heritage institutions. Digital preservation is as volatile and unsure, as it is expensive—so goes the argument.[19] However, digital media is not ethereal, and storage costs keep dropping, although maintenance and service contracts remain a problem. Furthermore, even virtual reality has a material foundation in the form of nano technological inscriptions on the computer's hard disk. Buildings might collapse and server systems might get flooded, but binary information is nearly always retrievable. Computer forensics teaches that it is more or less impossible to erase a hard drive; every digital inscription leaves a trace—if only at the nano level.

One might suspect that the archival mistrust regarding digital formats has to do with access, which of course is the flip side of every digital activity. Since preservation for most heritage institutions has always been prior to the type of access that comes without saying with digital formats, the current digitization trend forces archives to deal with the issue of opening themselves. Some institutions have, however, embraced the new situation. Library of Congress, for example, announced during spring 2009 that they would start uploading millions of sound clips and video files onto iTunes and YouTube. The library already offers most of that media material at its own Web site, but the expansion is part of a "broad strategy to 'fish where the fish are,' " according to Matt Raymond, the library's director of communications.[20] And in September 2009 it was also reported that the U.S. Academy of Television Arts & Sciences Foundation would upload its voluminous collection of interviews with TV industry legends. The oral histories of one medium, television, were hence "being made available to the public via another medium, the Internet. The academy founded its preservation arm [...] more than a decade ago. Its goal was to record interviews with stars, producers, writers and executives." All in order "to create a digital encyclopedia of TV history," to quote Karen Herman, the director of the archive. Yet, until the archive embarked on a digitization process, its stacks of videotapes "languished in a temperature-controlled vault," accessible only to researchers who visited the academy. On the Web, however, the material is now present both on a dedicated YouTube channel and at emmytvlegends.org; both sites "allow visitors to browse by people, shows, professions and topics, and flags highlights within the videos."[21]

At least in the U.S., it is the so-called Flickr Commons project that has paved the way for various heritage institutions new warm embrace of the Web. Flickr is one of most popular photo- sharing sites online, or as Luc Sante has stated: "Flickr is to photography what the Pacific Ocean is to water."[22] Flickr is owned by Yahoo and as a hybrid economy makes money through subsriptions and advertisement. The Flickr Commons project, however, is different. Driven together with the Library of Congress, the leading cultural institution exploring Web 2.0 possibilities, it's key goals are firstly to show "hidden treasures in the world's public photography archives, and secondly to show how input and knowledge can help make these collections even richer." The project started with the Library of Congress uploading some 3,000 photographs from the vast Farm Security Administration's photo archive—an archive which contains almost 180.000 photographs from the 1930s depression until World War II. The project got an overwhelmingly positive response from the Flickr community, and it not only brought public awareness to the Library of Congress' existing online collection, but also sparked creative interaction with the images as users helped provide Library curators with new information on photos. The Library of Congress' photos have received more than 15 million views, and the the Flickr Commons project today has some 50 participating heritage institutions.[23]

Then again, not all institutions are as engaged as the U.S. Library of Congress, and one major obstacle regarding "the digital" and the distrust of it within the heritage sector also has to do with the materiality of culture. The materality of the cultural artefact has (nearly) always been more important than the actual stored content at most memory institutions. Basically, this is what museums do; they collect original pieces of art and craft. Copies of theses cultural objects, be they pots or paintings, would not be worthy collecting even though a digital version of Hieronymus Boschs "The Garden of Delight" made up of 1,600 digital photographs (as the one on Google Earth) presents aspects of this painting that a visitor at Prado in Madrid could never see.

As a consequence, if a film for example has been shot on celluloid, the only way to stay true to its "originality" from a strict film archival perspective is to screen it on celluloid in a projector or in an editing table. Digitizing a feature film and viewing on an iPhone in mpeg4-format is hence perceived as an archival violation. Naturally, every digitization activity involves some kind of media transfer, where copying might lead to loss of information. This is especially the case with various forms of compressed file formats. The problem, however, is that historically there has been a proliferation of various storage formats. Archival holdings of moving images for example are sometimes almost impossible to view because they are fixed in outdated formats, let alone difficult to copy—if one doesn't consider such an activity as unethical (which some film archives actually do).

FIGURE 5: A digital Kane? Within the heritage sector the materality of the cultural artefact is still more important than the stored content.

It goes without saying that as long as the materiality of culture at heritage institutions is perceived as more important than the actual content itself—stored on various forms of carriers, be they paper, tinfoils or celluloid—the archival transition to the digital domain will be utterly slow and remain difficult to steer. Conceptualizing the digital as the archival default does not mean avoiding storage strategies, nor that the materiality of content will be neglected or thrown away. It simply means that for example preserved celluloid films, frozen down and vacuum sealed (which according to the Swedish Film Institute will make films last for 500 years), do not make sense *at all* in relation to the digital domain. Since resources and funding are always limited within the heritage sector, *access* needs to be the new guiding principle rather than preservation in years to come. The binary paradigm has made analog preservation strategies so obsolete that in the long run it will become difficult to finance them. The lack of preservational funding in many countries, and the indifferent attitude among politicians and policy makers regarding national heritage, has sometimes been caused by the ALM-sector itself. Heritage institutions in Europe at least, have for years complained that too little money has been spent on them. But the argument has remained the same: give us more money so that we can collect and store things in our stacks and vaults. However, the political impact, the public relations value or the attention of media of such claims often amounts to nothing. Increased funding for putting "films on shelfs" (as I once heard a FIAF representative stating) is hardly the most progressive way forward. Younger users brought up with the Internet will simply not accept that public money in years to come is spent on preservational strategies at heritage institutions that do not involve any form of access to the material.

So whether or not one likes the differences of cultural artifacts in digitized form dissolve into a pulsing stream of bits and bytes, heritage institutions are faced with the fact that the Web and sites like YouTube, Flickr or Wikipedia have become the new archival interfaces. These sites are naturally not archives in a traditional sense—they don't store and preserve material—but in terms of access they have established a radically new archival paradigm. For some archivist within the film heritage sector, the archival mode of online media has become evident predominantly with YouTube's collection of perhaps 200 million videos, making the Internet the world's largest vault for moving image material. Others have stressed the lack of quality and preservational strategies. Kristin Thompson have for example argued that the "celestial multiplex" is a myth, and that there will "never come a time when everything is available [online]." And besides most film "archives are more concerned about getting the money to conserve or restore aging, unique prints than about making them widely available."[24] Sadly, Thompson might be right, but such an attitude has inevitably led to a paradoxical situation. As heritage institutions insist on the importance of traditional and classical archival missions, "they will appear to be less useful, less accommodating, less relevant, and ultimately less important" than the new archival sites on the Web, not the least from the political perspective regulating funding. As Rick Prelinger has noted, everything that anyone does to bring especially film archives online is from now on always "going to be measured against YouTube's ambiguous legacy."[25] Like Google, YouTube has constantly been distributing itself. Whereas YouTube.com rapidly established itself as the default site for online video, with the consequence that professional content providers lined up for partnership, surfers also encountered YouTube videos everywhere on the Web. The circulation of videos, especially the ability to embed them at other sites, blogs and social networking pages is crucial for understanding the success of YouTube. The site was—and is—both a node and a network.[26]

SOCIAL TAGGING

Wikipedia informs us that social tagging is the "practice and method of collaboratively creating and managing tags to annotate and categorize content."[27] Folksonomy, on the other hand, describes the bottom-up classification systems that emerge from the act of social tagging. The ALM-sector has been hesitant towards letting users provide heritage material with new metadata. This is understandable. However, examples from the Web—predominantly Wikipedia—testify to the wisdom of the crowds. If crowd sourcing can be useful for other domains, there is no reason why the heritage sector should be an exception. The Flickr Commons project is a case in point. The report summary issued by the Library of Congress, "For the Common Good: The Library of Congress Flickr Pilot Project," stated that comments on the provided photographs "have turned out to be very interesting and informative." Furthermore, the project "significantly increased the reach of Library content and demonstrated the many kinds of creative interactions that are possible when people can access collections within their own Web communities. The contribution of additional information to thousands of photographs was invaluable." The displayed photographs had allowed viewers to make reminiscences and share knowledge. "Drawing on personal histories, Flickr members have made connections between the past and the present, including memories of farming practices, grandparents' lives, women's roles in World War II, and the changing landscape of local neighborhoods. Sometimes commenters have identified the precise locations of photos, and [...] offered corrections and additions by identifying locations, events, individuals, and precise dates."[28] Apparently, after verification, social tags and information provided by the community was incorporated into the library catalog. More than 500 records in the original catalog have been enhanced with new metadata that cites the Flickr Commons project as the source of the information changed or added.

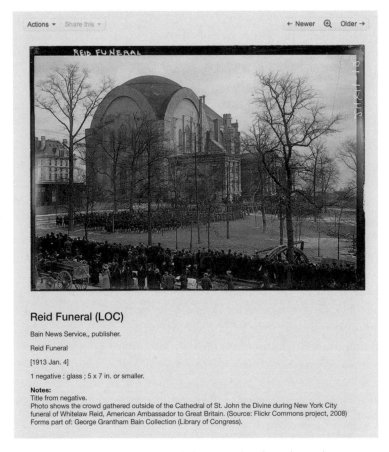

FIGURE 6: Library of Congress' Flickr project has through social tagging led to better data in more than 500 records of the original catalog.

Regarding social tagging, however, it remains important to note that even if the Web has spurred social interactivity and grassroot' activities, according to the so-called "90-9-1 rule," only a fraction of users do most of the tagging. In short, the "90-9-1 rule" stipulates that 90 percent of online audiences never interact, nine percent interacts perhaps a handful of times, and only one percent does most interacting. Nevertheless, on a global scale one percent of users might add up to tens of thousands of people. Still, social tagging has often been criticized because of the lack of control, especially in terms of terminology. Without a strict system it is likely to produce unreliable and inconsistent result; errors and contradictions are at times certainly the case. However, one might argue that the Web in general is moving towards an informational space where most data has to be filtered, valued and estimated. In addition, Wikipedia, YouTube and other "information spaces" of course vary a lot. Suffice it to say, they are not either/or. Some information provided by users might indeed be inadequate—and some information excellent. Nowhere else is there such an updated information on digital media, P2P, APIs and the semantic Web as on Wikipedia for example. It all depends on who does the interaction, who contributes and who tags. But heritage institutions should of course like the Library of Congress use the wisdom of the crowd, especially if catalog information is scarce. The socially tagged information can then be filtered through the institution. In an age when copy and paste are as normal as breathing in front of a computer, heritage institution needs to become aware that they cannot produce all information themselves. A more efficient and updated way of providing apt metadata is to re-use and edit information that already exists on the Web.

DATA MINING

Digitized collections of heritage material can today produce the most amazing things in terms of new knowledge structures. Different ways of data mining, that is the process of extracting more or less hidden patterns from huge amounts of data, has become an increasingly important tool to transform data into information. Data mining is, in short, the process of using computing power to retrieve new techniques for knowledge discovery. There are many nuances to this process, but roughly the steps are three. Firstly, one has to pre-process raw data, secondly mine the data, and finally interpret the results.[29] "More data is better data," Google claims, and in general Google is on its way to make statistical selection old-fashioned. Google already has enough data to make apt statistical analysis of basically anything with regards to the Web—you don't need to select, you simply mine everything.

However, data mining has also made its way into the heritage sector. An interesting project that gives a vivid impression of what is at stake is the so-called "Digging into Data Challenge," an international grant competition sponsored by four leading research agencies.[30] The idea behind the "Digging into Data challenge" is to answer questions like: "what do you do with a million books, or a million pages of newspaper, or a million photographs of artworks?" That is, "how does the notion of scale affect Humanities and social science research? Now that scholars have access to huge repositories of digitized data—far more than they could read in a lifetime—what does that mean for research?" The concept of data mining indicates that new techniques of large-scale data analysis can allow researchers to discover new relationships—or discrepancies. By performing computations on data sets that are "so large that they can be processed only using computing resources and computational methods developed and made economically affordable within the past few years," new knowledge and information can be deduced.

Within sciences as astronomy the "mining trend" has been going on for years; the SETI@home project, for example, a distributed computing project with more than five million Internet-connected PCs, tries to search for extra-terrestrial intelligence in space. But data mining technology can nowadays also be applied to the large collections of scanned heritage material across the globe. With books, newspapers, journals, films, artworks, and sound recordings being digitized on a massive scale, it is possible to apply data analysis techniques to large collections of diverse cultural heritage resources. Hence the "Digging into Data challenge" ask how these techniques might help scholars use digitized material to ask new questions. The goals of the initiative are: "to promote the development and deployment of innovative research techniques in large-scale data analysis; to foster interdisciplinary collaboration among scholars in the Humanities, social sciences, computer sciences, information sciences, and other fields, around questions of text and data analysis; to promote international collaboration; an to work with data repositories that hold large digital collections to ensure efficient access to these materials for research."[31]

As a process of extracting information from large digital sets of material, data mining does not work in the analog archive. It is, hence, a process that indicates what one can do, and what can happen once heritage material has been digitized. Within the ALM-sector there is sometimes a belief that when material has been digitized, the binary process has come to a halt. But in reality this is where the fun begins. When material exist in binary form, computers can start working on these digital assets deducing information on for example color settings in 10,000 digital impressionistic paintings or the clip rate in 5,000 Swedish newsreels. Scholars in the humanities always known that quantitative analysis will lead to better results than sample analysis. The best researcher is often the one who is able to go through as much material as possible. But since it has been more or less impossible to deduce patterns out of large sets of cultural objects prior to the usage of computers, the hermeneutical tradition of close qualitative readings have been favored. What data mining suggests, however, is that cultural and art sciences dealing with the past are now able to shift from a hermeneutical perspective to a kind of cultural science of heritage material—or as Daniel J. Cohen stated a few years ago:

> Quantity [can] may make up for a lack of quality. We humanists care about quality; we greatly respect the scholarly editions of texts that grace the well-tended shelves of university research libraries and disdain the simple, threadbare paperback editions that populate the shelves of airport bookstores. The former provides a host of helpful apparatuses, such as a way to check on sources and an index, while the latter merely gives us plain, unembellished text. But the Web has shown what can happen when you aggregate a very large set of merely decent (or even worse) documents. As the size of a collection grows, you can begin to extract information and knowledge from it in ways that are impossible with small collections, even if the quality of individual documents in that giant corpus is relatively poor.[32]

Basically, this is what Google has been doing in its Book Search Project. Another example of actual research in this field is the sort of "cultural analytics" that Lev Manovich has embarked upon. "The explosive growth of cultural content on the web including social media and the digitization efforts by museums, libraries, and companies since the 1990s make possible fundamentally new paradigm for the study of both contemporary and historical cultures," Manovich has stated. One of the reasons behind cultural analytics is that through various data mining sets, cultural objects in digital form as paintings, texts, photographs or films can as data files *per se* produce new forms of metadata. In other words, from one single numerical file a lot of data can be extracted—and from thousands of them entire data sets. Computer-based techniques for quantitative analysis and interactive visualization can, thus, be used to analyze patterns in massive cultural sets. Manovich is the leading figure behind the so called "software studies initiative" at the University of California, San Diego, with a firm belief "that a systematic use of large-scale computational analysis and interactive visualization of cultural data sets and data streams will become a major trend in cultural criticism and culture industries in the coming decades." At the core of the initiative lies the question what will actually happen when scholars start using interactive visualizations of large data sets as a standard tool in their work (like many scientists do already). Perhaps new cultural disciplines will "emerge out of the use of interactive visualization and data analysis of large cultural data sets?"[33]

FIGURE 7: Cultural analytics of Dziga Vertov's *The Man with the Movie Camera* (1929). In digitised form one can mine and run the film through a sophisticated computer grid and deduce average shot length and other forms of cinemetrics.

THINK DISTRIBUTED—OR STORAGE AS NETWORK

During the last three year the so-called cloud computing trend has transformed parts of the Web into a platform of distributed storage. In short, cloud computing defines a new kind of infrastructure for personified information, which no longer exists and resides locally on one's own computer, but online in the Internet's network. On a theoretical level the new digital cloud can be seen as something that substantially changed how we comprehend the computer as a machine. Today it seems clear that our computers cannot be understood as isolated and separate units. Concurrent with development of the Web, it has become impossible to differentiate one's own computer from the network it has become an unmistakable part of. Using the small free application Dropbox, for example, one can easily (by placing a file in a folder) use the Web as both a storage place and a file server and network between different computers and mobile devices.

What this shift implies for the heritage sector is still hard to say. However, as trust and reliability of online technology increases, institutions do have to acknowledge the possibilities that networked binary technologies offer. If the Web's network of networks of computers and servers can be perceived as one gigantic information processing machine, which through sophisticated and super-fast communication protocols share bits of data and strings of code, real archival centralization through new binary distributive methods is for example a possibility. It has been argued that Google is a post-media company that operates and thinks in distributed ways. Bits of Google are all over the Web, and even though there is a google.com-page—it too is but a node belonging to the company network. As is well known, the main purpose behind the Arpanet/Internet, set up in the 1960s during the cold war, was its decentralized character. If one part of the net was damaged, it would not mean that other areas stopped working. Within the heritage sector archivist are also afraid that their digital files will become corrupt and damaged. However, by using the networkable nature of new digital media networked preservation is an area with a number of interesting projects. The LOCKSS-project, that is "Lots of Copies Keep Stuff Safe," is, for example, an international community initiative that provides libraries with digital preservation tools in the form of open-source software, so that they can easily collect and preserve their own copies of authorized e-content. Furthermore, libraries cooperate in a P2P-network to ensure preservation of that content. By way of cryptographic hash functions, a damaged copy of a book or a journal can within LOCKSS easily be repaired from other peers in the network. In short, LOCKSS uses file sharing as a preservational model.[34]

Another example based on the same premise of distributed storage is the "Chronopolis. Preserving Our Digital Heritage"-project, a multi-member partnership run by the Library of Congress at the San Diego Supercomputer Centre. A key goal of the Chronopolis project is to provide cross-domain collection sharing for long-term preservation. Hence, it is part of a new breed of distributed digital preservation programs that tries to use the networkable nature of new digital technology. Long-term digital preservation is still an issue that most heritage institutions struggle with. The Chronopolis project addresses this critical problem by providing "a comprehensive model for the cyberinfrastructure of collection management, in which preserved intellectual capital is easily accessible, and research results, education material, and new knowledge can be incorporated smoothly over the long term." By integrating digital library resources, various data grids and persistent archive technologies, Chronopolis seems to be on its way to create a kind of trusted "preservation environments that span academic institutions and research projects, with the goal of long-term collection management, preservation, and knowledge generation."[35]

One of the more interesting aspects of the Chronopolis project is its cross-cultural approach between both the humanities and the natural sciences, and between commercial and government entities. In recent years, such institutions and companies have all produced reports and funded investigative efforts on aspects of the problems of data management and long-term digital preservation. What the Chronoplis project suggest is that the efforts of institutions as diverse as libraries and museums, science and engineering funding agencies, as well as supercomputing centers, should all be seen a complementary, "although these institutions may not have long histories of collaboration and have seemingly focused on very different disciplinary activities in the past."[36] On the Web as well as on the Internet, the network is everything, and new storage technologies of course tries to use and "think" preservation through the digital technology itself. There are, in fact, also various new sets of smaller distributive storage technologies. When one preserves a digital object in these systems it is, basically split up into chunks stored on various machines spread across a network in the manner of file sharing. These bits of data can then be replicated or encoded for redundancy—hence the storage capacity can be very reliable. The Open Source project "Celeste" is, for example, a highly available distributed, P2P-data storage system.[37]

CONCLUSION—THE ARCHIVE AS PLATFORM

Media critic Kevin Kelly has made the claim that sharing seems to be key to success in the digital domain. At the "Web 2.0 Summit" conference in San Francisco 2008, Kelly pointed out that because our media are converging, there would soon be only one common cultural platform. Everything is run by the same kind of shared Web-based machine independent of device. In his talk, Kelly stressed that in the future, three overall trajectories will probably characterize the Web: a move up into the "digital cloud," a move down into databases, and a move towards a kind of general sharing. According to him, information that is not accessible—will cease to exist.[38] Open source, various "mash-up" technologies and services, as well as open APIs are already progressing in this manner. One might even argue that if Gutenberg's movable pieces of type were the modules on which the art of printing rested, then almost analogous divisible binary program modules will—if shared—constitute the foundation of the information landscape of the future.

Today, a circulating binary flow of texts, images, sound and video characterizes the Web. Open APIs makes it possible for programmers to constantly develop new interfaces. Sharing metadata through open source and open APIs is also a way for the ALM-sector to increase a dynamic growth of new binary heritage services. Following Google, many websites have exposed their APIs and made them available to external developers, and even though there are numerous initiatives within the heritage sector, particularly concerning libraries, there is a general lack of data within the heritage domain. If data was more frequently re-used and shared, more sophisticated system could be built and creative mash-ups constructed, which in turn would mean that the collected data would reach a wider audience.

This article has dealt with different ways in which heritage institutions should use and think about digital technologies in general, and the Web in particular. My last proposition suggests that the ALM-sector should upgrade itself, and perceive itself as a sort of binary platform within the digital domain. The notion of platform, in fact, sums up what the article has tried to address, namely an increased focus on access and distribution, interactivity and sharing. The term "platform" can of course mean many things: a computing platform often describes some sort of software framework, and a political platform is a list of principles held by a political party. Yet as Jeff Jarvis has stated, "a platform enables. It helps others build value. [...] Networks are built atop platforms."[39] A number of popular social networking sites like to perceive themselves as more or less "empty" platforms to be filled by the communities using them. YouTube, for example, presents and views itself as a platform—and not as a regular media distributor (especially when copyright issues are at hand). For sure, there is a distinct politics of contemporary online platforms. However, I would argue that as a digital platform heritage institutions could better fulfill their basic democratic functions. If institutions would establish themselves on the Web and be open and collaborative with data and digital material, rather than claiming content as their own assets (like the National Portrait Gallery), users will naturally start adding value to such platforms.

ENDNOTES

1. "U.K. National Portrait Gallery threatens U.S. citizen with legal action over Wikimedia images" 14 July 2009—http://en.wikinews.org/wiki/U.K._ National_ Portrait_Gallery_threatens_U.S._citizen_with_legal_action_over_ Wikimedia_images [last checked 15 September 2009]. For a discussion, see also Wikimedia Commons "User:Dcoetzee/NPG legal threat"—http://com- mons. wikimedia.org/wiki/User:Dcoetzee/NPG_legal_threat[last checked 15 September 2009].

2. Cory Doctorow, "UK National Portrait Gallery threatens Wikipedia over scans of its public domain art" *boingboing* 20 July 2009—http://www.boing- boing.net/2009/07/20/uk-national-portrait. html [last checked 15 Septem- ber 2009].

3. Eric Felten, "Who's Art Is It, Anyway?" *The Wall Street Journal,* 30 July 2009— http://online.wsj.com/article/SB1000.html [last checked 15 September 2009]. For a discussion, see also Kenneth Hamma, "Public Domain Art in an Age of Easier Mechanical Reproducibility" *D-Lib Magazine,* No. 11 (2005)— http://

www.dlib.org/dlib/november05/hamma/11hamma.html [last checked 15 September 2009].

4. Astrid Verhausen, "Mass Digitisation by Libraries: Issues concerning Organisation, Quality and Efficiency," *Liber Quaterly*, No. 1 (2008)—http://webdoc. sub.gwdg.de/edoc/aw/liber/lq-1-08/ar ticle4.pdf [last checked 15 September 2009].

5. The funding provided from Google to various libraries taken part in the Book Search project is confidential. At a meeting in Munich in March 2009 with Klaus Ceynowa, the deputy Director General of the State Library of Bavaria, confessed however that around €50 million is what the library receives in funding.

6. "Europe's Digital Library doubles in size but also shows EU's lack of common web copyright solution," press release 28 August 2009—http://europa. eu/rapid/pressReleasesAction.do?reference=I P/09/1257&format [last checked 15 September 2009].

7. Lev Manovich, *Software Takes Command* (2008)—http://software studies.com/ softbook/manovich_softbook_11_20_2008.pdf, p. 19. [last checked 15 September 2009].

8. Ibid., 18.

9. Lawrence Lessig, *Remix: Making Art and Commerce Thrive in the Hybrid Economy* (London: Penguin Press, 2008).

10. Geert Lovink, "The Art of Watching Databases: An Introduction to the Video Vortex Reader." In Geert Lovink & Sabine Niederer, eds., *Video Vortex Reader: Responses to YouTube* (Amsterdam: Institute of Network Cultures, 2008), 9—http://networkcultures.org/wpmu/portal/publications/inc-readers/ videovortex/ [last checked 15 September 2009].

11. Lev Manovich, *The Language of New Media* (Cambridge, MA: MIT Press, 2001).

12. Paolo Cherchi Usai, "Äh, det är ju bara journalfilm: Varför ses inte 95% av museernas bestånd?" *Aura* No. 3–4 (1997): 111–117.

13. "YouTube Surpasses 100 Million U.S. Viewers for the First Time," Comscore press release 4 March 2009—http://comsc ore.com/index.php//Press_Events/ Press_Releases/2009/3/YouTube_Surpasses_100_Million_US_Viewers [last checked 15 September 2009].

14. For a discussion, see Jonathan Zittrain, *The Future of the Internet* (New Haven: Yale University Press, 2008).

15. Richard Wright has made similar claims on various media archival events during the last decade. For a discussion, see for example the panel "Institu-

tional Perspectives on Storage" at the MIT "Media in transition 6" conference in Boston, April 2009—http://mitworld.mit.edu/video/681/ [last checked 15 September 2009].

16. Clair Cain Miller, "Ad Revenue on the Web? No Sure Bet," *New York Times,* 24 May 2009—http://www.nytimes.com/2009/ 05/25/technology/start-ups/ 25startup.html [last checked 15 September 2009].

17. For a discussion around the Prelinger Archives, see http://www.archive.org/ details/prelinger [last checked 15 September 2009].

18. Matthew B. Kirschenbaum, *Mechanisms: New Media and the Forensic Imagination* (Cambridge, MA: MIT Press, 2008).

19. For a discussion see http://www.fiafnet.org as well as Paolo Cherchi Usai et al., *Film Curatorship: Archives, Museums, and the Digital Marketplace* (Vienna: Synema, 2008).

20. For a discussion see, Grant Gross, "Library of Congress embraces YouTube, iTunes," 27 March 2009, *IDg News Service*—http://www.networkworld.com/ news/2009/032709-library-of-congress-embraces-youtube.html [last checked 15 September 2009].

21. See, Brian Stelter, "Interviews With Legends of Television Hit the Web" 13 September 2009—http://www.nytimes.com/2009/09 /14/ business/media/ 14archive.html [last checked 15 September 2009].

22. Sante is quoted from, Noam Cohen, "Historical photos in web archives gain vivid new lives," *New York Times,* 19 January 2009—http://www.nytimes.com/ 2009/01/19/technology/internet/19link.html [last checked 15 September 2009].

23. For a discussion, see—http://www.flickr.com/commons [last checked 15 September 2009].

24. Kristin Thompson, "The Celestial Multiplex," 27 March 2007—blog post at http://www.davidbordwell.net/blog/?p=595 [last checked 15 September 2009].

25. Rick Prelinger, "The Apperance of Archives." Pelle Snickars & Patrick Vonderau, eds., In *The YouTube Reader* (Stockholm: National Library of Sweden, 2009), 272.

26. For a discussion, see *The YouTube Reader* (2009).

27. See—http://en.wikipedia.org/wiki/Social_tagging [last checked 15 September 2009].

28. Michelle Springer et al.,"For the Common Good: The Library of Congress Flickr Pilot Project" (2008)—http://www.loc.gov/rr/pri nt/flickr_report_ final.pdf [last checked 15 September 2009].

29. For information on "data mining", see Wikipedia—http://en.wikipedia.org/ wiki/Data_mining [last checked 15 September 2009].

30. For more information, see—http://www.diggingintodata.org/ [last checked 15 September 2009].

31. Ibid.

32. Daniel J. Cohen, "From Babel to Knowledge. Data Mining Large Digital Collections," *D-Lib Magazine* no. 3, 2006—http://www.dlib.org/dlib/march06/cohen/03cohen.htm [last checked 15 September 2009].

33. Lev Manovich, "Cultural Analytics"—http://lab.software studies.com/2008/09/cultural-analytics.html [last checked 15 September 2009].

34. For a discussion, see—http://www.lockss.org/lockss/Home [last checked 15 September 2009].

35. For a discussion, see—http://chronopolis.sdsc.edu/index.html [last checked 15 September 2009].

36. Christopher Jordan et al., "Encouraging Cyberinfrastructure Collaboration for Digital Preservation" (2008)—http://chronopolis. sdsc.edu/assets/docs/39_Jordan.pdf [last checked 15 September 2009].

37. See—http://www.opensolaris.org/os/project/celeste/ [last checked 15 September 2009].

38. Kevin Kelly's talk can be found at—http://www.youtube.com/watch?v=1So-S36pMo4 [last checked 15 September 2009].

39. Jeff Jarvis, *What Would Google Do?* (New York: HarperCollins, 2009), 32.

CHAPTER 13

ARE AMERICANS HUMAN?

EVELYN CH'IEN

'"Just beat it."
—Michael Jackson

WHEN THE FRENCH ask, with rhetorical irony, "Est-ce que les Americains sont humains?" it provokes. But in an increasingly technological world, Americans are playing Wii instead of sports; singers are lip syncing in public spaces because they are afraid of using their own, unmediated voices; guitar hero is replacing guitar playing; and Facebook steadily eroding the concept of friendship. These events illuminate the increasing hybrid human-machine relationships that now define current American culture. I encounter this hybridity in my profession. One of my courses is rap composition, and rap is heavily influenced by technology and a major departure from traditional instrument-based music. [1] In my course "Hip Hop Sound and Literature," I encounter questions like "Should I import a sound or use my voice to make sounds? Should I bring in my guitar or just use MIDI?" These are different ways of asking whether to use sounds already in the computer or to use the human voice or a live instrument. Linguist and jazz pianist Theo Van Leeuwen probes the question of whether the "vox humana" on a keyboard is simply a reproduction of human voice, or whether digitalization adds another dimension. [2] Through a series of historical examples about the instrumental appropriation of both sounds—birds, trains—and emotions—anger, happiness—he shows how, in the end, the creation of the vox humana remains still an abstraction of the human voice rather than the gritty real thing. Despite that, we can choose, and my students often do, to use the abstraction. We start with microphone and tweak the pitch, timbre and quality of the voice until isn't ours anymore.

RAP AS HYBRID TECH

In the world of electronic music, this abstraction frequently substitutes for the human, in the way that technology has pervaded so much of life; in the way we game, socialize and experience our mental physical lives. Music schools do not tend to acknowledge rap as a musical form, in part because the creation of it does not require learning an instrument in the musical tradition, but also because technology is an entirely different field than music and few can master both an instrument and audio technology. Rappers can produce without any awareness of musical notation, pitch, or knowledge of tonal architecture. Rap requires rhythm and a gift for wordplay; and a decent mixer. It is often considered poetry rather than music. But rap is not simply poetry, it is a new kind of hybrid, and rhetorical voice for its generation(s). Instead of dramatizing our voice we can distort it with the help of audio technology. We can make it sound superhuman and subhuman; super-fast, super-bass, electronic. If we return to literature to find our humanity, then the voice of rap, a new kind of literature, tells us that evolution of humanity has been at the mercy of machines. The question about humanity in relation to American life arises because the art is being created in sync with technology. The phenomena that humans engage in to find their humanity are all intervened by machines. So does this make us less human, inhuman, perhaps superhuman?

The gradual evolution to making non-human generated music, music that emanated because of machines, began with the gramophone.[3] Of course, human beings have created instruments that intervened in the emanation of human sound, but it was still human sound. Even if we had to learn circular breathing or train each phalange to move independently, the musical instrument was not independent of our influence and use of it. The beginning of recording and playback inaugurated the independence of instruments from human beings. Because rap music is such a force of technology, it demonstrates the most robust way in which an art form has been built by technology. In fact, such intervention could be said to have developed an entirely new system of writing—writing sound, tonal arrangements, and drafting collages.

Before computers took over the recording industry in the early 1990s in a startling break from human intelligence, the writing tool behind rap music was the needle. The needle was first referred to, significantly, as a stylus. Sometimes hovering, sometimes tearing over the gramophone or turntable, it inaugurated the mechanization of the voice: when humans could write acoustics with a stylus they took writing to a new level. In line with the function of a stylus, the needle's transmission of information from vinyl reconfigured the human relationship to the acoustic world, to their acoustic selves, carving sound and reproducing it in circumscribed space—leading to ideas about speakers and surround sound (decades after its invention) and creating a conception of audio-spatiality. The needle, like the human, became the center of the audio universe. The needle, like other stylus tools before it, showed another way to configure the environment, to translate notes to sounds to an environment structured by sound. In the hip-hop world the needle's role in centering acoustic environments changed the ghetto. The revolution that minorities hoped for in the sixties and seventies was not only socio-political; it was technological. Since the 1970s, we have advanced from basic turntables, to mixers, to virtual mixers, as well as computer-based audio software.[4] Although it has been argued that the power of rap is really lodged in keeping it real, it is clear that technology keeps getting its props from the rappers as the force of evolution for hip-hop. From turntable to computer, hip-hop's musical landscape has greatly altered.

RAP AGAINST THE MACHINE

The hip-hop movement engineered a dynamic relationship between human and machine.[5] To compete with such centrifugal audio force, humans would have to be as skilled, and in some ways as machine-like in precision, to out-perform the sound-making turntables that functioned as independent composers with their agile tiny needles. They would have to appropriate a machine mentality, striving to place attack notes right on the beat, or to hit the notes required. Rap demands such precise and controlled energy, but at the same time it ushered in a new trend in that if the song's structure could not be created by human powers, it could be produced in collabora-

FIGURE 1: J. Anthony Allen, now an assistant professor of music composition at McNally Smith College of Music, a former teaching assistant in "Hip-Hop Sound and Literature, a course I taught at the University of Minnesota, in the McNally Smith studios with engineer Andrew Hill.

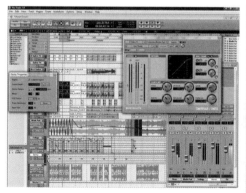

FIGURE 2 AND 3: Screenshot of Protools and of Reason (note the cables, which demonstrate the degree of physical reality the designers gave to the program), music software programs used in my class at the University of Minnesota, "Hip Hop Sound and Literature."

333

tion with technology. For example, precision could be doctored—with tools like pitch doctor to alter (obviously) pitch, for example. Because of the back-and-forth relationship between musician and machine, sometimes people would actually recreate machine noises. A former student of mine, Joe Battaglia, used to verbally mimic the act of back-spinning the record with the onomatopoetic sound rrprrprrp. Now our subjectivities have come to match the technology; we can imitate the machine while it creates percussion and all sorts of effects with the click of a button and move of mouse, with knowledge of programs like Garageband, Protools, Max MSP/Jitter.

RAPPERS AND SCRATCHERS

Rappers became turntables while scratchers controlled the needle, interrupting its writing to make their own turntable collages of sound. While rappers morphed themselves into super-turntable replicas, scratchers created a instrument with the machine instead of simply allowing the machine to reproduce sounds, hands moving to capture the needle's automatic looping and interrupting its flow to create a human-machine meta-flow with the records. Such ingenuity further inspired rappers to make instruments of themselves, to make themselves into human turntables and reproduce the sounds of scratching and beat-making and to make their voices follow, trip up, syncopate with or disrupt regular rhythmic patterns. A cipher of rappers can be seen spitting out the sounds of scratching and beating, emitting sounds like arrip arrip pa pa puh puh like the sound of a needle going back on a groove then hitting the part of the break-beat and in that moment morphing into turntables. The shape of the cipher evokes the groove's circular motion, mimicking the circular shape of a needle's repetitive journey, and connecting the rappers' movements to that of the needle, as a physical manifestation of the loop. Their structure is dictated by the passage of the writing needle; each person is represented by a groove.

With the initial movements of the needle grooving vinyl, the break-beat and scratching were born: the two principal structural foundations of rap music. The needle wrote the structure, while the verbal component follows its direction. Tricia Brook Rose writes, "Rap is fundamentally literate and deeply technological [...] The lyrical and musical texts in rap are a dynamic hybrid of oral traditions, post-literate orality, and advanced technology. Rap lyrics are a critical part of a rapper's identity, strongly suggesting the importance of authorship and individuality in rap music. Yet, sampling as it is used by rap artists indicates the importance of collective identities and group histories."[6] Because of the significance of this instrument of writing, rap music's evolution has been driven by technology. The musical composition and style of rap has been tied to the changing landscape of new mixers, sound libraries, and recording programs. Still, while scratch sounds can be downloaded from libraries and beats can be created with a variety of programs and compositions can be choreographed in greats scope and detail by software such as MAX/MSP, the needle remains the signifying symbol of rap music; scratch competitions are still held worldwide and clubs will still enjoy the presence of a spinner who can use the needle. The raw sound of generated by the needle and the spontaneous compositions that it is responsible for remain part of the identity of rap music.

The needle, the stylus—and the era of sound recording that it inaugurated—performs differently than the pen and to scholars such as Friedrich Kittler thus seems antithetical to writing ideals. But the needle's performance is that not merely of writing but also collaging.[7] Writing collaborates with the powers of machinery. And this cooperation with machinery is a juggling act between being co-opted and programmed by the machinery and noise—but the needle also did something to our psyches, allowed for automatic writing, and thus a kind of automatic talking. It penetrates us as much as the grooves from which the music bursts, and it generates an emotional flow, in the technical sense of flow. The way in which we insist on our own automatic behavior manifests itself in the utterance of rap, which is intrinsically an act of self-automation. Yet rap negotiates both the machine-like and the explosively creative.

MAKING MACHINE MENTALITIES

"Hail Mary. Mother of God. Got the whole host of angels in my iPod."
                                                            —Saul Williams.

Rap's encounter with the needle created a unique relationship between the human and the needle that later became a relationship between the human and the mixer, and even later recording software—each transition

335

reorganizing the human relationship to music yet again. But the transition was not immediate: as the idea of speaking over music or beats became appealing, the first attempts were spoken word, not rap. The emotional setting for rap had not yet been established and the human voice was still seen as separate from the beat, so that the performance of give-ad-take between voice and beat could not get off the ground. For example, in 1971—when rap was a mere fledgling art, Gil Scott Heron recorded "The Revolution Will not Be Televised." Little did he know that the revolution would be beat-scripted and later digitized. Adam Bradley writes, "Rap as we know it was born only after words started bending to the beat. It was founded on that dual rhythmic relationship [...] For all Muhammad Ali's brilliant rhyme and wordplay, he never said his lines over a beat. For all their smoothed-out patter, soul crooners like Barry White did it as singers rather than as rhymers."[8]

The turntable is the last thoroughly embodiable musical machine; the mixer is clearly a machine without human extension, as is software—few pretend to embody garageband, protools, logic, reason or any of the programs that create rap or other music on a computer — though performance artists make valiant efforts. DJ Singe says, "There's so much in [production] that's amazingly repetitive [...] I think when people are practicing scales on piano, there is this technical thing about what is correct, what is perfect—but there's a real physical aspect to that repetition. And one of the things that's really bugged out about doing it all in the computer is that it's absolutely repetitive in those same ways, but the gesture is not in sync [...] when I play the stuff back to do live shows, there is more relationship between the physical gestures and, like, stomping on my keyboard, in relationship to what's happening with the sound, which is really fun."[9] DJ Singe's experiences—trying to make the computer do performance work—are a new dimension of how technology can be integrated into stage work. The classroom is now a microcosm of this historical transformation, where students live in such a global mix that a single poetic voice is now not adequate stimulation to keep or attract attention. In a world without audio technology the voice is trafficked by molecules; in the millennium, a voice equals infinitely modifiable digital bits, a communal phenomenon emerging from splicing, compressing and other digital manipulations.

But the turntable is the last machine that *writes* music, rather than simply reproduces it. By embodying the turntable, rappers intervened in the mechanization process, interrupting and in some ways reversing the relationship between human and machine as mechanization. Rap—and its necessary partner, the DJ—now signify the synergistic relationship between the human and the machine: while rappers and DJs often reference their machines in their names, or the creative process that generates their flow (i.e. names such as Phlowtations or Grandmaster Flash), the machine became an extension of the human, not simply an appropriator of human sound but something that could, upon human prompting, generate its own compositions. In *Freestyle and the Art of Rhyme*, the rapper Supernatural raps an entire sequence describing the process of rap production, from the turntable scratch to the fader's adjustments. He acknowledges that the mechanical intervention significantly influenced the form of these compositions, and evolved the movement of rap; yet the artists acknowledged this trend and also extended their own creativity with the invention of new machinery. As early as the 70s praise for the machine was prevalent: "Jam Master Jay is the one in charge/Who makes beats that are really large/He is the master of a scratch and cut."[10]

The turntable created dance scenes of unparalleled flow as related in *Generation Ecstasy* and *Last Night A DJ Changed My Life*,[11] as well as *Can't Stop Won't Stop*, among others. As related in *Last Night a DJ Changed My Life*, the introduction of the machine as the emitting musical device upon which all activity was centered, began with the jukebox[12]; yet it was the introduction of the turntable that brought the human element back into the control of the machine; pre-dating the computer/human relationship as the focal point of a room. The scratcher and turntable master, however, controlled the turntable that controlled the crowd, and tech savvy entered the musical world with full force with the arrival of Grandmaster Flash, who knew that his technical expertise was the foundation for a cultural transformation:

> I knew what it was because I was going to the technical school for electronics. I knew that inside the unit it was a single pole, double throw switch, meaning that when it's in the center it's off. When it's to the left you're listening to the left turntable and when it's to the right you're listening to the right turntable. I had to go to the raw parts shop downtown to find me a single pole double throw switch, some crazy glue to glue this part to my mixer, an external amplifier and a headphone [...] After that, I mastered punch phasing—taking certain parts of a record where there's

a vocal or drum slap or a horn. I would throw it out and bring it back, keeping the other turntable playing. If this record had a horn in it before the break came down I would go—BAM, BAM, BAM-BAM—just to try this on the crowd.[13]

For one, the turntable/DJ as social axes made parties louder, and perhaps more of a single mindset; Saul Williams writes about hip-hop but the same message could apply to house or disco music; his *Dead Emcee Scrolls* emphasizes the spiritual hypnotism of rap and its capacity to synchronize group psyche:

There is no music more powerful than hip-hop. No other music demands an instant affirmative on such a global scale. When the beat drops, people nod their heads, 'yes,' in the same way that they would in conversation with a loved one, a parent, professor, or minister. Instantaneously, the same mechanical gesture that occurs in moments of dialogue as a sign of agreement which subsequently, releases increased oxygen to the brain and thus, broadens one's ability to understand, become the symbolic and actual gesture that connects you to the beat.[14]

BREAKBEAT AND RAP RHYTHM

It was the breakbeat that cemented the centrality of the turntable. Broughton and Brewster narrativize the breakbeat's beginning in a compelling way, starting on how it was commanded by the dance movement of breakdancing:

Before there was anything called hip hop, there was break dancing. It evolved, as an expression of male prowess, from the 'Good Foot' steps of James Brown, from eh robotic 'locking' and 'popping' moves of West Coast funk dancers, and from he extrovert dancing on TV's Soul Train. It took influences from such acrobatic styles as tap dancing and Lindy-hopping, even from kung fu [...] It is named after the 'break,' a jazz term for the part of the dance record where the melody takes a rest and the drummer cuts loose, this being the explosive, rhythmic section of a song which most appealed to the teenage show-offs (207). [...] Many dancers would completely forgo the rest of the music, standing against the wall until a

song's break came in. They were eventually known as b-boys, the 'b' almost certainly for 'break' (some say it was also for 'Bronx'). The stern 'b-
boy stance,' beloved of rappers even today—with shoulders cured inwards
and arms folded tightly under the chin—was not so much as signal of aggression as a b-boy's way of looking cool while he waited for a break.[15]

They continue, "The dance floor was soon spit between the meandering
moves of the hustlers and the youthful explosion of the breakers. When
a record reached its break, the entire room's energy level shot up. The
same thing was happening when certain oldies, notably James Brown
tracks, got an airing. It couldn't be long before the DJ would take notice."[16] Rap rhythm's alchemic properties to make communicative impressions are vivid n the dance movements that are part of hip-hop. David LaChapelle's film *Rize* includes dance sequences that last for several
minutes, inviting a reconception of the body as a rhythmic instrument.
The needle gave birth to a collective consciousness for music that reflects
the established computer network of human beings who feel connected
or wired together. The same accusations leveled at the computer for creating so much of a collective consciousness that the individual is eradi-
cated is often leveled at the rap and rave movements.

The predominance of the beat can be seen to drown out the possibility of individual musicality within the musical group. There are advantages to having a predominant beat, and to having a drummer gain
strength at a break and fade away. The advantage to a predominant beat
is that it introduced such danceable music, such arousing intensity. Since
the beat's constant predominance was enhanced with the automation of
the beat and thus the machination of music, its manipulation became
possible around the same time it became so central. With reverberation,
compression and hi- and lo-pass filters accessible with a mouse and keyboard, beat-making became easy. Varieties of beats exploded—dirty and
clean beats, beats with long lead-ins, and tinny or fat beats. Tempos could
be altered quickly and smoothly. Human emotion was, in short, amped.
But other instruments became subordinate to the beat, because subordinate to the unrelenting rhythmic patterns—but the human voice could
work around the beats with the greatest agility, thus becoming a powerful instrument in itself. Tricia Rose writes that "Rhythmic complexity,
repetition with subtle variations, the significance of the drum, melodic
interest in the bass frequencies, and breaks in pitch and time (e.g., sus-

pensions of the beat for a bar or two) are also consistently recognized features of African-American musical practices"[17] and then adds "one might wonder why the change from harmony to rhythm accompanied the advent of technology. It could have simply reinforced the centrality of melody and harmony. [...] it seems reasonable to suggest that recording technology has been the primary vehicle for providing access to black music and black cultural priorities, which have in turn had a critical impact on popular pleasure."[18]

In addition to African American musical practices, technology enabled the centrality of the percussion by increasing the varieties of drumbeats that could be arranged. With Reason and Logic and other beat-making programs, individuals could design the shape of the beat and where each instrument fell on the beat, giving unprecedented speed to creating variety and color to beats. Speed and sound were enhanced in ways never before associated with rhythm, and culture with rich histories of rhythm-making were the first to realize the advantage of what technology had to offer for rap and dance music. Scratchers made noises and beats that were unprecedented in variety. I've had students create beats from the sound of corks popping, bubblegum bubbles bursting, and the sound of a raindrop.

The ever-evolving beat launched a unique display of the human voice in the history of music. Because of the emotional capital generated by its relentless force, some contend that it evokes the voice patterns of multiple cultural rituals which are created by cathartic beat-making, while others say that machination forces humans to find emotional sources brought into being by machines. DJ Spooky asserts that technology can be made to evoke the ancient and pre-technological self before technology fragmented it—through rhythm science. Certainly, it is ironic that it is the reproduction of this music via technology that can bring out primal emotions in crowds, and specifically crowds:

> Rhythm science is not so much a new language as a new way of pronouncing the ancient syntaxes that we inherit from history and evolution, a new way of enunciating the basic primal languages that slip through the fabric of rational thought and infect our psyche at another, deeper level. Could this be the way of healing? Taking elements of our own alienated consciousness and recombining them to create new languages from old (and in doing so to reflect the chaotic turbulent reality we all call home) just

might be a way of seeking to reconcile the damage rapid technological advances have wrought on our collective consciousness.[19]

Whether the human voice became mechanized or was propelled to find ancient syntaxes, its countenance changed with the movement of rap. Rappers are conscious of the power of rhythm and create a beat by posturing, gesturing and using words to function as beats. Although DJ Spooky sees rhythm science[20] as a kind of art of bridging past and present, it is also a bridge of physical embodiment and technological infrastructure. Making the technology flow means imbuing it with the energy of the environment, and making one's words flow is revitalizing language with human energy, letting that energy flow. Rap is thus both rhythmically repetitive and yet electric with continual energy input. The attack and decay of each word emulates the cycles of nature. Simon Reynolds writes in *Generation Ecstasy*, the digital voice a recombination of digital packages of sound. His attribution of the new voice is simultaneous with the popularity of the sampler: "The sampler is a computer that converts sound into numbers, the zeros and ones of digital code. In its early days, the sampler was used primarily as a quote machine, a device for copying a segment of pre-recorded music and replaying it on a keyboard at any pitch or temp. But because the sound has been converted into digital data, the information can be easily rearranged. Early hip-hop sampling was like Frankenstein's monster, funk-limbs crudely bolted together, the stitching clearly audible. With its quasi-organic seamlessness, today's sampladelia is more like the *chimera*, that mythical monster."[21]

RAP MACHINES

To segue with the beat created by a machine, the rapper often mimicked machines to communicate this transformation, moving in robotic motion and lightening speed and producing such phenomena as the moonwalk; the lock-and-pop dance moves; the insane daring of spinning like tops on the head. They also created, with their voices, repetitive tropes that reflected the loop structure—intensive and multiple rhyming, rigid observance of the beat and maintenance of the same volume—loud. But the transformation of the human being to a human being who could conceive of themselves as rap generating machines would require half a century before it happened. While the gramophone was invented in the late 1800s along with the jukebox, however, the conception of rap did not happen until the early 1970s. Even modern rappers refer to themselves and their machines in one breath; in an interview Jean Grae says: "I'm a keyboard person and I know everyone's usually into their MPCs and people have been trying to get me into MPCs for years [...] My first machine was an SP12 and I loved it and I still love the sound of it, it's so gritty, you can't recreate that with an MPC; I would say the MPC is so much more clean, and I enjoy the clean sound that comes out of say the Triton or the Motif, but I'm an ASR10 and EPS-16+ plus kind of girl."[22] Grandmaster Flash also critiques Herc's early machinations: "Herc really slipped up. With the monstrous power he had he couldn't mix too well. He was playing little breaks but it would sound so sloppy. I noticed that the mixer he was using was a GLI 3800. It was a very popular mixer at that time. It's a scarcity today but it's still one of the best mixers GLI ever made [...]"[23]

Jean Grae's connection to a machine is shared by most rappers and scratchers, just like the i-generation who illustrate i-literacy by personalizing computers, desktops, cellphones and other devices, musicians have their favorite mixers, software and sound library resources (freesound-project.com, for example). Certain trends have passed through the rap movement, notably the gangsta rap movement that brought notoriety to rap in the 1980s. Significantly at this point, mixers became generally available, rappers enjoyed producing dirty beats and gangsta rap. Though there are legitimate and compelling historical and social explanations behind the production of gangsta rap that account for its aggressive and bass-dominated sound (well-examined by Jeff Chang in *Can't Stop Won't Stop*) without the available technology, gangsta rap would not have made the hypermasculined superhero quality sound that it had. While in concerts and block parties rappers would hit the mike and rhyme in bass with as much strength as possible, the technology made it possible to sustain certain rapping styles that would be beyond human capacity. Singing in extremely bass notes requires more horsepower, at loud volumes, than singing at normal voice with normal sound output. It also requires vocal agility to bend the voice around superfast or oddly scratched beats, but it is the rapper's inflections on words that creates meanings, not simply the words themselves: "The music, its rhythmic patterns, and the idiosyncratic articulation by the rapper are essential to the song's meanings."[24] In *Prime Mover: A Natural History of Muscle*, Steven Vogel writes:

Treble comes cheap while bass costs, as those of us who've built hi-fi systems learned early in the game. Tweeters are naturally tiny; the art lies in building a nonmonstrous woofer. Even now, fancy stereo systems use era amplifiers for their subwoofers. If you want to attract females or to announce your presence and territory, you do best with frequencies above at least 100 hertz.[25]

So the rapper who can manipulate his/her vocal cords to emulate this piece of machinery is admired. Vogel continues, "Even now, fancy stereo systems use era amplifiers for their subwoofers. If you want to attract females or to announce your presence and territory, you do best with frequencies above at least 100 hertz."[26] Low frequencies are proof of strength (as they require great muscle power) and produce aesthetic excitement.

Gangsta rap would profit from the machine's horsepower and many new rap pieces would have low pulsing beats and bass voicings and sharp attacks, which would require human strength and muscle power but merely a tweak of the dial on the machine or press of the keys. Such characteristics would continue to remain in rap music. On the other hand, rap would also benefit from extremely sharp attacks in voicing patterns, to harness the extremities of the vocal chords.[27]

SCRATCHING

"A scratch is *nothing* but the back-cueing that you hear in your ear before you push it out to the crowd. All you have to know is mathematically how many times to scratch it and when to let it go—when certain things will enhance the record you're listening to."
— Grandmaster Flash

Scratching made rap possible. With this technique, instead of playing records, or even recognizable parts of records, the DJ was able to chop previously recorded music up so finely that he was manipulating sounds—discrete noises that would not be recognizable after being manipulated from their original sources. "Hands whipping from one record to another, stopping lightening fast on the crossfader in between, shoulders dipping slightly in time to the beat, but running no risk of unplanned movement, fingers moving in millimeter-precise formation, each flick or slide or run controlled to a hair's breadth, and from the speakers a pounding beat with a barrage of scribbles and scratches running in and out of it, the bare bones of a song repeated and repeated and repeated, then let go, dropping into the climax of another."[28] The turntable's needle[29]—the composition of which graduated from gemstones to steel—is still what produces scratch, and any other sound of scratch in the mix are recordings of scratches. The phenomenon of scratch is true to its descriptive moniker: it is an attention-getting screech of noise. In isolation the screech is jarring, but multiply the scratches and they can be arranged into a series of pleasant rhythmic sensations, danceable and rappable.

While the verbal component of rap is often emphasized as its driving force, scratching constitutes a system of writing on its own, and has been the principal evolutionary force for rap music, generating the combinations of beats that have altered its verbal accompaniment. Scratchers also discovered the advantages of technical expertise: in the late eighties beat-juggling was invented, a technique involving the manipulation of the cross-fader switch, so that a basic scratch could be chopped up in all sorts of ways. "Today there is rarely anything like a simple scratch. A dedicated turntablist would be able to tell you the difference between the chirp, the tweak, the scribble, the tear, and the stab (or chop), not to mention the more advanced techniques of the transform, the hydroplane, the flare (a reverse transform), the orbit or the twiddle."[30] [...] "Instead of using a relatively long noise (a scratch) for your rhythm and cutting it up with the cross-fader to make a percussion sound, you use a record's individual drum beats more or less intact, juggling them, as the name suggests, to construct new and untold percussion patterns."[31]

The computer produces a kind of high in the user; which is why "surfing" feels so appropriate—sometimes the waves of information provide such a high that it is difficult to jump off the rolling temptations of infowaves. The emotional high also extends to technology that given us tools to use and manipulate acoustics. This sense of super-computerism surrounds the language of scratch and scratchers often say off-beat things about the potential for their compositions, such as the comment by Mix Master Mike: "I got inspired one day because down from the apartment complex there was a football field [...] I'd seen these three lights that landed on the field [...] out of my window, I kid you not, and that's where I got inspiration to like, maybe it was my scratching that got them to land, maybe I'm actually communicating with these intergalactic be-ings."[32] In fact, in comments by Mix Master Mike and DJ QBert of the Invisibl Skratch Piklz, (the latter group being legendary champion scratch-ers in world scratch competitions) each scratcher admits to being trans-ported while scratching and imagining themselves in a discourse with other populations in the galaxy:

> Mix Master Mike: scratching to me is like some other kind of intelligence [...] me and Qbert used to practice, that's when we'd made up the ques-tion and answer, I'd scratch the question and he'd scratch the answer... and so we wouldn't have to talk to each other all day [...]
>
> Qbert: I remember when he moved away, and I thought how am I going to bite it, how am I going to get his ideas... and so I imagined all these DJs from outerspace, like what would their style be—
>
> Mix Master Mike: He took that and just like went in his own world with it—
>
> Qbert: Since earth is like a primitive planet, what about the more ad-vanced civilizations, how does their music sound, so I would imagine what-ever they are doing and I guess that's how I come up with my ideas [...]

For these two scratchers, the activity of scratching is linguistic activity, a new way of communicating with nonhuman populations, of developing new frequencies for communication. Like the rappers, DJ Qbert finds noble vocation in his scratching:

> Rhythm is really important, it's like if you want to reach that spiritual kind of medium in your soul, it's like the Indians when they wanted to speak to the gods they would have like a rain dances and that would be with the drums, and after a while the drums would get hypnotic and stuff and they would go into a trance, and so music is trance-inducing, it gets you into that state [...] it's called the zone, or a nirvana [makes noises] it's like you're not playing the instrument, you're in the instrument and the universe is playing you [...] it's that kung fu stuff [...] I believe that everyone is one, one big ball of energy, kind of like the star wars thing of the force, everyone's connected and we're all like one big energy, we think we're separated but everyone affects everyone [...] when you find out you're not separated, say uh, everyone is a limb of a one whole thing why would you want to hurt your hand, hurt your fingers, hurt your arms,

345

when you know that that person is part of you [...] so in order to help people, teach people scratching and brighten their day, that's my destiny [...]

Qbert identities an attraction to rhythm with an attraction to communicate or convene with forces outside ourselves.

THE AGE OF THE SPEED OF LIGHT

"The urbanization of real time is in fact first the urbanization of one's own body plugged into various interfaces (keyboard, cathode screen, DataGlove or DataSuit), prostheses that make the super-equipped able-bodied person almost the exact equivalent of the motorized and wired disabled person."

— Paul Virilio

The sense of the possibility of speed—rather than perhaps speed itself—has influenced rap: it has made rap wordplay more daring and wildly associative; it has created a flow in which multilingual rappers are bound, and it has created new vocabulary. Combine the new emotional register wrought by the concept of the machine's speed with the agitation that accompanies the ending of a century,[33] and it produces a kind of frenzy that requires control, often obtained by rhythm and counting. Rhythm-based rap is a fitting emotional art form that harnesses this agitation and provides and aesthetic form of release for it. Rap has absorbed speed in its reproduction of it in beat arrangements, and thus voicings. It demands that humans DJ Spooky says,

I'd say this is going to be a century of hyper-acceleration [...] Mix culture, with its emphasis on exchange and nomadism, serves as a precedent for the hypertextual conceits that later arrived from the realms of the academy [...] The DJ spreads a memetic contagion. A thought storm brought about by annoyance and frustration with almost all the conventional forms of race, culture and class hierarchies. Hip-hop is a vehicle for that, and so are almost all forms of electronic music [...] At their best, these genres are about the morphology of structure—how forms and feelings transmute from one medium to another. Culture in this milieu affects

a digital triangulation. Language becomes its own form of digital code
[. . .] check the theater of the rhyme as it unfolds in time.[34]

Mos Def says, "Hip hop's relationship to education could be phenomenal. It could be extremely phenomenal, in the sense that hip hop is a medium where you can get a lot of information into a very small space, and
make it hold fast to people's memory. It's just a very radical form of information transferal [. . .] I mean, do you know how much information
—vital information—you could get across in three minutes?! [. . .] I mean,
the *Qur'an* is like that. The reason that people are able to hafiz is because
the entire *Qur'an* rhymes [. . .] Like, there's a rhyme scheme in all of that
[. . .] And it holds fast to your memory. And then you start to have a
deeper relationship with it on recitation."[35] And the results of the speed
of innovation of this collaboration created as an offshoot a revolution in
language and music—the wordplay, millions of voices rhyming in all their
different ways in the streets, all of this had a common denominator that
in combination with technology became a revolution.

Paul Virlio writes: "The revolutionary contingent attains its ideal form
not in the place of production, but in the street, where for a moment it
stops being a cog in the technical machine and itself becomes a motor
(machine of attack), in other words *a producer of speed*." Speed has become
an identifier of rap, something even detachable from the content. Adam
Bradley writes, "The fraternity of speed rappers includes artists as different from one another as Bone Thugs-N-Harmony, Big Daddy Kane, and
OutKast, all of whom occasionally rapped at tempos that stretched the
bounds of human breath control [. . .] Few, however, were as committed
to speed rapping as Tung Twista."[36]

LANGUAGE AS FLOW

In the case of rap, we absorb the effect of a changing world within our
linguistic system—namely speed. Speed defines the material culture built
around it. Wireless, cell phones, instant messaging, and accelerating musical rhythms demonstrate subjugation to speed. Speed obsolesces past
theories about language[37], forcing the construction of a new theory about
language's function and its evolutionary drive. It has intruded into our
pastimes of reflection and obsolesced the notions of quietude, solitude,

and the idea of waiting. Squeezing out as many words as possible in a time unit is the mode of speech.

Emotion, and its contagion, helped spread this appreciation of the new beat-driven language. The concept of the flow—an emotional continuum that includes the performer and its audience, began with the DJ movement and has influenced notions of the cause of language evolution. For example, in being subjugated to the search for the flow, language is driven by emotional gain and sensual reward—quick rhymes and rhythms (rather than the elucidation of meaning lucidly). The reward that certain sounds—mapped onto words—can bring about reverses the traditional causal design of how we conceive of language. The traditional design, as Rousseau wrote, has language beginning with naming and reference: It is about mapping meanings and creating a system of reference, and using sounds to achieve this aim. But for rappers, language is not only about producing not meaning but sounds. The verbal dance of rap and the flow strives for acoustic radiance and richness rather than simply clear utterance. [38] For rappers, the flow is identifiable on stage when words spill out in rhymes with such smooth continuity, such appropriate beat measure, that the rapping seems on par with breathing. At this point, rhymes and rhythm seem effortless. The audience can experience the flow vicariously, and for the rapper, the flow is emotional gold. It is specifically in the act of rapping and the world it engenders—scratching, beat-making and spinning—that the flow emerges into being. The components of acoustic stimulation—beats, voices and certain frequencies of music—may mimic the acoustic world of our own bodies or of the womb, but they also invoke a state of spiritual transcendence[39] or loss of self, perhaps from being overwhelmed by acoustic stimuli, that is related to the flow.[40] As Adam Bradley writes, "A wack flow is death to rap."[41]

Now how do these patterns affect the voice? Part of the synergy of beats and rhymes is that they protect each other from their own potential excesses. Beats without voices soon become monotonous. Rhymes in isolation expose the frailty of the human voice and the fallibility of the rapper's vocal rhythms. Together, however, beats and rhymes find strength: The voice gives the beat humanity and variety; the beat gives the rhyme a reason for being and a margin for error. This essential relationship is rap's greatest contribution to the rhythm of poetry: the *dual rhythmic relationship*.[42] Rap's most striking contribution to the American oral tradition is this rhythmic sophistication, rap's outward manifestation of the meter and rhythm of literary verse.[43]

> Certainly there are an infinite number of patterns you could generate with beats, and in the beginning they simply experimented with what would work on the dance floor: they simply speeded up the beat from, say 90 beats a minute to 110. Early hip hop featured simple syncopation—matching beats, or more specifically pulses to syllables—and that explains why early rappers often paused between syllables (hip ... hop ... you ... don't ... stop) and generally rapped slower than their lyrical descendants. Given the fact that early crews were built around the DJ, not the rapper, very few individual lyricists got the change to fully demonstrate—or cultivate—their mic skills. Instead, they worked in routines where each line of a verse might be broken down and distribute to one of four or five rappers in the crew.[44]

Cobb's description accurately describes the techniques of groups of rappers such as the Sugarhill Gang, Run DMC, and other groups which can be seen trading lines and tossing words to each other in a call-response structure. The invention of flow occurred simultaneous with the technologies of rap and turntablism. But then later, after the breakbeat was discovered and delivered to the dance floor by DJ Kool Herc—and later that powerful concept was polished into a steady constancy by DJ Grandmaster Flash—the voice patterns have now become too numerous and various to keep track of. Flash made sure that when the DJ wanted to, that the crowd wouldn't know that a breakbeat section had been edited or manipulated, that a DJ could simply choose to keep playing a breakbeat section for as long as he or she wanted. Flash also had to invent a cueing system so that a DJ could listen through records solitarily on the dance floor with a Sony MX8. He would count the revolutions on the vinyl (clocking) to pick the break-beat section with the dog paddle (fingers at edge of disc) or phone dial (spinning from inner part of disk); by flitting between two turntables with lighting hand speed he could create his own songs at will.[45] It is manual sampling that now has become part of the cut-and-paste technology that characterizes digital audio technology.

Thus, the explosion of sound as relevant to community bonding and social grouping has changed language forever. We are now experiencing communication faster and more varied acoustically and it is stretching our ears and our technology of reproduction. The speedy gestures and rhythm of rap is can be identifiably separate from its other features. In line with Paul Virilio's notion that humans are now telepresences in an electronic world, DJ Spooky (Paul Miller) uses terms like "geographic implosion" and "cartographic failure"[46] to provide a context for the dark side of music, which he describes as "unprecedented [...] phonographies and telephonies."[47] Miller floods us with words that seem like a spontaneous flow of, at times, unintelligibility, but the notion of the flow manages to provide a rhythm of beat and thought that seem more music than meaning-driven:

> Situationist style generative psychogeography—jumping from topic to topic, culture to culture, website to website, thought to thought, becomes rhyme time—we're looking at a life living in a tapestry woven of words and beats that give them cadence. I flip the script and float.[48].

The sensation of the flow, of floating, can happen when words are combined in such a way that the rhythmic pattern seems to generate the next word. Rap is probably the most effective form yet invented for doing this, because what happens between the beats and rhymes leave the audience in suspension and suspense. The audience hangs mid-rap until the beat arrives again, until the rhyme is concluded, only to embark upon another wave of words that generate another rhyme scheme.

Miller catches such a rhythm in his book—rather than being a linear read, it is a kind of tumble of ideas that does not believe in linear presentation, a multi-terraced terrain of thoughts, words and ideas that at times seems pell-mell but is definitely aura-creating. In the world of the DJ, the impression the sound montage creates is intended to overwhelm, to sweep away the audience in the flow. The best DJ music is irresistibly danceable, hypnotic in its sway.

As a result of such flow, rap is an international phenomenon, evolving not simply English but Spanish, French (NTM, Lyrikal Injection, MC Solaar), Chinese,[49] Korean, Japanese, Arabic, German and many more. Rap highlights the potential of language to accent the rhythms of these languages. Rap also infiltrated the rhythms and gestures of the deaf, as captured in performances of deaf rappers who gesture with rap rhythm, like MC Geezer or Signmark, who sign-rhyme to a beat.[50]

CUT, PASTE, SCRATCH, RAP

"Rap is a hidden transcript" —Tricia Brook Rose[51]

Such fast rhyming—often in a cipher—changes language and the way it is built. The needle's ability to scratch-sample also engendered the same methods in rap. Sampling technology, which started with the simple movement from one record to the other, has now become a cut-paste universe relying on sound libraries, past songs and other software. In parallel, rap is a cut-and-paste exercise in wordplay of ideas and rhymes. One student in my "Hip hop Sound and Literature" class, John Haine, put his song together by sampling the voice of Katie Couric while he wrote a rap about the Virginia Tech killings. Other students might sample sounds; two collaborating students, Matt Zeigler and Joe Battaglia, in a class of mine sampled airplane sounds in a piece on the Vietnam war. Both of these samples drove the themes of their raps. Tricia Rose writes:

> Sampling technology is also a means of composition, a means of (post) literate production. Using sounds and rhythms as building blocks, rap musicians store ideas in computers, build, erase, and revise musical themes and concepts [...] writing music in the age of electronic reproduction is a complex and dense process in which millions of sounds, rhythms, and melodies are made fantastically accessible. Eric Sadler describes how he writes music using the Bomb Squad's 20,000 record collection as his main source: 'You decide you are going to write some songs. You just work. You just write, write, write.'[52]

Russell Potter adds, "Unfortunately for up-and-coming rappers, the copyright laws maintain the status and position of that white Eurocentric romantic 'author,' such that their material assault upon the constructions of 'originality' faces legal as well as critical opposition. Nonetheless, there can be no question that the vernacular re-use of sonic material deemed to be 'property' situates hip-hop on the edge of a practice which questions, in a way all the theoretical eulogies for the 'death of the author' have not, the notion of originality and authorship." Rap has inaugurated a new concept of authorship: "To those who heard it at that time—a record made from nothing more than other records, a record made by a DJ, a postmodern collage of existing texts, the scratch-filled proof that turntables could be real instruments—it was as revolutionary moment in the history of music. Theoreticians heard the creaking of concepts like authorship, copyright, originality, musicianship."[53] Instead of words, entire phrases are added to the rap, and thus entire arrangements are created at once instead of gradually evolving. In rap, phrases appear, and the rapper who is the most effective or hyperactive search engine—capable of weaving random associations for the sake of rhyme—is the one who crafts the writing. Adam Bradley relates how Eminem rhymes "public housing systems" with "victim of Munchausen syndrome" and Asher Roth rhyme "Yiddish," "spinach," and "quidditch." Meanwhile a former student Jesse Morgenstern planted three internal rhymes: "obsession," "aggression," "discretion," "confession," and "depression" and here I preserve his orthography, intentionally misspelled in order to communicate the significance of the phonetic over the conventional spellings:

yo, it was 9-1-1, the war begun without a gun
Jus a 747[54] sendin peoples to heaven and down to hell
hearin funeral bells, but time will tell,
all the sounds and the smells,
seein angels that fell from up above
show no love fo all tha fake ass thugs
that I peeped shovin others to escape from tha rubble,
yo bartender, better make that shot of henny a double
cuz I'm in mournin, adornin a ribbon of hope,
tryin to cope wit tha fact I'm at the end of my rope.
The situation's lose-lose, I'm abused and confused,
all the oppression an aggression causin manic depression
makin confessions my obsession beats my betta descretion
got me guessin an pressin wanna teach em a lesson,
not fo peace,
jus wanna see the destruction decrease
or at least see the cease of all the beatings in tha streets
I'm one man, but I'm a try tha best that I can
fuck tha 'W' plan, we got's to make em understan
that we can't jus force an end like in iraq or japan.
it's not tha same
we may never reach tha end of the game
but feel the shame
if you's the sick mother-fucker to blame.

Of course, the words on the pages are much flatter than the oral expression. But what is important is to see how the writing evolves under the influence of the verbal agility. The rhythm commands the line breaks and the rhymes command word arrangement and breath control. The beat is internal to the writing.

> The orthography of rap not only exists within the songs but also the movie *Freestyle* for me was about the art of freestyle rappin, or comin up wit dope rhymes off the top of the dome. In this part of rap, an emcee can be horrible [sic] shut down by the group if they think that his rhymes were written down somewhere or even memorized. Writing would not get you anywhere in a freestyle battle. And it is just more fun comin up wit funny ass shit with your homies and see whos rhymes are quicker and bader. Although a huge part of rap music and culture is about writing and expressing ideas about who you are and what you believe in. A lot of great rap artists have written and produced material that will split ya wig […][55]

Two students, Joe Battaglia and Matt Zeigler, wrote about Cambodia in "They Kill Everything They See:" In their work they wanted to present a voice that narrated from a distance the situation in Vietnam, and a local voice of a soldier experiencing the war firsthand:

> The boats have landed touchdown helicopters, planes finding airships
> Air, rivers thick with mist—natives come out to see democracy
> Stretching as far, as far as the eye can see,
> Uniformly skilled to break skulls rules are void and null
> We're the wonderful, wonderful west, I digress we got your address
> Kick down the door now to make our arrest
>
> (second voice)
> It's about time what a journey
> Eyes bloodshot my gun sturdy
> I'll kill anyone unworthy
> I said I'll kill you—heard me?
> It's my turn your lose my gain
> I landed it's time for my reign
> How you gonna tell me my laws have flaws?
> I got two paws hitting you in your jaws

353

Rap's rhythmic versatility is also demonstrated in another piece by Saga-city, another former student, who wrote "Spittin" for a class on minor-ity literature. It was handwritten with graffiti-type lettering (an inge-nious and creative project). He drew upon work by Paul Beatty and bell hooks, capturing their argumentative force with his own rhetoric. His piece is half-and half-song, in a format that reflects the spirit of so much rap:

> The energy of my ancestors
> I put that to use
> Spit them head banger rhymes
> That straight up knock out your tooth
> KO punches get delivered
> To y'all pussy ass niggas
> Write 'til my hand gets locked in a state of permanent stiffness
> Skillz ridiculous
> While y'all throw up signs
> I give you the finger
> Then kick y'all in the chest
> To stay alive like Wyclef
>
> Scaling walls like Spiderman
> I'm a demon inside a man
> Matt's a living breathing corpse
> Got these dumb oxy morons
> Like an ungiving source
> You got this
> I locked this

The wordplay is evident: "I write the shit/You write the bull"; "Lyrical fitness is practiced/To perfect my tactics/Continue ripping the mic"; "Stay pornographic like Spice/it's scary how a Posh nigga"; and "Got these dumb oxy morons" demonstrate the fragmentation of words—bullshit and oxymoron; metaphor of fitness and being "ripped" or rip-ping the mic; and a reference to the Spice Girls. This rap concentrates on putting the rhythms toward the end of each phrase so they hit the beat, thus driving each line to the endbeat.

Working within the rules of freestyle, where the rhyme and the

354

rhythm are key to a winning performance, rappers battle for the last word that brings the most applause from the crowd. Speaking has never been more instinctual, more possessive of the flow. One night at a radio show in Middletown, three rappers commanded a few hours of the night—from midnight to around 3 A.M.—speaking to beats set up by a scratcher, DJ Sirius. About twelve tracks were made that night, some of them like this:

[Dave:]
Yo mom check it out that man yelling at you it be the big J-O-E
Yo I'm telling you, yo you know he's cool he is a fellow New Yorker
So where coming in with love and no kind of stalker...
[Matt:]
Now I'm not the stalker but I'm moving outside your house,
Just finding my beats in a way that I can turn it out
So I could do it just to be fit I'll be starting
Coming through like Nancy Kerrigan and Tonya Harding
[Joe:]
Tonya Harding that's how we be
Nancy Kerrigan—Why me??!!
I can't do it you best a know me—
Watch out and get a bump on your knee

What's notable about these tracks is the observance of the rules (each rapper gets four lines, and I've seen rappers get into a physical fight if one of them takes more) and the amount of popular culture history they draw upon. The rules change in track two, where each rapper gets two lines:

That's the gist
We could line these Jews up like *Schindler's List*
[...] Yo I'll put on my red like a Fascist
Put on my red like I just took the Praxis
Now just the Praxis they don't know half of this
We should be peaceful lets listen to Santana's *Abraxis*
[...] I'll stutter but I can still ho-ho-hover
Like M. Night Shyamalan's *Village* I'll smother
[...] Now that would just be fate but I know it's unmistakable

355

Like Samuel L. Jackson when he was in *Unbreakable*
Unbreakable but you could never see the spinach
I'm in two movies they call me Joaquin Phoenix

If the form of rap is rhyme structured to create beats, this rhyme has to
be stronger than much poetry has been before. Poetry has its techniques
of trochee, spondee, iambs, ellipses and countless terms, but none of
these quite capture the forcefulness of the beat that pervades rap. Significantly, this beat is created by word and language structure, not merely
by technology. Joe adds,

Beep boop bop bop I rhyme like Rjd2
You can't even see it R2d2
Whoa here I come again a dog in a tutu
Once again you can't even flow that's how I meet you

How I meet you in the middle of space
I got two things on my head recognize the face
I be the princess yes I confess
Got a light saber sword skill man I address

Meeting bleeding surviving into the night
This is how we're combining and also rising
Lyrics upon the beats upon molecular feats
And I rip rip bread for the Bird treats

Bird treats—heh recognize the gut—
I'm not giving her up like Jabba the Hut
Here we come again you know I'm foster, lost her,
Growl on a track like Chewbacca

Now you be Chewbacca but I'm Hans Solo
Sitting here or maybe driving up to Soho, tomorrow
That's alright how we go, surprising—
I'm not burning Andre Rising[56]

FIGURE 4: Joey Battaglia, aka Joey Batts, at Sully's in Hartford, CT (2010), a former student in my classes at Hartford and now a musician and MC in Connecticut.

CONCLUSION

The technology that accompanied the rise of hip-hop is now practiced by those who are distanced or even unfamiliar with diaspora, African-American or African history or even urban life. It is not simply that suburban Caucasians have become one of the largest consumer groups of hip-hop, but that communities that do not speak English or connect through English are now also a part of the rap universe (think of the 2005 *Live from Iraq* album). But a convergence of factors has enabled rap to be exported to the world from the United States—technology, mixing and recording soft—and hardware, cellphones and instant messaging. When the guardians of rap, like Bambaata, KRS-One, Public Enemy, among others, invented a vernacular that grew out of concrete projects and gang street life. Now their vernacular—clever, rhythmic, fast-talking code—is reincarnated in the pitched rapping of anyone from Jason Mraz (pop singer) to KJ 52 (Christian Evangelical rapper) to Kou Kou Ching (Taiwanese rappers) to Nelly Furtado (pop singer)—much of it saccharine and sweet and distinctly not from the hood—so that all the well-known voices of popular music today are inflected with the rap sound: fast, dexterously rhythmic, recalling scat and bebop.

Rap is ranting about social context; it's often a collection of references to its own cultural milieu—Cui Jian rants about the iron rice bowl, Kung Foo about the WTO for example. Dick Hebdidge, writes that subcultures often experience this alchemic transformation from being unrecognized noise to semantic power:

> Subcultures represent 'noise' (as opposed to sound); interference in the orderly sequence which leads from real events and phenomena to their representation in the media. We should therefore not underestimate the signifying power of the spectacular subculture not only as a metaphor for potential anarchy 'out there' but as an actual mechanism of semantic disorder: a kind of temporary blockage in the system of representation.[57]

The battling that rappers usually engage in is actually a subset of the larger battle between the rapper and the machine. As technology grows in sophistication, the rapper will have a greater range of musical production choices, but also a battle for their own voice in the mix.

ENDNOTES

1. Rap's origins is quintessentially American, spawned by American politics and urban life in the Bronx. In *Rhyme and Reason*, KRS-One declares, "A rapper can be from any culture, anywhere, but you gotta visit the Bronx [...] You will always be a rap *artist* until you visit the South Bronx [...] Go to 123 and Park and just stand there, and imagine the birth of a culture happening at this very spot."

2. N. Neumark, R. Gibson, and T. Van Leeuwen, eds., in press, *Voice: Vocal Aesthetics in Digital Arts and Media* (Cambridge, Mass: MIT Press).

3. Friedrich Kittler, *Gramophone, Film, Typewriter* (Palo Alto, CA: Stanford University Press, 1999).

4. For images, Google protocols, reason or any virtual software to see the detail to which virtual software adheres to its original machine (for example, in reason you can tab and flip to the back of the mixer and see all the cables—strictly aesthetic ingenuity).

5. To hear the difference between spoken word and rap, listen to Gil Scott Heron's "The Revolution Will Not Be Televised," released in 1971. Instead

358

of interacting with the beat his voice speaks over it. His humanity is not to be confused with the beat, or the machine that creates it. Now we have greater collaboration with machinery and even being technological selves. Before widespread internet use, humans conceived themselves, and their authentic selves, outside the digitized universe, whereas now, in 2009, we can meet people who feel surprisingly comfortable thinking that their authentic selves actually reside on Facebook or Myspace.

6. Tricia Rose, *Black Noise* (Wesleyan, CT: Wesleyan UP, 1994), 95.

7. Ibid.

8. Adam Bradley *Book of Rhymes: The Poetics of Hip Hop* (New York: BasicCivitas, 2009), 14.

9. DJ Singe (Beth Coleman) in an interview with Analog Tara, Pinknoises. com.

10. From Jam Master Jay, Run DMC.

11. Bill Brewster and Frank Broughton, *Last Night a DJ Saved My Life* (New York: Grove, 1999).

12. Ibid; " 'Juking' is derived from the Gullah dialect of the sea-island slaves of South Carolina and Georgia. It originally meant 'disorderly' or 'wicked' but became a common word in black vernacular for having sex. Like 'rock'n'roll,' which also started life as a euphemism for fucking, the verb 'juke' eventually came to mean 'dance.' " (47)

13. David Toop, *Rap Attack 2* (London: Serpent's Tail, 1992), 63.

14. Saul Williams, *The Dead Emcee Scrolls* (New York: MTV: 2006).

15. Brewster and Broughton, 207.

16. Ibid., 208

17. Rose, 67.

18. Ibid., 91.

19. Paul Miller, *Rhythm Science* (Cambridge, MA: MIT Press, 2004), 72.

20. Ibid. "Rhythm science is not so much a new language as a new way of pronouncing the ancient syntaxes that we inherit from history and evolution, a new way of enunciating the basic primal languages that slip through the fabric of rational thought and infect our psyche at another, deeper level. Could this be the way of healing? Taking elements of our own alienated consciousness and recombining them to create new languages from old (and, in doing so, to reflect the chaotic, turbulent reality we all call home) just might be a way of seeking to reconcile the damage rapid technological advances have wrought on our collective consciousness." (72)

21. Simon Reynolds, *Generation Ecstasy* (New York: Routledge, 1999), 45.

22. http://www.youtube.com/watch?v=6hs7p4tAMf4&feature= related, accessed on 29 April 2009.

23. David Toop, 62.

24. Rose, 88.

25. Ibid., 66.

26. Steven Vogel, *Prime Mover: A Natural History of Muscle* (New York: Norton, 2001), 66.

27. Age might also allow for the capacity to produce dramatic voicings—sometimes people speak in a monotone because they cannot hear differences in tone, or because of age. Some stores profit from the difference between the adult and adolescent ear by emitting sounds that teens find annoying to prevent them from loitering—but these do not turn away older clients who tend to enter and leave more quickly. In a minor revolt, ring-tone inventors rebelliously invented Mosquitotone, a tone whose frequency is usually beyond the hearing of adults but quite apparent to youth, that can be used in classrooms where often the professor will be ignorant while students text each other. See Mike Vitello, "A Ring Tone Meant to Fall on Deaf Ears," *The New York Times*, 12 June 2006.

28. Brewster and Broughton, 256.

29. Scratching is just one form of new form of writing that emerged at the end of the twentieth century, as this book has observed. The needle has been used before as a writing implement, specifically in the case of Nu Shu, a language originally embroidered in silk, and more generally in the art of engraving.

30. Brewster and Broughton, 262.

31. Ibid., 263.

32. See the film *Scratch*. Dir. Doug Pray. Palm Pictures. 2002.

33. Elaine Scarry writes about the role of counting in emergencies—to stabilize the environment so that practical needs can be met, as in the practice of resucitation. She also describes the specific emotional register of the *fin de siècle* humanity becomes more agitated, in an efforts to produce new kinds of linguistic matter and invigorate, or revitalize, our humanity. She writes, "When [...] one draws a picture of human will based on the poetic legacy of final decades, a very different portrait emerges: the many poems already evoked here [...] suggests that the end of the century inspires inaugurating linguistic acts, words, lines, passages, plays that invigorate the language not just of the next century but of a period far into the future"(see *Fin de Siecle Poetry*, ed., Elaine Scarry)... and later she asserts that at the finish of the century, "the world is alert to its need for poetry." Such a need for poetry at the end of the century

is exacerbated by the encroachment of technology upon our humanity. Such is the agitation that the words become engraved on the mind, and rap grooves them into our mentality by its technique.

34. Miller, 100.

35. James Spady, H. Samy Alim, and Samir Meghelli, *The Global Cipha* (Philadelphia, PA: Black History Museum Press, 2006), 129.

36. See Bradley, 38.

37. For example, it collapses the notion of absence, obliterating Derridean différance by producing ultimate presence.

38. Within the flow a spiritual layer is often tapped; in modern poetry such an event would be transcendence, and Eliot's *The Wasteland* voyages to the final utterances of "Shantih, Shantih Shantih," exemplifying the modernists' reach for transcending words, as the war had already taught them that language must be bended, contorted to fit the horror of their experiences.

39. Another technique of moving people from ordinary states to an imaginary world (*l'imaginal*, as the French call it) would be to use "big images, strong images of angels and supernatural things," such as appear in the *Apocalypse* [the biblical account of the end of the world]" said Juliette Binoche (19 July 2007, conversation with Evelyn Ch'ien, Patmos, Greece).

40. Rap's acoustic matter is centered on rhythm. As aforementioned, in her book *Emergence*, Temple Grandin claims that the existence of rhythm is one of the problems faced by autistic children when dealing with language. She recalls when she was given an assignment to write a poem and had no ability to internalize or conceive of rhythm. (Autism apparently blocks this capacity to have flow, in the sense of rapid-fire linguistic production, favoring instead a highly visual capacity.)

41. Bradley, 28.

42. Ibid., 37.

43. Ibid., 15.

44. William Jelani Cobb, *To the Break of Dawn: A Freestyle on the Hip Hop Aesthetic* (New York: New York University Press, 2007), 119.

45. Paraphrase from Brewster and Broughton, 216.

46. Ibid., 72.

47. Ibid., 72.

48. Ibid., 109.

49. Chinese legend Cui Jian (personal communication in 2000) told me that it's hard to rap in Chinese because of the tones: "Well, it's difficult because Chinese has tones. But you take some of the tones out and you can do it." Three

years later, bands like Yin Jiang and Kung Foo are proving that Chinese can be rap material.

50. Rap is often combined with other forms—in Paris during the Indian Summer exhibit series, on 10 December at the Ecole des Beaux Arts, Régine Magloire alternated between rapping in one mike and singing opera in the other, rendering Bizet's Carmen into a fast-talking rapper who could—in between rap verse—belt out the operatic score.

51. Rap music is, in many ways, a hidden transcript. Among other things, it uses cloaked speech and disguised cultural codes to comment on and challenge aspects of current power inequalities. Not all rap transcripts directly critique all forms of domination; nonetheless, a large and significant element in rap's discursive territory is engaged in symbolic and ideological warfare with institutions and group that symbolically, ideologically and materially oppress African Americans. In this way, raps music is a contemporary stage for the theater of the powerless. On this stage, rappers act out inversions of status hierarchy, tell alternate stories of contact with police and the educational process, and draw portraits of contact with dominant groups in which the hidden transcript inverts/subvers the public, dominant transcript. Often rendering a nagging critique of various manifestations of power via jokes, stories, gestures, and song, rap's social commentary enacts ideological insubordination. Lydia Yee, "Breaking and Entering." In *One Planet Under a Groove: Hip hop and Contemporary Art* (New York: Bronx Museum of the Arts, 2001), 18.

52. See Rose, 89.

53. Brewster and Broughton, 245.

54. Elaine Scarry later alerted me to the fact that the plane was indeed a 757, but this track was released before a change could be made.

55. Joe Braun, University of Minnesota midterm exam, 10 March 2006.

56. In Middletown, CT at a radio station in June 2004.

57. Dick Hebdidge, *Subculture: The Meaning of Style* (New York: Routledge, 1979), 90.

RETHINKING THE AMERICAN CENTURY

WILLIAM URICCHIO

For the better part of two decades, summer vacations on Cape Cod have had an unsettlingly international character. In small towns like Brewster and Harwich, an almost nostalgic sense of Americana plays itself out with well-landscaped and neatly shingled cottages, Saturday evening band concerts, flag-festooned general stores, and the comingled smells of the ocean, clambakes and pitch pines. The rhythms and rituals of Cape summers seem largely unchanged since Thoreau described them in the mid 19th Century, barring the joggers and SUVs. But a drive to the discretely designed malls and super-sized grocery stores that punctuate the peninsula—carefully sectored off reminders of life back in the real world—introduces something, well, unsettling. The young people staffing the meat and fish departments, the people behind the cash registers and bagging the groceries, nearly all speak quite proper but clearly accented English. Andrei, Elisaveta, Lyudmila, Szczepan... their nametags suggest what conversation confirms: Bulgarians, Romanians, Poles. They are hired by the thousands to handle the increased traffic in vacation destinations around the country. And while by the standards of their home economies they earn enough to make the summer trip worthwhile, by U.S. standards they are poorly paid.

The unsettling part of this East European presence has not so much to do with these invariably hard-working and underpaid workers; nor with the nation's increasingly outspoken anxieties about immigration and foreign workers (which somehow ignore this population). Rather, it turns on what I *think* might be going on in their minds as they tally up the bills for endless lines of heavily laden carts. The shopping rhythms of many coastal vacation destinations entail buying everything necessary for the extended family on the Friday or Saturday that rental properties change hands: thus, gargantuan purchases and bills that can easily exceed the average monthly earnings these workers will return to in Bulgaria. I wonder what they make of America when they spend their days in super-sized markets, packed to the florescent lights with every possible food-stuff? When the bulk of their exposure is to wealthy vacationers, relaxed and spending like there's no tomorrow? When their wages here, while generous compared to home, clearly would not equip them to live the lifestyle they spend their days serving? How does this fit with their ex-pectations of America? What stories will they tell when they return home, or regale their grandchildren with fifty years hence?

Many of these young people were born after the fall of the Berlin Wall. And while they have grown up in transitional economies and po-litical systems, they have also grown up with largely unfettered access to the fruits of American culture, or at least that portion represented by popular music, Hollywood film, television programs, and MySpace. The dream homes and lifestyles that predominate in "the movies" and sit-coms, and that are celebrated in MTV's *Cribs* and *My Super Sweet 16*, doubtless stand in sharp contrast to other information coming from America—the news for example—in which a far more sobering and even disquieting range of lifestyles is portrayed. The shock of summer life at the Cape or along North Carolina's Outer Banks or elsewhere is that it largely confirms the excesses of the American dream, giving them tangi-ble form without the proviso that vacations in the U.S. typically last two weeks, and that this represents a mere sliver of the socio-economic spec-trum. America the spectacle is confirmed as both real and quotidian. The State Department's cultural diplomacy section should be envious.

BEHIND THE FACADE

From De Tocqueville to Venturi to Baudrilliard, one of the recurrent ob-servations about America regards the difficulty of penetrating the many illusions it throws up and finding an underlying substance. Neil Harris, in his explorations of "humbug," has reframed this epistemological challenge as a mode of engagement rather than a site of anxiety.[1] Half empty or half full, the America described by these and other observers functions as a floating signifier, easy to spot but not necessarily connected or substantial. Consider that most "American" of Hollywood films, *Independence Day* (Twentieth Century Fox, 1996), in which the president of the U.S. saves the world from an alien attack on the 4th of July. Its flag-waving frenzy notwithstanding, the film was produced, directed and co-written by a German national (Roland Emmerich), and distributed by 20th Century Fox, a company controlled by Australian Rupert Murdoch. Or consider Milli Vanilli, one of the most popular pop music bands of the late 1980s and early 1990s, whose Grammy Award for Best New Artist was recalled when it was discovered that the singers' voices were not those of the band members. Brand "America" fit the bill not only because of the corporate slickness of the Milli Vanilli package, but indeed because of the humbug factor ("were they, or weren't they...?"). In fact, the band was put together by a German national, Frank Farian, and fronted by Robert Pilatus, a German-American, and Fabrice Morvan, a Frenchman (both of whom Farian discovered in a Tokyo dance club), and released on Hansa, BMG and Artista—German and Japanese owned labels. Or consider that most "American" of icons, Route 66, now the trademarked property of Tempting Brands B.V., a Dutch company. And even if we sidestep the issue of hip-hop's Afro-Caribbean roots, searching for its "American" component in the Turkish, Japanese, or Palestinian hip-hop scenes leaves one with a handful of superficialities.[2] These and many other examples suggest the increasingly complicated process of defining something as "American" in a world of multi-national ownership, high levels of mobility, and transnational taste cohorts.

DEFINING AMERICAN VALUES

The essays in this collection neatly bracket off roughly a century of dramatic change in the definitional dynamics of America. At one end, the decades around the transition from the 19th to the 20th Centuries witnessed a project of obsessive self-definition, as former West Europeans but a few generations removed from the boats struggled to distinguish themselves from the latest waves of immigrants. Their efforts drew upon—and as often as not, invented—historical antecedents both oppressive and aspirational drawn from the Puritans to the Founding Fathers. And at our end of the spectrum, we have something closer to *Brand America*, multinational in character, and if manufactured, produced in Asia. But while Brand America may be a floating signifier, undulating with the currents of the global economy, it is not a hollow one. It continues to re-enact and draw upon, often as caricature, key components of the great identity revival of the century past.

Coincidentally, this long century neatly overlaps the era of cinema, the mass circulation illustrated press, and the recorded sound industry, an overlap that partially accounts both for its persistence and status as caricature. Of course the media scene has changed, with the new patterns and possibilities of connectivity evident from the logics of ownership and production to the fine-grained particularities of reception. And these changes have enhanced global flows, and been drawn upon to redefine the dynamics of taste, culture and identity. But for all of the radical potential of these new media, we are still in a transition phase, with the heavy industries of legacy media exercising considerable influence over the system as well as over the production and flow of its texts. At least as viewed from the perspective of the symbolic order of things, the continuities threading together the past century seem impressive; but appearances can be deceiving.

Looking back to the late 19th Century, we can see that the preoccupation with self-definition was driven by the perfect storm of an influx of southern and eastern Europeans, the nation's rapid urbanization (with many cities doubling and even tripling in population within a decade or two), ensuing infrastructural problems, economic panics, food riots, labor unrest, and fears of socialism. Immigration, however, seemed a widely agreed upon cause for these and other problems, and triggered both an articulation and reification of what it meant to be an American. That articulation took two mutually-reinforcing forms: fears of what would be lost through the corrosive influences of the unwashed hoards; and a more assertive sense of the values that actively constituted being Amercian.

The fears did much to shape the media. Film censorship laws were designed to protect the innocent and weak of mind: children, "panicky" women and "simple-minded" foreigners. As Meredith C. Ward reminds us, cinema admission restrictions, lighting requirements and occasional police raids were based on fears regarding the "demoralizing" combination of darkness and a heterosocial space. Seating and behavioral regulations sought to minimize "contagion," whether of the moral or pathogenic variety. Sunday closings reflected the Blue Laws promoted by Sabbatarians, laws that sought to regulate the single free day available to most workers. Even the frequency of "high quality" films produced by companies such as Vitagraph sought to align with the project of cultural arbiters, the first decade of the century enjoying remarkably high levels of Shakespearean and Biblical films. While there are a number of ways to explain these films, echoing Kingsley Bolton, among them must surely be counted the thinly veiled nativist stance voiced by Thomas Weld in his 1886 advocacy of Shakespeare: "Nothing would so withstand the rush into our language of vapid, foreign dilutions as a baptism into Shakespeare's terse, crisp, sinewy Saxon." The film industry, for its part, tended to embrace these tropes particularly when trying to drive out foreign competition, with ritualistic expressions of concern over the lewd and immoral behavior in imported films.[3]

Beyond this repressive stance, there were, as Joel Frykholm, Peter Stanfield, Esther Sonnet and Ann-Kristin Wallengren document, clear and persistent textual assertions of American identity. Robust, red-blooded, white masculinity asserted its mastery over nature, technology, the social order, and narrative. The depicted moral universe enjoyed the clarity of a simple binary opposition, with good and bad writ large in the physiognomy of the actors' faces and played out in their gestures. Social mobility, whether through *deus ex machina* scenarios familiar from the work of Horatio Alger, or through strategic acts of violence, or through sheer hard work and perseverance, was almost always guaranteed. These traits, easily and often correctly understood as brutish and mean-spirited, also brought with them quite laudable connotations. In contrast to the more rigid and deterministic social structures of many European cultures, a modicum of control over one's destiny or position in life seemed a positive thing. Measured against endlessly nuanced and relativistic assessments of situations, a clear moral compass seemed a useful device. And instead of highly intellectualized and even effete responses to the world, red-blooded action seemed bold and decisive. Many popular American and European retellings of World War II fall back on these very traits when discussing the U.S.'s role, even if the tone is increasingly recriminatory from the American side. These and related traits are as persistent in popular cultural artifacts as the genres in which they are embedded—westerns, gang-ster films, detectives, adventure films, and so on, and yet, because they are more textural than formal, they have tended to elude the grasp of many media historians. The authors of this book have managed—through di-verse modes of textual engagement—to breathe life into the contexts, pat-terns and meanings of these elements, restoring their importance to the project and projection of national identity.

These two early 20th Century definitional strategies—one built upon anxieties and persistent puritanical proclivities, and the other upon the red-blooded man of action and adventure, able to right wrongs and leap to the top of social hierarchies in a single bound—have remained intact over the century, benchmarks of American identity. The rhetoric of the Tea Party and its right-wing followers c. 2010, with its anti-immigrant frenzy, its bible-thumping appeals for "family values," its calls for red-blooded, manly intervention ("nuke 'em!"), and its binary moral uni-verse (perhaps best articulated by George W. Bush's cry of "with us or against us"), seems willfully anachronistic, bordering on the hysterical. And although embedded in the mythos of "the land of opportunity" and desperately trying to reclaim the positive connotations of these terms, the ever more vociferous incantation of this rhetoric seems increasingly at odds with a world of global interdependencies and population flows. Indeed, one might read this as a nostalgic retreat to a less complicated time, a time of greater possibility, an imaginary time. At least on the sur-face, the continuities that bookend the 20th Century are striking; but the underlying differences are also profound. The fiercely self-confident identity that emerged in the early 20th Century was rooted in the linkage between American society and American culture; one hundred years lat-er, that linkage has been largely decoupled and re-worked as a purely cul-tural enterprise, as a brand. Little wonder that this discursive tradition and the media products it has produced, like *Independence Day*, are seen as "American" regardless of the citizenship or originating culture of the me-dia artifact. Little wonder that, at least within European critical quarters, these products have garnered descriptors such as those offered by Wal-lengren: "bad taste, commercialism, immaturity, materialism, shallow-ness, violence, vulgarity." And little wonder that the global public lines up to consume it.

BEYOND THE TEXT

At the start of the 20th Century, the many attempts to define "insiders" and "outsiders" were encountered—by the "outsiders"—in complex and contradictory ways. On one hand, we have ample evidence of certain films—and lectures, and books—being embraced by working class and immigrant audiences as agencies of "uplift" and assimilation. Despite this, immigrants' displays of cultural competence on a textual level were often discounted. For mainstream Americans, an Italian immigrant's deep familiarity with, say, Dante's or Shakespeare's work or the medieval histories retold through marionette shows, did not necessarily translate into much beyond curiosity, despite proscriptive rhetoric that would seem to extol it. On the other hand, as Jan Olsson demonstrates, immigrants also embraced the film medium itself as an emblem of modernity and Americanization, in a sense rendering textual particulars beside the point. Crossing the threshold into a cinema was the defining act, not the film on the screen, or even the language spoken by the audience and *explicateurs*. This shift from textual centricity to medium centricity, at least as it pertains to identity, would continue to grow throughout the century. Of course, this narrative of encounters and implications leaves out the experiences of those populations precluded from all but a few cinemas, at least if we take New York City's 600+ nickelodeons as an example. Asian- and African-Americans were barred from most commercial venues, complicating the notion of "outsider" and as Gregory Lee reminds us, requiring a reassessment of our categories and methods of study.

This condition, this inscription of the medium itself within the cultural domain of America, has been a powerful force for Hollywood, and one carefully cultivated in the course of the long *pas de deux* between the industry and the government. To say "the medium," of course, overstates the case; in fact, the alignment with American identity turns on particular deployments of the medium. Hollywood has become synonymous with those deployments, a legacy of a particular mode of production, a circumscribed if not formulaic notion of narrative, and a reliance on particular signifying practices. The result is a kind of predictability, one already inherent in the notion of genre, but one that goes beyond to include big budgets, stars, happy endings, and the requisite critiques of superficiality, commercialism, and the rest. And while exceptions abound, *grosso modo*, Hollywood-type production has emerged as a default, or better, a vernacular for the medium's expressive capacities regardless of the national identities of the creative team or the production company. Similar patterns have appeared in the popular music industry and they are increasingly apparent in television programming as well, although the historical processes involved are quite different. In the case of European television, for example, a pincers move of U.S.-sponsored study trips encouraged leading figures in the industry to visit the U.S. and learn about its production practices; this was combined with U.S. State Department-backed initiatives to push U.S. programming directly into the European market. The results, as discussed by scholars such as Jerome Bourdon, encouraged a "self-inflicted" Americanization of the medium, with the U.S. established as a professional benchmark that others sought to emulate.[4] Widespread copying of American formats, techniques, and presentation strategies, together with franchising, were not so much read as "American" as they were "professional," a category that the American industry just happened to both define and embody.

The slippages between the terms "Hollywood" and "American" (much to the dismay of American independent film makers)—like the slippage between "Fordism" and "American" to an interbellum generation of concerned German critics, or "McDonaldsization" and "American" closer to our present—all speak to related processes in which the site of identity is decoupled from a specifically textual domain. Here, the organization of labor and the qualities of uniformity and standardization (already addressed by Horkheimer and Adorno) have been singled out for attention, and form the basis for an identity claim. In certain ways, this resonates with the immigrant's visit to the nickelodeon, and through it, participation in modernity and the American experience.

The essays by Lisa Parks, Pelle Snickars and Evelyn Ch'ien point in very different ways to similar conflations between today's new media technology and American identity. Whether imagined as an American's inalienable "right" to television, a right articulated at a moment of technological change and service vulnerabilities, or as the inexorable logic of standardizing access to information through search engines such as Google, or as the technologies at the disposal of the DJ and hip-hop artist, the implied slippage of technologies and systems with American values remains ongoing. As with *Independence Day*, the underlying national identity of the developers seems less important than the American character of the supervening system (perhaps to the relief of Sergey Mikhaylovich Brin as well as the army of multinationals in Google's service). The identity process is a curious one, one that seems to operate at a different level of abstraction than similar processes in most other nations

Significantly, some of the most forward-looking and fiercest supporters of the new values possible in the networked community have not been American. From Linux, prominent in the world of free and open software and initiated and led by Finn Linus Torvalds, to WikiLeaks, founded by Chinese dissidents, directed by Australian Julian Assange, and populated by international journalists, the new media's radical agenda has been generated elsewhere. To the extent that the most visible industries are understood as American, regardless of the underlying realities, it makes sense that their critics are not necessarily American, again, regardless of the underlying realities (Richard Stallman's GNU project, for example).

THE OTHER 'AMERICAN CENTURY'

Henry Luce's call to create the "American Century," published as an editorial in *Life* magazine on February 17, 1941, addressed the expansion of the nation's political, economic, moral and cultural influence in the midst of a world at war. It was a forward look, an appeal, and above all a highly influential catalyst, capturing and giving voice to a widespread ambition. The American Century charted throughout the pages of this book speaks to a different dynamic. It begins with the most outspoken period of the nation's obsession with self-definition and identity, and it continues on into our present, where many of those characteristics have slipped their mooring: they are still around, but free floating and undulating in both reference and meaning. Roughly one hundred years separate "now" from "then", a century, thus. The claim in invoking, but also modifying the meaning of, Luce's phrase, is not that we have somehow reached the end of history. Rather, it is to suggest that we have run a particular course, witnessed a particular cycle. This "alternative" "American Century" began with a fabric of cultural identity closely coupled to the nation's social realities, and ended with an identity that was largely uncoupled from those social realities, an identity culture as brand that could be applied regardless of a creator's or owner's national affiliations or an object's location or site of manufacture. This "alternative" American Century also

371

coincided with the emergence of mass media (film and the illustrated press), and ended with the proliferation of networked media and personal media. Media have been integral to this Century as projection, as mirror, as site of displacement, and as a locus of identity.

Identity is more than a sticker that can be affixed to an object of choice, and one of the striking things to emerge from a long view of this "other" "American Century" is the nature of the objects and processes that in the eyes of the world bear the American brand, even if the label is missing. As in any country, histories, habits, laws, cuisines, the work of the nation's artists, poets, builders and much more offer obvious sites to interrogate in the search for identity. However, for the course of the Century, Brand America has been unique in appropriating logics of production (from Ford to McDonald's), forms of media (from the Hollywood film to television formats; from Google to FaceBook), and even modes of distribution (the supermarket). This alignment reflects both overt attempts by the corporate world and (at times) agencies of the U.S. government, as well as the active ceding of identity to America by global publics. The latter process can be seen in the decisions made by audiences, in the ease with which foreign talent (writers, directors, actors, singers) are recast as Americans, and in the actions of taste elites who articulate and support what is NOT American through criticism and subsidy funds. The value of the brand may be contested, but its parameters and characteristics are surprisingly clear.

One of this collection's clear implications concerns the academic field of American Studies. Although significant differences in perspective and history mark those institutions active within the U.S. and those outside, the institutional tradition on both sides leans heavily on the disciplines of history and literary studies. As with all area studies, the field has been relatively open to new impulses and opportunistic with regard to good ideas in neighboring disciplines. The authors in this collection, however, have posed some important challenges to the disciplinary status quo, and the field could benefit greatly by taking heed.

Lee's chapter makes a compelling appeal to end the exotic marginalizing of non-white subjects. In complimentary fashion, Corrado Neri's essay offers a nuanced set of culturally specific readings, taking up the ever-slippery notion of "realism" as a marker of cultural distinction and addressing the issue of cultural transfer between the U.S. and China. The nuance that Neri brings to the reading of Sun Yu's films and contexts needs to be extended to the work of Chinese-Americans in America. Lee hits the nail on the head when he says that what is at stake "is not just minority history but a history that interrogates and calls for a revision of the story of the totality that would be American history were it written." The records of cultural and political engagements by Asian-Americans, African-Americans and Latin-Americans are at times quite limited— consider their frequent absence from certain sectors of the film exhibition scene in the early 20ᵗʰ Century. Yet we can no longer be content to apply Wittgenstein's seventh proposition from the *Tractatus* "whereof one cannot speak, thereof one must be silent." Systematic attention, integrated and contextually coherent research design, and creative archival strategies can go far toward restoring long silenced voices, and helping us reconfigure our histories.

Media have been fundamental to the American experience, both at home and abroad, and the study of the uses and reception of American media would seem to merit an equally foundational place in American Studies' training and research agenda. As the combined essays in this collection demonstrate, a rich variety of approaches to media artifacts and processes can yield powerful insights. Parks' reminder of the elaborate interconnections among audiences, television companies and the government offers a multi-dimensional portrait of a medium that, despite all the new competition from games, cell phones, the Internet and so on, enjoyed its highest ever average viewing time this year. And Michael Renov reminds us of the new situation we inhabit, in which cameras are ubiquitous and people can post, mix and remix their own and others' work, creating their own texts and entering as participants into the public debate. Considering the global perceptions of many media forms as American, and considering the fast changing media scene particularly as it builds social networks and offers ways to circumvent long established filters and barriers, the need for greater understanding is pressing. The field urgently needs to redouble its efforts in this sector.

Finally, as Snickars reminds us, the archives, too, are undergoing a profound transformation, and beyond the overtones of Americanization alluded to earlier with regard to new digital technologies, American Studies like any other academic field would do well to play an active, critical and demanding role in the process. The use of social networking tools, the gathering of new information sources and the development of aggregating and accessing strategies, together with the enhanced means of collaborating with other interested colleagues, all point to the potential advantages of participating with the archives as they continue to change.

One might argue that there are several American Centuries; but the century mapped out in this book helps us to locate a common dynamic that will pose ever-greater challenges to the field. This dynamic turns on the shift from coherent and socially-grounded cultural identities, to those that are cut off from the social, and more free floating. These new identities tend to adhere to media forms like Hollywood, Google and hip-hop technology, regardless of their "real" national cultural grounding. And as such, this process—and its implications for future area studies—requires much deeper interrogation.

Like Hollywood and Fordism, supermarkets are sometimes seen as American or at least as evidence of Americanization. The anecdote with which I opened this essay referred to my shopping experiences on Cape Cod; my supermarket, in this case Stop-and-Shop, is in fact owned by Ahold—a Dutch company that I know as Albert Heijn through its supermarkets in the Netherlands. Yet in the Dutch context, where supermarkets began to proliferate in the 1950s, the concept seems American. Marshall Plan-sponsored study trips to America promoted the idea of self-service, one-stop shopping, hoping to spread economic efficiency to cultures peppered with small butcher shops, bakeries, cheese and dairy stores, vegetable markets, and so on. And thanks to these promotional trips, recurrent media images of the "American way of life," and the coincident increase in supermarkets, the concept was quickly branded as "American." The concept caught on, and the hard work of the locals soon took the form of Ahold, the UK's Tesco, France's Carrefour, and more—global supermarket chains that eventually competed for market share within the U.S. The red, white and blue festooned supermarket that reads as proudly American, might in fact be celebrating the Netherlands, UK or France.

ENDNOTES

1. Neil Harris, "The Operational Aesthetic." In Tony Bennett, ed., *Popular Fiction: Technology, Ideology, Production, Reading* (London: Routledge, 1990), 401–412.
2. See for example, Ian Condry, *Hip-Hop Japan: Rap and the Paths of Cultural Globalization* (Durham: Duke University Press, 2006).
3. For more details on these developments, see Roberta Pearson and William

Uricchio, *Reframing Culture: The Case of the Vitagraph Quality Films* (Princeton, N.J.: Princeton University Press, 1993).

4. Jerome Bourdon, "Imperialism, Self-inflicted? On the Americanizations of Television in Europe." In William Uricchio, ed., *We Europeans? Media, Representations, Identities* (Chicago: University of Chicago Press, 2008), 93–108.

CONTRIBUTORS

KINGSLEY BOLTON is a Professor at the City University of Hong Kong and Stockholm University. His latest book is *Chinese Englishes: A Sociolinguistic History* (Cambridge: Cambridge University Press, 2003).

EVELYN CH'IEN is an Associate Professor at the University of Minnesota and she is a member of IETT, Université de Lyon, Lyon, France. Her latest book is *Weird English* (Cambridge, MA: Harvard University Press, 2005).

JOEL FRYKHOLM is a Research Fellow at Stockholm University where he was awarded his doctorate in 2009 for the thesis *Framing the Feature Film Multi-Reel Feature Film & American Film Culture in the 1910s* (Stockholm: Acta Universitatis Stockholmiensis, 2009).

GREGORY B. LEE is a Professor at the City University of Hong Kong. His latest book is *China's Lost Decade: Cultural Politics and Poetics 1978–1990 in Place of History* (Lyon: Tigre de Paiper, 2009).

CORRADO NERI is an Assistant Professor at the University of Jean Moulin, Lyon 3. His latest book is *Ages inquiets: cinemas chinois, une representation de la jeunesse* (Lyon: Tigre de Papier, 2009).

JAN OLSSON is a Professor of Cinema Studies at Stockholm University. His latest book is *Los Angeles Before Hollywood: Journalism and American Film Cul-*

ture, 1905–1915 (Stockholm: National Library of Sweden, 2008; distribution Wallflower Press, London and Columbia University Press, New York).

LISA PARKS is a Professor at the University of California, Santa Barbara. Her latest book is *Cultures in Orbit: Satellites and the Televisual* (Durham, N.C.: Duke University Press, 2005).

MICHAEL RENOV is a Professor at the University of Southern California. His latest book is *The Subject of Documentary* (Minneapolis: University of Minnesota Press, 2004).

PELLE SNICKARS is Head of Research at the Swedish National Library. He has co-edited *The YouTube Reader* (Stockholm: National Library of Sweden, 2009) with Patrick Vonderau. Snickars is the co-editor of the fortcoming, *Moving Data: the iPhone and My Media* (Columbia University Press, 2011).

ESTHER SONNET is a Principal Lecturer at the University of Portsmouth. She has co-edited *Mob Culture: Hidden Histories of the American Gangster Film* (New Brunswick, N.J.: Ruthers University Press, 2005) with Lee Grieveson and Peter Stanfield.

PETER STANFIELD is a Senior Lecturer at the University of Kent. His latest book is *Body and Soul: Jazz and Blues in American Film, 1927–63* (Urbana: University of Illinois Press, 2005).

WILLIAM URICCHIO is a Professor at the Massachusetts Institute of Technology and Utrecht University. His latest book is *We Europeans? Media, Representations, Identities* (Chicago: The University of Chicago Press, 2009).

ANN-KRISTIN WALLENGREN is an Associate Professor at Lund University. Her latest book is *UR-bilder: Utbildningsprogram som tv-genre* (Lund: Arkiv, 2005).

MEREDITH C. WARD is a Lecturer at Johns Hopkins University. She is currently finishing her dissertation at Northwestern University on the role of noise in American film culture.

BIBLIOGRAPHY

Abbreviations
AMPAS Academy of Motion Picture Arts and Sciences
MPW Moving Picture World

AARP.org. "Get Ready for Digital TV." *AARP.org* (8 March 2007), http://www. aarp.org/money/consumer/articles/digital_tv.html.

Abel, Richard. *Americanizing the Movies and "Movie-Mad" Audiences, 1910–1914.* Berkeley: University of California Press, 2006.

—. *The Red Rooster Scare: Making Cinema American, 1900–1910.* Berkeley: University of California Press, 1999.

Acland, Charles, ed. *Residual Media.* Minneapolis: University of Minnesota Press, 2007.

Adams, James Truslow. "Why We Glorify Our Gangsters." *New York Times* (13 December 1931): SM1.

Agnew, David Hayes. *Theatrical Amusements.* Philadelphia: Wm. S. Young, 1857.

Alm, Martin. *Americanitis: Amerika som sjukdom eller läkemedel: svenska berättelser om USA åren 1900–1939.* Lund: Nordic Academic Press, 2002.

Anchimbe, Eric A. "World Englishes and the American Tongue." *English Today* 88, vol. 22, no. 4 (2006): 3.

Andrejevic, Mark. *I Spy: Surveillance and Power in the Interactive Era.* Lawrence: University Press of Kansas, 2007.

Ang, Ien. *Watching Dallas: Soap Opera and the Melodramatic Imagination.* London: Routledge, 1985.

Angell, James A. *Psychology: An Introductory Study of the Structure and Function of Human Consciousness*. New York: Henry Holt, 1904.

Arbetarbladet, "Svenska gangsterfilmen: Friskt vågat, hälften vunnet." *Arbetarbladet* (28 November 1974): 9.

Arbetaren, "Gangsterfilmen." *Arbertaren* (22 November 1974): 10.

Attali, Jacques. *Noise: The Political Economy of Music*. Translated by Brian Massumi. Minneapolis: University of Minnesota Press, 1989.

Bailis, Stanley. "The Social Sciences in American Studies: An Integrative Conception." *American Quarterly* 26, no. 3 (1974): 202–224.

Bank, Rosemarie K. *Theatre Culture in America, 1825–1860*. Cambridge, UK: Cambridge University Press, 1997.

Barthes, Roland. *Camera Lucida: Reflections on Photography*. Translated by Richard Howard. New York: Hill and Wang, 1981.

—. *Mythologies*. Translated by Annette Lavers. New York: Hill and Wang, 1972.

Barton, H. Arnold. "A Heritage to Celebrate: Swedes in America, 1846–1996." *Scandinavian Review* 84, no. 2 (Autumn 1996): 4–10.

Baudrillard, Jean. *Amérique*. Paris: Grasset, 1986.

Bazin, André. "The Ontology of the Photographic Image." In *What Is Cinema?*, translated by Hugh Gray. Berkeley: University of California Press, 1967.

Beach, Rex, and James McArthur. *The Spoilers: A Play in Four Acts*. Stage Play Manuscript, the William Selig Papers, Margaret Herrick Library, AMPAS.

Beach, Rex. "Book Review." *Duluth News Tribune* (21 September 1913): 5.

Bell, Alexander Melville. *Elocutionary Manual: The Principles of Elocution, with Exercises and Notations for Pronunciation, Intonation, Emphasis, Gesture, and Emotional Expression*. Washington: John C. Parker, 1878.

Belpedio, James R. "Fact, Fiction, Film: Rex Beach and *The Spoilers*." Ph.D. diss., University of North Dakota, 1995.

Bender, James F. *NBC Handbook of Pronunciation*. New York, Thomas Y. Crowell, 1943.

Benton, Mike. *The Illustrated History of Crime Comics*. Dallas: Taylor Publishing, 1993.

Bergeron, Regis. *Le Cinema chinois: 1905–1949*. Lausanne: Alfred Eibel editeur, 1977.

Berry, Chris, and Mary Farquhar. *China on Screen. Cinema and Nation*. New York: Columbia University Press, 2006.

Bertellini, Giorgio. "Southern Crossings: Italians, Cinema, and Modernity." Ph.D. diss., New York University, 2001.

Binde, Zhou 周斌德. "百年中國電影與中外文化" ["One hundred years of Chinese cinema and its relation to foreign cultures."] In Theory People, http://theory.people.com.cn/BIG5/49167/ 3855547.html (accessed 25 June 2009).

Blackton, John Stuart. "Literature and the Motion Picture—A Message." Introduction to Robert Grau, *Theatre of Science: A Volume of Progress and Achievement in the Motion Picture Art*, xxvii . New York: Broadway Publishing Company, 1914.

Bo, Chen陳播. *Zhongguo zuoyi dianying yundong* 中國左翼電影運動 [*Chinese Left Wing Cinema*.] Beijing: Zhongguo dianying, 1993.

Boas, Franz. "Changes in Bodily From of Descendents of Immigrants." *American Anthropologist* 14, no. 2 (April–June 1912): 530–562.

Bondebjerg, Ib. "Culture, Media and Globalisation." In *Humanities: Essential Research for Europe*, 71–88. Copenhagen: Danish Research Council for the Humanities.

Bonfiglio, Thomas Paul. *Race and the Rise of Standard American*. Berlin/New York: Mouton de Gruyter, 2002.

Borde, Raymond, and Etienne Chaumeton. *Panorama du film noir americain*. Paris: les Editions de Minuit 1955; translated by Paul Hammond, *A Panorama of American Film Noir, 1941–1953*. San Francisco: City Lights Books. 2002 [1955].

Bordwell, David, and Kristin Thompson. *Film Art: An Introduction*. New York: McGraw-Hill, 2001.

Bordwell, David, Janet Staiger and Kristin Thompson. *The Classical Hollywood Cinema: Film Style and Mode of Production to 1960*. New York: Columbia University Press, 1985.

Boston Journal. "Boston Reopens with Film Play." *Boston Journal* (21 November 1914): 5.

—. Advertisement for the Boston Theatre. *Boston Journal* (21 November 1914): 5.

Bottomore , Stephen. "The Story of Percy Peashaker: Debates About Sound Effects in the Early Cinema." In *The Sounds of Early Cinema*, edited by Richard Abel and Rick Altman, 134–142. Bloomington: Indiana University Press, 2001.

Bourdon, Jerome. "Imperialism, Self-inflicted? On the Americanizations of Television in Europe." In *We Europeans? Media, Representations, Identities*, edited by William Uricchio, 93–108. Chicago: University of Chicago Press, 2008.

Bradley, Adam. *Book of Rhymes: The Poetics of Hip Hop*. New York: BasicCivitas, 2009.

Brewster, Bill, and Frank Broughton. *Last Night a DJ Saved My Life*. New York: Grove, 1999.

Brinkley, Alan. *The Publisher: Henry Luce and His American Century*. New York: Knopf, 2010.

Broadbandinfo.com. "DTV Transition: Wal-Mart Selling Digital TV Converter Boxes." *Broadbandinfo.com* (14 February 2008), http://www.broadbandinfo.

com/news-archives/2008/ dtv-transition-wal-mart-selling-digital-tv-converter-boxes.html (accessed 18 March 2009).

Brown, H. Rap. "Die, Nigger, Die!" In *The Sixties Papers: Documents of a Rebellious Decade*, edited by Judith Clavir Albert and Stewart Edward Albert, 151–158. New York: Praeger, 1984.

Browne, Nick. "Society, and Subjectivity: On the Political Economy of Chinese Melodrama." In *New Chinese Cinemas. Forms, Identities, Politics*, edited by Nick Browne, et al., 40–56. Cambridge: Cambridge University Press, 1994.

Buruma, Ian, and Avishai Marglit. *Occidentalism*. London: Atlantic, 2005.

Bush, W. Stephen. "Facing an Audience." *MPW* 9, no. 10 (16 September 1911): 389.

Cameron, Ian, and Elizabeth Cameron. *Heavies*. London: Studio Vista, 1967.

Cantor, Norman F., ed. *The American Century: Varieties of Culture in Modern Times*. New York: HarperCollins, 1997.

Carbine, Mary. "The Finest Outside the Loop: Motion Picture Exhibition in Chicago's Black Metropolis, 1905–1928." *Camera Obscura* 23 (May 1990): 9–41.

Carmichael, Stokely. "What We Want." In *The Sixties Papers: Documents of a Rebellious Decade*, edited by Judith Clavir Albert and Stewart Edward Albert, 137–144. New York: Praeger, 1984.

Carpenter, William B. *Principles of Mental Physiology*, 4th ed. London: Kegan Paul, 1896.

Carr, Harry C. "Blowing Up Movie Town: Wonderful Moving Picture Reel Played; A Complete Placer Mine Dynamited; Rex Beach's Novel, 'The Spoilers.'" *Los Angeles Times* (18 July 1913): III:1.

Casey. "Giving 'The Spoilers' at the Salt Lake Theatre the 'Once Over.'" Cartoon. *Salt Lake Telegram* (9 September 1914): 2.

Castro, Brian. *Birds of Passage*. North Ryde, NSW: Angus & Robertson, 1989.

Chafe, William Henry. *The Rise and Fall of the American Century: United States from 1890–2009*. New York: Oxford University Press, 2009.

Chalby, Jean K., and Glen Segell. "The Broadcasting Media in the Age of Risk: The Advent of Digital Television." *New Media & Society* 1, no. 3 (1999): 351–368.

Chambers, Jack. "Talk the Talk?" *PBS.org*, http://www.pbs.org/speak/ahead/mediapower/media/ (accessed on 9 June 2010).

Chanan, Michael. *The Cuban Image*. London: BFI Publishing, 1985.

Charlotte Observer. " 'The Spoilers' Fine Production." *Charlotte Observer* (18 April 1916): 8.

—. " 'The Spoilers.' Amusements. *Charlotte Observer*" (17 April 1916): 5.

—. Advertisement for the Academy of Music. *Charlotte Observer* (15 April 1916): 5.

Chicago Tribune. "The Spoilers Spoiled." News of the Theaters. *Chicago Tribune* (31 October 1906): 8.

—. "The Spoilers." News of the Theaters. *Chicago Tribune* (6 November 1906): 8.

—. Advertisements for the Sunday's Tribune. *Chicago Tribune* (5 December 1914): 15.

—. Advertisements for the Sunday's Tribune. *Chicago Tribune* (20 December 1914): 9.

Chronopolis. "Federated Digital Preservation Across Space and Time." *Chronopolis.sdsc.edu*, http://chronopolis.sdsc.edu/index.html (accessed 15 September 2009).

Civilrights.org. "Digital Television Transition Organizer Tool Kit." *Civilrights.org*, www.civilrights.org/dtv/toolkit/ (accessed 18 March 2009).

—. "Transition in Trouble: Action Needed to Ensure a Successful Digital Television Transition." *Civilrights.org*, http://www.civilrights.org/publications/reports/dtv/introduction.html (accessed 17 March 2009).

Clarens, Carlos. *Crime Movies: An Illustrated History*. New York: Norton, 1980.

Clark, Paul. *Chinese Cinema: Culture and Politics Since 1949*. New York: Cambridge University Press, 1987.

Cobb, William Jelani. *To the Break of Dawn: A Freestyle on the Hip Hop Aesthetic*. New York: New York University Press, 2007.

Cohen, Daniel J. "From Babel to Knowledge. Data Mining Large Digital Collections." *D-Lib Magazine*, no. 3 (2006), http://www.dlib.org/dlib/march06/cohen/03cohen.htm (accessed 15 September 2009).

Cohen, Noam. "Historical photos in web archives gain vivid new lives." *New York Times* (19 January 2009), http://www.nytimes.com/2009/01/19/technology/internet/19link.html (accessed 15 September 2009).

Collier, John. "Motion Pictures for Y.M.C.A. Work." *Motography* 8, no. 13 (21 December 1912): 493–495.

Columbus Daily Inquirer. " 'The Spoilers' at the American." At the Movies. *Columbus Daily Inquirer* (13 December 1914): 2.

—. "Great Crowd Attends 'Spoilers' at Grand." At the Movies. *Columbus Daily Inquirer* (13 December 1914): 2.

—. Advertisement for the American Theatre in Columbus, Georgia. *Columbus Daily Inquirer* (13 December 1914): 2.

—. Advertisement for the Bonita Theatre. *Columbus Daily Inquirer* (28 December 1915): 6.

Commercial Advertiser. (15 March 1833).

Comscore. "YouTube Surpasses 100 Million U.S. Viewers for the First Time."

Comscore press release (4 March 2009), http://comscore.com/index.php// Press_Events/Press_Releases/2009/ 3/YouTube_Surpasses_100_Million_ US_Viewers (accessed 15 September 2009).

Condry, Ian. *Hip-Hop Japan: Rap and the Paths of Cultural Globalization.* Durham: Duke University Press, 2006.

Confiant, Raphaël. *Case à Chine.* Paris: Mercure de France, 2007.

Corbin, John. "How the Other Half Laughs." *Harper's New Monthly Magazine* 98 (December 1898): 30–48.

Cox, William R. *Hell to Pay.* New York: Signet, 1958.

Crary, Jonathan. *Suspensions of Perception: Attention, Spectacle, and Modern Culture.* Cambridge, MA: MIT Press, 2001.

Curtin, Michael. *Redeeming the Wasteland: Television Documentary and Cold War Politics.* New Brunswick, NJ: Rutgers University Press, 1995.

Dagens Nyheter. "Gulager lanseras för gangsterfilm." *Dagens Nyheter* (28 June 1974): 10.

—. "Spännande yta djupt innehåll." *Dagens Nyheter* (19 April 1974): 9.

Dahlquist, Marina. " 'Swat the Fly.' Educational Films and Health Campaigns 1909-1914." In *Kinoöffentlichkeit/Cinema's Public Sphere,* edited by Corinna Müller, 211-225. Marburg: Schüren Verlag, 2008.

—. "Teaching Citizenship via Celluloid." In *Early Cinema and the 'National,'* edited by Richard Abel, Giorgio Bertellini, and Rob King, 118-132. New Barnet: John Libbey Publishing, 2008.

Dala-Demokraten. "En USA-gangster kom till Sverige." *Dala-Demokraten* (28 October 1974): 6.

Davis, Michael M., Jr. *The Exploitation of Pleasure: A Study of Commercial Recreations in New York City.* New York: Department of Child Hygiene of the Russell Sage Foundation, 1911.

de Grazia, Victoria. *Irresistible Empire: America's Advance through 20ᵗʰ-Century Europe.* Cambridge, MA: The Belknap Press of Harvard University Press, 2005.

de Guignes, Joseph. *Recherches sur les navigations des Chinois du côté de l'Amérique, et sur quelques peuples situés à l'extrémité orientale de l'Asie.* Paris: Académie des inscriptions et belles-lettres, 1761.

De Rosalia, Giovanni. "Scene Sicilane: Lu Cinematografu." *Follia di New York* (7 November 1909): 4.

Digging into Data. http://www.diggingintodata.org/ (accessed 15 September 2009).

Dikötter, Frank. *Sex, Culture and Modernity in China.* London: Hurst & Company, 1995.

Dissanayake, Wimal, ed. *Melodrama and Asian Cinema*. Cambridge: Cambridge University Press, 1993.

Dobbs, Lou. *Exporting America: Why Corporate Greed Is Shipping American Jobs Overseas*. New York: Warner Business Books, 2004.

—. *Independents Day: Awakening the American Spirit*. New York: Viking, 2007.

—. *War on the Middle Class: How the Government, Big Business Are Waging War on the American Dream and how to Fight Back*. New York: Viking, 2006.

Doctorow, Cory. "UK National Portrait Gallery threatens Wikipedia over scans of its public domain art." *Boingboing* (20 July 2009), http://www.boingboing.net/2009/07/20/uk- national-portrait.html (accessed 15 September 2009).

DTVAnswers (NAB). "DTV Roadshow." DTVAnswers (NAB), http://www.dtvanswers.com/ roadshow/ (accessed 17 March 2009).

—. "Summary of the DTV Roadshow." DTVAnswers (NAB), http://www.dtvanswers.com/ roadshow/ (accessed 17 March 2009).

Duluth News Tribune. "Orpheum," Amusements. *Duluth News Tribune* (22 May 1914): 5.

—. "Orpheum." *Duluth New Tribune* (16 May 1914): 6.

Dyer, Richard. *Heavenly Bodies: Film Stars and Society*, 2nd ed. London: Routledge, 2003.

Eggerton, John. "KARE: Man Shoots TV Over Converter Confusion." *Broadcasting and Cable* (20 February 2009), http://www.broadcastingcable.com/article/174518-KARE_Man_Shoots_ TV_Over_Converter_Confusion.php.

Eliason, Norman E. "American English in Europe." *American Speech* 32, no. 3 (October 1957): 166–169.

Ellroy, James. *American Tabloid: A Novel*. New York: Knopf, 1995.

—. *Blood's a Rover: A Novel*. New York: Knopf, 2009.

—. *The Cold Six Thousand: A Novel*. New York: Knopf, 2001.

Ennis, Harry. "Selig's Great Picture," Motion Picture Department. *New York Clipper* 62, no. 10 (18 April 1914): 8.

—. "Strand, New York's Newest Playhouse, Opens Saturday, April 11," Doings in Filmdom. *New York Clipper* 62, no. 9 (11 April 1914): 14.

—. "Success Prefaces 'The Spoilers.' " Motion Picture Department. *New York Clipper* 62, no. 9 (11 April 1914): 14.

Europa.eu. "Europe's Digital Library doubles in size but also shows EU's lack of common web copyright solution." Europa.eu press release (28 August 2009), http://europa.eu/rapid/press ReleasesAction.do?reference=I P/09/1257&format (accessed 15 September 2009).

Evening Sun. (16 December 1909, New York): 10.

Expressen. "En ovanlig regidebutant som lyckas långa stycken." *Expressen* (29 October 1974): 28.

—. "Publiken ska skratta och rysa." *Expressen* (27 October 1974): 38.

Falk, Julia S. *Linguistics and Language: A Survey of Basic Concepts and Implications.* New York: Wiley, 1978.

Faulkner, W. G. *The Literary Digest* 47, no. 3 (19 July 1913): 97–98.

FCC. "Updated Maps of All Full-Service Digital TV Stations Authorized by the FCC." FCC, http://www.fcc.gov/dtv/markets/ (accessed 17 March 2009).

Felten, Eric. "Who's Art Is It, Anyway?" *The Wall Street Journal* (30 July 2009) http://online.wsj.com/article/SB1000.html (accessed 15 September 2009).

Ferguson, Niall, *Colossus: The Rise and Fall of the American Empire* (New York: Penguin, 2005).

FLICKR. http://www.flickr.com/commons (accessed 15 September 2009).

Fox's Talkshow with Spike Ferensten, season 3, episode 3, available at http://www.hulu.com/watch/36608/talkshow-with-spike-feresten-cable-psa#s-p1-st-i1, accessed Dec. 3, 2008.

Frankel, Robert. *Observing America: The Commentary of British Visitors to the United States, 1890–1950*. Madison, Wis.: University of Wisconsin Press, 2007.

Franklin, Benjamin. "Securing the Friendship of the Indians," (1750). http://www.historycarper.com/resources/twobf2/letter 12.htm (accessed on 9 June 2010).

Fromkin, Victoria, and Robert Rodman. *An Introduction to Language*, 5th ed. New York: Holt, Rinehart & Winston, 1993.

Frykholm, Joel. "Framing the Feature Film: Multi-Reel Feature Film and American Film Culture in the 1910s." Ph.D. diss., Stockholm University, 2009. Stockholm: Acta Universitatis Stockholmiensis, 2009.

Fu, Poshek. *Between Shanghai and Hong Kong. The Politics of Chinese Cinema*. Stanford: Stanford University Press, 2003.

Funk & Wagnall's New Practical Standard Dictionary. New York: Funk & Wagnall, 1946.

Gabaccia, Donna. "Little Italy's Decline: Immigrant Renters and Investors in a Changing City." In *The Landscape of Modernity: New York City, 1900–1940*, edited by David Ward and Oliver Zunz. Baltimore: Johns Hopkins University Press, 1997 [1992].

Garcia, Cristina. *Monkey Hunting*. New York: Alfred Knopf, 2003.

Gates, Henry Louis, Jr., and Cornel West. *The African-American Century: How Black Americans Have Shaped Our Country*. New York: Free Press, 2000.

Geng, Song. *The Fragile Scholar. Power and Masculinity in Chinese Culture*. Hong Kong: Hong Kong University Press, 2004.

Gilfoyle, Timothy J. "City of Eros: New York City, Prostitution, and the Commercialization of Sex, 1790–1920." Ph.D. diss., Columbia University, 1988.

Gleason, Arthur H. "Last Stand Marionette." *Collier's* 44, no. 5 (23 October 1909): 16, 24, 26.

Gledhill, Christine. "Klute I: A contemporary film noir and feminist criticism." In *Women in Film Noir*, edited by E. Ann Kaplan, 6–21. London: BFI, 1980.

Glessner, Bonnie. " 'The Spoilers' in Eight Reels." *Los Angeles Times* (9 September 1913): II:6.

Globe and Commercial Advertiser. "The American Type." *Globe and Commercial Advertiser* (17 December 1909): 10.

Godard, Jean-Luc. "La Photo du Mois." *Cahiers du Cinema*, no. 92 (February 1959), reprinted in translation in *Cahiers du Cinema: The 1950s—Neo Realism, Hollywood, New Wave*, edited by Jim Hillier. Cambridge, MA: Harvard, 1985.

Gorky, Maxim. "Lumière." In *Kino: A History of the Russian and Soviet Film*, translated by Leda Swan and edited by Jay Leyda, 407–409. Princeton, NJ: Princeton University Press, 1983.

Göteborgs-Posten. "Roligare när jag kan komma frivilligt." *Göteborgs-Posten* (21 April 1974): 37.

—. "Samhällsdebatt utan pekpinnar—så vill Thelestam göra film." *Göteborgs-Posten* (27 October 1974): 37.

Grandgent, Charles H. "The Dog's Letter." In *Old and New Sundry Papers*. Cambridge, MA: Harvard University Press, 1920.

Gravlee, Clarence G. et. al. "Boas' *Changes in Bodily Form*: The Immigrant Study, Cranial Plasticity, and Boas' Physical Anthropology." *American Anthropologist* 105, no. 2 (2003): 326–332.

Gravlee, Clarence G., H. Russell Bernard, and William R. Leonard. "Heredity, Environment, and Cranial From: A Re-Analysis of Boas' Immigrant Data." *American Anthropologist* 105, no. 1 (2003): 123–136.

Gross, Grant. "Library of Congress embraces YouTube, iTunes." *IDg News Service* (27 March 2009) http://www.networkworld.com/news/2009/032709-library-of-congress-embraces-youtu be.html (accessed 15 September 2009).

Gundle, Stephen. *Glamour: A History*. Oxford: Oxford University Press, 2008.

Gunning, Tom. "The Cinema of Attractions: Early Film, Its Spectator, and the Avant-Garde." *Wide Angle* 8, no. 3–4 (1986): 63–70. Reprinted in *Early Cinema: Space, Frame, Narrative*, edited by Thomas Elsaesser and Alan Barker. London: British Film Institute, 1990.

—. *The Films of Fritz Lang: Allegories of Vision and Modernity*. London: BFI, 2000.

Hadju, David. *The Ten-Cent Plague: The Great Comic Book Scare and How It Changed America*. New York: Farrar, Straus, Giroux, 2008.

Hallam, Julia, and Margaret Marshment. *Realism and Popular Cinema*. Manchester: Manchester University Press, 2000.

Hamelink, Cees. *Trends in World Communication: On Disempowerment and Self-Empowerment*. Penang: Southbound, and Third World Network, 1994.

Hamma, Kenneth. "Public Domain Art in an Age of Easier Mechanical Reproducibility." *D-Lib Magazine,* no. 11 (2005), http://www.dli b.org/dlib/november05/hamma/11hamma.html (accessed 15 September 2009).

Handlin, Oscar. *Race and Nationality in American Life*. Boston: Little, Brown and Company, 1957 [1948].

Hansen, Miriam. "The Mass Production of the Senses: Classical Cinema as Vernacular Modernism." *Modernism/Modernity* 6, no. 2 (1999): 59-77.

—. *Babel and Babylon. Spectatorship in American Silent Film*. Cambridge, MA: Harvard University Press, 1991.

Harris, Neil. "The Operational Aesthetic." In *Popular Fiction: Technology, Ideology, Production, Reading*, edited by Tony Bennett, 401–412. London: Routledge, 1990.

Harrison, Louis Reeves. "Jackass Music." *MPW* 8, no. 3 (21 January 1911): 124–5. Sketches by H. F. Hoffman.

—. "Managerial Stupidity." *MPW* 7, no. 24 (10 December 1910): 1400.

Harrison's Reports. (30 January 1960): 18.

—. (9 January 1960): 6.

Hart, Jeffrey A. *Technology, Television, and Competition: The Politics of Digital TV*. Cambridge: Cambridge University Press, 2004.

Hayward, Susan. *Cinema Studies. The Key Concepts*. London and New York: Routledge, 2003.

Hebdidge, Dick. *Subculture: The Meaning of Style*. New York: Routledge, 1979.

Hedges, Chris. "American Psychosis." In *Adbusters* (Summer 2010): no page numbers. Vancouver, British Columbia.

Hoffman, H. F. "What They Want for Christmas." *MPW* 7, no. 26 (24 December 1910): 1482.

Hoffmann, Charlotte. "The Spread of English and the Growth of Multilingualism with English in Europe." In *English in Europe: The Acquisition of a Third Language*, edited by Jasone Cenoz and Ulrike Jessner. Clevedon: Multilingual Matters, 2000.

Hom, Marlon K. *Songs of Gold Mountain: Cantonese Rhymes from San Francisco Chinatown*. Berkeley: University of California Press, 1987.

Huebner, Grover G. "The Americanization of the Immigrant." *Annals of the American Academy of Political and Social Science* 27, The Improvement of Labor Conditions in the United States (May 1906): 191.

Huizinga, Johan. *Life and Thought in America*, (1926). Translated by Herbert H. Rowen, *America: A Dutch Historian's Vision, from Afar and Near*. New York: Harper & Row, 1972.

—. *Man and Masses in America*, (1918). Translated by Herbert H. Rowen, *America: A Dutch Historian's Vision, from Afar and Near*. New York: Harper & Row, 1972.

Idaho Statesman. Advertisement for the Isis Theatre in Boise, Idaho. *Idaho Statesman* (14 September 1914): 10.

Irwin, Elisabeth. "Where the Players Are Marionettes and the Age of Chivalry Is Born Again in a Little Theater in Mulberry Street." *Craftsman* 12, no. 6 (September 1907): 667–669.

Jantz, Richard L., and Corey S. Sparks. "Changing Times, Changing Faces: Franz Boas' Immigrant Study in Modern Perspective. "*American Anthropologist* 105, no.2 (2003): 333–337.

Jarvis, Jeff. *What Would Google Do?* New York: HarperCollins, 2009.

Jean Grae. Interview. http://www.youtube.com/watch?v=6hs7p4tAMf4&feature =related (accessed 29 April 2009).

Jenkins, Keith, ed. *The Postmodern History Reader*. London: Routledge, 1997.

Jerome, Lucy B. "The Marionettes of Little Sicily." *New England Magazine* 41 (February 1910): 745–750.

Jihua, Cheng程季華. *Zhongguo dianying fazhan shi* 中國電影發展史 [History of Chinese Cinema.] Beijing: Zhongguo dianying chubanshe, 1963.

Johansen, Jorgen Dines, and Svend Erik Larsen. *Signs in Use: An Introduction to Semiotics*. Translated by Dinda L. Gorlee and John Irons. London: Routledge, 2002.

Johnson, Claudia D. "That Guilty Third Tier: Prostitution in Nineteenth-Century American Theaters." *American Quarterly* 27, Special Issue on Victorian Culture in America, no. 5, (December 1975): 575–584.

Jordan, Christopher, et al. "Encouraging Cyberinfrastructure Collaboration for Digital Preservation." *Chronopolis* (2008), http://chronopolis.sdsc.edu/assets/ docs/39_Jordan.pdf (accessed 15 September 2009).

Junxian, Wei. *Zhongguoren faxian Meizho chu kao*. Taibei: Shshi chuban gongsi, 1975.

Kansas City Star. (30 May 1915): 15.

—. Advertisement for the Orpheum Theatre in Kansas City. *Kansas City Star* (30 May 1914): 3.

—. Advertisement for the serial publication of Rex Beach's *The Net. Kansas City Star* (1 September 1912): 11.

—. Advertisement for the Willis Wood Theater in Kansas City. *Kansas City Star* (14 December 1914): 9.

—. Advertisements for the Empress Theater. *Kansas City Star* (29 May 29 1915): 3.

Keil, Charlie, and Shelley Stamp, eds. *American Cinema's Transitional Era: Audiences, Institutions, Practices*. Berkeley: University of California Press, 2004.

Kelly, Kevin. "Web 2.0 Summit 08: Kevin Kelly (Wired)." http://www.youtube. com/watch?v=1S0-S36pM04 (accessed 15 September 2009).

Kerlan-Stephens, Anne, and Marie-Claire Quiquemelle. "La Compagnie cinématographique Lianhua et le cinéma progressiste chinois : 1930–1937." *Arts Asiatiques,* no. 61 (2006): 5.

Kirschenbaum, Matthew B. *Mechanisms: New Media and the Forensic Imagination*. Cambridge, MA: MIT Press, 2008.

Kittler, Friedrich *Gramophone, Film, Typewriter*. Palo Alto, CA: Stanford University Press, 1999.

Klein, William, II. "Authors and Creators: Up by Their Own Bootstraps." *Communications and the Law* 14, no. 3 (September 1992): 41–72.

Korman, Gerd. "Americanization at the Factory Gate." *Industrial and Labor Relations Review* 18, no. 3 (April 1965): 396–419.

—. *Industrialization, Immigrants, and Americanizers: The View from Milwaukee, 1866–1921*. Madison, Wis: Wisconsin State Historical Society, 1967.

Krutnik, Frank. *In a Lonely Street: Film Noir, Genre, Masculinity*. London: Routledge, 1991.

Kutner, C. Jerry. "Beyond the Golden Age: Film Noir Since the '50s." http:// www. brightlightsfilm.com/54/noirgolden

Kvällsposten. "Succé i Polen för Gangsterfilmen." *Kvällsposten* (13 September 1975): 13.

La Sorte, Michael. *La Merica: Images of Italian Greenhorn Experience*. Philadelphia: Temple University Press, 1985.

Labov, William. *Sociolinguistic Patterns*. Philadelphia: University of Pennsylvania Press, 1972.

Lai, Linda. "Big Road, an Eclectic Text." *Linda Lai Floating Site*, http://www.lindalai-floatingsite. com/contents/writings/Bg/index.html (accessed 27 June 2009).

Lawrence, William Witherle. *Medieval Story and the Beginning of the Social Ideals of English-Speaking People*. New York: Columbia University Press, 1911.

Laymen, Richard, and Julie M. Rivett, eds. *Selected Letters of Dashiell Hammett 1921–1960*. Washington, DC: Counterpoint Press, 2001.

Lee, Gregory B. "From America to Amérique." Lecture at Stockholm University (25 September 2008).

—. *Chinas Unlimited: Making the Imaginaries of China and Chineseness*. Honolulu: University of Hawai'i Press, 2003.

—. *Troubadours, Trumpeters, Troubled Makers: Lyricism, Nationalism and Hybridity in China and Its Others*. Durham, NC: Duke University Press, 1996.

Legendre, A.-F. *L'Illustration: Journal Universel* (26 December 1925).

Lessig, Lawrence. *Remix: Making Art and Commerce Thrive in the Hybrid Economy*. London: Penguin Press, 2008.

Lewis, Sinclair. *Babbitt*. New York: Harcourt, Brace and Company, 1922.

LOKSS. http://www.lockss.org/lockss/Home (accessed 15 September 2009).

Los Angeles Times. " 'The Spoilers' Is Thrilling." *Los Angeles Times* (6 August 1913): III:2.

—. "Clune's Auditorium," Dramatic Reviews. *Los Angeles Times* (24 May 1914): III:3.

—. "Rex Beach's 'The Spoilers' Returns to Clune's." *Los Angeles Times* (4 October 1914): III:1.

—. "The Woodley." *Los Angeles Times* (7 February 1915): II:6.

—. "The Woodley." *Los Angeles Times* (11 February 1915): III:3.

Lovink, Geert. "The Art of Watching Databases: Introduction to the Video Vortex Reader." *Video Vortex Reader: Responses to YouTube*, edited by Geert Lovink and Sabine Niederer. Amsterdam: Institute of Network Cultures, 2008. http://networkcultures.org/wpmu/portal/ publications/inc-readers/videovortex/ (accessed 15 September 2009).

Luce, Edward. "Goodbye American Dream." *Financial Times* (1 August 2010), Life and Arts: 1-2.

Luce, Henry R. "The American Century." *Life* 10, no. 7 (17 February 1941): 61–65. Reprinted in *Diplomatic History* 23, no.2 (Spring 1999): 159–171.

Lyons, Arthur. *Death on the Cheap: The Lost B Movies of Film Noir*. New York: Da Capo Press, 2000.

Lyotard, Jean-Francois. *The Postmodern Condition: A Report on Knowledge*. Translated by Geoff Bennington and Brian Massumi. Manchester: Manchester University Press, 1984.

MacNeil, Robert, and William Cran. *Do You Speak American?* New York: Doubleday, 2005.

Madison, Frank H. "Springfield, Ill. Picture Shows." *MPW* 7, no. 25 (17 December 1910): 1420.

Maltby, Richard. "Why Boys Go Wrong: Gangsters, Hoodlums, and the Natural History of Delinquent Careers." In *Mob Culture: Hidden Histories of the American Gangster Film*, edited by Lee Grieveson, Esther Sonnct, and Peter Stanfield, 41–66. New Brunswick, NJ: Rutgers University Press, 2005.

Manovich, Lev. "Cultural Analytics." (2008) http://lab.softwarestudies.com/2008/09/cultural- analytics.html (accessed 15 September 2009).

—. *Software Takes Command*. (2008) http://softwarestudies.com/softbook/manovich_softbook_ 11_20_2008.pdf (accessed 15 September 2009).

—. *The Language of New Media*. Cambridge, MA: MIT Press, 2001.

Marquez, Jose. "Join LISTA on Digital Justice Day and Volunteer in ATLANTA." http://network.nshp.org/forum/topics/join-lista-on-digital-justice (accessed 4 November 2009).

Martin. "Working the Sound Effects." *MPW* 9, no. 11 (23 September 1911): 873.

Matthews, Brander. "A Standard of Spoken English." In *Essays on English*. New York: Charles Scribner's Sons, 1921.

—. "Puppet Shows, Old and New." *The Bookman* 40, no. 4 (December 1914): 379–388.

McCrum, Robert, William Cran and Robert MacNeil. *The Story of English*. London: Faber & Faber, BBC publications, 1986.

McCrum, Robert. *Globish*. London, New York: Penguin Viking, 2010.

McPharlin, Paul. *The Puppet Theater in America: A History*. New York: Harper & Brothers, 1949.

McQuade, James. "Rex E. Beach: Author of The Spoilers Sees Filmed Story Passed by Chicago Censors, and Gives an Interesting Interview to World Representatives." *MPW* 19, no. 12 (21 March 1914): 1506.

—. "Studebaker to Be Opened by 'The Spoilers,' " Chicago Letter. *MPW* 20, no. 4 (25 April 1914): 520.

—. "The Spoilers." *MPW* 20, no. 2 (11 April 1914): 186–87.

Mead, Theodore H. *Our Mother Tongue*. New York: Dodd, Mead and Company, 1890.

Meals on Wheels Association of America. "Keeping Seniors Connected." Meals on Wheels Association of America, http://www.mowaa.org/Page.aspx?pid=338 (accessed 17 March 2009).

Mechanismstudios. "Cameras in Digital Convert Boxes! BEWARE!!!!" (16 February 2009), http://www.youtube.com/watch?v=TQ4iIM8Eljc (accessed 18 March 2009).

Mencken, H. L. *American Language. An Inquiry into the Development of English in the United States*, Supplement II. New York: Alfred A. Knopf, 1948.

Menzies, Gavin. *1421: The Year China Discovered the World*. New York: Harper Collins, 2002.

Meyer, Richard J. *Jin yan: The Rudolph Valentino of Shanghai*. Hong Kong: Hong Kong University Press, 2009.

Michie, Helena, and Ronald Thomas, eds. *Nineteenth-Century Geography: The Transformation of Space from the Victorian Age to the American Century*. New Brunswick, NJ: Rutgers University Press, 2003.

Miller, Clair Cain. "Ad Revenue on the Web? No Sure Bet." *New York Times* (24 May 2009) http://www.nytimes.com/2009/05/25/technology/start-ups/25 startup.html (accessed 15 September 2009).

Miller, Paul. *Rhythm Science*. Cambridge, MA: MIT Press, 2004.

Milne, Tom. *Mamoulian*. London: BFI, 1969.

Milroy, Lesley. "Standard English and Language Ideology in Britain and the United States." In *Standard English: The Widening Debate*, edited by Tony Bex and Richard J. Watts. London and New York: Routledge, 1999.

Mobärg, Mats. "Media Exposure vs. Educational Prescription: The Case of British and American English in Sweden." In *The Major Varieties of English: Papers from MAVEN97, Växjö 20–22 November 1997*, edited by Hans Lindquist, Staffan Klintborg, Magnus Levin and Maria Estling, 241–248. Växjö University: Acta Wexionensia, 1998.

Moffitt, Jack. *The Hollywood Reporter* (3 July 1958): 3.

Moore, R. Laurence, and Maurizio Vaudagna, eds. *The American Century in Europe*. Ithaca, N.Y.: Cornell University Press, 2003.

Morey, Anne. " 'Would You Be Ashamed to Let Them See What You Have Written?' The Gendering of Photoplaywrights, 1913–1923." *Tulsa Studies in Women's Literature* 17, no. 1 (Spring 1998): 83–99.

Morning Olympian. " 'The Spoilers' Pack the Ray." *Morning Olympian* (31 December 1914): 4.

—. "Rex Beach's 'The Spoilers' at Ray." *Morning Olympian* (30 December 1914): 4.

—. Advertisement for the Ray Theater in Olympia, Washington. *Morning Olympian* (30 December 1914): 4.

Morosco, Oliver. "Tomorrow—The Future of the Photoplay." *Motography* 15, no. 1 (1 January 1916): 9.

Motion Picture Herald. (12 July 1958): 905.

—. "The Last Mile." (31 January 1959): 433.

—. Product Digest Section (23 January 1960): 565.

—. Product Digest Section (25 June 1960): 749.

—. Product Digest Section (3 October 1959): 437.

—. Product Digest Section (6 May 1961): 276.

—. Product Digest Section (January 16, 1960): 557.

—. Product Digest Section, (9 November 1957): 593.

MPW "Plucky (Akron) Exhibitor Wins His Case: Ch. 1: To Prison in Wagon." *MPW* 1, no. 9 (6 April 1907): 113.

—."Hazel B's" letter to Clarence E. Sinn, the "Cue Music Man." "Music for the Picture." *MPW* 8, no. 7 (18 February 1911): 353.

—. The 'World Reviewer,' "The Picture the Audience Likes." *MPW* 8, no. 6 (11 February 1911): 310.

—. 7, no. 25 (3 December 1910): 1303.

MUBI. "*You Only Live Once.*" http://www.theauteurs.com/films/3557.

Murtaugh, John, and Sarah Harris. *Cast the First Stone.* New York: McGraw-Hill, 1957.

Naremore, James. *More Than Night: Film Noir and Its Contexts.* Berkeley: University of California Press, 1998.

Needham, Joseph. *Science and Civilization in China.* Cambridge: Cambridge University Press, 1971.

Neumark, N., R. Gibson, and T. Van Leeuwen, eds. *Voice: Vocal Aesthetics in Digital Arts and Media.* Cambridge, MA: MIT Press. In press.

New York Dramatic Mirror. "An Interview with Lawrence S. McCloskey, Scenario Editor of the Lubin Manufacturing Company." *New York Dramatic Mirror* 69, no. 1798 (4 June 1913): 25, cont. on 32.

—. " 'Spoilers' to Open. Selig Production Will Be Opening Attraction at the Strand Theater." *New York Dramatic Mirror* 71, no. 1840 (25 March 1914): 30.

—. "First Showing of 'Spoilers': Selig Company Host to Distinguished Audience at Orchestra Hall—Film Pleases." *New York Dramatic Mirror* 71, no. 1841 (1 April 1914): 22.

—. "Strand Theater Opens. In Blaze of Glory Selig's 'The Spoilers' is Well Received at Opening of Large Theater." *New York Dramatic Mirror* 71, no. 1843 (15 April 1914): 31.

—. 62, no. 1618 (25 December 1909): 15.

New York Evening Post. (1931, no date given). In *City Streets* press file: AMPAS.

New York Evening World. "Marionettes and Moving Pictures." *New York Evening World* (15 December 1909): 18.

New York Herald. "Where Puppet Knights Battle Gloriously As Lurid Tale Is Told." *New York Herald* (20 February 1910): III:8.

—. Letter writer to the *New York Herald.* *New York Herald* (1 and 2 November 1842).

New York Times. (12 December 1957): 35.

—. (25 February 1931). Undated clipping from *New York Times* at AMPAS.

—. " 'The Spoilers' Produced." *New York Times* (6 November 1909): 9.

—. " 'The Spoilers' Produced: Daniel Frohman's Presentation of the Dramatization of Beach's Novel." *New York Times* (29 January 1907): 9.

—. "Hope for Parisi of the Marionettes." *New York Times* (21 April 1908): 6.

—. "Marionettes Back, Speaking English." *New York Times* (22 May 1910): 7.

—. "New Strand Opens: Biggest of Movies; Handsome Theatre at Broadway and 47th Street Seats Almost 3,500 People." *New York Times* (12 April 1914): 15.

—. "The Old Puppet Show Is to Be Restored to Favor." *New York Times* (4 May 1913): SM5.

New York Tribune. (17 December 1909): 4.

Nichols, Bill. *Blurred Boundaries*. Bloomington, IN: Indiana University Press, 1994.

Nielsenwire. "6.5 Million U.S. Homes Unready for Digital TV Transition." *Nielsenwire* (22 January 2009), http://blog.nielsen.com/nielsenwire/media_entertainment/65-million-us-homes- unready-for-digital-tv-transition/ (accessed 18 March 2009).

Norlin, George. *Things in the Saddle: Selected Essays and Addresses*. Cambridge, MA: Harvard University Press, 1940.

North American. "Film of 'The Spoilers' Is Good Movie Drama: Nine-Thousand Feet of Pictures Give Fine Version of Rex Beach's Novel; Action Is Sustained." *North American* (10 November 1914): 14.

O'Brien, Geoffrey. "In Cold Blood." *Film Comment* (May–June 2006): 22–23.

O'Dell, Tom. "Culture Unbound: Americanization and Everyday Life in Sweden." Ph.D. diss., Lund University, 1998.

Olsson, Jan. *Los Angeles Before Hollywood: Journalism and American Film Culture, 1905–1915*. Stockholm: National Library of Sweden, 2008.

—. "Trading Places: Griffith, Patten and Agricultural Modernity." *Film History* 17, no. 1 (2005): 39–65.

OpenSolaris. "Celeste." *OpenSolaris*, http://www.opensolaris.org/os/project/celeste/ (accessed 15 September 2009).

Pang, Laikwan, and Hu Junbin. *Projecting a Nation. Chinese National Cinema Before 1949*. Hong Kong: Hong Kong University Press, 2003.

—. *Building a New China in Cinema. The Chinese Left-Wing Cinema Movement, 1932–1937*. Boston: Rowman and Littlefield, 2002.

Paredes, Mari Castaneda. "Television Set Production at the US-Mexico Border: Trade Policy and Advanced Electronics for the Global Market." In *Critical Cultural Policy Studies: A Reader*, edited by Justin Lewis and Toby Miller, 272–281. Malden, MA: Blackwell, 2003.

—. "The Complicated Transition to Broadcast Digital Transition in the United States." *Television and New Media* 8, no. 2 (2007): 91–106.

Parfrey, Adam, ed. *It's A Man's World: Men's Adventure Magazines, the Postwar Pulps.* Los Angeles: Feral House, 2003.

Pearson, Roberta, and William Uricchio. *Reframing Culture: The Case of the Vitagraph Quality Films.* Princeton, NJ: Princeton University Press, 1993.

Peiss, Kathy. *Cheap Amusements: Working Women and Leisure in Turn-of-the-Century New York.* Philadelphia: Temple University Press, 1986.

Philadelphia Inquirer. " 'The Barrier' in Film." *Philadelphia Inquirer* (18 February 1917): 11.

—. " 'The Spoilers': Rex Beach's Novel Seen in Films at Chestnut Street Opera House." *Philadelphia Inquirer* (10 November 1914): 13.

—. "Opera House," The Film Drama. *Philadelphia Inquirer* (8 November 1914): II:15.

—. "Thrilling Picture Realism." *Philadelphia Inquirer* (1 November 1914): 14.

—. Advertisement for Nixon's Colonial. *Philadelphia Inquirer* (23 March 1920): 3.

—. Advertisement for the Chestnut Street Opera House. *Philadelphia Inquirer* (8 November 1914): II:16.

—. Advertisement for Tuxedo Tobacco. *Philadelphia Inquirer* (28 August 1913): 5.

Philadelphia Record. "Opera House—'The Spoilers.' " *Philadelphia Record* (2 November 1914): 6.

—. "Opera House—'The Spoilers.' " *Philadelphia Record* (8 November 1914): 7.

—. "Rescript from Life: 'The Spoilers' Told a Story that Had Been Enacted in Alaska." *Philadelphia Record* (1 November 1914): 7.

Phillips, Henry Albert. "How I Came to Write For the Motion Pictures: The Interesting Facts Brought to Light for the First Time in an Interview with Rex Beach." *Motion Picture Magazine* 9, no. 4 (May 1915): 95–98.

Phillipson, Robert. *Linguistic Imperialism Continued.* London and New York: Routledge, 2009.

Place, Janey. "Women in Film Noir." In *Women in Film Noir*, edited by E. Ann Kaplan, 35–67. London: British Film Institute, 1980.

Potter, Claire Bond. *War on Crime: Bandits, G-Men, and the Politics of Mass Culture.* New York: Rutgers University Press, 1998.

Prelinger Archives. http://www.archive.org/details/prelinger (accessed 15 September 2009).

Prelinger, Rick. "The Apperance of Archives." In *The YouTube Reader*, edited by Pelle Snickars and Patrick Vonderau, 268-274. Stockholm: National Library of Sweden, 2009.

Prison Planet forum blog. "Camera and mic found in digital convertor box paid for by Feds." Prison Planet Forum blog (17 February 2009), http://forum.prisonplanet.com/index.php?topic= 87074 (accessed 18 March 2009).

Privatt, Kathy L. "The New Theater of Chicago: Democracy 1; Aristocracy 0." *Theatre History Studies* 24 (June 2004): 103.

Production Code Administration. *City Streets file*: AMPAS.

Quiquemelle, Marie-Claire and Jean-Loup Passek, eds. *Le Cinéma chinois*. Paris : Centre George Pompidou, 1985.

Quizz [pseud.]. " 'The Spoilers' (Selig) Nine Reels." Current Film Events. *New York Clipper* 62, no. 11 (25 April 1914): 16.

Raymond, Alex. *Rip Kirby 1946–1948*. San Diego: The Library of American Comics, IDW Publishing, 2009.

Renov, Michael. *The Subject of Documentary*. Minneapolis: University of Minnesota Press, 2004.

Reynolds, Simon. *Generation Ecstasy*. New York: Routledge, 1999.

Ribot, Theodule. *Psychologie de l'attention*. Paris: F. Alcan, 1889. English translation as *The Psychology of Attention*. Chicago: The Open Court Publishing Company, 1896.

Rich, J. Dennis, and Kevin L. Seligman. "The New Theatre of Chicago, 1906–1907." *Educational Theatre Journal* 26, no. 1 (March 1974): 61–62.

Riggs, Marlon. "Tongues Re-Tied." In *Resolutions: Contemporary Video Practices*, edited by Michael Renov and Erika Suderburg. Minneapolis: University of Minnesota Press, 1996.

Roberts, Randy, and James S. Olson. *John Wayne: American*. New York: The Free Press, 1995.

Robertson, Roland. *Globalization: Social Theory and Global Culture*. London: Sage, 1992.

Rogoway, Mike. "Time Running Short to Make Digital TV Leap." *The Oregonian* (1 November 2008) (accessed 18 March 2009).

Rose, Tricia. *Black Noise*. Wesleyan, CT: Wesleyan University Press, 1994.

Ross, Edward A. *The Old World and the New*. New York: Century Publishing, 1914.

Rothkopf, David. "In Praise of Cultural Imperialism." *Foreign Policy*, no. 107 (Summer 1997): 45.

Rousseau, Victor. "A Puppet Play Which Lasts Two Months." *Harper's Weekly* 52, no. 2702 (3 October 1908): 15–16.

Said, Edward, W. *Orientalism*. New York, Vintage, 1979.

Salt Lake Telegram. "At the Theatres." *Salt Lake Telegram* (29 September 1914): 3.

—. "Do You Think That You Would Be a Competent Stage Director? Cast the Willard Mack-Marjorie Rambeau Players for The Spoilers and Earn Tickets." *Salt Lake Telegram* (22 August 1912): 10.

—. "Rex Beach's Gripping Drama Opens at Wilkes Tonight." *Salt Lake Telegram* (15 April 1917): 12.

—. "Scene from Rex Beach's Play to be Shown at the Salt Lake." *Salt Lake Telegram* (5 September 1914): 5.

—. "Telegram Readers Cast Characters in 'The Spoilers': Many Join Contest for Rex Beach's Dramatized Story." *Salt Lake Telegram* (24 August 1912): 10.

—. "Vitalizing a Romance." *Salt Lake Telegram* (9 September 1914): 2.

—. "What Part Do You Want to See Your Favorite Stock Actor Play?" *Salt Lake Telegram* (23 August 1912): 12.

—. "Winners of 'The Spoilers' Cast Contest." *Salt Lake Telegram* (26 August 1912): 10.

—. Advertisement for the Rex Theatre. *Salt Lake Telegram* (1 July 1915): 10.

—. Advertisement for the Rex Theatre. *Salt Lake Telegram* (2 July 1915): 8.

—. Advertisement for the Salt Lake Theatre. *Salt Lake Telegram* (12 September 1914): 31.

—. Advertisement for the Salt Lake Theatre. *Salt Lake Telegram* (5 September 1914): 15.

—. Advertisement for the Salt Lake Theatre. *Salt Lake Telegram* (7 September 1914): 6.

San Jose Mercury News. " 'The Spoilers.' At the Theatres." *San Jose Mercury News* (17 January 1915): 14.

—. " 'The Spoilers' at the Liberty Theatre Today: Wonderful Film Story Is Romance of Alaska." *San Jose Mercury News* (20 January 1915): 8.

—. "A 'Thriller' Movie at the Victory: Rex Beach's 'Spoilers' Filmed with William Farnum in the Lead." *San Jose Mercury News* (21 September 1914): 3.

—. "Important Events of the Week: When, Where and How to Get There." *San Jose Mercury News* (20 September 1914): 8.

Sargent, Epes Winthrop. "Advertising for Exhibitors." *MPW* 9, no. 11 (23 September 1911): 876.

Sato, Tadao. "Le Cinéma japonais et le cinéma chinois face la tradition." In *Le Cinéma chinois*, edited by Marie-Claire Quiquemelle and Jean-Loup Passek, 77–84. Paris : Centre George Pompidou, 1985.

—. *Le Cinéma japonais*. Paris : Centre Georges Pompidou, 1997.

Scarry, Elaine, ed. *Fin de Siecle Poetry*. Johns Hopkins University Press, Baltimore, 1994.

Scheffauer, Herman. "The Last Refuge of 'Romance.' " *Lippincott's Monthly Magazine* 91, no. 594 (January 1913): 120–122.

Selig Polyscope Co. "Selig's 'The Spoilers.' " Four-page publicity brochure, the William Selig Papers, AMPAS.

Senses of Cinema. "You Only Live Once." http://archive.sensesofcinema.com/contents/cteq/08/48/you-only-live-once.html.

Silver, Alain, and James Ursini, eds. *Film Noir Reader, Vol. I*. New York: Limelight Editions, 1996.

—. *Film Noir Reader, Vol. II*. New York: Limelight Editions, 1999.

Silver, Alain, James Ursini, and Robert Porfiro, eds. *Film Noir Reader, Vol III*. New York: Limelight Editions, 2002.

Sjögren, Olle. "Det blågula stjärnbaneret. Om amerikanska smältbilder i svensk film" ["The Swedish Star-Spangled Banner: An Essay on Blended Images in Film."] In *Networks of Americanization: Aspects of the American Influence in Sweden*, edited by Rolf Lundén and Erik Åsard, 130–161. Uppsala: Uppsala universitet, 1992.

Slater, David, and Peter J. Taylor, eds. *The American Century: Consensus and Coercion in the Projection of American Power*. Malden, MA: Blackwell, 1999.

Smith, Henry Nash. *Virgin Land: The American West as Symbol and Myth*. Cambridge, MA: Harvard University Press, 1950.

Smitherman, Geneva. "Foreword." In *Roc the Mic Right: The Language of Hip Hop Culture*, edited by H. Samy Alim. New York: Routledge, 2006.

Snickars, Pelle, and Patrick Vonderau. *The YouTube Reader*. Stockholm: National Library of Sweden, 2009.

Sonnet, Esther, and Peter Stanfield. " 'Good Evening, Gentleman, Can I Check Your Hats Please?': Masculinity, Dress and the Retro Gangster Cycles of the 1990s." In *Mob Culture: Hidden Histories of American the Gangster Film*, edited by Lee Grieveson, Esther Sonnet, and Peter Stanfield, 163–184. New Brunswich, NJ: Rutgers University Press, 2005.

Sonnet, Esther. "Ladies Love Brutes: Reclaiming Female Pleasures in the Lost History of Hollywood Gangster Cycles 1929–31." In *Mob Culture: Hidden Histories of the American Gangster Film*, edited by Lee Grieveson, Esther Sonnet, and Peter Stanfield, 93–119. New Brunswick, NJ: Rutgers University Press, 2005.

Spady, James, H. Samy Alim, and Samir Meghelli. *The Global Cipha*. Philadelphia, PA: Black History Museum Press, 2006.

Sparks, Corey S., and Richard L. Jantz. "A Reassessment of Human Cranial Plasticity: Boas Revisited." *Proceedings of the National Academy of Sciences* 99, no. 23 (2002): 14636–14639.

Spigel, Lynn, and Jan Olsson, eds. *TV after Television*. Durham, NC: Duke University Press, 2004.

Springer, Michelle, et al. "For the Common Good: The Library of Congress Flickr Pilot Project." (2008), http://www.loc.gov/rr/pri nt/flickr_report_final.pdf (accessed 15 September 2009).

Staff Writer. "An Original Critique." *MPW* 9, no. 9 (9 September 1911): 705.

—. "At Coney Island." *MPW* 8, no. 27 (8 July 1911): 1571.

—. "Facts and Comments." *MPW* 9, no. 8 (2 September 1911): 604.

—. "Facts and Comments." *MPW* 10, no. 1 (7 October 1911): 20.

—. "In the Educational Field." *MPW* 8, no. 11 (10 March 1911): 584.

—. "The Lost Gallery." *MPW* 9, no. 3 (29 July 1911): 397.

—. In the Educational Field: "BRAINS"—"Using the Brains"—"The Cinematograph a Stimulus to the Brain." *MPW* 8, no. 7 (18 February 1911): 352.

Stag Magazine. "THE FBI'S DEATH DUEL WITH BABY FACE NELSON." *Stag Magazine* 9, no. 5 (May, 1958).

—. *Amazing Detective Cases. Stag Magazine* (December, 1958).

Staiger, Janet. *Interpreting Films: Studies in the Historical Reception of American Cinema*. Princeton: Princeton University Press, 1992.

—. *Perverse Spectators: The Practices of Film Reception*. New York: New York University Press, 2000.

Stamp, Shelley. *Movie-Struck Girls: Women and Motion Picture Culture After the Nickelodeon*. Princeton, NJ: Princeton University Press, 2000.

Stanfield, Peter. *Hollywood, Westerns and the 1930s: The Lost Trail*. Exeter: University of Exeter Press, 2001.

Stead, W.T. *The Americanisation of the World, or The Trend of the Twentieth Century*. London: Review of Reviews, 1901.

Steene, Birgitta. "The Swedish Image of America." In *Images of America in Scandinavia*, edited by Poul Houe and Sven Hakon Rossel, 145–192. Amsterdam, Atlanta, GA: Rodopi, 1998.

Steinberg, Jacques. "Digital TV Beckons, but Many Miss the Call." *The New York Times* (28 January 2009), http://www.nytimes.com/2009/01/29/arts/television/29ears.html (accessed 18 March 2009).

Steiner, G. *After Babel: Aspects of Language and Translation*. Oxford: Oxford University Press, 1975.

Stelter, Brian. "Digital TV Delay Runs into Protest." *The New York Times* (16 January 2009), http://www.nytimes.com/2009/01/17/technology/17digital.html (accessed 17 March 2009).

—. "Interviews With Legends of Television Hit the Web." *The New York Times* (13

September 2009), http://www.nytimes.com/2009/09/14/business/media/14archive.html (accessed 15 September 2009).

—. "Switch to Digital TV Wins a Delay to June 12." *The New York Times* (4 February 2009), http://www.nytimes.com/2009/02/05/business/media/05digital.html (accessed 17 March 2009).

Straw, Will. "Urban Confidential: The Lurid City of the 1950s." In *The Cinematic City*, edited by David B. Clarke. London: Routledge, 1997.

Studlar, Gaylyn. "A Gunsel is Being Beaten: Gangster Masculinity and the Homoerotics of the Crime Film, 1941–1942." In *Mob Culture: Hidden Histories of the American Gangster Film*, edited by Lee Grieveson, Esther Sonnet, and Peter Stanfield, 120–145. New Brunswick, NJ: Rutgers University Press, 2005.

Suyuan, Li酈蘇元, and Hu Jubin 胡菊彬. *Zhonggguo wusheng dianying shi* 中國無聲電影史 [History of Chinese Silent Cinema.] Beijing: Zhongguo dianying, 1997.

Svenska Dagbladet. " 'Gangsterfilmen' fellanserad i Sverige." *Svenska Dagbladet* (2 July 1975): 9.

—. "Mickey Spillane i Mumindalen..." *Svenska Dagbladet* (29 October 1974): 13.

Sydsvenska Dagbladet. "En splittrad regidebut." *Sydsvenska Dagbladet* (29 October 1974): 10.

Talmadge, Thomas DeWitt. *Sports That Kill.* New York: Funk and Wagnall, 1875.

Teo, Stephen. "Il genere *wenyi*: una esegesi del melodramma cinese" [The *wenyi* genre: the Chinese melodrama.] In Festival del cinema di Pesaro, *Stanley Kwan. La via orientale al melodramma.* Roma: Il Castoro, 2000.

—. *Hong Kong. The Extra Dimensions.* London: BFI Publishing, 1997.

The Black Panther Party. "Platform and Program." In *The Sixties Papers: Documents of a Rebellious Decade*, edited by Judith Clavir Albert and Stewart Edward Albert, 159–164. New York: Praeger, 1984.

The Hollywood Reporter. (21 January 1958): 3.

—. (3 July 1958): 3

—. (6 March 1958): 4.

—. (6 November 1957): 3.

The Internet Movie Database. City Streets. http://www.imdb.com/title/tt0021750/

—. "*You Only Live Once* user reviews." http://www.imdb.com/title/tt0029808/usercomments.

The Sun. (1 June 1913, New York): IV:12.

Thompson, Kristin. "The Celestial Multiplex." Blog post (27 March 2007), http:// www.davidbordwell.net/blog/?p=595 (accessed 15 September 2009).

—. *Exporting Entertainment: America in the World Film Market 1907–1934*. London: BFI Publishing, 1985.

Toop, David. *Rap Attack 2*. London: Serpent's Tail, 1992.

Torres, Sasha. *Black, White and in Color: Television and Black Civil Rights*. Princeton, NJ: Princeton University Press, 2003.

Trudgill, Peter. *Dialects in Contact*. Oxford: Basil Blackwell, 1986.

Tsivian, Yuri. *Early Cinema in Russia and its Cultural Reception*. Translated by Alan Bodger. New York: Routledge, 1994.

Turnbull, Robert. *The Theatre, in Its Influence upon Literature, Morals, and Religion*. Hartford: Canfield and Robins, 1837.

Usai, Paolo Cherchi, et al. *Film Curatorship: Archives, Museums, and the Digital Marketplace*. Vienna: Synema, 2008.

—. "Äh, det är ju bara journalfilm: Varför ses inte 95% av museernas bestånd." *Aura* 3, no. 3–4 (1997): 111–117.

Vahimagi, Tise. *The Untouchables*. London: British film Institute, 1998.

Variety. (22 April 1931).

—. (6 November 1957): 6.

—. "Gangsterfilmen (The Gangster Movie)." *Variety* (1 November 1974): 9.

—. " 'The Spoilers.' " *Variety* 34, no. 7 (17 April 1914): 22.

Vasey, Ruth. *The World According to Hollywood, 1918–1939*. Exeter: University of Exeter Press, 1997.

Verhausen, Astrid. "Mass Digitisation by Libraries: Issues concerning Organisation, Quality and Efficiency." *Liber Quaterly*, no. 1 (2008), http://webdoc.sub. gwdg.de/edoc/aw/liber/lq-1-08/ar ticle4.pdf (accessed 15 September 2009).

Vernet, Mark. "Film Noir on the Edge of Doom." In *Shades of Noir*, edited by Joan Copjec, 1–32. London: Verso, 1993.

Vitello, Mike. "A Ring Tone Meant to Fall on Deaf Ears." *The New York Times* (12 June 2006).

Vizetelly, Francis H. *How to Speak English Effectively*. New York: Funk and Wagnall's, 1933.

Vogel, Steven. *Prime Mover: A Natural History of Muscle*. New York: Norton, 2001.

Von Harleman, G. P. "Chicago Letter." *MPW* 20, no. 13 (27 June 1914): 1812.

Wallengren, Ann-Kristin. "Samhällsbyggarnas tv-undervisning. Estetik och ideologi i utbildningsprogram för televisionen" ["Television Teaching by the Builders of Modern Society. Aesthetics and Ideology in Educational Programmes for Television."] In Ann-Kristin Wallengren and Cecilia Wadensjö, *Om tilltal, bildspråk och samhällssyn i utbildningsprogrammen*, 19–125. Stockholm: Stiftelsen Etermedierna i Sverige, 2001.

Wandres, Jenna. "AAPD Releases DTV Transition Music Video." (3 December 2008), http://www.civilrights.org/dtv/index.jsp?page=3 (accessed 18 March 2009).

Wandres, Jenna. "LCCREF Video Tells the Story of a DTV Assistance Center at Work." (5 March 2009), www.civilrights.org/dtv/index.jsp?page=2 (accessed 17 March 2009).

Warhol, Andy. *The Philosophy of Andy Warhol: From A to B and Back Again.* New York: Harcourt Brace Jovanovich, 1975.

Warshow, Robert. "The Gangster as a Tragic Hero." (Original date of publication 1948.) In *The Immediate Experience: Movies, Comics, Theatre & Other Aspects of Popular Culture*, 85–88. Cambridge, MA/London: Harvard University Press, 2001).

Washington Post. (30 December 2008).

—. "The White Open Spaces," Editorial. *Washington Post* (16 August 2007), http://www.washingtonpost.com/wp-dyn/content/article/2007/08/15/AR2007081502128.html (accessed 17 March 2009).

Weber, Ian, and Vanessa Evans. "Constructing the Meaning of Digital Television in Britain, the United States and Australia." *New Media & Society* 6, no. 4 (2004): 435–456.

Webster, Noah. *Dissertations on the English Language.* Boston: Isaiah Thomas, 1789.

Weitzel, Jason. "Pulling Free TV Signals out of Berks County's Thin Air." *Reading Eagle.com* (Penn.) (February 2, 2009), http://readingeagle.com/articleprint.aspx?od=123746 (accessed 18 March 2009).

Wikimedia Commons. "User:Dcoetzee/NPG legal threat." http://commons.wikimedia.org/wiki/ User:Dcoetzee/NPG_legal_threat (accessed 15 September 2009).

Wikinews. "U.K. National Portrait Gallery threatens U.S. citizen with legal action over Wikimedia images." (14 July 2009), http://en.wikinews.org/wiki/U.K._National_Portrait_Gallery_threatens_U.S._citizen_with_legal_action_over_Wikimedia_images (accessed 15 September 2009).

Wikipedia. "Data Mining." http://en.wikipedia.org/wiki/Data_mining (accessed 15 September 2009).

—. "Social Tagging." http://en.wikipedia.org/wiki/Social_tagging (accessed 15 September 2009).

—. "You Only Live Once (film)." http://en.wikipedia.org/wiki/You_Only_Live_Once_%28film%29.

William Selig Papers. Edith Ogden Harrison to Sam Lederer, manager of the Studebaker Theatre Chicago. (11 May 1914), William Selig Papers, AMPAS.

—. Rex Beach to William Selig. (28 November 1913), William Selig Papers, AMPAS.

—. Rex Beach to William Selig. (9 June 1913), William Selig Papers, AMPAS.

Williams, Raymond. *Marxism and Literature*. New York: Oxford University Press, 1977.

Williams, Saul. *The Dead Emcee Scroll*. New York: MTV: 2006.

Wing, W. E. "Interest in 'Spoilers': High Expectations for Film Adaptation of Rex Beach's Story." *New York Dramatic Mirror* 70, no. 1809 (20 August 1913): 28.

Wise, Gene. " 'Paradigm Dramas' in American Studies: A Cultural and Institutional History of the Movement." *American Quarterly* 31, no. 3 (1979): 293–337.

Witt, Richard. "Today: TV Static. Tomorrow: Broadband." Google Public Policy Blog (12 December 2007), http://googlepublicpolicy.blogspot.com/2007/12/today-tv-static-tomorrow -broadband.html (accessed 17 March 2009).

Wolfram, Walt. "Do You Speak American? Language Change: The Truth About Change." (2010), http://www.pbs.org/speak/ahead/change/change/ (accessed on 9 June 2010).

Wollen, Peter. *Signs and Meaning in the Cinema*. Bloomington, IN: Indiana University Press, 1969.

Wong, Shawn. *Homebase*. New York: Penguin Books, 1993.

Woods, Frank E. "What Are We Coming To?" *MPW* 21, no. 3 (18 July 1914): 443.

Wright, Richard. "Institutional Perspectives on Storage" at the MIT "Media in transition 6." Conference in Boston (April 2009), http://mitworld.mit.edu/video/681/ (accessed 15 September 2009).

Xianggang Zhongguo dianying xuehui 香港中國電影學會. *Tansuo de niandai*, 探索的年代 [*Origins of Chinese Cinema*.] Hong Kong, Hong Kong Arts Center, 1984.

Xiaolan, Dai戴小蘭. *Zhongguo wusheng dianying* 中國無聲電影 [*Chinese silent Cinema*.] Beijing: Zhongguo dianying, 1996.

Xiaomei, Chen, and Jinhua, Dai. *Occidentalism: A Theory of Counter-discourse in Post-Mao China*. New York and Oxford: Oxford University Press, 1995.

Xiongping, Jiao焦雄屏. *Shidai xianying: Zhong Xi dianying lunshu* 時代顯影：中西電影論述 [*Historical Developments: Discussion of Oriental and Western Cinemas*]. Taibei: Yuanliu, 1998.

Yee, Lydia. "Breaking and Entering." In *One Planet Under a Groove: Hip hop and Contemporary Art*. New York: Bronx Museum of the Arts, 2001.

Yingjin, Zhang. *Chinese National Cinema*. New York and London: Routledge, 2004.

Yu, Sun孫瑜. *Da lu zhi ge* 大路之歌 [*Song of The Big Road*.] Taibei: Yuanliu, 1990.

—. *Yinhai fanzhou—huiyi wo de yisheng* 銀海泛舟—回憶我的一生 [*Floating on the screen. Memories of my Life*.] Shanghai : Shanghai Wenyi chubanshe, 1987.

Zeidel, Robert F. *Immigrants, Progressives, and Exclusion Politics: The Dillingham Commission, 1900–1927*. DeKalb, Illinois: Northern Illinois University Press, 2004.

Zhang, Zhen. *An Amorous History of the Silver Screen: Shanghai Cinema, 1896–1937*. Chicago: University of Chicago Press, 2006.

Zhiwei, Xiao. "Cinema cinese. Il periodo del muto 1896–1936" ["Silent Chinese Cinema 1896–1936."] In *Storia del cinema mondiale, Vol. 4*, edited by Gian Piero Brunetta, 715–737. Torino: Einaudi, 2001.

Zittrain, Jonathan. *The Future of the Internet*. New Haven: Yale University Press, 2008.

Bartlett, Lanier, 66; *The Spoilers* (1914), 13, 62–100, 379, 381–2, 384, 386, 390–8, 401, 403

Barton, H. Arnold, 225n. 19, 379

Battleship Potemkin (1925), 228–9

Baudrillard, Jean, 252, 269n. 8, 379

Bazin, André, 273, 283n. 2, 379

Beach, Rex Ellingwood, 13, 62–100, 379, 381, 389–92, 394–5, 397, 403; *The Barrier* (1917), 88–9, 99n. 102, 395; *The Iron Trail* (1913), 88, 99n. 101; *The Net*, 65–6, 94n. 19, 389; *The Ne'er Do Well* (1916), 65; *The Spoilers* (1905/1914), 13, 62–100, 379, 381–2, 384, 386, 390–8, 401, 403

A Beijinger in New York (Beijingren zu Niuyue, 1993), 266

Beijingren zu Niuyue (1993), *see A Beijinger in New York* (1993)

Bell, Alexander Graham, 130

Bell, Alexander Melville, 130, 150n. 15, 379

Belpedio, James R., 93n. 7, 379

Bender, James F., 133, 151n. 21, 379

Benjamin, Walter, 52

Bennett, Constance, 171

Benton, Mike, 213n. 6, 379

Bergeron, Regis, 228, 235, 245n. 4, 248n. 18, 379

Bergman, Hjalmar, 222; *Dollars (Dollar,* 1938), 222

Bernard, H. Russell, 60n. 16, 386

Berry, Chris, 246, 379

Bertellini, Giorgio, 61n. 29, 225n. 20, 379, 383

Billy the Kid, 22, 194

Binde, Zhou, 231, 246–7n. 10, 379

Binet, Alfred, 117

Binoche, Juliette, 361n. 39

Biro, Charles, 188; *Crime Does Not Pay* (1942–1955), 188–9

The Birth of a Nation (1915), 92

Bizet, Georges, 362n. 50

Black Panther Party, 279–81, 283n. 16, 400

Blackton, John Stuart, 99n. 107, 380

Blake, Robert, 199–200, 202; *The Purple Gang* (1960), 186, 190–1, 198–200, 202

Blondell, Joan, 171

Bo, Chen, 245n. 4, 380

Boas, Franz, 45–8, 52, 57, 60n. 16, 380, 386, 388, 399

Bogart, Humphrey, 202

Bolton, Kingsley, 7–33, 125–53, 367, 376

Bondebjerg, Ib, 152n. 40, 380

Bonfiglio, Thomas Paul, 128–31, 133–5, 146,

150n. 9, 150n. 14, 151n. 22–3, 151n. 26, 380

Bonnie and Clyde, *see* famous gangsters: Parker, Bonnie; famous gangsters: Barrow, Clyde

Boone, Daniel, 22

Booth, Ernest, 178; *Ladies of the Mob* (1928), 178, 180

Borde, Raymond, 160, 181–2n. 8, 380

Bordwell, David, 92–3n. 3, 232, 247n. 12, 380

Borzage, Frank, 235; *Seventh Heaven* (1927), 231, 235

Bottomore, Stephen, 109, 122n. 38, 380

Bourdieu, Pierre, 145

Bourdon, Jerome, 370, 375n. 4, 380

Bowie, Jim, 22

Bradley, Adam, 336, 347–8, 352, 359n. 8, 361n. 36, 361n. 41–3, 380

Brewster, Bill, 338, 359n. 11–2, 359n. 15–6, 360n. 28, 360n. 30–1, 361n. 45–8, 362n. 53, 380

Brin, Sergey Mikhaylovich, 370–1

Brinkley, Adam, 31n. 6, 380

Bronson, Charles, 207

Broughton, Frank, 338, 359n. 11–2, 359n. 15–6, 360n. 28, 360n. 30–1, 361n. 45–8, 362n. 53, 380

Brown, H. Rap, 279, 383n. 15, 381

Brown, James, 338–9

Browne, Nick, 246n. 8, 381

Buruma, Ian, 245–6n. 5, 381

Bush, George W., 24, 26, 368

Bush, W. Stephen, 114, 118–9, 123n. 55–6, 381

Butterfly Hu, *see* Die, Hu

Cagney, James, 202

Caldo, Joseffi, 38, 58n. 3

Cameron, Elizabeth, 213n. 11, 381

Cameron, Ian, 213n. 11, 381

Campbell, Colin, 67–8, 70, 83; *The Spoilers* (1914), 13, 62–100, 379, 381–2, 384, 386, 390–8, 401, 403

Caniff, Milton, 214n. 35; *Terry and the Pirates* (1934–46), 214n. 35

Cantor, Norman F., 31n. 5, 381

Capra, Frank, 235; *It Happened One Night* (1934), 235

Carbine, Mary, 121n. 22, 381

Carmichael, Stokely, 278, 283n. 13, 381

Carpenter, William B., 118, 124n. 83, 381

Carr, Harry C., 67–8, 95n. 25, 381

films; juvenile delinquency films; noir
films; prison films; Swedish films
The Fly Pest (1909), 40–1
Fonda, Henry, 155, 158; *You Only Live Once*
(1937), 155–84, 191, 393, 398, 401, 403
Frankel, Robert, 32n. 15, 385
Frankenstein (1931), 247–8n. 17
Franklin, Benjamin, 128–9, 150n. 8–9, 385
Friedman, Thomas L., 24
Friendly, Fred, 276
Frohman, Charles, 65, 71
Frohman, Daniel, 65, 94n. 12, 394
Fromkin, Victoria, 150n. 6, 385
Frykholm, Joel, 13, 62–100, 367, 376, 385
Fu, Poshek, 245n. 4, 385
Fuller, Samuel, 192; *Crimson Kimono* (1959),
192
Furtado, Nelly, 357

Gabaccia, Donna, 36–7, 57, 58n. 1, 385
Gandhi, Mahatma, 272, 276
gangster films: *711 Ocean Drive* (1950), 193;
Al Capone (1959), 186, 188, 190–1, 193–5,
201, 206; *Baby Face Nelson* (1957), 186–
90, 192, 194, 197–8, 202–4, 206, 212n. 2,
213n. 13; *The Big Operator* (1959), 193,
202; *The Black Hand* (1950), 193; *Black
Orchid* (1953), 193; *The Bonnie Parker Story*
(*Lady With a Gun, Tommy Gun Connie*,
1958), 186, 190–1, 194–5, 198, 201–2,
206–7; *Bugsy* (1991), 196–7; *The Captive
City* (1952), 193; *Chicago Syndicate* (1955),
193, 206; *Dillinger* (1945), 191, 209–10;
Edge of the City (1957), 193; *The Enforcer*
(1951), 193; *Gang Busters* (1955), 188; *The
Garment Jungle* (1957), 193; *Guns Don't
Argue* (1957), 188, 190; *Hoodlum Empire*
(1952), 193; *Inside the Mafia* (1959), 192;
*King of the Roaring 20s – The Story of Arnold
Rothstein* (1961), 187; *Little Caesar* (1931),
167, 174–7, 192, 202–5; *Love Me or Leave
Me* (1955), 187; *Ma Barker's Killer Brood*
(1960), 186, 190, 195, 207; *Machine Gun
Kelly* (1958), 186, 190–1, 198, 200, 205,
207; *Mad Dog Coll* (1961), 186–8, 191–2,
199–202, 205; *Miller's Crossing* (1990),
196–7; *The Mob* (1951), 193; *Mobsters*
(1991), 196–7; *Murder, Inc.* (1960), 186,
191, 193–6, 202, 206, 212–3n. 4; *Never
Love a Stranger* (1958), 193; *On the Waterfront* (1954), 193; *Once Upon a Time in
America* (1984), 188; *Party Girl* (1958),
187; *Pay or Die* (1960), 193; *Pete Kelly's*

Blues (1955), 187; *The Petrified Forest*
(1936), 202; *Portrait of a Mobster* (1961),
187–91, 201, 206–8; *Pretty Boy Floyd*
(1960), 186, 190, 198, 201, 206; *The
Public Enemy* (1931), 163, 167, 174–6, 202;
The Purple Gang (1960), 186, 190–1, 198–
200, 202; *The Racket* (1951), 163, 193; *The
Rise and Fall of Legs Diamond* (1960), 186,
190–1, 193–4; *Rumble on the Docks* (1956),
193; *The Scarface Mob* (1960/62), 187–8;
Scarface: Shame of a Nation (1931), 167,
176, 192, 202; *Some Like It Hot* (1959),
187; *Underworld USA* (1961), 193; *The
Untouchables* (1987), 196; *see also* gangster
TV series; Swedish films: gangster films
gangster novels: *Al Capone*, 188; *Hell to Pay*
(1958), 210–1, 215n. 42, 383; *The Hoods*
(1953), 188; *The Mobster* (1960), 188;
Portrait of a Mobster (1958), 187–91, 201,
206–8
gangster TV series: *Gangbusters* (1952), 188,
190; *The Lawless Years* (1959–61), 187; *The
Roaring 20s* (1960–62), 188, 190; *The
Untouchables* (1959–63), 187–8, 191, 212n.
1; *see also* gangster films
gangsters, *see* famous gangsters; gangster
films; gangster novels; gangster TV series
Gao Zhanfei, *see* Zhanfei, Gao
Garbo, Greta, 19; *The Divine Woman*
(1927), 19
Garcia, Cristina, 257, 385
Garnett, Paul, 178
Gates, Jr., Henry Louis, 31n. 5, 385
Gaynor, Janet, 171, 242
Geng, Song, 248n. 27, 385
Gibson, Ross, 358n. 2, 393
Gilfoyle, Timothy J., 123n. 62, 386
Gish, Lillian, 234–5, 242
Gleason, Arthur H., 51–2, 54, 59n. 6, 61n.
22, 386
Gleason, Lev, 188; *Crime Does Not Pay*
(1942–1955), 188–9
Gledhill, Christine, 182n. 24, 182n. 26–7,
386
Glessner, Bonnie, 68, 95n. 27, 386
Godard, Jean-Luc, 204, 214n. 31, 386
Gone with the Wind (1939), 214n. 38
Gordon, Leo, 203
Gorky, Maxim, 56, 102–4, 108, 116, 120,
120n. 1–6, 121n. 12, 121n. 14, 386;
Revenge, 121n. 12; *see also Baby's Breakfast*
(1895)
Graham, Stephen, 130